"At a time when globalization is unprecedentedly challenged, Prof[...] new thinking on how business impacts can better be tackled throug[...] laborative regulation system that organically optimizes the differe[...] public institutions, private sector and the civil society, so that globalization can be sustained as it was, and sustainable as it should be."

Dr. Liang Xiaohui,
Peking University, China

"The theory of Collaborative Regulation corresponds very well to real life negotiations on responsible business conduct, which my experience as Chair of the tough negotiations on the OECD Guidelines for Multinationals has certainly illustrated. Professor Buhmann's theory reflects the importance of representation and involvement of stakeholders. I would recommend this book because it provides useful insights in the crucial role stakeholders could and should play in regulating globalisation."

Prof. Dr. Roel Nieuwenkamp,
Chair OECD Working Party on Responsible Business Conduct

"The planet that we all share appears increasingly challenged by disputes over the environment, internet, resources, human rights, etc. Karin Buhmann acknowledges that we cannot easily find solutions. In this book, she uses thoughtful arguments and case studies to posit a new global governance approach which involves civil society and could be seen by a wide range of actors as legitimate. Buhmann calls this 'collaborative regulation' to balance power disparities. She has produced a thoughtful, insightful, original, and important book for scholars of human rights, law, international relations, governance and political science."

Dr. Susan Ariel Aaronson,
George Washington University, USA

Power, Procedure, Participation and Legitimacy in Global Sustainability Norms

Globalisation of the market, law and politics contributes to a diversity of transnational sustainability problems whose solutions exceed the territorial jurisdictional limits of nation states in which their effects are generated or occur. The rise of the business sector as a powerful global actor with a claim to participation in and potential contributions to, as well as adverse impacts on, sustainability complicates the regulatory challenge. Recent decades' efforts to govern transitions towards sustainability through public or hybrid regulation display mixed records of support and results. In combination, these issues highlight the need for insights on what conditions multi-stakeholder regulation for a process that balances stakeholder power and delivers results perceived as legitimate by participants and broader society.

This book responds to that need. Based on empirical experience on public–private regulation of global sustainability concerns and theoretical perspectives on transnational regulation, the book proposes a new theory on collaborative regulation. This theory sets out a procedural approach for multi-stakeholder regulation of global sustainability issues in a global legal and political order to provide for legitimacy of process and results. It takes account of the claims to participation of the private sector as well as civil society organisations and the need to balance power disparities.

Karin Buhmann is Professor in the Department of Management, Society and Communication at Copenhagen Business School. Her dedicated charge is the field of Business and Human Rights. Her teaching and research interests are in the areas of business responsibilities for human rights, corporate social responsibility, sustainability and public–private regulation. She has published widely on these and related areas.

Globalization: Law and Policy

Globalization: Law and Policy builds an integrated body of scholarship that critically addresses key issues and theoretical debates in comparative and transnational law and the principles of governance and policy on which they are developed. Volumes in the series focus on the consequential effects of globalization, including emerging frameworks and processes for the internationalization, legal harmonization, juridification, and democratization of law among increasingly connected political, economic, religious, cultural, ethnic, and other functionally differentiated governance communities. Legal systems, their harmonization and incorporation in other governance orders, and their relationship to globalization are taking on new importance within a coordinated network of domestic legal orders, the legal orders of groups of states, and the governance frameworks of non-state actors. These legal orders engage a number of important actors, sources, principles, and tribunals – including multinational corporations as governance entities, contract and surveillance as forms of governance that substitute for traditional law, sovereign wealth funds and other new forms of state activity, hybrid supranational entities like the World Bank and the International Monetary Fund, and international tribunals with autonomous jurisdiction, including the International Criminal Court, the World Trade Organization, and regional human rights courts. The effects have been profound, especially with respect to the role of states, and especially of developed states as their long time position in global affairs undergoes significant transformation. Comparative and transnational law serve as natural nexus points for vigorous and sometimes interdisciplinary approaches to the study of state and non-state law systems, along with their linkages and interactions. The series is intended as a resource for scholars, students, policy makers, and civil society actors, and includes a balance of theoretical and policy studies in single-authored volumes and collections of original essays.

Larry Catá Backer is the W. Richard and Mary Eshelman Faculty Scholar, Professor of Law and International Affairs at the Pennsylvania State University. Previously he served as Executive Director of the Comparative and International Law Center at the University of Tulsa. He has published widely on comparative and transnational law.

Also in the series:

Multinationals and the Constitutionalization of the World Power System
Edited by Jean-Philippe Robé, Antoine Lyon-Caen and Stéphane Vernac
ISBN: 978-1-472-48292-1

https://www.routledge.com/Globalization-Law-and-Policy/book-series/GLOBLP

Power, Procedure, Participation and Legitimacy in Global Sustainability Norms

A Theory of Collaborative Regulation

Karin Buhmann

Routledge
Taylor & Francis Group

LONDON AND NEW YORK

First published 2018
by Routledge

2 Park Square, Milton Park, Abingdon, Oxfordshire OX14 4RN
52 Vanderbilt Avenue, New York, NY 10017

Routledge is an imprint of the Taylor & Francis Group, an informa business

First issued in paperback 2019

British Library Cataloguing in Publication Data
A catalogue record for this book is available from the British Library

Library of Congress Cataloging in Publication Data
Names: Buhmann, Karin.
Title: Power, procedure, participation, and legitimacy in global
    sustainability norms : a theory of collaborative regulation / Karin
    Buhmann.
Description: Abingdon, Oxon [UK] ; New York : Routledge, 2017. |
    Series: Globalization : law and policy | Includes bibliographical
    references and index.
Identifiers: LCCN 2017008255| ISBN 9781138696082 (hardback) |
    ISBN 9781315525440 (web pdf) | ISBN 9781315525433 (epub) |
    ISBN 9781315525426 (mobipocket / kindle)
Subjects: LCSH: Corporate governance—Law and legislation. | Social
    responsibility of business—Law and legislation. | Corporate
    governance—International cooperation. | Non-state actors
    (International relations) | Sustainability—Government policy. |
    Human rights.
Classification: LCC K1327 .B86 2017 | DDC 346/.06—dc23
LC record available at https://lccn.loc.gov/2017008255

ISBN: 978-1-138-69608-2 (hbk)
ISBN: 978-0-367-27345-3 (pbk)

Typeset in Times New Roman
by Swales & Willis Ltd, Exeter, Devon, UK

For Nicholas, in appreciation of the concern that he and his contemporaries born in the 1990s harbour over the state of the world that their parents' generation will be leaving them with

Contents

Tables

Abbreviations

BHR	Business and Human Rights
BIAC	Business and Industry Advisory Committee
BOP	bottom of the pyramid
CSR	Corporate Social Responsibility
Draft UN Norms	Draft Norms on the Responsibilities of Transnational Corporations and Other Business Enterprises with Regard to Human Rights
ECOSOC	United Nations Economic and Social Council
EITI	Extractive Industries Transparency Initiative
EU	European Union
FSC	Forest Stewardship Council
GAL	Global Administrative Law
GRI	Global Reporting Initiative
ICC	International Chamber of Commerce
ICCPR	International Covenant on Civil and Political Rights
ICESCR	International Covenant on Economic, Social and Cultural Rights
ICJ	International Court of Justice
ILO	International Labour Organization
IOE	International Organisation of Employers
ISO	International Organization for Standardization
MDGs	Millennium Development Goals
MNC	multinational corporation
MNE	multinational enterprise
MSF	European Commission's Multi-Stakeholder Forum
NCP	National Contact Point
NGO	non-governmental organisation
OECD	Organisation for Economic Co-operation and Development
OEIWG	Open-Ended Intergovernmental Working Group (on treaty on Business and Human Rights)
OHCHR	Office of the High Commissioner for Human Rights
PEFC	Programme for the Endorsement of Forest Certification
SDGs	Sustainable Development Goals
SME	small and medium-sized enterprise
SR	Social Responsibility
SRSG	Special Representative of the UN Secretary-General on Business and Human Rights
TNC	transnational corporation

UDHR	Universal Declaration of Human Rights
UN	United Nations
UNGPs	United Nations Guiding Principles on Business and Human Rights
US	United States
USCIB	United States Council for International Business
WBCSD	World Business Council for Sustainable Development
WTO	World Trade Organization

Acknowledgements

This work has been greatly assisted by support from a number of institutions and individuals. I am grateful to the Danish Research Council for the Social Sciences for a grant for the research project 'The legal character of CSR (Corporate Social Responsibility): reflections between CSR and public international law, and implications for corporate regulation' (2006–2010), which funded much of the research and international activities that inform the current work. I am also grateful to the Research Council for its grant for the collaborative research project 'Ny styrings- og retsformer i multi-level governance: Statens rolle mellem international, transnational, national og sub-national styring af bæredygtigt skovbrug' ['New forms of governance and law in multi-level governance: the role of the State in international, transnational, national and sub-national governance of sustainable forestry'] (2010–2013), which also in various ways fed into the research that informs the current book. Both projects were significant for my ability to perform research and for freeing time to undertake the advanced post-doctoral research treatise (Danish 'disputats'), parts of which have informed this book.

For institutional hosting, my thanks go to institutions where I was employed or was a visiting scholar: the Department of Society and Globalisation at Roskilde University, where the research idea that informs this book was conceived and the initial years of work carried out; the Institute for Food and Resource Economics at the University of Copenhagen, where much of the research was carried out; the Department of Communication, Business and Information Technologies at Roskilde University, where the work that informs this book was finalised and published as my disputats treatise; and finally the Department of Intercultural Communication and Management at Copenhagen Business School (CBS), where substantial parts were rewritten into this book. For inspiring short-term research visits in 2007, 2009–2010 and 2013 I am grateful to the Danish Institute for Human Rights, Columbia Law School in New York City, and the School of Law at the University of Nottingham. I wish to extend my thanks to Hans Otto Sano, Benjamin Liebman and Mary Footer, respectively, for their efforts to make those visits possible.

The Committee that assessed the treatise provided useful comments and suggestions, which have inspired parts of the current book. I was lucky to have my work assessed by a Committee composed of individuals with a combined high and relevant expertise in the field on which I wrote, together representing international law, human rights law and human rights and business, sociology of law, and business ethics. I am grateful to Nicola Jägers, Errol Meidinger and Jacob Dahl Rendtorff for their suggestions.

During the years that I have been working on the research for this book I have benefited from the views and advice of a large number of individuals. For fruitful discussions and encouragement I would like in particular to thank Annali Kristiansen, Anne Lise Kjær, Beate Sjåfjell, Ben Cashore, Bettina Lemann Kristiansen, Cedric Ryngaert, David Kinley,

David Monciardini, Errol Meidinger, Håkan Hydén, Inger-Johanne Sand, Jan Wouters, Jette Steen Knudsen, Johanna Alkan Olsson, Jørgen Dalberg-Larsen, Linda Nielsen, Knud Sinding, Lynn Roseberry, Mary Footer, Margaret Jungk, Mette Morsing, Michael Addo, Nils Åkerstrøm Andersen, Radu Mares, Rass Holdgaard, Steen Thomsen, Surya Deva and Sune Skadegaard Thorsen, as well as colleagues at the departments and institutions where I worked or was a visiting scholar.

I wish to extend my gratitude to the research librarians, financial and secretarial staff and supportive heads of departments at the institutions where I was hosted during my work feeding into this book.

I wish also to acknowledge inspiring discussions that I was fortunate to have in 2007 and 2008 with SRSG John Ruggie and members of his team, especially Lend Wendland and Vanessa Zimmermann, which also contributed interesting perspectives for my research that fed into this work. Similarly, conversations with Søren Mandrup Petersen and Ursula Wynhofen at the UN Global Compact, and with Genevieve Besse and Dominique Bé at the European Commission and the European Social Fund, respectively, assisted my work. In this context I also wish to acknowledge the participation and engagement of Gunther Teubner at a workshop on reflexive law held in Copenhagen in November 2007, funded under the grant from the Danish Research Council for the Social Sciences noted above.

Further thanks go to my editors Alison Kirk and Alexandra Buckley at Ashgate and now Routledge for their support and patience, to Larry Catá Backer for encouraging conversations on the book idea, to Jacqueline Tedaldi for very useful comments and for doing a wonderful job editing the text and references, to Aishwarya Pramod and Deepika Vundavalli for useful suggestions for the text, and to the Governing Responsible Business (GRB) research environment and the Department of Intercultural Communication and Management, both at CBS, for financial support for language and text editing.

Most of all, I wish to thank my son Nicholas for his patience and forbearance when I was working strange hours, physically absent or, maybe even more demanding, simply mentally absent with my mind preoccupied by the research that informed this book and much of my other work during part of his childhood and much of his adolescence.

Karin Buhmann
Copenhagen, January 2017

Part 1

Sustainability, transnational economic activity and regulatory challenges

1 Introduction

Overview: This chapter introduces the issue of the book in regards to sustainability challenges and challenges of regulating these at a global level as well as regulatory challenges and legitimacy issues related to the inclusion of non-state actors, such as businesses, in super-national law-making. It describes how this book responds to those challenges and sets out the objective of developing a theory on collaborative regulation. Moving on, the chapter describes the method that has been applied in terms of empirical cases and the applied theoretical framework. Finally, it introduces key terms and sets out delimitations.

1.1 Setting the stage

1.1.1 Sustainability challenges

The early 21st century abounds in transnational sustainability problems whose solutions exceed the territorial jurisdictional limits of the nation states in which their effects are generated or occur. Transnational economic activity is a significant factor for many of these problems. Yet recent decades' efforts to govern transitions towards sustainability in public, private or hybrid organisations display mixed records of results and outcomes. Recent history has shown that political support, which governments may give to international organisations like the United Nations (UN) to regulate such problems by hard law, is not easily forthcoming or uniform. The difficulties that marked the process of reaching a global climate change agreement in the years up to the 2015 Paris Climate Change Accord[1] are a case in point.

Across the globe, organisations of many types encounter difficulty in adequately meeting environmental and social sustainability challenges. The diversity of processes and outcomes calls for insights into what drives and impedes processes of clarifying what constitutes acceptable conduct. There is a particular need for knowledge on what makes for effective processes for defining norms for such conduct, and for the norms to become accepted with a view to integrating them into organisational practice.

The natural and social sciences have documented acute global sustainability challenges related to climate change and resource depletion[2] and business-induced human rights and

---

1 United Nations/Conference of the Parties, Framework Convention on Climate Change (2015) *Adoption of the Paris Agreement*, UN Doc. FCCC/CP/2015/L.9/Rev.1.

2 Andonova, L. B., Betsill, M. M. and Bulkeley, H. (2009) 'Transnational climate governance', *Global Environmental Politics*, Vol. 9, No. 2, pp. 52–73; Rockström, J. (2009) 'Planetary boundaries: Exploring the safe operating space for humanity', *Ecology and Society*, Vol. 14, No. 2, article 32; Intergovernmental Panel on Climate Change (2012) 'Summary for policymakers', in C. B. Field, V. Barros, T. F. Stocker, Qin D., D. J. Dokken, K. L. Ebi, M. D. Mastrandrea, K. J. Mach, G.-K. Plattner, S. K. Allen, M. Tignor and P. M. Midgley (eds), *Managing the Risks of Extreme Events and Disasters to Advance Climate Change Adaptation*, Special Report, Cambridge: Cambridge University Press, pp. 3–22.

labour abuse.[3] Public and private actors' overexploitation of natural and human resources enhances economic imbalance and destabilises the global ecology.[4] The exercise of power, competition, need for and use of natural resources and labour pitch organisations against each other within and across private and public domains. The understanding of sustainable development and sustainability in a more general sense of societal objectives has undergone a significant evolution from the 1987 'Brundtland Report'[5] through the 1992 Rio Declaration on Environment and Development[6] and the 2000 Millennium Development Goals (MDGs)[7] to the 2015 Sustainable Development Goals (SDGs).[8] The evolution of global policy objectives on sustainability displays an expansion of issues related to sustainability from environmental to broad social concerns. From the original environmental and developmental focus, the understanding has expanded to a broader and integrated view that sustainability assumes a convergence between the three pillars of economic development, social equity and environmental protection.[9] The adoption of the SDGs underscores that sustainability concerns are not tied to specific economies, regions or developmental stages, but are simply global in reach and significance.

The transnational nature of sustainability challenges limits the political and jurisdictional powers of states and international organisations, leading to governance gaps.[10] Despite some progress, particularly in natural resource law,[11] regulation of sustainability often relies on market-based sanctions[12] and informal law.[13] Pragmatic socio-legal approaches to processes

3 Frynas, J. G. (2008) 'Corporate social responsibility and international development: Critical assessment', *Corporate Governance: An International Review*, Vol. 16, No. 4, pp. 274–281; Ruggie, J. G. (2013) *Just Business: Multinational Corporations and Human Rights*, New York: W. W. Norton & Company.

4 Brundtland, G., Khalid, M., Agnelli, S., Al-Athel, S., Chidzero, B., Fadika, L., Hauff, V., Lang, I., Shijun, M., Botero, M. M. de and Singh, M. (1987) *Report of the World Commission on Environment and Development: 'Our Common Future'*, UN Doc. A/42/427 Annex, 4 August; Zelli, F. and Asselt, H. van (2013) 'Introduction: The institutional fragmentation of global environmental governance: Causes, consequences, and responses', *Global Environmental Politics*, Vol. 13, No. 3, pp. 1–13.

5 Brundtland et al. (1987) *Report of the World Commission on Environment and Development*.

6 United Nations General Assembly (1992) *Rio Declaration on Environment and Development* (United Nations Conference on Environment and Development: Annex 1: Declaration on Environment and Development), UN Doc. A/CONF.151/26 (Vol. I), 12 August.

7 United Nations General Assembly (2000) *United Nations Millennium Declaration*, UN Doc. A/Res/55/2, 18 September.

8 United Nations General Assembly (2015) *Transforming Our World: The 2030 Agenda for Sustainable Development*, UN Doc. A/Res/70/1, 21 October.

9 Drexhage, J. and Murphy, D. (2010) *Sustainable Development: From Brundtland to Rio 2012: Background Paper Prepared for Consideration by High Level Panel on Sustainability at Its First Meeting, 19 September 2010*, New York: United Nations.

10 Ruggie, J. G. (2004) 'Reconstituting the global public domain – issues, actors and practices', *European Journal of International Relations*, Vol. 10, No. 4, pp. 499–531; Abbott, K. W. and Snidal, D. (2012) 'Taking responsive regulation transnational: Strategies for international organizations', *Regulation and Governance*, Vol. 7, No. 1, pp. 95–113.

11 McIntyre, O. (2016) 'The making of international natural resource law', in C. Brölman and Y. Radi (eds), *Research Handbook on the Theory of International Lawmaking*, Cheltenham: Edward Elgar, pp. 442–465.

12 Cashore, B., Auld, G. and Newsom, D. (2004) *Governing through Markets: Forest Certification and the Emergence of Non-State Authority*, New Haven, CT: Yale University Press; Bush, S. R., Belton, B., Hall, D., Vandergeest, P., Murray, F. J., Ponte, S., Oosterveer, P., Islam, M. S., Mol, A. P. J., Hatanaka, M., Kruijssen, F., Ha, T. T. T., Little, D. C. and Kusumawati, R. (2013) 'Certify sustainable aquaculture?', *Science*, Vol. 341, No. 6150, pp. 1067–1068.

13 Buhmann, K. (2006) 'Corporate social responsibility: What role for law? Some aspects of law and CSR', *Corporate Governance: The International Journal of Business in Society*, Vol. 6, No. 2, pp. 188–202.

of turning societal needs into aspirational norms that may transform into changed practices recognise a multiplicity of governance forms,[14] but still fail to fully explain the dynamics that trigger change and deliver solutions. Discursive evolution of norms of conduct has proven significant for their uptake,[15] but the evolution of norms related to sustainability has also been shown to be vulnerable to capture by specific interests and power relations.[16]

Climate change has been high on the global sustainability agenda in recent years.[17] Yet global sustainability concerns go beyond climate change, often related to economic practices with social and environmental impacts. Excessive natural resource exploitation, land-grabbing and sub-standard labour conditions in global supply chains are frequent occurrences that also have high sustainability relevance. Such practices pose risks to the environment and human lives currently as well as in a longer-term sustainability perspective of balancing current needs with those of the future. Investments and trade have caused depletion of large stretches of tropical forests, which not only harms the environment and adds to climate change, but also affects the socio-economic conditions of communities. The transnational character of these economic activities often involves or affects numerous private and public actors in several states or regions. This causes challenges for singular or even sector-wide private self-regulatory initiatives, and reduces the effectiveness of self-regulation by individual actors on their own.

The challenges that marked the road to the Paris Climate Change Accord for years are telling of the difficulties that the conventional international law-making process encounters in regard to developing and adopting norms of conduct related to sustainability problems. By contrast to the situation when the state-centric international legal system was created, actors to be regulated are increasingly not public but private. Moreover, despite overall convergence, political interests are highly dispersed at national, regional or even sectoral levels. Failures by the international society to address societal challenges and needs of global concern have drawn attention to the impact that private actors have on society and the responsibility that firms of all sizes have for such impacts. The combination of, on the one hand, the weaknesses encountered by the existing public institutional structures to deal with such problems and, on the other, increased societal awareness of the impact and perceived societal responsibilities of business has placed pressure on the UN, which is the world's key international organisation concerned with social and economic growth and sustainability, set up under a state-centrist international law and policy regime. At the same time, the immensity and encompassing character of global sustainability challenges have also drawn attention to the limitations of singular initiatives like the private or sectoral Corporate Social Responsibility (CSR) guidelines, reporting schemes and codes of conduct.

---

14 Lobel, O. (2005) 'The Renew Deal: The fall of regulation and the rise of governance in contemporary legal thought', *Minnesota Law Review*, Vol. 89, pp. 7–27.

15 Risse, T. and Kleine, M. (2010) 'Deliberation in negotiations', *Journal of European Public Policy*, Vol. 17, No. 5, pp. 708–726; Buhmann, K. (2014) *Normative Discourses and Public–Private Regulatory Strategies for Construction of CSR Normativity: Towards a Method for Above-National Public–Private Regulation of Business Social Responsibilities*, Copenhagen: Multivers.

16 Buhmann, K. (2011) 'Integrating human rights in emerging regulation of corporate social responsibility: The EU case', *International Journal of Law in Context*, Vol. 7, No. 2, pp. 139–179; Fairbrass, J. (2011) 'Exploring corporate social responsibility policy in the European Union: A discursive institutionalist analysis', *JCMS: Journal of Common Market Studies*, Vol. 49, No. 5, pp. 949–970; Kinderman, D. (2013) 'Corporate social responsibility in the EU, 1993–2013: Institutional ambiguity, economic crises, business legitimacy and bureaucratic politics', *JCMS: Journal of Common Market Studies*, Vol. 51, No. 4, pp. 701–720.

17 Rockström (2009) 'Planetary boundaries'; Andonova et al. (2009) 'Transnational climate governance'.

Through the SDGs, the UN General Assembly also sent a message that sustainability and responsibility for sustainable development are global in reach and not limited to particular countries or regions. This is a call to the world on the need to solve impending dilemmas: first, that political and regulatory issues confronting global sustainability development challenges are on the rise; and, second, that there is a need to find novel ways to govern the sustainability impact of economic activities, whether those are linked to the private sector or the public sector or a combination.

Adding to the complexity is the fact that much norm creation related to sustainability is transnational and trans-systemic in process as well as intended applicability. The trans-systemic character transgresses not only conventional boundaries between public and private, international and national law, but also boundaries between the legal, the political and the economic systems.

The past has shown that the evolution of new sustainability concerns is dynamic and often goes beyond our current imagination. When labour issues rose high on the agenda in the 1990s, few suspected that climate change mitigation would move forcefully on to the global sustainability agenda in terms of both public and private regulation. The governance and exploitation of water as a resource for transport, production and sale and a condition for human health are among emerging challenges, as is the exploitation of the land or sea areas around the Arctic or Antarctic. In view of the natural resources available, it may not be far-fetched to speculate that even outer space may be among future challenges for sustainability. Against this backdrop and against the CSR area in general, the field of business and human rights stands out. As explained below, this field has undergone a major transition in less than two decades: contention and disagreement have been turned around into multi-stakeholder development and agreement on guidance for both public and private actors. The human rights field has broad relevance across public and private governance, because many human right issues are directly linked to public policy objectives of a social, economic or political character. This applies whether the issues at stake are at risk of harm caused by the private sector, or whether businesses may contribute to improved delivery of services or other public goods.

1.1.2 Regulatory and legitimacy challenges

Traditionally, non-state actors like businesses do not have a role in international law. This means that they have neither obligations nor a right to participate in law-making. The lack of obligations leads to a situation of impunity or at least a severe lack of normative guidance for firms in regard to their impacts on society. The non-inclusion in international efforts to regulate is a challenge too: it may contribute to alternative ways to influence law-making, but inclusion also causes legitimacy issues because firms are not democratically representative or elected for that role, and because of a risk of capture of the process.

In fact, non-state actors such as civil society organisations increasingly take some part in negotiations within the framework of the UN or other international organisations, which is conventionally state-centric in terms of both rule-making and duty-bearers. Based on the consultative status that many such organisations enjoy with the UN, non-governmental organisations (NGOs) have long participated in such activities. The involvement of non-state actors in regulatory processes also causes legitimacy challenges to process as well as outputs. For example and as elaborated below, in the environmental or human rights field, civil society organisations typically represent the voice of those affected. Business associations, which may also hold consultative status, have in some cases been admitted to such processes. The explicit inclusion of business in such multi-stakeholder regulatory processes under the UN on sustainability issues is a novelty that further underscores the legitimacy challenge, which in this case is dual. It is not only about involving for-profit non-state actors in international law-making, a role traditionally exercised by sovereign states. It is also about involving the very organisations whose actions the new regulation is intended to shape with a view to reducing their adverse impact or enhancing positive impact, in the evolution of new norms for their conduct. It is not surprising that this may cause apprehension lest businesses capture the process. However, as we shall see below, the exclusion of business may be damaging for the result, too. This calls for a compromise that involves stakeholders broadly while balancing power and avoiding undue effects of the interests of one or more types of stakeholders or their networks.

From the process-oriented perspective, international law is a system aimed at achieving common values and providing an operational system for securing these. It continuously needs to adapt to a changing political world and remain conscious of the context in which rules are to be applied.[18] The growth of global or regional sustainability concerns that are transnational in cause or effect makes it pertinent to ask how the international regulatory system, including the UN, may adapt its law-making processes to respond to such challenges. Besides the 2015 climate change breakthrough, recent years have also witnessed a major ground-breaking development in the field of business and human rights. The 2015 Paris Climate Change Accord[19] has received wide acclaim and attention, well deserved in view of the urgency of the matter and the long and winding road to success, which has witnessed several disappointments on the way, in particular the 2009 COP 15 meeting in Copenhagen. The agreements on the 2008 UN Framework[20] and the 2011 UN Guiding Principles on Business and Human Rights (UNGPs)[21] have received less attention and acclaim outside human rights circles, but the processes to those results represent important innovation too and potential lessons for future collaborative regulation. The Paris Climate Change Accord was reached through a largely political process led by individual governments in collaboration with the UN under the set-up agreed to in the 1992 UN Framework Convention on Climate Change and the Kyoto Protocol.[22] The process towards the UN Framework and the UNGPs was on a much smaller scale, but also with wide-ranging implications. It was a more typical UN process for development of specific norms of conduct in a contentious field in that it was directed by the key UN body (in this case the Commission on Human Rights, later the Human Rights Council) and charged on an individual mandate-holder. However, it differed from

18 McDougal, M. (1964) 'The policy-oriented approach to law', *Virginia Quarterly Review*, Vol. 40, pp. 626–632; McDougal, M. and Reisman, W. M. (1981) *International Law in Contemporary Perspective*, Mineola, NY: Foundation Press; Higgins, R. (1994) *Problems and Process: International Law and How We Use It*, Oxford: Clarendon Press.

19 United Nations/Conference of the Parties, Framework Convention on Climate Change (2015) *Adoption of the Paris Agreement*.

20 United Nations Human Rights Council (2008) *Protect, Respect and Remedy: A Framework for Business and Human Rights*, Report of the Special Representative of the Secretary-General on the issue of human rights and transnational corporations and other business enterprises, John Ruggie, UN Doc. A/HRC/8/5 (2008), 7 April.

21 United Nations Human Rights Council (2011) *Guiding Principles on Business and Human Rights: Implementing the United Nations 'Protect, Respect, Remedy' Framework*, Report of the Special Representative of the Secretary-General on the issue of human rights and transnational corporations and other business enterprises, UN Doc. A/HRC/17/31, 21 March.

22 Bodansky, D. and Rajamani, L. (2016) 'Evolution and governance architecture of the climate change regime', in D. Sprinz and U. Luterbacher (eds), *International Relations and Global Climate Change: New Perspectives*, Boston, MA: MIT Press, available at SSRN, https://papers.ssrn.com/sol3/papers.cfm?abstract_id=2168859 (accessed 22 December 2016).

typical UN law-making through its broad multi-stakeholder inclusion, and it extended the view of actors treated as political or actual holders of responsibilities in addition to states' duties under international law.

Criticism has been levelled at the UN Framework and the UNGPs for limiting their focus to the 'negative' aspect of firms respecting human rights (not doing harm) rather than also setting guidance for how companies may contribute to fulfilling human rights (doing more good).[23] Yet the two instruments probably did help pave the way for a process launched in 2014 by the UN Human Rights Council towards an international treaty on business and human rights (BHR). The instruments' delimitation to respecting human rights has been explained as a pragmatic choice that helped ensure broad agreement on the UN Framework[24] and does not prevent or discourage firms' engagement in human rights fulfilment. Indeed, the latter is increasingly addressed in the general organisational literature on CSR as 'political CSR'.[25]

Studies of regulatory strategy, new modes of governance and public–private regulation to address public policy concerns suggest that the effectiveness and legitimacy of non-coercive or co- or self-regulatory alternatives to formal state regulation depend on a number of factors. These include: the intensity of the regulatory intervention required for the purpose of a particular public policy objective; the intervention capacity of governmental actors; the economic benefits for companies and the extent to which companies or an industry may be motivated to engage in self-regulation as a form of pre-emptive regulation based on enlightened self-interest; reputational sensitivity in relation to the company's or industry's environment as well as competitors; and alignment between the salient public policy objectives and the culture that exists within a particular industry or series of companies.[26] Most of these studies address the effectiveness of the resulting

23 See, for example, Cernic, J. L. (2010) 'Two steps forward, one step back: The 2010 UN report by the UN Special Representative on Business and Human Rights', *German Law Journal*, Vol. 11, pp. 1264–1280; Bilchitz, D. (2013) 'A chasm between "is" and "ought"? A critique of the normative foundations of the SRSG's Framework and the Guiding Principles', in S. Deva and D. Bilchitz (eds), *Human Rights Obligations of Business: Beyond the Corporate Responsibility to Respect?*, Cambridge: Cambridge University Press, pp. 107–137; Wettstein, F. (2013) 'Making noise about silent complicity: The moral inconsistency of the "Protect, Respect and Remedy" Framework', in S. Deva and D. Bilchitz (eds), *Human Rights Obligations of Business: Beyond the Corporate Responsibility to Respect?*, Cambridge: Cambridge University Press, pp. 243–268.

24 Buhmann, K. (2012) 'The development of the "UN Framework": A pragmatic process towards a pragmatic output', in R. Mares (ed.), *The UN Guiding Principles on Business and Human Rights: Foundations and Implementation*, Leiden: Martinus Nijhoff, pp. 85–105; Knox, J. H. (2012) 'The Ruggie Rules: Applying human rights law to corporations', in R. Mares (ed.), *The UN Guiding Principles on Business and Human Rights*, Antwerp: Brill, pp. 51–83; Sanders, A. (2015) 'The impact of the "Ruggie Framework" and the "United Nations Guiding Principles on Business and Human Rights" on transnational human rights litigation', in J. Martin and K. E. Bravo (eds), *The Business and Human Rights Landscape: Moving Forward, Looking Back*, Cambridge: Cambridge University Press, pp. 288–315; see also Wettstein, F. (2015) 'Normativity, ethics, and the UN Guiding Principles on Business and Human Rights: A critical assessment', *Journal of Human Rights*, Vol. 14, No. 2, pp. 162–182.

25 See, for example, Scherer, A. G. and Palazzo, G. (2011) 'The new political role of business in a globalized world – a review of a new perspective on CSR and its implications for the firm, governance, and democracy', *Journal of Management Studies*, Vol. 48, No. 4, pp. 899–931; Scherer, A. G., Rasche, A., Palazzo, G. and Spicer, A. (2016) 'Managing for political corporate social responsibility: New challenges and directions for PCSR 2.0', *Journal of Management Studies*, Vol. 53, No. 3, pp. 273–298.

26 For overviews, see Saurwein, F. (2011) 'Regulatory choice for alternative modes of regulation: How context matters', *Law and Policy*, Vol. 33, No. 3, pp. 334–366; Cafaggi, F. and Renna, A. (2012) *Public and Private Regulation: Mapping the Labyrinth*, CEPS Working Document No. 370, October, Brussels: Centre for European Policy Studies, esp. at pp. 4–9.

norms of conduct contained in a rule or other governance instrument – and not the process to generate the rule. This book, by contrast, looks at the process for the creation of norms or amendment of prior norms. Its focus is on participation in a rule-making process and on procedures for balancing power interests among participants in order for the rule-making to be legitimate and effective in delivering relevant and appropriate norms. The book is driven by the socio-legal idea of a compliance pull as significant either for governance systems that lack strong enforcement institutions or where, as in the case of human rights and many other sustainability-related issues, prevention is much more desirable than a cure. That is so because a remedy is rarely able to fully repair the damage done: an arm lost in an occupational health and safety accident cannot be replaced; a childhood lost to factory labour cannot be relived; lethal chemicals polluting drinking water or agricultural land do not disappear overnight; and the impacts of environmental damage on the possibility of farmers or fishing people providing for themselves and their families may persist for years to come. Studies indicate that, even where a remedy is provided, its effectiveness is questionable,[27] thus further underscoring that, however important a remedy is, prevention of harm occurring is of paramount significance. To build a compliance pull from within, the law-making process takes centre stage. Several legal philosophers,[28] political scientists,[29] socio-legal scholars,[30] and international and transnational law experts[31] agree that the regulatory process must be structured in such a way that the processing of input into output has a high degree of legitimacy. Yet there is a need for theory-based insights into what it takes to transform the ideals into practice.

1.1.3 How this book contributes

This book responds to a need for insights on developing norms and rules for transnational sustainability governance. It addresses the conditions for such processes to generate a normative output that is broadly accepted as being legitimate in terms of both process and outcome.

The analysis takes its point of departure in the evolution of norms of conduct for business with regard to sustainability-related issues within a set of public–private multi-stakeholder initiatives that were launched and finalised between 1998 and 2011. Within a general context that was sometimes referred to as CSR, all of these hybrid initiatives addressed social aspects of business impact on society. Some, in particular, addressed business impact on human rights, laying part of the ground for what is today increasingly referred to as

---

27 Daniel, C., Wilde-Ramsing, J., Genovese, K. and Sandjojo, V. (2015) *Remedy Remains Rare: An Analysis of 15 Years of NCP Cases and Their Contributions to Improve Access to Remedy for Victims of Corporate Misconduct*, Amsterdam: OECD Watch.

28 Especially Habermas, J. (1996) *Between Facts and Norms: Contributions to a Discourse Theory of Law and Democracy*, translated by W. Rehg, Cambridge: Polity Press/Blackwell.

29 Risse, T. (2000) '"Let's argue": Communicative action in world politics', *International Organization*, Vol. 54, No. 1, pp. 1–39; Risse and Kleine (2010) 'Deliberation in negotiations'.

30 For example, Teubner, G. (1983) 'Substantive and reflective elements in modern law', *Law and Society Review*, Vol. 17, No. 2, pp. 239–285; Berger-Walliser, G. and Shrivastava, P. (2015) 'Beyond compliance: Sustainable development, business, and pro-active law', *Georgia International Law Journal*, Vol. 46, No. 2, pp. 417–475.

31 For example, Picciotto, S. (2003) 'Rights, responsibilities and regulation of international business', *Columbia Journal of Transnational Law*, Vol. 42, No. 1, pp. 131–152; Cohen, J. and Sabel, C. (2005) 'Global democracy?', *NYU Journal of International Law and Politics*, Vol. 37, No. 4, pp. 763–797; Burca, G. de (2008) 'Developing democracy beyond the state', *Columbia Journal of Transnational Law*, Vol. 46, No. 2, pp. 221–278.

Business & Human Rights (BHR). The BHR acronym reflects that the debate on business responsibilities for human rights has matured to the stage of becoming an institutionalised normative discourse. BHR is related to the general CSR discourse, on which it feeds, but also branches off into an autonomous discourse, which is increasingly shaping the conception of CSR.[32] A process launched by the UN in 2005 and its outcome – the 2008 UN 'Protect, Respect and Remedy' Framework and the 2011 UNGPs – broke ground by generating progress in a field that had been marked by failures to reach agreement. It also broke ground through a multi-stakeholder process that included business enterprises in a dual active role: as participants, and as bearers of potential new human rights duties. Business participation was a result of the emerging recognition that businesses do have responsibilities for their impacts on society, and of an awareness that the exclusion of business in a previous initiative to develop norms on business responsibilities for human rights (the Draft UN Norms, see below) had contributed to the failure of that initiative to achieve the legitimacy required for its successful adoption, even within a regulatory forum composed of government representatives. The outcome, the process and the participants raise issues of legitimacy of a character that are typically addressed in social science studies as output, throughput and input legitimacy. The approach here is pragmatic socio-legal. This allows for exploring past effort at regulating sustainability with varying degrees of non-state actor participation and results, with a view to providing insights for future collaborative regulation of sustainability-related issues.

1.2 Objective, method, key terms and delimitations

1.2.1 Objectives

In view of the issues set out above, the overall task here is to engage in a discussion on whether and how to involve non-state actors in rule-making processes occurring at the supranational level, that is, above nation states. Such processes may take place under the auspices of international organisations, but they may also occur under the auspices of hybrid organisations that are set up or function with a combination of public and private actors. Hybrid organisations may be completely private but still, like the International Organization for Standardization (ISO), develop rules through a process that involves both private and public actors, as was the case for the ISO 26000 Social Responsibility (SR) Guidance Standard. They may also be organised within a public international organisation but involve private actors – whether for-profit or non-profit – in a manner that makes them very direct partners in law-making processes, including processes to update normative standards and guidance. Developed through a multi-stakeholder process, the ten principles of the UN Global Compact offer an example of the latter. Thus, the task here is not to develop specific delimitations of what degree of international legal personality companies should enjoy.

In the social sciences, the term *legitimacy* has a number of nuances that turn around a common core on acceptance, representativeness and coherence with the norms and needs of society. As elaborated in Chapter 4, in legal science legitimacy entails an acceptance of norms that are representative of the views and interests of those to whom the norms apply, whether as rights-holders or duty-bearers. In political science, legitimacy often refers to power and the exercise of authority as results of a perception that this is representative of

---

32 See, further, Buhmann, K. (2016) 'Juridifying corporate social responsibility through public law: Assessing coherence and inconsistencies against UN guidance on business and human rights', *International and Comparative Corporate Law Journal*, Vol. 11, No. 3, pp. 194–228.

those over whom the power or authority is exercised. In organisation and management studies, legitimacy sometimes refers more narrowly to a particular organisation, but still denotes an action being appropriate within a socially constructed system of norms, values, beliefs and definitions.[33] In this work, legitimacy refers to a process of law-making that is acceptable as being representative in a balanced way of the views and needs of those to whom the resulting norms will apply, and to the normative output as acceptable because it was developed through a legitimate process.

In terms of new theory on hybrid law-making on sustainability this book proposes and develops the concept of *collaborative regulation*. The concept refers to a process that ensures throughput legitimacy for making rules that (typically, but not necessarily) relate to sustainable conduct, and output legitimacy of the resulting output, with a view to the output having an inherent compliance pull that invites parties to follow the norms, whether or not they are backed by a strong enforcement regime. More specifically, collaborative regulation involves private and public stakeholders[34] in rule-making through a procedure aimed at balancing power disparities while allowing for an exchange of views, needs and expectations in such a way as to enable the appreciation of interests across functional categories of systems, and stimulate the evolution and agreement on norms and their practical implementation in organisational practice.

Against the backdrop of current and likely future sustainability and regulatory challenges, some of which are described above and in the following, the book offers insights into how collaborative regulation can be undertaken so as to produce norms of conduct that are legitimate with regard to the process as well as the norms resulting from the process.

In order to inform and stimulate such collaborative regulation, the book provides an overview of theories on compliance pull and legitimate law-making, describes how communication between stakeholders with conflicting and often competing interests and concerns can be brought together to develop an understanding of societal needs and expectations in relation to sustainability (depending on context as a process of regulated self-regulation), and discusses the significance of participation, power relations and power disparities for the way in which stakeholders engage with the process and give their support to the output. It draws on selected empirical examples of past public–private sustainability regulation to develop insights for the design and management of processes of sustainability regulation that involves participants with diverse concerns and experiences, and networks that affect their power and interests at stake. Against this backdrop, it develops a method for collaborative regulation, setting out the overall foundations as well as specific steps. It proposes future avenues for the implementation of collaborative regulation in practice. Ideally, procedural equalisation of the participation of non-state actors in super-national law-making related to global or regional concerns, such as generally social or environmental sustainability, will be regulated in an international treaty embodying the steps set out in the method described in Part 3. Such a treaty could be developed by the UN, being the global organisation charged with the promotion of social and economic growth with respect for human rights, labour rights, the environment, and peaceful development. A treaty might

---

33 Suchman, M. (1995) 'Managing legitimacy: Strategic and institutional approaches', *Academy of Management Review*, Vol. 20, No. 3, pp. 571–610, at p. 574.

34 The concept of *collaborative regulation* that is proposed and developed here is distinct from that of *collaborative governance*, which is a narrower idea that refers to sustainability governance standards with a particular focus on the standards as such, a stronger private focus dealing with the private character and role of private organisations in filling public governance voids, and collaboration between existing standards and their organisations (see Rasche, A. (2010) 'Collaborative Governance 2.0', *Corporate Governance*, Vol. 10, No. 4, pp. 500–511).

also be developed by regional organisations such as the African Union, Council of Europe, Organization of American States and/or ASEAN. Pending the evolution of such a treaty, the book offers steps to be followed by regulatory processes that aim to understand and handle power disparities so that such disparities do not become an obstacle to the effectiveness of the regulatory process to deliver on its objectives. The steps aim to, provide the process and the output with the legitimacy required to gain support and a compliance pull.

1.2.2 Empirical cases

For the empirical part, the study draws on six processes of public–private development of norms of conduct on sustainability-related issues that took place in a super-national context, that is, above the national level, and in terms of subject matter, participants or process going beyond the conventional state-centrist system for international law-making. Covering a period from 1998 to 2011 and reaching up to the present time, the six cases take the reader through a period of major changes in relation to the failures and successes of the level of detail, normative background, and support for norms of conduct for business impact on society. The diversity of these examples offers insights into the importance of power issues, process design and management, and the practical implications of legitimacy related to the process and output of a law-making process that takes place outside the space and institutional set-up of the national and the state-centrist international regimes. The cases, which serve as examples, are: the process towards the so-called Draft UN Norms and their output (Norms on the Responsibilities of Transnational Corporations and Other Business Enterprises with Regard to Human Rights) 1998–2004;[35] the process towards the UN Global Compact 1999–2000 and some later changes;[36] the process of the European Commission's Multi-Stakeholder Forum (MSF) on Corporate Social Responsibility 2002–2004 with later developments in 2006, including the main output, a report issued in 2004;[37] the European Union's (EU) CSR Alliance, launched in 2006 and still operating;[38] the two mandates of the Special Representative of the UN Secretary-General (SRSG) on Business and Human Rights 2005–2008 and 2008–2011, which resulted in the UN 'Protect, Respect and Remedy' Framework[39] and the UNGPs;[40] and the process of the ISO towards the 26000 SR Guidance Standard and its output, commonly referred to as ISO 26000.[41]

The six processes have been selected to present major initiatives to regulate business impact on society from a perspective informed by the CSR concept during a recent time period, initiated within different super-national contexts ranging from the UN's human rights institutional set-up through the executive arm of the UN, the Secretary-General and his office, to the EU

---

35 Sub-Commission on the Promotion and Protection of Human Rights (2003) *Norms on the Responsibilities of Transnational Corporations and Other Business Enterprises with Regard to Human Rights*, UN Doc. E/CN.4/Sub.2/2003/12/Rev.2.
36 United Nations Global Compact, http://www.unglobalcompact.org/ (last accessed 27 December 2016).
37 European Multi-Stakeholder Forum on CSR (2004) *Final Results and Recommendations*, 'Final Report', 29 June, http://forum.europa.eu.int/irc/empl/csr_eu_multi_stakeholder_forum/info/data/en/CSR%20Forum%20final%20report.pdf (last accessed 15 February 2013, website has been removed).
38 BusinessEurope, *European Alliance for CSR*, https://www.businesseurope.eu/european-alliance-csr (last accessed 5 December 2016).
39 UN Human Rights Council (2008) *Protect, Respect and Remedy*.
40 UN Human Rights Council (2011) *Guiding Principles on Business and Human Rights*.
41 ISO (2010) *ISO 26000 – Social Responsibility*, http://www.iso.org/iso/iso_catalogue/management_standards/social_responsibility.htm (last accessed 5 December 2016).

(a particular type of public international organisation with political and law-making powers that differs from other international organisations) and finally ISO, a private organisation. The regulatory processes either are finished or have delivered normative outputs.

The study mainly relies on official reports and other statements having fed into the processes, which are officially available, generally on the internet.[42] For the Draft UN Norms and ISO 26000, where such statements are few or not widely available, academic articles sharing insights from individuals close to the processes have been applied to supplement the publicly available documents.

Within the broader context of evolution of norms of conduct on sustainability and business impacts on society, the case of the evolution of normative guidance on BHR offers an interesting example that places more general CSR initiatives into perspective. It offers a unique case for analysis of how public organisations can develop new norms on sustainable economic activity in collaboration with economic actors as well as affected stakeholders (victims) and communities, civil society and other organisations with vested interests.

The case of the evolution of normative guidance on human rights for business is interesting because it has undergone a major change from failure to success with significant influence on CSR. It is relevant because it relates not only to human rights in a narrow sense but also to a series of other related or often interrelated sustainability concerns. These range from issue areas like the environment and anti-corruption to multifaceted sectoral or geographic sustainability concerns like the exploitation of natural resources whether renewable (e.g. oil palm and bio-fuel) or non-renewable (e.g. rare earth minerals). The connection to resources makes the lessons of the course towards normative guidance on business and human rights valuable in a number of contexts that extend beyond human rights in the narrow sense. The insights for collaborative regulation are relevant whether focused on labour, land, agricultural products, minerals, water, knowledge or other resources to be managed in a manner that is mindful of the range of interests at stake and does not unduly favour short-term gains over longer-term needs and values.

1.2.3 Theoretical framework

Social science literature on collective decision-making through deliberation and related practices recognises that it is 'almost impossible' to empirically observe actors' motivations for the decisions made and that, as a result, research tends to consider the institutional conditions that affect both processes and outputs, based on specific cases, and employing a mix of inductive and deductive reasoning.[43] The current study adopts a similar approach.

---

42 For the identification of texts, official websites of the initiatives have been used: United Nations Global Compact, http://www.unglobalcompact.org/ (last accessed 27 December 2016); Business and Human Rights Resource Centre, UN Secretary-General's Special Representative on Business and Human Rights (SRSG portal), https://business-humanrights.org/en/un-secretary-generals-special-representative-on-business-human-rights (last accessed 27 December 2016); European Multi-Stakeholder Forum on CSR (2002–2004) EU MSF homepage through the EU Commission's website, http://circa.europa.eu/irc/empl/csr_eu_multi_stakeholder_forum/info/data/en/csr%20ems%20forum.htm (last accessed 15 February 2013, webpage has been removed); CSR Alliance: not one single website, but information at the website of the European Commission DG Enterprise and Industry at http://ec.europa.eu/enterprise/policies/sustainable-business/corporate-social-responsibility/european-alliance/index_en.htm (last accessed 12 March 2013, website has been removed), CSR Europe at http://www.csreurope.org/pages/en/alliance.html (last accessed 12 March 2013, website has been removed), and BusinessEurope at https://www.businesseurope.eu/european-alliance-csr (last accessed 5 December 2016).

43 Risse and Kleine (2010) 'Deliberation in negotiations', at p. 711.

The cases differ from conventional legal study cases in a number of ways. Being processes towards an output, they have an iterative character. They progress without a clear procedural format, with interaction based on negotiations, formal documents and speeches, reports, and less formal statements by different participants. No judgments or final decisions are involved, and with the partial exception of the UN Human Rights Council's resolution, which formally 'welcomed' the SRSG's 'UN Framework' in 2008 and the Council's adoption in 2011 of the UNGPs, the outputs are not made by formal law-makers but as consensus-like products of the public–private multi-stakeholder process. With variations, the cases are all regulatory initiatives with a multi-stakeholder composition including both public (intergovernmental and some governmental) and non-state participants (companies and civil society organisations). Each of the outputs is a result of the multi-stakeholder debates, negotiations and efforts to affect the final output to promote or protect the interests of each particular participating stakeholder or stakeholder group.

These features call for a research method allowing for the analysis of processes as these evolve, to understand the initiatives that serve as case studies as procedural modes of regulation, to understand the interests of involved stakeholders, and to analyse their influence with regard to the output. It also needs to assess the public–private regulatory process against the backdrops of their political and legal backgrounds and setting, identify functionality and deficiencies with regard to legitimacy, and identify weaknesses for legitimate rule-making on businesses' societal impacts, with a particular focus on public–private multi-stakeholder processes at the super-national level. In this respect, the current work draws on a research project that applied a combination of theory on legitimate law-making, reflexive law theory, and discourse theory.[44] For the current purposes, a theory background that consists of deliberative legitimate law-making in general and in global governance is applied along with socio-legal theory on law-making that aims at stimulating organisational change in line with societal needs and expectations related to sustainability. Deliberative law-making leaning on and inspired by theory developed by Jürgen Habermas provides the former, while reflexive law theory, originally developed by Gunther Teubner, provides the latter. The analysis of past public–private law-making both confirms the appropriateness and relevance of reflexive law for hybrid regulation of sustainability concerns and such regulation taking place in a super-national context, and identifies imbalanced power disparities as a major obstacle to the effectiveness and legitimacy of such regulatory processes. This also confirms a gap in reflexive law theory identified by other scholars. The analysis applies legitimate law-making theory to fill the gap in reflexive law theory. Based on this, the book offers an advanced theory of reflexive law that has been enriched by habermasian theory on legitimate law-making as a new theoretical framework for collaborative regulation.

1.2.4 Key terms

Law-making is used synonymously with *rule-making* as a broad term that includes not only conventional hard or soft law, but also processes of developing other forms of normative codes and guidance for conduct for organisations.[45]

---

44 For the full study and explanation of methodology, see Buhmann (2014) *Normative Discourses and Public–Private Regulatory Strategies for Construction of CSR Normativity.*
45 Compare also Kingsbury, B. (2009) 'The concept of "law" in global administrative law', *European Journal for International Law*, Vol. 20, No. 1, pp. 23–57.

Super-national (super = above) law-making occurs above the level of the nation state. While super-national law-making includes international, transnational and regional law-making because these occur above the nation state, 'super-national' should not be confused with 'supra-national' as that term is applied in the specific context of EU law, that is, with reference to the specific legal order of the EU with regard to the state-like powers that EU institutions possess in that particular context when the law-making powers have been con-ferred to the EU from member states. Without such conferral of powers, the EU does not have the legal basis to legislate but it can promote self-regulation. This is the case for the EU-initiated efforts to develop CSR norms that are included among the cases studies.

Super-national law-making often targets concerns of a *transnational* character. They may be transnational for a number of reasons, such as because the organisations addressed are multinational corporations whose operations take place in more than one state, making it difficult for one state to fully regulate the concerns at hand, or because they relate to impacts such as environmental damage or climate change that may occur in other states than where the action that caused the harm took place. It is important to note that the actions addressed do not need to have a transnational character. In many cases, the pertinent issue responds to public policy concerns or needs that are highly relevant to and within individual states or local communities. In such cases, the concerns are often shared by several states or com-munities across borders, bringing additional relevance to efforts to deal with problems at the super-national level.

The terms transnational corporation (TNC) and multinational corporation (MNC) are used interchangeably by the international organisations that play a role in emergent rule-making for sustainable business conduct. The Organisation for Economic Co-operation and Development (OECD) and International Labour Organization (ILO) prefer 'MNC', while the UN prefers 'TNC' for referring to an economic entity or group operating in more than one country.[46] TNC is the term generally used in this work.

1.2.5 Delimitations

In discussing regulatory strategies employed to promote normativity on business impacts on sustainability and business self-regulation on CSR, this book is neither a positive nor a negative appraisal of CSR as a phenomenon or a normative paradigm, or of the idea that businesses take responsibility for their impact on society. To the extent that it discusses CSR, it takes the CSR discourse as a given and as a social phenomenon that plays a role in relation to social expectations and business conduct with regard to economic activities and sustainability, and as a discourse that is observable and therefore may be observed in a scholarly way.

This work is also not about whether business entities are holders of duties under inter-national law, or whether they should be. Rather, it is about the regulatory modalities directed towards defining such duties or encouraging business to take related responsi-bility. Such modalities and insights into the design of law-making to ensure legitimacy of process and output will be significant for the outcomes of future efforts to promote sustainability and responsible conduct with private actors, regardless of whether specific

---

46 See Wouters, J. and Chané, A. (2013) *Multinational Corporations in International Law*, Working Paper No. 129, Leuven: Leuven Centre for Global Governance Studies, at pp. 2–3.

duties will be developed in international law for business impacts on society. Such efforts are currently under way under a UN-initiated process that aims to develop a treaty on setting out binding obligations on business and human rights, although it is currently uncertain whether businesses or only states will be direct duty-bearers.

In this book law, including international law, is treated as a discipline that gains meaning, use and justification by relating to, and providing solutions to, developments outside of law. Law is informed by and responds to political developments, economic challenges, moral claims and other social phenomena. In this sense, international law may be considered to be based in part on politics and to involve the pursuit of social ends, but through use of legitimate power.[47] The study recognises that moral claims and social expectations may influence the political drive to formulate, develop or change law. Still, this is a study of law and regulatory strategies based on legal theory, and not one of morals, economics and politics. It is a study of what factors shape the legitimacy of hybrid regulatory processes and their normative outputs, with a variety of actors seeking to shape normativity on business responsibilities in a sustainability context.

This study differs from the mainstream of studies on CSR by taking a legal theory-informed perspective.[48] Both in the general CSR context and within the legal context, it differs from the mainstream by taking a public regulatory approach to the topic. With past decades' increase in intergovernmental and national governmental regulatory initiatives on CSR, legal scholarship with a public regulatory approach is, however, also increasing. In the context of the current study, legal theory offers a relevant perspective, as a theory concerned with the creation and institutionalisation of norms of conduct and modalities for providing such institutionalisation. The actual application and implementation of norms of conduct by companies and their compliance are not addressed here. Scholars from fields such as organisational and management studies may wish to engage in such analysis.[49] This may add important complementary insights to the current work's analysis and proposal for a theory for collaborative regulation. Finally, general interviews, focus group studies or qualitative or quantitative assessments of the application or impact of the initiatives studied have not been employed in this study. Such methods could be relevant, but are left by this author to future research, or perhaps to a follow-up to the current study.

1.2.6 Structure

This book deals with the issue of collaborative regulation of sustainability challenges through three parts. Part 1 sets out: the limitations that conventional international law places on business in terms of duties as well as rights to participate in rule-making; innovative suggestions by scholars in the past to deal with this; and the public, private and hybrid efforts at developing norms of conduct for business that have tried to address this problem. It also describes the connection between CSR, sustainability and super-national governance needs and sets out

---

47 See Koskenniemi, M. (1989) *From Apology to Utopia: The Structure of International Legal Argument*, Helsinki: Finnish Lawyers' Publishing Company, at p. 3.

48 This is particularly so in a European, and even more particularly in a continental European, context. Anglo-Saxon legal environments have produced a large part of the existing legal scholarship-informed studies of CSR and regulatory strategies employed in a legal context.

49 Compare the limited analysis of CSR instruments in Lambooy, T. (2009) 'Private regulation: Indispensable for responsible corporate conduct in a globalizing world?', in *Law and Globalization*, Bocconi School of Law Student-Edited Papers, Saarbrucken: VDM Publishing, pp. 90–133, esp. at pp. 127–128.

key actors and their sometimes complementary but often competing interests. Finally, Part 1 introduces the empirical cases.

Part 2 first explains the theory basis, which is set in socio-legal instrumental approaches to regulation as a modality to change conduct with a proactive view to prevent harm before it occurs and the deliberative approach to legitimate law-making that was introduced by Jürgen Habermas and has been expanded by other social scientists. Moving on, it describes how the instrumental regulatory theory of reflexive law is a theory on inducing normative change and self-regulation in organisations through a process of learning that is based on a qualified form of stakeholder communication. Reflexive law notes the importance of balancing power disparities in such a setting but does not explain how this can be done. Drawing on the empirical case studies, Part 2 moves on to show that reflexive law is a relevant regulatory strategy for super-national law-making that offers a way around the limitations caused by political and jurisdiction boundaries on law-making pertaining to transnational sustainability concerns. Drawing on the empirical cases it also demonstrates the significance of the reflexive law theory to prescribe how power disparities should be managed. It argues lacuna in the case for developing a new theory on collaborative regulation that fills this lacuna, in order for reflexive law approaches to be able to deliver regulatory outputs that are legitimate as a result of a legitimate process. Finally, the theoretical complementarity between deliberative law-making theory and reflexive law is introduced.

Part 3 develops the theory of collaborative regulation, in which proceduralisation is a key concept. Drawing on deliberative law-making theory, proceduralisation offers a way to provide for broad participation in a reflexive regulatory or other law-making process while at the same time equalising such participation to balance power disparities among participants and leaving the development of the normative output with participants in the process. Part 3 sets forth the theory foundations for collaborative regulation and outlines concrete steps to be taken for collaborative regulation. The focus is on proceduralisation in public–private sustainability regulation to frame a process that is legitimate and effective in connecting input to output in a manner that generates broad support. Part 3 proposes that an international treaty could set out these steps in order to provide for a formalised inclusion of non-state actors in super-national law-making while at the same time setting procedural rules for balancing power disparities. Pending such a treaty, it proposes a model for a collaborative regulatory process at the super-national level, leaning on proceduralisation to ensure legitimate multi-stakeholder law-making on sustainability concerns.

2 Regulatory innovation

Non-state actors and sustainability norms

Overview: The chapter opens by elaborating on the place of TNCs in international law. The limited role of TNCs in terms of holding international obligations and taking part in international law-making is set against the role of states as the primary actors in the conventional system of international law, which is state-centric in regards to rights, duties and participation in law-making. While TNCs have been awarded considerable rights in international economic rights unmatched by corresponding obligations for their adverse societal impacts, rights-holders in regards to human rights are typically victims of human rights abuse or their representatives. Further, Chapter 2 explains that civil society organisations, which may represent victims but can also be associations of business, can obtain consultative status with international organisations like the UN, and in this capacity have access to a limited form of participation in international law-making, primarily to provide input to the process. The chapter proceeds to explain how international law-making theory has proposed to increase the participation of business in supernational law-making to develop norms of conduct for businesses order to provide for stronger support among them for the resulting normative directives. Next, it explains how regulatory innovation has occurred in practice through various types of public, private and public-private (hybrid) initiatives that have emerged in recent decades to set normative guidance for business conduct with regard to societal impacts. Following this, the connection and inter-relationship between sustainability, Corporate Social Responsibility (CSR) and governance needs are discussed. Finally, the chapter sets out the key actors in public-private law-making aiming at governing business conduct with regards to societal impacts, and explains the quite considerable and often conflicting power interests at play with public organisations, businesses and business organisations, the labour movement and NGOs representing civil society.

2.1 Regulation of companies in conventional international law

With the globalisation of the economy, the role of companies in international law has become an issue in tandem with the increased information available on their adverse impacts on society. The rights that companies have achieved under international economic law has not been balanced by duties for companies to limit or account for their adverse social impact. Because international law conventionally regulates states, the regulation of companies is typically an indirect effect of states' international obligations. The strength and quality of such regulation are therefore easily affected by ineffective implementation, law enforcement and other governance gaps.

The transnational character of TNCs causes challenges for nation states with regard to regulation and enforcement relating to TNC conduct or impacts outside the home state. As a result, scholars and international organisations have been wondering how international society produces and promotes norms that encourage TNCs to conduct themselves in accordance with human rights and other societal needs or expectations.

Being original subjects of international law, states are both duty-bearers (and rights-holders) and participants in the law-making process. States therefore are in full control of the rules that apply to themselves, and are able to bring up their concerns or needs in the process of law-making. When international law-making extends rule-bearing personality (even if initially on a political and soft law basis) beyond states and the international organisations that are also created by states (such as the UN), it is therefore relevant to ask what practical implications that might have for the possible involvement of new duty-bearers in the rule-making process. The situation of business organisations differs from that of NGOs and other civil society organisations representing victims in regard to the emergence of new rules. While organisations representing victims represent *rights-holders* and do so whether the harm has been caused by states or businesses, business organisations are potential *duty-bearers* under new super-national rules. Being non-state actors, businesses do not currently have formal access to international law-making. Like other non-state actor organisations, organisations for business may apply for consultative status with the UN, but this does not translate into a role comparable to that of states. Even so, the role of businesses as not only potential bearers of new duties under international law but also participants in the regulatory process is not without significance.

Among other points, legitimacy issues that arise in regard to the idea of business participation concern the capacity of such actors to influence outcomes towards reducing the extent of potential new duties for themselves. As will be elaborated below, the experience of EU efforts at CSR rule-making shows that this is a valid concern. The issue of how skilfully managed involvement can help generate support for the process and its outcome has been much less discussed. While on the one hand the involvement of companies in super-national law-making pertaining to their conduct and social impact may raise risks of capture, on the other hand the exclusion of companies may raise claims that the rule-making process is deficient in legitimacy with regard to those subjected to the resulting duties.

International law-making differs from the law-making process in national legal systems. Domestic law in democratic societies is normally created in processes that involve several actors within that state. Through various formalised representative and consultative measures, civil society and sometimes certain private actors are granted rights to provide input for rule-making. On the other hand, international law is formally made by the international community, composed of states and state representatives. Civil society organisations enjoying consultative status have formalised but somewhat limited opportunities for bringing forward suggestions. In principle, business associations (such as organisations for a specific sector or firms of a particular size) can qualify for such status as well as NGOs representing the environment, human rights victims and so on. NGOs have historically taken a stronger interest in social or environmental sustainability-related law-making processes than business associations.

At the national level, non-state actors may feed into the international law-making process through interacting with national actors formally involved in the law-making process. At the international level, such interaction risks taking on a less formalised and less transparent lobbying character, precisely because non-state actors and particularly business organisations often do not enjoy formal rights to participate in rule-making and therefore resort to other avenues of influence. As a result of the number of actors formally and informally involved as well as differences between countries in regard to national business interests, organisations and their access to national actors, the process of international law-making is both more complex and less transparent than national law-making.[1]

---

1 Szasz, P. C. (1995) 'General law-making processes', in O. Schachter and C. C. Joyner (eds), *United Nations Legal Order*, Vol. I, Cambridge: Cambridge University Press, pp. 35–108; and Hannum, H. (1995) 'Human rights', in O. Schachter and C. C. Joyner (eds), *United Nations Legal Order*, Vol. I, Cambridge: Cambridge University Press, pp. 319–348.

The traditional view in international law was that individuals did not have an independent position in the international legal system: what role, rights and privileges they enjoyed was based on states' consent. Under modern international law this situation has changed somewhat. Especially with the development of international human rights law, individuals (especially as victims of human rights violations caused by states) have been granted legal rights at the international level, and obligations have been imposed on individuals under customary international law and international criminal law. Still, the attribution of rights and obligations has not been met by similar access to participation in law-making.

Traditionally, TNCs were not seen to possess international legal personality. The international governance system that was created in 1945 with the establishment of the UN did not take into account that a few decades later some of the world's largest business organisations would be on a par with some of the world's large states in terms of the size of their economies, and that global transnational trade and the number of TNCs would grow as they did during the second half of the 20th century. The Universal Declaration of Human Rights (UDHR) makes reference to all organs of society, but businesses were not originally intended to be included among these 'organs', nor thought to belong there. It simply was not conceivable in the late 1940s that the private sector would attain the economic and political power that it soon came to have, nor the capacity to cause societal harm that in the latter decades of the 20th century led to severe concern about business impact on society.

In recent decades some scholars have begun to question whether this view holds under current conditions, because it excludes these companies from international legal sanctions and allows a situation of impunity for their actions.[2] Even if it has rarely occurred until now, international legal personality can, in principle, be bestowed upon a company as an individual organisation, just as on any other individual. This does not imply that companies need be granted wide or general international legal personality, that is, to match that of states. It also does not foreclose less radical approaches, like inviting companies to participate in or be consulted on the processes of formulating rules pertaining to business conduct and societal impact. Given their status as so-called legal persons, companies already enjoy individual legal personality in most jurisdictions. This means that, in addition to enjoying rights, a company as such can be penalised as an organisation if it is found to violate the law. By contrast, the International Criminal Court can penalise only individuals, not companies as organisations.

International law already recognises a purpose-based differentiation of international legal personality for certain non-state actors. The International Court of Justice (ICJ) has reasoned that the international legal personality of international organisations extends only to the needs to fulfil assigned tasks in context.[3] Following that line of thinking, any international legal personality of companies may also be delimited to the purpose at hand. However, as expectations of companies and especially TNCs expand so that they are increasingly seen as new duty-bearers on a political, ethical, soft or even hard law basis, it might be considered to grant companies certain limited purpose-oriented rights to take part in international law-making that looks to expanding their duties to correspond with widely held societal views and expectations of rights and responsibility. This means that companies may be involved, but there is no assumption in international law that companies should by default enjoy the same degree of participation in international law-making as states or the same decision-making powers as states. The idea of involving for-profit non-state actors in international law-making processes aiming to introduce constraints on the societal impact of business by

2 For a detailed overview, see Wouters and Chané (2013) *Multinational Corporations in International Law.*
3 International Court of Justice (1949) *Reparations for Injuries*, Advisory Opinion, ICJ Reports, pp. 178–179.

developing norms of conduct may seem like letting the fox into the hen-house. However, the experience of the process towards the UNGPs of involving some of the large business associations that had previously been among the hardest opponents on norms on business responsibilities for human rights[4] offers a different perspective, even if the model offered by the process towards the UNGPs is in need of some revision, as explained in later chapters. The purpose would be to develop rules that enjoy a strong pull towards compliance from within, because those to whom they apply have taken part in developing them and perceive the rule-making process and the output as legitimate. Legitimacy would require the role of companies to be balanced by that of others, such as civil society organisations. The inclusion of non-state actors would be in addition to that of states and international organisations that are already members of the pertinent international law-making process by default.

The fact that intergovernmental regulation of the private sector's social or environmental impact on society so far generally has the form of soft law (not legally binding, but often said to be morally and politically binding) rather than hard law (legally binding) does not make it devoid of legal relevance. Soft law is guiding, and in international law often serves as proto-law or as the precursor of later instruments of hard international law (whether in the name of a treaty or another legally binding instrument under another name, typically 'convention'). Soft international law is particularly prevalent in areas of human rights, international economic relations and environmental protection. Soft law norms are typically faster agreed to by states compared to their transformation into legally binding treaty obligations, which is often protracted and sometimes more susceptible to politically based delay or even rejection. For example, the UDHR was developed in three years (1945–1948), but it took almost 20 years to transform its standards into the legally binding treaties of the International Covenant on Economic, Social and Cultural Rights (ICESCR)[5] and the International Covenant on Civil and Political Rights (ICCPR),[6] both adopted in 1966. Additionally, the UN Declaration on the Right to Development,[7] adopted in 1986, has not yet been turned into a treaty, and negotiations have been halted.

International law-making is typically formal and aligned with the state-centred structure of international law, the closer it gets to adopting conventional types of hard and sometimes soft law. By contrast, the more informal process of developing the preceding instruments, or 'law-in-the-making', can enable non-state actors to contribute through national, NGO or lobbyist channels. The variety of international law instruments with varying degrees of binding or guiding force (especially in international soft law) contributes to the limited transparency of the law-making process.[8]

Soft law is not enforceable in front of courts of law. It may, however, be sanctioned through other means, including economic or political or by 'naming and shaming'.[9] To a company, responses from buyers, customers, investors, regulators or media may be a powerful driver for adopting specific conduct. By contrast to some regional human rights law,

4 See Chapter 4, section 4.4 and discussion in Ryngaert, C. and Buhmann, K. (2012) 'Human rights challenges for multinational corporations working and investing in conflict zones', Introductory article for special issue of *Human Rights and International Legal Discourse*, Vol. 6, No. 1, pp. 3–13.

5 International Covenant on Economic, Social and Cultural Rights, GA Res. 2200A (XXI), UN Doc. A/6316 (1966), 993 UNTS 3.

6 International Covenant on Civil and Political Rights, GA Res. 2200A (XXI), UN Doc. A/6316 (1966), 999 UNTS 171.

7 United Nations (1986) *Declaration on the Right to Development*, UN Doc. A/RES/41/218, 4 December.

8 Hajer, M. A. (1995) *The Politics of Environmental Discourse: Ecological Modernization and the Policy Process*, New York: Clarendon Press; Szasz (1995) 'General law-making processes'.

9 Cashore et al. (2004) *Governing through Markets*; Burke, R. J., Martin, G. and Cooper, C. L. (2011) *Corporate Reputation: Managing Opportunities and Threats*, Farnham: Ashgate.

international law in the field of human rights, environment and climate change mitigation is already marked by an enforcement regime that is weak in terms of 'hard' sanctions, that is, sanctions like fines and prison sentences that can be executed. Even for states much international law in sustainability-related areas is enforced through 'naming and shaming' through critique from treaty bodies. In other words, the line between what is hard and soft law is therefore thin in this area. International law that is hard in the sense of being legally binding may not be much more felt in practice by those who violate it than international law that is soft in the sense of not being legally binding. As a result, in international law and particularly in the sustainability-related fields, it need not be crucial whether a law-making process leads to hard or soft law, as often the fact that new norms emerge by itself carries sanction opportunities that are not necessarily effectively stronger if the norm is adopted as legally binding.

2.2 Regulatory innovation in theory: involving non-state actors in super-national law-making

Already when the issue of international codes of conduct for TNCs was in its infancy in legal theory, the issue of business participation in the norm-making process did occupy some international law scholars. Writing in 1964, Wolfgang Friedmann argued that the development of such rules with little or no direct TNC participation would be detrimental to the effectiveness as well as the implementation of the codes.[10] Writing in the 1980s, Jonathan Charney explained that failure to include TNCs in negotiations under international organisations to produce norms for their behaviour was likely to result in rules that would not accurately reflect the realities of TNC interest and power. Charney speculated that this could cause TNC resistance to implementation should the international community try to convert the soft codes into binding international or national law, or in other words would cause TNC resistance to compliance and to being subjected to rules developed without their participation. Failure to allow direct TNC participation in the development of potential international law pertaining to their activities and impacts would mean that the proposed codes 'do not resolve the underlying political and economic issues, they merely convert them into *legal* issues'.[11] Charney argued that direct TNC involvement in the norm-making process would facilitate interaction within the international legal system, including about the interests, needs and conditions of stakeholders and those subjected to the rules, and would promote commitment.

Charney argued that greater participation by corporations might in fact strengthen the system of international law by recognising their increasing power and reducing the drive to protect business interests through lobbying of states. With reference to the relative success of the ILO and OECD in international law-making setting norms of conduct for business with regard to their societal impacts (also explained in the next section), Charney suggested that TNCs be granted limited procedural rights to enable them to participate through formal and informal avenues in the development and enforcement of international law-making relevant to their interests.[12] Business participation in international law-making could be complemented and balanced by awarding other non-state interest groups (e.g. NGOs) similar rights of participation.[13] Charney noted that, owing to the conflicting interests and

10 Friedmann, W. (1964) *The Changing Structure of International Law*, London: Stevens & Sons; Charney, J. I. (1983) 'Transnational corporations and developing public international law', *Duke Law Journal*, Vol. 32, pp. 748–788.
11 Charney (1983) 'Transnational corporations and developing public international law', at p. 754.
12 Ibid., esp. at pp. 775–780.
13 Ibid., esp. at p. 780.

concerns of states and various non-state actors, independent participation of non-state actors in the creation and enforcement of international law would be best achieved through an iterative process.[14] Indeed, scholars have more recently argued that a pluralist global order must recognise a plurality of actors in duties as well as in law-making, and that participation by non-state actors does not challenge the primacy of states in law-making.[15]

The dynamic character of international law and its course of gradually expanding the recognition of legal personality beyond sovereign states and resembling groups, such as rebel movements, have demonstrated themselves in several other ways that testify to an ability to adapt to conditions of change in the external environment. The granting of limited international personality to international organisations is a case in point, as is the establishment of limited duties applying to legal persons in international environmental law.[16] Provided the political will is present, governments can in principle develop and adopt legally binding international obligations for companies to reduce their adverse impacts on society or promote positive impacts.[17] Indeed, the ability of international society to adopt such rules may be significant for long-term faith in international organisations to handle global problems.[18]

Although states are the original primary actors in international law, international law does involve a plurality of actors and sources of law. Policy- and process-oriented international law scholars like Rosalyn Higgins and Myres McDougal have argued in favour of a process-oriented approach to the system of international law, recognising that international law is a constantly evolving process of decision-making.[19] Higgins and Robert McCorquodale have emphasised the participation of individuals in the international legal system, as holders of rights and increasingly of duties and as claim-makers.[20] McCorquodale also emphasises the ability to participate in the creation, development and enforcement of international law. Noting that NGO participation has become accepted in international law-making,[21] and that to 'look solely at the end process (i.e. the ratified treaty) without any examination of the process by which that law is made, ignores the *discursive context, power structures and interests involved* in international law',[22] he observes that a measure of non-state actors' participation in international law-making is consistent with the dominant state-based concept of the international legal system, with participation still largely dependent on state consent.[23] Arguably, increased participation by for-profit non-state actors may be a corollary to the

14 Ibid., esp. at pp. 775–780, 787–788.
15 Noortmann, M. (2001) 'Non-state actors in international law', in B. Arts, M. Noortmann and B. Reinalda (eds), *Non-State Actors in International Relations*, Aldershot: Ashgate, pp. 59–76, at p. 72, with references to Charlesworth, H. and Chinkin, C. (2000) *The Boundaries of International Law: A Feminist Perspective*, Manchester: Manchester University Press; see also McCorquodale, R. (2010) 'The individual and the international legal system', in M. D. Evans (ed.), *International Law*, 3rd edn, Oxford: Oxford University Press, pp. 284–310; and discussion below.
16 For example, the *1969 Convention on Civil Liability for Oil Pollution Damage*, 973 UNTS 3.
17 Shaw, M. N. (2008) *International Law*, 6th edn, Cambridge: Cambridge University Press, at p. 197; De Schutter, O. (2010) *International Human Rights Law*, Cambridge: Cambridge University Press, at pp. 55, 395–399.
18 Steiner, H. J., Alston, P. and Goodman, R. (2008) *Human Rights in Context*, 3rd edn, Oxford: Oxford University Press, at p. 1385.
19 McDougal (1964) 'The policy-oriented approach to law'; McDougal and Reisman (1981) *International Law in Contemporary Perspective*; Higgins (1994) *Problems and Process*.
20 Higgins (1994) *Problems and Process*, at pp. 49–50; McCorquodale (2010) 'The individual and the international legal system', esp. at pp. 299–305.
21 McCorquodale (2010) 'The individual and the international legal system', at pp. 301–304.
22 McCorquodale, R. (2006) 'The individual and the international legal system', in M. D. Evans (ed.), *International Law*, 2nd edn, Oxford: Oxford University Press, pp. 308–332, at p. 325 (emphasis added).
23 McCorquodale (2010) 'The individual and the international legal system', at pp. 305–306.

already extensive participation by civil society organisations, which are non-profit non-state actors. To avoid capture and legitimacy risks, it must take place within a clearly demarcated process with clearly demarcated roles. Clearly defined procedures are already applied by specific fields of law, such as national administrative law, for related purposes. We revert to this in Chapter 4 and onwards.

Multi-level regulatory and governance theories have contributed to innovating the thinking on actors and processes in international and related public law in order to accommodate the emergence of new actors and new concerns.[24] Common to these is a recognition of the role of non-state actors and a recognition that corporations already in practice engage in law-making at the transnational level through a number of networks or technical specialised structures in addressing global sustainability concerns. As will be elaborated below in this and subsequent chapters, scholars like Friedmann, Charney, Teubner and more recently Sol Picciotto and Berger-Walliser with Shrivastava have long speculated that the integration of companies will benefit their understanding and acceptance of the regulatory needs at hand, and that this would be supportive of compliance.[25] Despite differing points of departure, those observers note that an integration, recognition and formalisation is required in order to ensure the representation of the interests both of potential bearers of duties or responsibilities (such as companies) and of those whose interests are legally or de facto subjected to impact by the actions of other non-state actors (in other words, those who are victims of the adverse impacts caused by companies).

A broader integration of non-state actors in the law-making process, including not-for-profit organisations like NGOs and other civil society organisations, is perhaps even more important in relation to the sustainability issues that grow increasingly more global as well as local within diverse global contexts. Such inclusion may help ensure the representation of concerns and interests beyond a few selected organisations that may not necessarily represent all interests and stakeholders in a balanced manner. Additionally, it offers a way forward for dealing with representative legitimacy deficits increasingly apparent with globalisation, the growth of the political economy, and its impact on the role of and reliance on law to regulate societal interests and concerns at a global level.

Among pragmatic takes on the evolution of law across borders and across the public and private, national and international sphere, observations made by scholars of 'Global Administrative Law' (GAL) draw attention to the legal relevance of new forms of law. These new forms of law are evolving through public–private, networking and/or multi-stakeholder processes, involving actors who do not have a formal law-making role at the international level but who nevertheless produce rules of conduct that have law-like effects, often at multiple levels and addressing subjects transnationally.[26] The pragmatic approach of GAL demonstrates that it is possible to observe novel and often hybrid developments in an international or transnational regulatory context and deal analytically with those new phenomena

24 For example, Kingsbury, B., Krisch, N. and Stewart, R. B. (2005) 'The emergence of global administrative law', *Law and Contemporary Problems*, Vol. 68, No. 3, pp. 15–61; Lobel (2005) 'The Renew Deal'; Picciotto, S. (2008) 'Regulatory networks and multi-level governance', in O. Dilling, H. Martin and G. Winter (eds), *Responsible Business: Self-Governance and Law in Transnational Economic Transactions*, Oxford: Hart, pp. 315–341.

25 Friedmann (1964) *The Changing Structure of International Law*; Charney (1983) 'Transnational corporations and developing public international law'; Teubner (1983) 'Substantive and reflective elements in modern law'; Picciotto (2003) 'Rights, responsibilities and regulation of international business'; Berger-Walliser, G. and Shrivastava, P. (2015) 'Beyond compliance'.

26 Krisch, N. and Kingsbury, B. (2006) 'Introduction: Global governance and global administrative law in the international legal order', *European Journal of International Law*, Vol. 17, No. 1, pp. 1–13, at pp. 12–13; McIntyre, O. (2012) 'The human right to water as a creature of global administrative law', *Water International*, Vol. 37, No. 6, pp. 654–669.

without getting lost in debates on how to classify them within the conventional boxes of public or private law.

Moreover, of considerable relevance to the issue of transnational rule-making, GAL draws attention to problems that these new forms of processes for producing rules and resulting substantive rules or 'law' encounter with regard to legitimacy, transparency and accountability. By deploying legal constructs that are well established in national procedural administrative law, GAL offers an approach and vocabulary for questioning and developing law in the field of super-national decision-making.[27] For example, likening it to the right of affected individuals to hearing or consultation, which is an essential procedural guarantee in national administrative law,[28] GAL scholarship has drawn on the participatory rights perspective that is familiar from due process in national administrative and constitutional law. GAL scholars apply this to analyse and discuss already existing rights of participation that have been granted to some private parties before some global institutions (such as certain activities of the World Trade Organization (WTO) and ILO).[29] It has been observed that, although consultation and participation are not fully efficient for ensuring broad participation, such processes of dialogue mimic parliaments and courts towards establishing transnational legal and governance dialogue and preventing conflicts.[30]

The GAL approach has been applied to several examples that are highly relevant in the context of sustainability regulation, typically related to regulation that is either developed by or executed by set-ups that combine private and governmental actors. The ISO has adopted a large number of standards that harmonise product and process rules around the world through broadly participatory processes involving both private and public actors.[31] ISO's SR Guidance Standard ISO 26000 is a case in point.[32] ISO 26000 is neither private self-regulation nor government regulation, but rather a hybrid public–private regulatory scheme that was developed with the participation of groups that consisted of major stakeholders. The UN Global Compact and the Forest Stewardship Council (FSC) can also be considered as examples of GAL.[33]

---

27 See also Anthony, G., Auby, J. B., Morison, J. and Zwart, T. (2011) 'Values in global administrative law: Introducing the collection', in G. Anthony, J. B. Auby, J. Morison and T. Zwart (eds), *Values in Global Administrative Law*, Oxford: Hart, pp. 1–16, at p. 2.

28 Kingsbury et al. (2005) 'The emergence of global administrative law', at p. 37.

29 Cassese, S. (2011) 'A global due process of law', in G. Anthony, J. B. Auby, J. Morison and T. Zwart (eds), *Values in Global Administrative Law*, Oxford: Hart, pp. 17–60.

30 Ibid., at p. 60.

31 Kingsbury et al. (2005) 'The emergence of global administrative law', at pp. 20–23. Other examples noted by Kingsbury et al. include: 1) Administration by formal international organisations established by treaty or executive agreement, such as the UN High Commissioner for Refugees' effective assumption of regulatory and other administrative tasks related to conducting refugee status determination and managing refugee camps. 2) Administration based on collective action by transnational networks of cooperative arrangements between national regulatory officials. These are characterised by the absence of binding formal decision-making structure and the dominance of informal cooperation between state regulators. Although the resulting arrangements, like the pressure exerted by WTO law for mutual recognition of regulatory rules and decisions among member states, have an administrative rather than a judicial character, they are noted to have the potential of being very effective. 3) Distributed administration conducted by national regulators under treaty, network or other cooperative regimes, with national regulatory agencies taking decisions on issues of foreign or global concern, for example on biodiversity conservation or greenhouse gas emissions and arrangements for mutual recognition of standards and certifications.

32 ISO 26000 was adopted in 2010 after a multi-stakeholder preparatory process over several years, available at http://www.iso.org/iso/iso_catalogue/management_standards/social_responsibility.htm (last accessed 5 December 2016).

33 Meidinger, E. (2006) 'The administrative law of global private–public regulation: The case of forestry', *European Journal of International Law*, Vol. 17, No. 1, pp. 47–87; Buhmann, K. (2009) 'Regulating corporate

Multi-level structures of governance – including an increasing role for administrative bodies with political mandates and/or substantive technical expertise – make law and politics increasingly inter-tangled. Hybrid forms of law that include elements conventionally considered to belong to the fields of politics or economics have emerged.[34] The blurring of boundaries is also observed in the increasing debate on transnational law. Much of the large body of transnational law that has emerged in recent decades may appear to be private, but it is fundamentally public in character.[35] Transnational or hybrid law in such fields as human rights, labour, environmental and public health law is a core example of this.[36] The tendency towards such blurring of boundaries between politics, law and economics can become self-perpetuating when knowledge-oriented regulation of such areas as environmental protection, food safety and consumer safety leads to delegation to expert bodies to define details.

Participation by experts from within authorities may contribute precision knowledge on the issue at stake, but does not necessarily ensure that norms of conduct deliver the intended action and results. Participation by concerned actors in defining contents[37] as well as the autonomy and cognitive processes of concerned knowledge-oriented organisations[38] ideally provides the resulting regulation with a high degree of precision as to the target policy objective. Yet the effectiveness of hybrid regulation can also be reduced, owing to lack of cohesion between the various systems from which such regulation results, or in the context in which it is brought to prove its worth. Conflicts of interest between the economic system and the international human rights system are a case in point. In the relationship between trade law and human rights law, both as fields of international law, it is often the effectiveness of international human rights law that becomes compromised.[39] In other words, the protection of social aspects is marginalised in favour of economic ones. The emergence and growth of international trade law and international human rights law as specific legal systems illustrate the conflicts that may result from such fragmentation of international law.[40] Lack of coherence between international trade law and international human rights law is part of the reason why various sustainability-concerned actors have resorted to regulatory innovation, including hybrid or intergovernmental codes of conduct or guidance on sustainability concerns.

Yet other scholars have addressed the emergence of informal law and the participation of non-state actors from the process perspective of law-making. So far mainly sketching the foundations of what may become an institutionalisation and formal recognition of the

social and human rights responsibilities at the UN plane: Institutionalising new forms of law and law-making approaches?', *Nordic Journal of International Law*, Vol. 78, No. 1, pp. 1–52.

34 Sand, I.-J. (2000) *Changing Forms of Governance and the Role of Law: Society and Its Law*, Arena Working Paper No. WP 00/14, Oslo: University of Oslo, at footnote 6; Sand, I.-J. (2012) 'Hybridization, change and the expansion of law', in N. Å. Andersen and I.-J. Sand (eds), *Hybrid Forms of Governance: Self-Suspension of Power*, Houndmills: Palgrave Macmillan, pp. 186–204.

35 Koh, H. K. (2002) 'Opening remarks: Transnational legal process illuminated', in M. Likosky (ed.), *Transnational Legal Processes: Globalisation and Power Disparities*, Colchester: Butterworths, pp. 327–332, at p. 331.

36 Ibid.

37 Sand (2000) *Changing Forms of Governance and the Role of Law*, at footnote 2.

38 Sand, I.-J. (1997) *Fragmented Law – from Unitary to Pluralistic Legal Systems: A Socio-Legal Perspective of Post-National Legal Systems*, Arena Working Paper No. 18, Oslo: University of Oslo, at pp. 13–14.

39 Sand (2000) *Changing Forms of Governance and the Role of*, after footnote 90; United Nations Human Rights Council (2008) *Protect, Respect and Remedy*.

40 See also Koskenniemi, M. (2006) *Fragmentation of International Law: Difficulties Arising from the Diversification and Expansion of International Law*, International Law Commission – Report of the Study Group of the International Law Commission, UN Doc. A/CN.4/L.682, Part C.3.(ii).

inclusion of non-state actors in law-making 'beyond the state', parts of the debate turn on the feasibility of a 'global democracy without a global state' and what this may entail in terms of law-making process, forms of law, and accountability.[41] Accountability is often understood to consist of *ex post* sanctions, but may also be *ex ante*, such as processes that induce reporting and accounting for processes to identify and manage adverse impacts on society. Grainne de Burca has proposed a 'democratic-striving approach' as an iterative approach to deal with the dilemma of legitimacy and transnational governance. Critiquing some approaches for taking insufficient issue with the challenges in providing above-national governance with legitimacy as 'in denial', 'wishful thinking' or 'compensatory', de Burca notes that the democratic-striving approach 'acknowledges the difficulty and complexity of democratizing transnational governance yet insists on its necessity, and identifies the act of continuous striving itself as the source of legitimation and accountability'.[42] De Burca reasons that such an approach offers a way around the risk of too limited specificity or focusing too much on formal or *ex post* issues, such as due process and legal accountability, while giving insufficient consideration to questions of democratic representation and participation.[43] She observes that there is relevance in regarding democracy as a concept that can be transposed from the state to the transnational level, and therefore in designing mechanisms of participation or representation in transnational governance that offer functions similar to those which representation and participation have in national democratic systems.[44] From this iterative perspective it recognises the significance of inclusive participation for effective processes of rule-making.[45] The approach proposed by de Burca acknowledges that strengthening the democratic character of transnational governance is both feasible and significant and that, given the fluidity and evolving character of above-national governance, an approach to include non-state actors can be both dynamic and iterative work-in-progress.

2.3 Regulatory innovation in practice: public, private and hybrid law-making for sustainability and business conduct

Several types of regulatory innovation have occurred in response to the challenges set out above in relation to regulating the impact of transnational business. Early ground-breaking international soft law developments include the Guidelines for Multinational Enterprises adopted in 1976 by the OECD as an Annex[46] to the OECD Declaration on International Investment and Multinational Enterprises,[47] and the Tripartite Declaration of Principles

---

41 For example, Cohen and Sabel (2005) 'Global democracy?'; Habermas, J. (2008) 'The constitutionalization of international law and the legitimation process of a constitution for world society', *Constellations*, Vol. 15, No. 4, pp. 444–455; Hachez, N. and Wouters, J. (2011) *A Glimpse at the Democratic Legitimacy of Private Standards: Democratic Legitimacy as Public Accountability*, Working Paper, March, Leuven: Katholieke Universiteit Leuven – Leuven Centre for Global Governance Studies; Scott, C. D., Cafaggi, F. and Senden, L. (2011) 'The conceptual and constitutional challenge of transnational private regulation', *Journal of Law and Society*, Vol. 38, No. 1, pp. 1–19.

42 Burca (2008) 'Developing democracy beyond the state', at p. 237, with further details from p. 249.

43 Ibid., at pp. 238–249.

44 Ibid., at p. 247.

45 Ibid., at p. 253.

46 OECD (1976) *OECD Guidelines for Multinational Enterprises*, Paris: OECD, http://search.oecd.org/official documents/publicdisplaydocumentpdf/?cote=CES(2000)17&docLanguage=En (last accessed 27 December 2016). The Guidelines underwent major revisions in 2000 and 2011.

47 OECD (2011) *Declaration on International Investment and Multinational Enterprises*, most recently revised 25 May 2011. Most recent and earlier versions available at http://www.oecd.org/daf/inv/investment-policy/oecd declarationoninternationalinvestmentandmultinationalenterprises.htm (last accessed 20 November 2016).

Concerning Multinational Enterprises and Social Policy adopted in 1977 by the ILO.[48] The OECD's Guidelines are recommendations from home states to corporations based in those states to observe certain principles when they operate in host states. Revised in 2000 and 2011, the Guidelines are open to accession by non-OECD states. In addition to the promotion of responsible business conduct in issue areas that include human rights, labour and industrial issues, environment and anti-corruption, the Guidelines incorporate a remedy modality with extraterritorial reach. Introduced with the 2000 revision, National Contact Points (NCPs) are state-based non-judicial remedy institutions. They handle complaints of alleged violations of the Guidelines, including those that occurred in states that do not adhere to the Guidelines, provided the company in question operates out of one that does.[49] The ILO's Declaration aims to engage TNCs in complying with the ILO's social conventions and recommendations regardless of whether the host state is bound by these. It was followed in 1998 by the ILO's Declaration on Fundamental Principles and Rights at Work ('ILO 1998 Declaration'),[50] which refers to the core labour principles of freedom of association and collective bargaining, non-discrimination in employment, elimination of forced labour and elimination of child labour and underscores the obligations of all member states to respect ILO core labour principles. It declares that all ILO members – whether or not they have ratified the ILO conventions that protect the core labour rights – have an obligation to respect and protect those principles arising from the very fact of their ILO membership (art. 2). In combination with the 1977 Declaration the message to corporations is that core labour rights should be respected globally, regardless of how the rights are covered by national law in countries of operation. Additionally, launched in 2000 as a voluntary instrument for business conduct, the UN Global Compact has overall issue areas of human rights, environment, labour and anti-corruption that are each underpinned by one major international law instrument.[51]

The UN launched its first major attempt to develop norms of conduct for TNCs in the 1970s. Even though this was an early effort it is not without significance to the situation of the UN venturing into such a comprehensive endeavour as compared to more specialised organisations with more limited topical or regional focus, such as the ILO or OECD. Led by the Commission on Transnational Corporations,[52] the Draft UN Code of Conduct for TNCs[53] listed duties for TNCs to respect host countries' development goals, observe their domestic law, respect fundamental human rights, and observe consumer

48 ILO, *Tripartite Declaration of Principles Concerning Multinational Enterprises and Social Policy* (MNE Declaration), originally adopted in 1977 by the ILO Governing Body, http://www.ilo.org/empent/Publications/WCMS_094386/lang--en/index.htm (last accessed 27 December 2016).

49 Buhmann, K. (2015) 'Defying territorial limitations: Regulating business conduct extraterritorially through establishing obligations in EU law and national law', in J. L. Cernic and T. Van Ho (eds), *Human Rights and Business: Direct Corporate Accountability for Human Rights*, The Hague: Wolf Legal Publishers, pp. 179–228.

50 ILO (1998) *Declaration on Fundamental Principles and Rights at Work*, Adopted by the International Labour Conference, 86th session, Geneva, June, 37 I.L.M. 1233, http://www.ilo.org/public/english/standards/decl/declaration/text/ (last accessed 17 January 2013).

51 United Nations General Assembly (1948) *Universal Declaration of Human Rights*, GA Res. 217A (III), UN Doc. A/810, 10 December; United Nations General Assembly (1992) *Rio Declaration on Environment and Development*; ILO (1998) *Declaration on Fundamental Principles and Rights at Work*; and United Nations General Assembly (2003) *United Nations Convention against Corruption*, UN Doc. A/58/422, 31 October.

52 Established by the Economic and Social Council under Resolution 1913 (LVII) of 5 December 1974.

53 *Development and International Economic Cooperation: Transnational Corporations*, Draft Code of Conduct on Transnational Corporations (1990) Last version of the proposed Draft Code: UN Doc. E/1990/94, 12 June.

and environmental protection objectives.[54] The project was abandoned at the beginning of the 1990s, however, partly owing to opposition and divergence of investment-related interests among certain governments.[55] As seen above, the ILO and OECD were more successful in their efforts undertaken in the 1970s at the same time as the Draft UN Code of Conduct project was first introduced.

Several private or public–private hybrid initiatives have emerged across sectors or in relation to specific sectors. Ranging from principle-based standards over certification, reporting and process to guidance standards,[56] most embody a normative aspect that firms commit to on a voluntary basis; and some have modalities attached to certify adherence to or provide transparency on practices. While adherence to a code of conduct may be an integrated part of a legal contract and non-adherence therefore can lead to legal liability, many of these regulatory set-ups are based on market-based sanctions rather than legal sanctions. According to somewhat similar socio-legal,[57] political science[58] and economics[59] theories, the assumption is that stakeholder interaction and transparency on company practices and potential risks to a firm's 'social licence to operate' will encourage firms to self-regulate and adopt certain practices in order to stay in accordance with buyers' or consumers' preferences. Early codes were spurred by political and civil society concerned with the social impact of sourcing in ways that would contribute to upholding apartheid[60] or frustration with international regulatory developments. Set up by civil society organisations and firms in the timber industry, the FSC emerged as a response to limited regulatory output of the Rio 1992 Summit in relation to sustainable forestry. The extractives sector has witnessed public–private codes evolve in relation to products like diamonds,[61] security,[62] corruption and payment practices.[63] Process, management, reporting and/or labelling instruments directed at business practices have undergone a shift from general

54 For discussions of the Draft Code of Conduct, see Lansing, P. and Rosaria, A. (1991) 'An analysis of the United Nations proposed Code of Conduct for Transnational Corporations', *World Competition*, Vol. 14, No. 4, pp. 35–50; Bendell, J. (2004) *Barricades and Boardrooms: A Contemporary History of the Corporate Accountability Movement*, Technology, Business and Society Programme Paper No. 13, Geneva: United Nations Research Institute for Social Development, at pp. 12–13. Particularly on its human rights aspects, see Mayer, A. E. (2009) 'Human rights as a dimension of CSR: The blurred lines between legal and non-legal categories', *Journal of Business Ethics*, Vol. 88, pp. 561–577.

55 Lansing and Rosaria (1991) 'An analysis of the United Nations proposed Code of Conduct for Transnational Corporations'.

56 For an explanation of this typology, refer to Rasche (2010) 'Collaborative Governance 2.0'.

57 In particular, reflexive law (see further Chapter 4) and responsive law; see Nonet, P. and Selznick, P. (1978) *Law and Society in Transition: Toward Responsive Law*, New York: Harper/Colophon.

58 Cashore, B. (2002) 'Legitimacy and the privatization of environmental governance: How non-state market-driven (NSMD) governance systems gain rule-making authority', *Governance: An International Journal of Policy, Administration, and Institutions*, Vol. 15, No. 4, pp. 503–529; see also Cashore et al. (2004) *Governing through Markets*.

59 Ayres, I. and Braithwaite, J. (1992) *Responsive Regulation: Transcending the Deregulation Debate*, New York: Oxford University Press, which should not be confused with 'responsive law'. 'Responsive regulation' is an economic and political science-oriented theory which seeks to explain the way that a plurality of motivations for compliance interact, and to propose combined use of compliance and enforcement theories, including deterrent and cooperative regulatory enforcement strategies.

60 Global Sullivan Principles, http://hrlibrary.umn.edu/links/sullivanprinciples.html (last accessed 30 December 2016).

61 The Kimberley Process, a joint government, industry and civil society initiative, which seeks to curb the trade in conflict diamonds through a certification programme, available at http://www.kimberleyprocess.com/ (last accessed 27 December 2016).

62 Voluntary Principles on Security and Human Rights, http://www.voluntaryprinciples.org/files/voluntary_principles_english.pdf (last accessed 30 December 2016).

63 Extractive Industries Transparency Initiative (EITI), www.eiti.org (last accessed 27 December 2016).

principles of ethical conduct[64] towards a more detailed reference to instruments and standards of international human rights and labour law. Major instruments such as the artisanal and industry production process tool SA 8000,[65] the reporting tool Global Reporting Initiative (GRI)[66] and the original FSC principles reference international human rights law (including core international labour standards), and therefore by implication lean on those as normative sources. In the late 1990s, corporate environmental performance was entered into the ISO's process codes with the ISO 14000 series standard and occupational health and safety with the OHSAS 18000 series. Adopted in 2010 to non-state actor as well as governmental social responsibility, ISO 26000[67] includes several human and labour rights aspects.

An indication of emergent coherence among public and hybrid codes, ISO 26000, the 2011 revision of the OECD's Guidelines and guidance at the UN Global Compact website refer to the UNGPs and apply similar understandings of key concepts like social risk-based due diligence. This due diligence concept was introduced by the UN Framework and elaborated by the UNGPs. It entails a process to identify risks and manage adverse impacts caused by the firm to society. The uptake by the OECD's Guidelines expands its application from human rights to CSR issues in general.[68]

Not only NGOs but also TNCs already in practice enjoy a degree of access to international law-making processes through their international organisations enjoying consultative status with organisations like the UN. Through such organisations civil society has long been involved both formally and informally in international law-making. In sustainability-related areas, consultative status is mainly but not exclusively held by organisations representing actual or potential victims of state or corporate abuse. Article 71 of the UN Charter empowers the UN Economic and Social Council (ECOSOC) to 'make suitable arrangements for consultation' with an NGO 'which are concerned with matters within its competence'.[69] Some international business associations, including associations like the International Chamber of Commerce, have been granted consultative status under this provision. In addition, NGOs may have access to UN conferences. At least since around the 1992 Rio Conference on Environment and Development, NGO participation and influence have become significant.[70] They have become recognised in formality and in theory, including as contributing to the deliberative process of UN law-making to make the latter more democratic and better informed, but do not grant a formal negotiating role.[71] In addition, many NGOs have made use of later decades' development in information technology to access and scrutinise information, form networks and represent constituencies in places far from where UN meetings take place.[72]

---

64 For example, Caux Round Table, www.cauxroundtable.org (last accessed 27 December 2016).

65 Social Accountability International, Social Accountability (SA) 8000, version 2008, http://www.sa-intl.org/_data/n_0001/resources/live/2008StdEnglishFinal.pdf (last accessed 27 December 2016). SA 8000 was developed by Social Accountability International, an NGO.

66 Global Reporting Initiative, https://www.globalreporting.org/ (last accessed 27 December 2016).

67 ISO (2010) *ISO 26000*.

68 For details, see Buhmann, K. (2015) 'Business and human rights: Understanding the UN Guiding Principles from the perspective of transnational business governance interactions', *Transnational Legal Theory*, Vol. 6, No. 1, pp. 399–434.

69 *United Nations Charter* (1945), UNTS 993, art. 71.

70 Hajer (1995) *The Politics of Environmental Discourse*; Arts, B. (2001) 'The impact of environmental NGOs in international conventions', in B. Arts, M. Noortmann and B. Reinalda (eds), *Non-State Actors in International Relations*, Aldershot: Ashgate, pp. 195–210.

71 Hachez, N. (2008) 'The relations between the United Nations and civil society: Past, present and future', *International Organizations Law Review*, Vol. 5, No. 1, pp. 49–84, at pp. 62–63, 69.

72 Ibid., at pp. 69–70, 73 with references.

While international lawyers may tend to see NGO influence in terms of the formal consultative status, political science studies and some socio-legal scholars have demonstrated that the role of NGOs in practice transcends the pure consultative role and includes actual informal participation in negotiations with impact on actual law-making.[73] Studies have also demonstrated that companies and business organisations in practice have considerable influence on actual law-making through a number of channels, ranging from formal consultative status with degrees of actual participation in negotiations to defensive lobbying of states and taking the lead offensively through self-regulation, which may feed into international standard setting.[74]

2.4 Corporate Social Responsibility, sustainability and governance needs

Much of the regulatory innovation described above has taken place partly against the backdrop of the idea of firms having social responsibilities. CSR is a contested concept. To some, CSR indicates genuine efforts by profit-driven organisations to self-regulate and create a change in behaviour with the purpose of balancing economic and social impacts. To others, CSR suggests 'green-washing',[75] disguising adverse social impacts and exploiting governance gaps.[76] CSR is a dynamic phenomenon, which tends to expand to encompass new sustainability concerns, such as in recent years climate change.[77] No commonly agreed single definition of CSR exists, but most usages assume that businesses take action to promote their positive impact on society and reduce adverse impact. Assumptions that such action is done on a voluntary basis (underscored by the EU Commission's definitions of CSR from 2001 to mid-2011) have led to the CSR idea being discussed as distinct from law, despite one of the leading academics in CSR already in 1979 defining CSR to include legal responsibilities on a par with economic and ethical responsibilities,[78] both in the narrow sense of compliance with the letter of the law and in a broader sense of respecting the spirit of the law.[79] The core of the CSR idea is about business impact on society and assumes a

---

73 For example, Reinalda, B. (2001) 'Private in form, public in purpose: NGOs in international relations theory', in B. Arts, M. Noortmann and B. Reinalda (eds), *Non-State Actors in International Relations*, Aldershot: Ashgate, pp. 11–40 with references; compare from a legal perspective Chinkin, C. (2000) 'Normative development in the international legal system', in D. Shelton (ed.), *Commitment and Compliance: The Role of Non-Binding Norms in the International Legal System*, Oxford: Oxford University Press, pp. 21–42, esp. at p. 35; and, specifically with regard to human rights law-making at the UN, see Hannum (1995) 'Human rights'; Charnovitz, S. (1997) 'Two centuries of participation: NGOs and international governance', *Michigan Journal of International Law*, Vol. 18, No. 2, pp. 183–286.

74 For example, Arts (2001) 'The impact of environmental NGOs in international conventions'; Kolk, A. (2001) 'Multinational enterprises and international climate policy', in B. Arts, M. Noortmann and B. Reinalda (eds), *Non-State Actors in International Relations*, Aldershot: Ashgate, pp. 211–225. Compare also Kinley, D. and Nolan, J. (2008) 'Trading and aiding human rights in the global economy', *Nordic Journal of Human Rights Law*, Vol. 7, No. 4, pp. 353–377.

75 Green-washing denotes that an action is being made to look environmentally responsible, even if it remains questionable as to its environmental impacts.

76 Sheehy, B. (2015) 'Defining CSR: Problems and solutions', *Journal of Business Ethics*, Vol. 131, No. 3, pp. 625–648.

77 Matten, D. and Moon, J. (2008) '"Implicit" and "explicit" CSR: A conceptual framework for a comparative understanding of corporate social responsibility', *Academy of Management Review*, Vol. 33, No. 2, pp. 404–424, at pp. 406–407.

78 Carroll, A. B. (1979) 'A three-dimensional conceptual model of corporate performance', *Academy of Management Review*, Vol. 4, No. 4, pp. 497–505.

79 Schwartz, M. S. and Carroll, A. B. (2003) 'Corporate social responsibility: A three-domain approach', *Business Ethics Quarterly*, Vol. 13, No. 4, pp. 503–530.

convergence between economic development, social equity and environmental protection. This corresponds to the understanding of sustainability set out above, and indeed CSR is inherently related to sustainability.

Looking back, social practices related to the exploitation of labour were high on the CSR agenda in the 1990s following the exposure of sub-standard labour practices of large apparel TNCs and other firms. A common feature of many sustainability concerns is that they arise in relation to resources – labour, water, forests, land, minerals or others. Legal standards drawn from international law, for example international labour law standards expressed in the ILO's fundamental conventions, have long played a strong normative role in CSR instruments such as SA 8000, the UN Global Compact and the original principles of the FSC. Regulatory innovation driven by public institutions and international organisations like the OECD and the UN to promote corporate uptake of such standards through approaches that stimulate self-regulation often takes place in the shadow of mandatory law. The underlying message is that, if political will is sufficiently strong, political barriers to establishing hard law requirements can be overcome.

With its first policy documents on CSR, the EU defined CSR as a concept whereby companies decide voluntarily to contribute to a better society and a cleaner environment,[80] and as behaviour by businesses over and above legal requirements, voluntarily adopted because businesses deem it to be in their long-term interest.[81] In 2011 the EU Commission changed its definition of CSR into being for companies to take responsibility for their impact on society.[82] The change, which was partly introduced in order to ensure consistency between EU policies to promote CSR through legislative measures as well as the state duty element that had been noted by the UN Framework and was elaborated by the UNGPs, confirms the dynamic character of CSR.

CSR expectations often relate closely to sustainability in the sense that adverse social or environmental impacts are seen to harm the sustainability of conditions for the existence of humans, other beings in the natural environment, and even business. Sustainability is also a dynamic concept reflecting knowledge and concerns in relation to practices to balance current needs with those of the future. The evolution of the UN Global Compact's focus issues testifies to this dynamic character of both CSR and sustainability. The initial issue areas (human rights, labour and environment) adopted in 2000 were expanded to four after a UN treaty on anti-corruption had been adopted in 2004. In the early 2000s, climate change became a focus issue, reflecting global concern with the effects of greenhouse gases. More recently and since their adoption in September 2015, the 17 SDGs have been the dominant focus on the UN Global Compact's website, which serves as the Compact's key promotional information channel.

The dynamic evolution of both the concept of CSR and the idea of sustainability confirms that societal actors are concerned with the impact of economic and other practices, and that novel sustainability issues may be expected to keep arising. A report prepared in 2010 for UN discussions on sustainable development noted that, despite increased knowledge of the adverse impact of economic and other practices, 'unsustainable trends continue and sustainable development has not found the political entry points to make real

80 Commission of the European Communities (2001) *Promoting a European Framework for Corporate Social Responsibility*, COM(2001)366.

81 Commission of the European Communities (2002) *Communication from the Commission Concerning Corporate Social Responsibility: A Business Contribution to Sustainable Development*, COM(2002)347, at pp. 4–5.

82 European Commission (2011) *A Renewed EU Strategy 2011–2014 for Corporate Social Responsibility*, Communication from the Commission to the European Parliament, the Council, the European Economic and Social Committee and the Committee of the Regions, Brussels, 25 October, COM(2011)681, at 3.1.

progress'.[83] Terminologies may change and the CSR concept may date or be dated (as evident already with ISO 26000's focus on social responsibility rather than only *corporate* social responsibility, intended to signal the need for responsible practices among public and private actors alike), but concerns with balancing the needs of today with those of the future will persist. As technological evolution brings resources within ever closer reach even beyond the boundaries of this planet while those on the planet are being depleted,[84] the need to govern sustainable use of resources is likely to grow. This too reflects the need to innovate governance modalities to respond to such practical needs.

While organisational and some business ethics scholarship often understands 'law' in a positivist sense of 'black-letter law' and statutory requirements, various branches of legal theory and socio-legal studies have long taken an interest in CSR, the correlation between ethical directives on business and the boundaries of law as evolving norms of conduct, and the potential and implications that CSR has for the continuous evolution of law. Since the early 20th century, lawyers have discussed the merits of CSR from the corporate law perspective[85] and the potential of corporate governance to help deliver on public policy objectives,[86] the division of public and private roles of law,[87] and international law.[88] International human rights lawyers have taken a particular interest in CSR. The focus on societal impacts resonates well with concerns about the capacity of business activity to cause human rights harm and the risk of impunity arising from governance gaps.[89] Whereas much of the early literature prior to the adoption of the UN Framework and UNGPs focused on the potential of CSR with regard to business responsibilities for human rights, since the UN Framework was agreed some scholars of international human rights law have argued for a return to more conventional legal approaches to remedy and legal accountability.[90] Simultaneously, hybrid sustainability instruments keep expanding and becoming interrelated, as evidenced by the mutual interconnection of the UNGPs, the OECD's Guidelines, the UN Global Compact, ISO 26000 and others.[91]

83 Drexhage and Murphy (2010) *Sustainable Development*.
84 Rockström (2009) 'Planetary boundaries'.
85 Berle, A. A., Jr (1931) 'Corporate powers as powers in trust', *Harvard Law Review*, Vol. 44, No. 7, pp. 1049–1074; Dodd, E. M., Jr (1932) 'For whom are corporate managers trustees?', *Harvard Law Review*, Vol. 45, No. 7, pp. 1145–1163, both in response to the ruling in *Dodge v. Ford Motor Co.*, Ruling by the Michigan Supreme Court, 170 N W. 668 (Mich. 1919), at 684, whether a decision by Ford Company not to pay dividends to its shareholders in order to spend it on social causes was in accordance with the fiduciary duties of the management.
86 Teubner, G. (1985) 'Corporate fiduciary duties and their beneficiaries: A functional approach to the legal institutionalization of corporate responsibility', in K. J. Hopt and G. Teubner (eds), *Corporate Governance and Directors' Liabilities*, Berlin: Walter de Gruyter, pp. 149–177.
87 Epstein, E. M. (1998) 'Business ethics and corporate social policy', *Business and Society Review*, Vol. 37, No. 1, pp. 7–39, at p. 25; Backer, L. C. (2006) 'Multinational corporations, transnational law: The United Nations' Norms on the Responsibilities of Transnational Corporations as a harbinger of corporate social responsibility in international law', *Columbia Human Rights Law Review*, Vol. 37, Winter, pp. 287–389.
88 Mares, R. (2006) *Institutionalisation of Corporate Social Responsibilities: Synergies between the Practices of Leading Multinational Enterprises and Human Rights Law/Policy*, Lund: Lund University, Faculty of Law; Zerk, J. A. (2006) *Multinationals and Corporate Social Responsibility: Limitations and Opportunities in International Law*, Cambridge: Cambridge University Press.
89 Jägers, N. (2002) *Corporate Human Rights Obligations: In Search of Accountability*, Antwerp: Intersentia; Clapham, A. (2006) *Human Rights Obligations of Non-State Actors*, New York: Oxford University Press.
90 Bilchitz (2013) 'A chasm between "is" and "ought"?'; Deva, S. (2013) 'Treating human rights lightly: A critique of the consensus rhetoric and the language employed by the Guiding Principles', in S. Deva and D. Bilchitz (eds), *Human Rights Obligations of Business: Beyond the Corporate Responsibility to Respect?*, Cambridge: Cambridge University Press, pp. 78–104.
91 Buhmann, K. (2016) 'Public regulators and CSR: The "social licence to operate" in recent United Nations instruments on business and human rights and the juridification of CSR', *Journal of Business Ethics*, Vol. 136, No. 4, pp. 699–714.

2.5 Actors, interests and significance for the construction of norms on sustainable economic conduct

As sustainability-related practices and expectations are continually subject to revisions and adaptations, social actors seek to influence company conduct towards adherence to whatever standards and ideas are claimed to be part of socially responsible conduct at a given time. As part of this process, politicians and law-makers at national and above-national levels joined by trade unions, NGOs, companies and others also seek influence on what is to be understood by sustainability and how to shape organisational conduct accordingly. Governance and regulatory innovation have to take account of the diversity of actors and interests, because perceptions of benefit or loss from regulatory initiatives may affect support for or struggles against the launch of a regulatory activity or its outcome. Evolution of new norms and their implementation leads to institutionalisation. For this reason, the process as well as its outcome can have huge significance for actors whose functions may stand to either gain or lose from the new norms. The CSR stage offers a useful point of departure for understanding the diversity of actors, interests and convergence as well as divergence.

It has been observed in regard to CSR norms and their implementation that power and participation are two significant but somewhat unexplored issues in relation to CSR.[92] CSR is subject to struggles not only in the sense of defining relations between different actors and social groups and between the market and the state, but also in relation to participation in decision-making. Similarly, it has been noted that power relations between stakeholders have an influence over what issues are raised, what networks and alliances are formed, and what outputs result from discursive activities in the field of CSR.[93] These concerns also apply to sustainability in a more general sense.

Promoting particular forms of sustainability action through new norms or an institutionalisation of such norms can support the implementation of policy goals of national governments or international organisations (such as the UN) whose objectives relate to social or environmental impacts on society. Governments and international organisations therefore have much to gain from specific understandings of what CSR is or should mean. Other organisations too have much at stake in regard to both the process and its outcomes. Overall, we may distinguish between three general outcomes that will impact the process through which participants engage to preserve their interests and therefore their power. These outcomes are: change in the form of new binding rules (a 'hard institutionalisation'); change in the form of non-legally binding rules, for example new soft law or policy (a 'soft institutionalisation'); or no change in the law (corresponding to a preservation of the status quo).

A *'hard'* institutionalisation leads to the formulation of legal duties for businesses in international law, that is, for businesses to become duty-bearing subjects under international law. A hard institutionalisation could also result in the establishment of duties for businesses in regional (e.g. EU) law and national law in addition to those that they already have. A *'soft'* institutionalisation is formulated in terms of a clearer definition and (a degree of but not necessarily global) consensus on what is understood by the social responsibilities of businesses in the pertinent issue area. This could also entail a clearer delimitation of the boundaries between state duties and business responsibilities, and a clearer understanding and measure

---

92   Prieto-Carron, M., Lund-Thomsen, P., Chan, A., Muro, A. and Bhushan, C. (2006) 'Critical perspectives on CSR and development: What we know, what we don't know, and what we need to know', *International Affairs*, Vol. 82, No. 5, pp. 977–989, at p. 984 with references.

93   Ibid.

of consensus on disputed terms. A soft institutionalisation means that businesses are seen to have some social responsibilities, but without being subjected to legally binding requirements. Third, *status quo* means that the processes of attempting to reach either a hard or a soft institutionalisation are unsuccessful. Under the status quo, companies will be subjected mainly to their own norms and disparate economic and related sanctions, especially from investors and consumers. Of course, nation states may introduce specific requirements. For reasons of economic competition between states, such measures are, however, likely to be limited. To illustrate the implications, the following draws on the example of the human rights responsibilities of business.

A 'hard' institutionalisation in the form of legally binding requirements ensuring that businesses do not violate human rights and that they contribute actively to the realisation of human rights or act in socially responsible ways will mean significant restrictions in terms of permissible conduct and resource priorities for many businesses around the globe. Consequently, it will have potentially significant economic effects on many actors in the private sector, be they TNCs, suppliers or even buyers. A hard institutionalisation will affect the economies of many companies, at least in the short term. Therefore, much economic power may be related to businesses' social responsibilities being 'voluntary'. Indeed, this has marked much of the business-led discourse on CSR, as elaborated below in relation to the Draft UN Norms and the EU's Multi-Stakeholder Forum on CSR.

Companies that prefer minimal legal constraints may well prefer that international law should abstain from introducing obligations pertaining to their actions. A construction of understandings of corporate social responsibilities that would entail a preservation of international law as it was at the outset would allow them to pursue economic gain without the constraints of taking responsibility for their societal impacts. Some companies may also prefer a limitation of connections between norms on responsible business conduct and international law standards that may serve as guidance. Such limitations, or the rolling-back of connections already established, for example in the UN Global Compact and UNGPs, will reduce expectations of companies to respect the pertinent norms or standards. It could be less risky from a legal or even reputational perspective. From a short-term perspective, there may be economic gains to be made from observing only national law where it offers lower protection of, for example, labour conditions than that offered by ILO conventions. The medium- and longer-term costs may, however, be considerable, in terms of the effect both obviously on the host society and on the company's image and relations to other firms and to society.

Despite the overall reason being fundamentally different, the international labour movement also has interests at stake in avoiding a specific institutionalisation of labour-related CSR under international law. Voices belonging to the international labour movement argue that concerns promoted as CSR are already met by international and national labour law.[94] For them, the establishment of new legal obligations for businesses in a form other than national or international labour law, and monitored and enforced fully or in part by labour organisations, may be a loss of power.

Companies that have already established themselves as socially responsible and as companies which respect human rights and perhaps even contribute actively to their realisation may

---

94 See also Kell, G. and Levin, D. (2002) 'The Global Compact Network: An historic experiment in learning and action', Paper presented at the Academy of Management Annual Conference 'Building Effective Networks', Denver, CO, 11–14 August, http://www.unglobalcompact.org/docs/news_events/9.5/denver.pdf (last accessed 22 December 2016), at p. 9; International Labour Office (2003) *Corporate Social Responsibility: Myth or Reality?*, Labour Education Series 2003/1, Geneva: ILO.

perceive a legal construction of a 'level playing field' through the introduction of international law requirements as an opportunity for economic benefits. Such effects may occur in the short to medium term until other businesses catch up with the new legal requirements. Such an institutionalisation may also, arguably, ease the resource burden on many governments with regard to realisation of positive (typically social or economic) human rights obligations and lead to better conditions for many individuals. In terms of societal economics, these positive pay-offs may be large, especially in some states. For many socially, environmentally and human rights-concerned NGOs, there will be an important political message in their being able to demonstrate the success of their long struggles for businesses to be made to take more responsibility. Through this, NGOs will also be able to make a claim to power, and to be taken seriously in future regulatory efforts in relation to globalisation and its effects. Conversely, lack of success can entail a loss of power, as explained in the next paragraph.

A softer institutionalisation of current social expectations towards more specific expecta-tions of businesses in the form of 'soft', that is, non-binding, responsibilities would still have significant implications for a large number of companies globally, be they TNCs, suppliers or even buyers. For companies that do not already live up to human rights expectations, voluntary expectations could be much easier to handle in terms of resources and economic effects than legally binding requirements. A softer institutionalisation would still also have the potential of benefiting societies at large and create spill-over effects in terms of respect for and fulfilment of human rights in states, but most likely less than if requirements on companies were made mandatory. For NGOs that have been fighting for a hard institutionalisation of social responsibil-ities for companies, the political loss of not being able to demonstrate the power to successfully influence and take part in inducing a change in duty-bearing subjectivity at the level of inter-national law as well as in some regional and national legal contexts would be considerable.

A status quo situation would mean results somewhat along the lines of the soft institu-tionalisation scenario, but with effects stronger for most actor types. For some parts of the trade union movement, keeping the status quo in terms of avoiding a hard institutionalisa-tion would mean preserving a large part of their power in being able to claim to be the relevant organisations and experts when it comes to labour law and legal aspects of CSR. The status quo would indicate that international society is unable to agree on soft or hard nor-mative constraints to limit the adverse impact of business on human rights, or to strengthen the positive contributions that business may make to human rights. This could be seen as a significant weakness of the international legal system to regulate non-state actors' adverse societal impact. It would underscore the inability of international law to fill governance gaps resulting from an absence of strong and coherent action by states to address adverse impact through their national legal systems. In the case of the status quo, the effects on perceptions of the international legal machinery to adapt to changed circumstances and requirements, such as the effects of globalisation on trade, human rights and social conditions, could be considerable. An inability of international law to adapt (even if only through soft law or pre-law) would be welcomed by some and disappoint others.

These dynamics played out in different ways in each of the empirical cases that inform the current study. The introduction of the empirical case studies in the next chapter and dis-cussion in later chapters will show how specific groups were driven by their power interests in change or preservation of normative guidance for CSR, its character in terms of potential hard or soft law, its degree of detail, and the extent to which it referred to international law instruments for guidance.

3 A multiple case study representing a diversity of processes and outputs for business conduct and sustainability

Overview: This chapter opens by setting the context for the case studies by outlining how the interaction between society and law in the field of business impact on society entails a juridification of CSR, and how a series of international policy developments since the early 1990s have had increasing normative implications for the role of business in society. Following this, the chapter introduces the six case studies that inform the subsequent chapters. First, the United Nations' efforts to develop normative directives or guidance for business in regards to human rights are set out. The course from contention and disagreement on the 'Draft UN Norms' on Business and Human Rights to the agreement that emerged with the two outputs of the process of the Special Representative of the UN Secretary-General (SRSG) on Business and Human Right is described, and the Draft Norms and UN Framework and UN Guiding Principles on Business and Human Rights are briefly introduced. The aftermaths to both is briefly described, with an emphasis on implications for next steps. In regard to the Draft UN Norms this entailed recommendations from the UN's Office of the High Commissioner for Human Rights for an onward process to be more inclusive of non-state actors, including business. For the SRSG process, the aftermath entailed an academic debate, some of which challenges the legitimacy of the SRSG process and outputs, and a process initiated in 2014 to develop an international treaty on Business and Human Rights. Next, four additional cases are introduced. Representing multi-stakeholder processes with broader objectives of governing business conduct not just with regard to human rights, the UN Global Compact, the European Union's Multi-Stakeholder Forum on CSR and EU CSR Alliance and finally the ISO 26000 Social Responsibility Guidance Standard are described with an emphasis on the processes that led to those outputs and their success in delivering the intended outputs.

3.1 Context: juridification and international policy developments

3.1.1 Juridification of CSR

Developments having taken place over the past decades demonstrate that the regulation of business impact on society is increasingly becoming a field of interaction between society and law. Normative standards for business conduct to reduce adverse impact on society and/ or enhance positive contributions beyond simply creating jobs have come to be seen by a range of social actors as a topic to be regulated at the national as well as international level. The drive towards normative standards for CSR through national law, super-national regulation and international soft and hard law indicates that a juridification of CSR is taking place. This juridification is not just about reactive responses, such as attributing accountability or even liability to firms for their adverse impact on society, but as much about the proactive measures to provide normative directives and guidance for responsible business conduct. This may be observed in several ways, as described in the following. The legal system has been called upon to act to restrain the adverse impact of business on human rights. Not only a number of national legal systems but also international law has taken up that call, although not all efforts have been successful. CSR normativity has increasingly come to be related to specific norms of conduct established in law, particularly international human rights and labour law. In several national legal systems, statutory requirements on CSR reporting have been adopted, some of which go back to policies that specifically aim to proactively shape business conduct towards enhanced contributions to the implementation of public policy objectives.[1] Juridification does not necessarily indicate a change in the perception of CSR as 'voluntary' but that law is being brought into the picture to offer direction to business policies and action to limit adverse societal impact and enhance positive impact.[2]

From ideas on how businesses preserve their 'social licence to operate' to the plethora of CSR standards that have emerged in recent decades, theory and practice show that CSR is increasingly defined by normative guidance that is drawn from legal instruments. While at the beginning of the 21st century CSR was still mainly understood to be voluntary actions beyond the requirements of the law, CSR already then turned on business paying attention to societal needs and expectations typically grounded in law such as international human rights, labour or environmental law.[3] Many such CSR expectations of firms emerge in the shadow of the law in the sense that business conduct and impacts may be regulated by hard law in case firms do not self-regulate.[4] Indeed, the birth of the UN Global Compact built on this rationale, which was spelled out to business in the speech[5] that the then Secretary-General of the UN, Kofi Annan, delivered to the World Economic Forum in January 1999. And increasingly governments are introducing regulation that pertains directly to firms' CSR actions by requiring them to be transparent about their CSR policies, their implementation and results, or requiring them to deploy a portion of their income by donating to or investing in CSR-related activities. Countries around the globe are adopting CSR disclosure legislation based on the assumption that this will either drive firms to have an increased understanding of external concerns and expectations of them and better integrate this into their policies and actions, or promote corporate (economic) accountability vis-à-vis groups that critically scrutinise such reports and policies against reality. In these cases, CSR as

1 Buhmann, K. (2013) 'The Danish CSR reporting requirement as reflexive law: Employing CSR as a modal-ity to promote public policy', *European Business Law Review*, Vol. 24, No. 2, pp. 187–216; Buhmann (2016) 'Juridifying corporate social responsibility through public law'.
2 Buhmann (2015) 'Business and human rights'; Buhmann (2016) 'Public regulators and CSR'.
3 Epstein, E. M. (1993) 'Regulation, self-regulation and corporate ethics: Mutually reinforcing conditions for achieving socially responsible and publicly accountable business behaviour', in *Fundamental Subjects of the Contemporary Study of Business Administration (Essays in Honor of Professor Mizuho Nakamura)*, Japanese edn, Tokyo: Bunshindo, pp. 305–316; Elkington, J. (1998) *Cannibals with Forks: The Triple Bottom Line of 21st Century Business*, Gabriola Island, BC: New Society Publishers; see also discussions in Schwartz and Carroll (2003) 'Corporate social responsibility'; and Buhmann (2006) 'Corporate social responsibility: What role for law?'
4 Schwartz and Carroll (2003) 'Corporate social responsibility'.
5 Annan, K. (1999) 'Secretary-General proposes Global Compact on human rights, labour, environment, in address to World Economic Forum in Davos', Address of Secretary-General Kofi Annan to the World Economic Forum in Davos, Switzerland, 31 January, UN Press Release SG/SM/6881, 1 February, http://www.un.org/News/Press/docs/1999/19990201.sgsm6881.html (accessed 17 December 2016), also reprinted in McIntosh, M., Waddock, S. and Kell, G. (eds) (2004) *Learning to Talk: Corporate Citizenship and the Development of the UN Global Compact*, Sheffield: Greenleaf Publishing, pp. 28–31.

such remains technically voluntary, but the risk of economic, reputational or other sanctions aims at driving organisational change,[6] or at least having policies for CSR in place becomes an economic necessity for many firms. Non-financial disclosure requirements have been introduced by a number of states or regions, ranging from disclosure of the sourcing of 'conflict' minerals, for example for IT hardware,[7] to concessions and payments[8] and general CSR policies and their implementation.[9] The '2 per cent CSR laws' introduced by Mauritius and India[10] go a step further by simply requiring firms to set aside and invest a percentage of their profits in activities that are beneficial to society.

Recent processes of juridification of CSR and interaction between society and law have been underscored by previous decades' expanded focus on the human rights responsibilities of business. The juridification of CSR is, at least until now, primarily a proactively oriented process, seeking to set and promote standards of conduct. It is complemented by social and economic sanctions, such as consumers' decisions to change buying patterns and investors' decisions to divest from or not to invest in particular companies.

The powerful connection between social norms and international law in relation to business practices and their societal impact may be exemplified by the change in the practice of slavery on plantations in the United States (US) through the abolition laws passed in various states in the 19th century. A practice that has been a characteristic of numerous societies across times and regions, slavery is inherently related to today's social sustainability concerns with forced labour, sub-standard labour practices, trafficking and generally the exploitation of fellow humans for economic gain. In the US prior to abolition, the practice of slavery was defended by some as a rational economic practice and countered by others as a practice that was immoral, as it treated humans inhumanely.[11] The evolution of the moral idea that slavery is unacceptable became cemented into an international law ban in the 20th century. Views held by the Quakers and other religious groups who found the use of products made through slavery immoral helped shift buying practices in the US in the 18th and 19th centuries.[12] Combined with political issues and economic factors related to industrialisation,[13] governments began to

6 Gond, J. P. and Herrbach, O. (2006) 'Social reporting as an organisational learning tool? A theoretical framework', *Journal of Business Ethics*, Vol. 65, pp. 359–371; Buhmann (2013) 'The Danish CSR reporting requirement as reflexive law'.

7 United States Congress, Dodd–Frank Wall Street Reform and Consumer Protection Act (2010 – H.R. 4173), https://www.govtrack.us/congress/bills/111/hr4173, section 1502 (conflict minerals) (last accessed 22 December 2016). See also Drimmer, J. and Phillips, N. (2012) 'Sunlight for the heart of darkness: Conflict minerals and the first wave of SEC regulation of social issues', *Human Rights and International Legal Discourse*, Vol. 6, No. 1, pp. 131–158.

8 The EU Transparency Directive (2013/50/EU) ('the Transparency Directive') requires the disclosure of payments made to governments by both listed and large non-listed companies active in the extractive industry or in the logging of primary forests.

9 The Danish mandatory CSR reporting requirement in section 99a of the Act on Financial Statements, introduced in 2008 with effect from financial years 2009 onwards, was originally a relatively limited requirement that certain large companies publish information on their CSR policies, their implementation and outcomes. See Buhmann (2013) 'The Danish CSR reporting requirement as reflexive law'.

10 Section 135 of the India Companies Act 2013, *Gazette of India*, New Delhi, 30 August; Pillay, R. (2015) *The Changing Nature of Corporate Social Responsibility: CSR and Development – the Case of Mauritius*, Abingdon: Routledge.

11 Stauffer, J. (2008) *Giants: The Parallel Lives of Frederick Douglass and Abraham Lincoln*, New York: Twelve Publishing.

12 Ferrell, C. F. (2006) *The Abolitionist Movement*, Westport, CT: Greenwood Publishing.

13 Kaufmann, C. D. and Pape, R. A. (1999) 'Explaining costly international moral action: Britain's sixty-year campaign against the Atlantic slave trade', *International Organization*, Vol. 53, No. 4, pp. 631–668.

make the practice of slave labour illegal. Although slavery sadly continues in various forms, including human trafficking, international society's ban on the practice with the development of international human rights law (UDHR art. 4, ICCPR art. 8, ILO Conventions Nos 29 and 105) is a strong indication of how moral perceptions related to acceptable and unacceptable economic practices may become legally institutionalised.

Developments that have occurred from the time when morally based concerns arose in regard to products produced through slavery to the creation of international labour law in the early 20th century show that human and labour rights have gradually come to be a part not only of what is associated with corporate responsibility but also of soft and hard law. During the 20th century, broader concerns with labour conditions for the individuals who produce goods that are traded in an increasingly global market have worked their way from private groups in national settings (for example, the college wear movement and the Fair Labor Association) to the international level. They have become the subject of soft law regulation by intergovernmental organisations, as well as a large number of hard law treaty provisions adopted by the ILO and entrenched in UN and regional human rights law.

3.1.2 International policy developments with normative implications

At the political level, the 1990s were a decade of major UN summits on a range of issues related to the environment, human rights and development. However, explicit reference to the role of the private sector emerged only towards the end of the decade. Neither the Declaration from the 1992 Rio Summit on Sustainable Development[14] nor the Declaration and Programme of Action from the World Summit on Human Rights in Vienna in 1993[15] made clear references to the responsibility of the private sector for the environment and human rights respectively. By contrast, the ILO's 1998 Declaration on Fundamental Principles and Rights at Work ('ILO 1998 Declaration')[16] refers to the core labour principles of freedom of association and collective bargaining, non-discrimination in employment, elimination of forced labour and elimination of child labour.

Already the Declaration from the 1995 World Social Summit in Copenhagen[17] had encouraged countries that had ratified the ILO core labour conventions to implement them. It also called upon other countries to respect the principles embodied in the ILO core conventions. Indicative of a shift under way in international concern about TNCs, the Social Summit Declaration recognised that TNCs have an enormous impact on human rights through their employment practices, in their environmental policies and in their support of corrupt regimes or advocacy for policy change. It called for corporate human rights standards, implementation and independent audits. The shift indicated by the Social Summit Declaration became more obvious when leading declarations from UN summits from the early 2000s specifically suggested a role for the private sector. Adopted in 2000 by the UN General Assembly, the UN MDGs[18] established a number of goals to be implemented during 2000–2015. These goals included ensuring environmental sustainability and a global partnership for development, which was to build on an open trading and financial system, decent and productive

---

14 United Nations General Assembly (1992) *Rio Declaration on Environment and Development.*
15 United Nations General Assembly (1993) *Vienna Declaration and Programme of Action*, UN Doc. a/conf.157/23, 25 June.
16 ILO (1998) *Declaration on Fundamental Principles and Rights at Work.*
17 *Report of the World Summit for Social Development*, UN Doc. A/CONF/166/9.
18 United Nations General Assembly (2000) *United Nations Millennium Declaration.*

work for youth, cooperation with pharmaceutical companies to provide access to affordable essential drugs in developing countries, and cooperation with the private sector to make the benefits of new technologies available. This relatively limited enumeration of fields of collaboration with the private sector was important nevertheless. This was the first official UN document explicitly to recognise a role for the private sector in relation to human rights-related issues, such as health services and education. At the 2002 World Summit on Sustainable Development in Johannesburg, NGOs encouraged states to adopt a framework convention on corporate accountability.[19] The Johannesburg Declaration and Plan of Action,[20] adopted by governments at the Summit, did not go that far, but it encouraged business to show environmental and social responsibility. Participating governments committed themselves to encourage industry to improve social and environmental performance through voluntary initiatives, including codes of conduct, certification and public reporting on environmental and social issues, and an open dialogue between enterprises and stakeholders, including the communities in which they operate. Most recently, the SDGs, adopted in 2015 by the UN General Assembly, not only recognise that sustainable development is of global relevance rather than defined by specific economic indicators but also call for partnerships that include the private sector.

For most practical purposes, a distinction was not made between CSR and business responsibilities for human rights prior to the adoption of the UN Framework in 2008. In the late 20th century, human rights simply came to be an integrated part of CSR normativity related to societal impacts, where international law standards for practical purposes had served as the normative baseline in private or hybrid instruments on business conduct. This was seen in SA 8000 and the FSC, which originated as private responses to public governance gaps, and the Global Compact, which was the first major multi-stakeholder initiative for CSR initiated by a public international organisation. With the evolution of what is amounting to an explicit UN-based regime on business and human rights,[21] it has become increasingly evident that there are clear differences between CSR in general and corporate responsibilities for human rights, particularly with regard to state duties. Still, overlaps with CSR in terms of a societal push for corporate responsibility and for diverse types of regulatory efforts at various levels are reminders of the strength of social concerns and expectations as powerful agents of normative change that may be strengthened through the appropriate rule-making process.

Moving into the 21st century, what is clear is that neither TNCs nor small and medium-sized enterprises (SMEs) function independently of political, communicative and economic developments surrounding them. This can be seen from the global information flows on the societal impacts of business, to the knowledge of governance gaps or public frustration with the often limited specific and actionable results from international meetings to address such impacts or the gaps in law and governance that allow businesses to cause adverse societal impacts. Nor are businesses independent of social expectations. To many individuals, ranging from consumers to investors, investigative journalists or politicians, it is of little

19 Lugt, C. van der (2004) 'Growing big, learning that small is beautiful', in M. McIntosh, S. Waddock and G. Kell (eds), *Learning to Talk: Corporate Citizenship and the Development of the UN Global Compact*, Sheffield: Greenleaf Publishing, pp. 129–145, at p. 131.

20 United Nations (2002) *Report of the World Summit on Sustainable Development*, UN Doc. A/CONF.199/20.

21 Buhmann (2014) *Normative Discourses and Public–Private Regulatory Strategies for Construction of CSR Normativity*; Buhmann, K. (2018) *Changing Sustainability Norms through Communication Processes: The Emergence of the Business and Human Rights Regime as Transnational Law*, Cheltenham: Edward Elgar.

significance that international human and labour rights law does not formally address companies directly as duty-bearers. Many individuals simply expect companies to respect those rights, regardless of their formal legal duties. Social expectations of business have generated pressure on international organisations like the UN or OECD or in some cases regional intergovernmental organisations (like the EU) to come up with regulatory frameworks that correspond to such social expectations or even to transfer them into binding rules or at least non-binding formal guidance.

The combination of such tendencies and related pressures from stakeholders has played a role in the evolution of private and hybrid standards, some of which were more successful than others. The subsequent sections and chapters will focus on a selection of these that will serve as case studies for the remainder of the book. Among private initiatives, the ISO 26000 SR Guidance Standard is among one of the main private initiatives that broadly covers and offers guidance on human rights as well as other social concerns including labour rights, and environmental and consumer issues and community involvement across sectors. Key initiatives launched by public international organisations include a small series of efforts launched by the UN during the late 20th century and early 21st century and by the EU in the early 21st century to develop normative frameworks to regulate business conduct in order to reduce its adverse impact not just within home states but particularly outside those. An understanding of the previous efforts launched by public international organisations frames an understanding of whether, why and how some processes made a difference and stand out in the evolution of norms of conduct to restrain adverse impacts on society, and therefore why they are relevant cases for analytical insights for collaborative regulation of sustainability issues.

3.2 UN initiatives on normative guidance on business and human rights: from contestation and disagreement to deliberation and negotiated agreement

Initiatives by intergovernmental organisations to establish behavioural norms for business enterprises with a particular focus on their extraterritorial conduct and impact respond in part owing to documented impacts, information and expectations by various stakeholders. They are also – sometimes creative – reactions to the limited practical-political or legal capacity of such intergovernmental organisations to legislate directly with effect for companies with regard to the issue at stake. Creativity sometimes results in novel forms of regulatory initiatives, processes to turn policy into guiding norms, and eventually perhaps legally binding rules.

In the second half of the 1990s, the UN Sub-Commission on Prevention of Discrimination and Protection of Minorities addressed the impact of TNCs on the enjoyment of human rights, labour rights and the right to development in several reports. The Sub-Commission[22] was an expert body under the UN Commission on Human Rights, which itself was composed of politically appointed representatives from 53 UN member states. A report issued by the Sub-Commission in 1995 noted that TNCs were assuming power resembling that

---

22 The Sub-Commission was a subsidiary body of the UN Commission on Human Rights. It comprised 26 human rights experts from around the globe. Its mandate included human rights standard-setting and preparing studies of current human rights issues in all parts of the world. The Sub-Commission was initially subsumed under the auspices of the UN Human Rights Council, which was established on 3 April 2006 by the UN General Assembly as a replacement to the Commission on Human Rights. The Human Rights Council decided to terminate the mandate of the Sub-Commission after the Council's 58th session (2006).

of states. It argued that, as a corollary, TNCs ought to share responsibility for development and human rights, especially in poor states.[23] A 1996 report proposed a 'New International Regulatory Framework' for corporate governance, to be based in public international law. The proposal for that framework took a two-pronged approach to corporations and observed both their positive contributions and their adverse impacts on society. Among positive contributions, the proposal noted businesses' capacity to actively contribute to economic and social development, including labour relations, human rights, environmental protection and technology transfer. On adverse impacts, the report described the ability of corporations to infringe human rights. The report argued that an international regulatory framework to control TNC activity should be established, explaining that a uniform system applicable across borders was necessary to avoid powerful economic actors abusing weak governance or economic differences between states.[24] Soon after, a 1998 report specifically on TNCs took the point up, arguing that international law must adapt to regulate corporations.[25] Jointly these reports represent a shift in approaches to corporate regulation from national economic law to public international law, and from profit motives to a social role for corporations.[26] From around the beginning of the 2000s, a limited number of general comments issued by expert committees set up under UN human rights treaties also began to address the role and responsibilities of the private sector and the obligation of states to regulate corporations in order to live up to the states' duty to protect human rights.[27]

In 1998, an expert working group under a Sub-Commission of the then UN Human Rights Commission began work on a document that eventually became known as the Draft Norms on the Responsibilities of Transnational Corporations and Other Business Enterprises with

23 Sub-Commission on Prevention of Discrimination and Protection of Minorities (1995) *The Realization of Economic, Social and Cultural Rights: The Relationship between the Enjoyment of Human Rights, in Particular, International Labour and Trade Union Rights, and the Working Methods and Activities of Transnational Corporations*, UN Doc. E/CN.4/Sub.2/1995/11, 24 July.

24 Sub-Commission on Prevention of Discrimination and Protection of Minorities (1996) *The Impact of the Activities and Working Methods of Transnational Corporations on the Full Enjoyment of Human Rights, in Particular Economic, Social and Cultural Rights and the Rights to Development, Bearing in Mind Existing International Guidelines, Rules and Standards Relating to the Subject-Matter*, UN Doc. E/CN.4/Sub.2/196/12, 2 July.

25 Sub-Commission on Prevention of Discrimination and Protection of Minorities (1998) *The Realization of Economic, Social and Cultural Rights: The Question of Transnational Corporations*, UN Doc. E/CN.4/Sub.2/198/6, 10 June.

26 Backer (2006) 'Multinational corporations, transnational law', at pp. 322–327.

27 In particular, the Human Rights Committee (2004) *Nature of the General Legal Obligation on States Parties to the Covenant*, General Comment 31, UN Doc. CCPR/C/21/Rev.1/Add.13 clarified that governments' obligations extend to protecting individuals 'against acts committed by private persons or entities that would impair the enjoyment of Covenant rights in so far as they are amenable to application between private persons or entities'. See also Lucke, K. (2005) 'States' and private actors' obligations under international human rights law and the Draft UN Norms', in T. Cottier, J. Pauwelyn and E. Bürgi (eds), *Human Rights and International Trade*, Oxford: Oxford University Press, pp. 148–163; see further United Nations Human Rights Council (2007) *Background Paper: Mapping States Parties' Responsibilities to Regulate and Adjudicate Corporate Activities under Seven of the United Nations' Core Human Rights Treaties: Main Trends and Issues for Further Consideration, Prepared for Meeting between the SRSG on Human Rights and Business and Treaty Bodies*, 19 June; and United Nations Human Rights Council (2007) *Report of the Special Representative of the Secretary-General on the Issue of Human Rights and Transnational Corporations and other Business Enterprises: Addendum: State Responsibilities to Regulate and Adjudicate Corporate Activities under the United Nations Core Human Rights Treaties: An Overview of Treaty Body Commentaries*, UN Doc. A/HRC/4/35/Add.1, 13 February.

Regard to Human Rights[28] (commonly referred to as 'the Draft Norms').[29] The Draft Norms aimed to set standards of conduct for all companies with respect to human rights. The major novelty introduced by the Draft Norms was an explicit recognition in a text aiming at eventually becoming an international law instrument that transnational corporations and other business enterprises, as organs of society, are responsible for promoting and securing the human rights set forth in the UDHR.[30] According to the Draft Norms,

> [w]ithin their respective spheres of activity and influence, transnational corporations and other business enterprises have the obligation to promote, secure the fulfilment of, respect, ensure respect of and protect human rights recognized in international as well as national law, including the rights and interests of indigenous peoples and other vulnerable groups.[31]

These are normally obligations of states under international human rights law. Despite – or perhaps because of – never being formally adopted, the Draft Norms became a significant point of debate and contention, illustrative of some of the strong and differentiated stakes related to business impact on human rights and regulation of business conduct. The Human Rights Commission discussed the Draft Norms in 2004, but rather than adopting them requested the Office of the High Commissioner for Human Rights (OHCHR) to make a report on the scope and legal status of existing initiatives and standards relating to the human rights responsibilities of corporations.[32] In 2005 the Commission adopted a resolution proposing a mandate for a new so-called UN human rights special procedure, a Special Representative of the Secretary-General to deal with the issue of business and human rights. A Harvard professor with previous UN experience, John Ruggie was appointed soon after as the mandate-holder, typically referred to as 'the SRSG'. His work in that UN capacity led to the UN Framework and UNGPs on Business and Human Rights, described below in this chapter.

After the debate that led to the resolution setting out the mandate of the SRSG, the Human Rights Commission did not deal further with the Norms, and neither did the Human Rights Council that took over from the Commission in 2006. The drafting process as well as parts

---

28 Sub-Commission on the Promotion and Protection of Human Rights (2003) *Norms on the Responsibilities of Transnational Corporations and Other Business Enterprises with regard to Human Rights*.

29 Sub-Commission on the Promotion and Protection of Human Rights (1998) *Resolution*, 1998/8, 20 August. In 2001 the mandate was extended by another three-year period (Sub-Commission on the Promotion and Protection of Human Rights (2001) *Resolution 2001/3*, UN Doc. E/CN.4/SUB.2/RES/2001/3, 15 August). The drafting history of the Norms has been described in detail in Weissbrodt, D. and Kruger, M. (2003) 'Norms on the Responsibilities of Transnational Corporations and Other Business Enterprises with Regard to Human Rights', *American Journal of International Law*, Vol. 97, No. 4, pp. 901–922. See also Backer (2006) 'Multinational corporations, transnational law', at pp. 321–327; and Hillemans, C. F. (2003) 'UN Norms on the Responsibilities of Transnational Corporations and Other Business Enterprises with Regard to Human Rights', *German Law Journal*, Vol. 4, No. 10, pp. 1065–1080. The drafting of the Norms partly took its point of departure in three reports prepared by the Sub-Commission on Prevention of Discrimination and Protection of Minorities (footnotes 23, 24 and 25 above), which addressed the emerging power of TNCs and their impact on the enjoyment of international human and labour rights and the right to development.

30 Sub-Commission on the Promotion and Protection of Human Rights (2003) *Norms on the Responsibilities of Transnational Corporations and Other Business Enterprises with Regard to Human Rights*, Preamble.

31 Ibid., para. 1.

32 Commission on Human Rights (2004) *Decision 2004/116*, UN Doc. E/CN.4/2004/L.73/Rev.1, 16 April.

of the substantive elements of the Norms, however, is important for an appreciation of the SRSG process and its output. Moreover, the process leading to the Draft Norms is very relevant for the purposes of the current study, as is the aftermath within the UN's key human rights bodies, the Commission on Human Rights and OHCHR.

3.2.1 The Draft UN Norms: process, output and aftermath

The working group that developed the Draft Norms was charged with examining the working methods and activities of transnational corporations.[33] The rationale for the working group's task included the rise of power of business enterprises, and the need to address societal impacts resulting from the limited power of states vis-à-vis increasingly stronger corporations.[34] The group's agenda focused on the activities of transnational corporations and their effects 'on the enjoyment of civil, cultural, economic, political and social rights, including the right to development, the right to a healthy environment and the right to peace'[35] as well as standards for TNC conduct current at the time, and standard-setting activities.

The initial aim of formulating a code of conduct[36] evolved into the much more ambitious aim of formulating a text that might develop into binding norms.[37] A novelty in terms of international law text typologies, the term 'Norms' was not applied by the working group to its draft text until early 2002.[38] In parts of the business community the Draft UN Norms were either seen or by some actors perhaps for political purposes claimed to be already close to a legally binding text.[39] Parts of the debate during the time the Draft Norms were being developed as well as after they were rejected by the Commission on Human Rights have discussed the Draft Norms as a text that was intended to be a legally binding document from the outset. Comments made by the Draft Norms' primary author suggest that the ambition was a more modest aim of drafting a 'law-in-process' text. A mistaken presentation of the text as constituting a draft for a binding document, which marked part of the debate during and immediately following the negotiation process, probably expresses a combination of interests among groups or individuals opposed to the idea of formalised business responsibilities for human rights in arguing that the text should be rejected and in questioning its legitimacy, as well as an interest in reviving the Draft Norms among others

---

33 See footnote 29 above.

34 *Report of the Sessional Working Group on the Working Methods and Activities of Transnational Corporations*, 2nd session, UN Doc. E/CN.4/Sub.2/2000/12, para. 26; *Report of the Sessional Working Group on the Working Methods and Activities of Transnational Corporations*, 3rd session, UN Doc. E/CN.4/Sub.2/2001/9, preamble.

35 *Report of the Sessional Working Group on the Working Methods and Activities of Transnational Corporations*, 1st session, UN Doc. E/CN.4/Sub.2/1999/9, para. 9.

36 Ibid.

37 *Report of the Sessional Working Group on the Working Methods and Activities of Transnational Corporations*, 2nd session; *Report of the Sessional Working Group on the Working Methods and Activities of Transnational Corporations*, 3rd session; *Report of the Sessional Working Group on the Working Methods and Activities of Transnational Corporations*, 4th session, UN Doc. E/CN.4/Sub.2/2002/13; see also Weissbrodt and Kruger (2003) 'Norms on the Responsibilities of Transnational Corporations and Other Business Enterprises with Regard to Human Rights'.

38 *Report of the Sessional Working Group on the Working Methods and Activities of Transnational Corporations*, 4th session, para. 14.

39 Webb, T. (2004) 'Comment: Lobby groups and NGOs should rethink their approach to the UN Norms', *Ethical Corporation*, 23 April.

who have felt that the subsequent efforts that delivered the UN Framework and UNGPs have not gone far enough, and finally inadequate knowledge of the complexity and reality of international law-making. The road from turning an initial normative idea into adoption of binding rules is complex and involves both political and legal regulatory challenges. The process from suggestion to actual adoption of a binding international law instrument often involves years of negotiations, which typically produce a soft law declaration or recommendations as the first output of a recognised international law character. Moreover, such a process does not necessarily succeed in turning open-ended wording in soft law instruments into the detailed standards of conduct found in hard law instruments.

Indeed, the primary author of the Draft Norms, David Weissbrodt, has indicated that, while the Draft Norms might evolve into a binding instrument[40] and while they were 'more than aspirational statements of desired conduct[, going] beyond the voluntary guidelines found in the UN Global Compact, the ILO Tripartite Declaration, and the OECD Guidelines for Multinational Enterprises',[41] the Draft Norms themselves were 'not legally binding, but [if adopted would have been] similar to many other UN declarations, principles, guidelines and standards that interpret existing law and summarize international practice without reaching the status of a treaty'.[42] In other words, they would have been like other international soft law instruments: politically and morally guiding, but not legally binding.

When the working group set out on the drafting process, members of the group and from the Sub-Commission to which it reported observed that '[t]he working group should explore ways to bring the various constituencies together, in order to develop a widely accepted and effective set of standards which would address the human rights responsibilities of TNCs and the States in which they operate'.[43] In line with the way that international human rights instruments are typically drafted, NGOs representing human rights victims were an integral part of these constituencies from the outset, whereas TNCs and other business enterprises were not treated in quite the same way. The working group 'intend[ed] to consider developing a code of conduct for TNCs based on the [elaboration of business-relevant] human rights standards' and felt that '[s]uch a code would attempt to involve in a constructive manner the relevant business community and NGOs'. The working group member preparing the code of conduct would do so 'in cooperation with NGOs having expertise on the subject'.[44] An invitation to submit relevant background materials to the working group at its next session was extended to 'NGOs and other interested parties'[45] but not explicitly to the business community. This was repeated at the working group's second and third sessions.[46] Initially,

---

40 Weissbrodt and Kruger (2003) 'Norms on the Responsibilities of Transnational Corporations and Other Business Enterprises with Regard to Human Rights', at p. 913; Weissbrodt, D. and Kruger, M. (2005) 'Human rights responsibilities of businesses as non-state actors', in P. Alston (ed.), *Non-State Actors and Human Rights*, New York: Oxford University Press, pp. 315–350, at p. 339.

41 Weissbrodt and Kruger (2003) 'Norms on the Responsibilities of Transnational Corporations and Other Business Enterprises with Regard to Human Rights', at p. 913; compare also Weissbrodt, D. (2006) 'UN perspectives on "business and humanitarian and human rights obligations"', Proceedings of the Annual Meeting (American Society of International Law), Vol. 100, 29 March – 1 April, pp. 135–139.

42 Weissbrodt (2006) 'UN perspectives on "business and humanitarian and human rights obligations"', at p. 136.

43 *Report of the Sessional Working Group on the Working Methods and Activities of Transnational Corporations*, 1st session, para. 25.

44 Ibid., para. 32.

45 Ibid., para. 35.

46 *Report of the Sessional Working Group on the Working Methods and Activities of Transnational Corporations*, 2nd session, para. 61; *Report of the Sessional Working Group on the Working Methods and Activities of Transnational Corporations*, 3rd session, para. 62, compare para. 51 second-last sentence.

the sessions included opportunities for experts and representatives of UN specialised agencies, NGOs and civil society to make comments to the working group reports and debates. Later, TNCs and other business enterprises and other interested parties including labour unions were also invited to submit their views and recommendations.[47] Two public meetings were held towards the end of the drafting process.[48] Towards the end of the process it was noted that '[i]t was necessary to have the input and involvement of companies, unions, NGOs and other interested parties in considering the appropriate legal nature of the document that the working group was drafting'.[49] Multi-stakeholder consultations at the later stages of the Draft Norms preparation process included the International Business Leaders Forum and the World Business Council for Sustainable Development (WBCSD).[50]

Some business representatives welcomed the process and the objective of clarifying norms of conduct for businesses in relation to their human rights impacts, while a small number of large business organisations and business associations felt that business was not given a sufficient say in the process or involved at a sufficiently early stage.[51] The International Chamber of Commerce (ICC), which represents national chambers of commerce and has the promotion of business interests as its objective, opted out of consultations on the grounds that the organisation 'objects to the principles on which the Norms are based and their overall approach' and therefore did 'not consider it appropriate or useful for us to get involved in a discussion on the details of the Norms'.[52] Similar allegations of a non-inclusive process were reportedly made by a representative of the international group of the Confederation of British Industry.[53] In terms of substance too, conflicting stances were at play around and following the presentation of the Draft Norms. Focusing on the desirable form of shaping the social responsibilities of business, that conflict was very much articulated as an 'either or' between voluntary action, on the one hand, and hard law and enforceable accountability, on the other.

After approving the working group's final text[54] in August 2003,[55] the Sub-Commission transmitted the Draft Norms to the Human Rights Commission for adoption. As part of

---

47 *Report of the Sessional Working Group on the Working Methods and Activities of Transnational Corporations*, 2nd session; *Report of the Sessional Working Group on the Working Methods and Activities of Transnational Corporations*, 3rd session; *Report of the Sessional Working Group on the Working Methods and Activities of Transnational Corporations*, 4th session, para. 3; see also Weissbrodt and Kruger (2003) 'Norms on the Responsibilities of Transnational Corporations and Other Business Enterprises with Regard to Human Rights'.

48 *Report of the Sessional Working Group on the Working Methods and Activities of Transnational Corporations*, 4th session, paras 3, 36.

49 *Report of the Sessional Working Group on the Working Methods and Activities of Transnational Corporations*, 2nd session, para. 29.

50 Kinley, D., Nolan, J. and Zerial, N. (2007) 'The politics of corporate social responsibility: Reflections on the United Nations Human Rights Norms for corporations', *Company and Securities Law Journal*, Vol. 25, No. 1, pp. 30–43, at pp. 35–42; see also the discussion in Nolan, J. (2005) 'The United Nations' compact with business: Hindering or helping the protection of human rights?', *University of Queensland Law Journal*, Vol. 24, No. 2, pp. 445–466.

51 Hearne, B. (2004) 'Proposed UN Norms on human rights: Is business opposition justified?', *Ethical Corporation*, 22 March; Backer (2006) 'Multinational corporations, transnational law', at pp. 321–327.

52 Hearne (2004) 'Proposed UN Norms on human rights'.

53 Ibid.

54 Sub-Commission on the Promotion and Protection of Human Rights (2003) *Norms on the Responsibilities of Transnational Corporations and Other Business Enterprises with Regard to Human Rights*.

55 Sub-Commission on the Promotion and Protection of Human Rights (2003) *Resolution 2003/16*, UN Doc. E/CN.4/Sub.2/2003/L.11, 15 August.

the preparations for adoption, the Sub-Commission recommended that the Commission invite governments, UN bodies and specialised agencies, NGOs and 'other interested parties' to submit comments on the Draft Norms.[56] The Sub-Commission at the same time requested the working group that had drafted the text to receive information from governments, NGOs, business enterprises, individuals, groups of individuals and other actors concerning the possible negative human rights impact of business activities and to invite transnational corporations and other business enterprises concerned to provide comments.[57]

Thus, while the process did involve a measure of business participation, the Draft Norms were as a point of departure developed based on the structure for conventional human rights instruments that address states as duty-bearers, and are concerned with non-state actors in the capacity of victims, *not* as potential duty-bearers or in the capacity of human rights abusers in their own right. The inclusion of business organisations as participants in the drafting process was not strongly worded in documents setting out the process, nor in the structure for providing input or comments to the text.

Despite their novelty, the Draft Norms resemble much other early international law in terms of a drafting process that may begin with a law-in-process product, which may gradually become couched and adopted in a traditional form of international soft law and even hardened into international treaty law through a process of revisions, refinements and sometimes more radical amendments.

3.2.2 The Human Rights Commission's rejection of the Draft Norms and OHCHR recommendations for an inclusive onward process

When the Draft Norms reached the Human Rights Commission at its 2004 session, the text was received with hesitation by a number of member states, particularly some with strong corporate lobbies against regulation of human rights responsibilities of business.[58] Prior to this session, extensive lobbying by groups in favour of as well as groups opposed to the Draft Norms had taken place. A small but influential number of large associations of business or employers, including the ICC, the International Organisation of Employers (IOE) and the United States Council for International Business (USCIB), lobbied against the Norms.[59] A group of NGOs had urged the Commission to avoid a rushed decision to reject the text.[60] The Commission decided not to proceed to adopting the Draft Norms at the session in 2004, and issued a resolution stating that the text 'contain useful elements and ideas for consideration by the Commission'.[61] Testifying to the level of disagreement on the need for and form of international regulation of business responsibilities for human rights within the Commission, the final paragraph stated that the Draft Norms had 'not been requested by the Commission' and that, 'as a draft proposal, [the document] has no legal standing'.[62]

---

56 Ibid., para. 3.
57 Ibid., para. 5.
58 Kinley, D. and Chambers, R. (2006) 'The UN Human Rights Norms for corporations: The private implications of public international law', *Human Rights Law Review*, Vol. 6, No. 3, pp. 447–497.
59 Warhurst, A. and Cooper, K. in association with Amnesty International (2004) *The 'UN Human Rights Norms for Business'*, 26 July, Bradford on Avon: Maplecroft, at p. 15 with references.
60 Warhurst and Cooper (2004) *The 'UN Human Rights Norms for Business'*.
61 Commission on Human Rights (2004*) Decision 2004/116*, preamble and para. (a).
62 Ibid., para. (c).

The Human Rights Commission's decision not to explicitly mention the Draft Norms in the 2005 resolution[63] setting out the mandate of the SRSG was criticised by NGOs, some states and others.[64]

In the immediate aftermath of its 2004 decision, the Human Rights Commission asked the OHCHR to develop a report on the scope and legal status of existing initiatives and standards relating to the human rights responsibilities of corporations.[65] The report was to feed into the discussion of the Draft Norms at its 2005 session and help form the basis for deciding on the onward course options for strengthening standards on business responsibilities for human rights and means of implementation.

The Commission's request to the OHCHR for the report, as well as several points made in that report, indicates that both institutions had critically considered the process leading to the Draft Norms and saw a need to ensure that onward initiatives included a measure of business participation from an early stage.

In asking for recommendations from the High Commissioner, the Human Rights Commission actually requested the OHCHR to consult with all relevant stakeholders in compiling the report, and explicitly noted that those included not just states, relevant international organisations and NGOs, but also transnational corporations and associations for employers and employees.[66] The resulting report[67] also noted that its own findings and recommendations were based on a consultative and multi-stakeholder process. Unusually for a UN product related to human rights, the report mentioned business before other non-state stakeholders consulted.[68] The report also observed that, according to the horizontality doctrine of international human rights law, states have an obligation to protect individuals against human rights violations by the actions of third parties, such as companies. It observed that market mechanisms and contractual terms in business-to-business relationships may be brought in to support companies in addressing human rights issues in their operations, but also warned that market-based initiatives are not necessarily comprehensive in their coverage, nor a substitute for legislative action. The report concluded that there was a need for further discussion towards an agreed framework identifying business responsibilities for human rights. It recommended that the Human Rights Commission act on the momentum that existed at the time in order to define and clarify the human rights responsibilities of business entities.[69] Importantly, following the Commission's dismissal of the Draft Norms and also taking into account the more successful launch of the UN Global Compact, it stressed a need for continued stakeholder consultation and consensus-building in the onward process.[70]

---

63 Commission on Human Rights (2005) *Human Rights and Transnational Corporations and Other Business Enterprises*, UN Doc. E/CN.4/2005/L.87, 15 April.

64 See, for example, the comment by the representative of Mauritania on the occasion of the Human Rights Commission's vote on the resolution calling for the appointment of a Special Representative on business and human rights, United Nations (2005) *Press Release: Commission Requests Secretary-General to Appoint Special Representative on Transnational Corporations*, Commission on Human Rights, 20 April, http://www.unhchr. ch/huricane/huricane.nsf/view01/F92E35AD92F360D3C1256FEA002BF653?opendocument (last accessed 19 January 2013, website has been removed).

65 Commission on Human Rights (2004) *Decision 2004/116*.

66 Ibid.

67 OHCHR (2005) *Report of the United Nations High Commissioner on Human Rights on the Responsibilities of Transnational Corporations and Related Business Enterprises with Regard to Human Rights*, UN Doc. E/CN.4/2005/91, 15 February.

68 Ibid., see both para. 2 and Annex 1.

69 Ibid., para. 52.

70 OHCHR, in cooperation with the Global Compact Office (2004) *Consultation on Business and Human Rights: Summary of Discussions*, at pp. 11–12.

At its 2005 session the Commission resolved to ask the UN Secretary-General to appoint an expert to serve as Special Representative of the Secretary-General with a mandate drafted by the Commission. The mandate holder was instructed to adopt a broad and consultative multi-stakeholder approach that was to involve businesses as well as civil society organisations, the Global Compact, states and the UN. The mandate tasked the SRSG with identifying and clarifying standards of corporate responsibility and accountability for transnational corporations and other business enterprises with regard to human rights. It set a number of sub-tasks related to the role, implications, best practices and methodologies for businesses and states with regard to promoting business respect for human rights.

3.2.3 The SRSG process and the UN Framework and UNGPs

As noted, the task of the mandate defined by the Commission on Human Rights to move the debate on business and human rights forward was charged by Kofi Annan to Professor John Ruggie, who came to be referred to as SRSG in this capacity. Ruggie was a political scientist, whose background was as a Harvard academic as well as UN Assistant Secretary-General. In the latter capacity, he had been involved in establishing the Global Compact together with Georg Kell, who later became the Compact's first CEO.

The SRSG mandate on business and human rights evolved over two three-year terms.[71] The first term resulted in the UN 'Protect, Respect and Remedy' Framework, which was received favourably by the UN system in 2008 without the lobbying that 'killed' the Draft Norms.[72] Also received well by business and civil society comments to the Human Rights Council, the Framework formed the basis for the task of the SRSG's second term, which resulted in the UNGPs. The UNGPs were developed by the same type of broadly consultative multi-stakeholder process as the UN Framework, and were formally adopted by the Human Rights Commission in 2011. Hence, being the normative outputs resulting from the two SRSG terms, the UN Framework and UNGPs were not the personal projects of Professor Ruggie, but rather the result of decisions made by the UN at the highest levels.

The mandate prescribing the SRSG's task followed the recommendations by the OHCHR report on inclusiveness, which therefore framed the multi-stakeholder process from the outset. The Human Rights Commission's instructions for the SRSG's consultation process to include business in the consultation process add a perspective that has not been noted much in the literature. In particular, the inclusion of business resulted not only from the SRSG but from the recommendations of two prominent UN human rights bodies, the Human Rights Commission (and after 2006 the Council) and the OHCHR. Against that backdrop, the SRSG also influenced the process by developing the particular form in which stakeholder consultation was practised during the two terms of the mandate.

In addition to recommendations for how to go about stakeholder consultation as part of the process, the substantive task described under the mandate for the SRSG's first term

---

71 For the two mandates, see Commission on Human Rights (2005) *Human Rights and Transnational Corporations and Other Business Enterprises*; and United Nations Human Rights Council (2008) *Mandate of the Special Representative of the Secretary-General on the Issue of Human Rights and Transnational Corporations and Other Business Enterprises*, Human Rights Council Resolution 8/7, June.

72 De Schutter, O. (2013) 'Foreword', in S. Deva and D. Bilchitz (eds), *Human Rights Obligations of Business: Beyond the Corporate Responsibility to Respect?*, Cambridge: Cambridge University Press, pp. xv–xxii.

was comprehensive.[73] It encompassed: the identification and clarification of standards of corporate responsibility and accountability for business with regard to human rights; the elaboration of the role of states in effectively regulating and adjudicating the role of business with regard to human rights, including through international cooperation; and research and clarification of the implications for business of concepts such as 'complicity' and 'sphere of influence'. It also encompassed the development of materials and methodologies for undertaking human rights impact assessments of the activities of business; and the compilation of a compendium of best practices of states and business.[74] In practice, the SRSG and his team mainly focused their work on the first three issues. Owing to formal UN requirements each main annual report delivered by the SRSG had to be limited to 30 pages. In addition, a number of detailed and much longer studies were issued as 'addenda' to the formal reports.[75]

A small team comprising four to six individuals seconded by the OHCHR and a few national governments and companies assisted the SRSG in his work. The SRSG and his team adopted a method of work that involved meetings with a large number of stakeholders, including human rights NGOs, businesses, academics and other specialists on CSR, and that moved the bulk of the meetings from UN headquarters in Geneva or New York to venues closer to stakeholders, including in some cases operational sites for extractive or other large companies as well as meetings with civil society organisations and others.[76] During the first three-year term, the SRSG with his team held around 15 sectoral, regional or topical consultations and workshops.[77] During the second term, around 14 regional and multi-stakeholder consultations were held, some of which were structured to be conducted online.[78] In addition to meetings and consultations, the SRSG received a large number of written submissions from stakeholders, in particular civil society organisations.[79]

---

73 The mandate was described as follows:

'1   To identify and clarify standards of corporate responsibility and accountability for transnational corporations and other business enterprises with regard to human rights;

2   To elaborate on the role of States in effectively regulating and adjudicating the role of transnational corporations and other business enterprises with regard to human rights, including through international cooperation;

3   To research and clarify the implications for transnational corporations and other business enterprises of concepts such as "complicity" and "sphere of influence";

4   To develop materials and methodologies for undertaking human rights impact assessments of the activities of transnational corporations and other business enterprises;

5   To compile a compendium of best practices of States and transnational corporations and other business enterprises.'

(Commission on Human Rights (2005) *Human Rights and Transnational Corporations and Other Business Enterprises*, para. 1)

74 Commission on Human Rights (2005) *Human Rights and Transnational Corporations and Other Business Enterprises*.

75 The reports and addenda are available through the SRSG portal at the website of the Business and Human Rights Resource Centre, https://business-humanrights.org/en/un-secretary-generals-special-representative-on-business-human-rights (last accessed 27 December 2016).

76 The reports and addenda are available through the SRSG portal at the website of the Business and Human Rights Resource Centre, https://business-humanrights.org/en/un-secretary-generals-special-representative-on-business-human-rights (last accessed 27 December 2016).

77 The reports and addenda are available through the SRSG portal at the website of the Business and Human Rights Resource Centre, https://business-humanrights.org/en/un-secretary-generals-special-representative-on-business-human-rights (last accessed 27 December 2016).

78 Information available at website of the Business and Human Rights Resource Centre, UN Secretary-General's Special Representative on Business and Human Rights (SRSG portal), 'Consultations, meetings and workshops', https://business-humanrights.org/en/un-secretary-generals-special-representative-on-business-human-rights/consultations-meetings-workshops (accessed 17 December 2016).

79 Available through the website of the Business and Human Rights Resource Centre, https://business-humanrights.org/en/un-secretary-generals-special-representative-on-business-human-rights.

The SRSG's first ('interim') report, issued in the spring of 2006 less than a year after the mandate appointment, sought to clear the table for onward negotiations towards agreement on what responsibilities businesses have for human rights and practical guidance. As part of that exercise, the SRSG made clear that he did not intend to re-awaken the Draft UN Norms, because too much controversy and antagonism had taken place around those to be favourable for the onward process that the SRSG envisaged.[80] In their comments on the interim report and suggestions to the SRSG for his further work, civil society mainly called for regulation of companies through a conventional international law mechanism. Business organisations argued in favour of voluntary mechanisms. A certain softening of stances took place, however. This entailed a measure of recognition by both sides that a sort of framework regulation setting general norms of conduct would be acceptable, and that detailed regulation could be left to businesses.[81]

Each of the subsequent annual reports from the SRSG to the Human Rights Council under both mandate terms developed, tested and refined elements of the UN Framework and the UNGPs step by step. This included building on consultations during the mandate and responses from consultation audiences to ideas that were often tested on such audiences.[82]

The third annual report of the first mandate term, issued in 2008, includes the recommendations that are now known as the UN Framework. This 'Framework', which forms an integrated part containing the final recommendations of the SRSG's first term, was presented under the title of a 'policy framework', carefully avoiding any reference to legal standards or 'norms'. The Framework comprised the three 'pillars' of *protect, respect and remedy*, and the report set out what is in fact a highly normative framework for states to *protect* against human rights violations by companies, for companies to *respect* human rights, and for states and companies to provide judicial as well as non-judicial *remedy* to (alleged) victims of human rights violations by companies.

The UN Framework does not create new human rights, but explains the implications for both businesses and states of existing human rights standards. Based on analyses by the SRSG team of a large number of factual cases and reports which involved or alleged human rights abuse by companies, the Framework observed that all human rights may be relevant in terms of business responsibilities. The Framework does, however, refer to the International Bill of Human Rights and the ILO core labour conventions as the minimum normative standards that businesses should observe.[83] The former consists of the UDHR, the ICESCR and the ICCPR. The latter consists of the eight ILO treaties on the abolition and elimination of slavery, forced labour and child labour, on the protection of labour unions and the right to organise and engage in collective negotiation, and on freedom from discrimination in the workplace. Those eight conventions, and the human rights that they protect, correspond to the labour rights covered by Principles 3, 4, 5 and 6 of the UN Global Compact.

For pragmatic reasons the SRSG during his first term opted for a product that did not fall squarely within established categories of international law. He has explained that agreement

80 United Nations Commission on Human Rights (2006) *Interim Report of the Special Representative of the Secretary-General on the Issue of Human Rights and Transnational Corporations and Other Business Enterprises*, UN Doc. E/CN.4/2006/97, 22 February.
81 Buhmann (2014) *Normative Discourses and Public–Private Regulatory Strategies for Construction of CSR Normativity*, chaps 4, 7; Buhmann (2018) *Changing Sustainability Norms through Communication Processes*, chap. 5, section 5.7.
82 Buhmann (2014) *Normative Discourses and Public–Private Regulatory Strategies for Construction of CSR Normativity*, chaps 4, 7.
83 United Nations Human Rights Council (2008), para. 58.

on such a product would likely be a protracted process (as indeed international law-making often is). He felt it was important to aim for a text that could deliver a more immediate impact to reduce business-related human rights abuse without waiting for the even more uncertain outcome of an international law soft or hard law-making procedure.[84] His decision was to develop a document explaining the implications for firms of already existing international law (Pillar Two – the corporate responsibility to respect human rights), at the same time effectively reminding states of the extent of their existing obligations under international human rights law (Pillar One – the state duty to protect human rights against abuse caused by others, including non-state actors such as businesses), and making recommendations for both states and businesses for effective, transparent and legitimate grievance mechanisms (Pillar Three – access to remedy for victims of business-related human rights abuse).

The third annual report, issued in 2011 at the end of the second SRSG term, contains the UNGPs, which are the recommendations that the SRSG was asked by the Human Rights Council to develop in order to 'operationalize' the UN Framework. Accordingly, the UNGPs take their point of departure in the UN Framework and develop the recommendations that are set out under the three pillars into specific steps to be taken by governments at their different levels, companies regardless of form and locality, and governments and businesses to provide better access to remedy for affected stakeholders. Among the 31 principles, all with commentaries, ten relate to Pillar One, the state duty to protect, 14 relate to Pillar Two, the corporate responsibility to respect, and seven to Pillar Three, access to remedy. Among the Pillar Two principles, several elaborate on actions that businesses should take to spell out their human rights commitments into policies and human rights (risk-based) due diligence. The due diligence process introduced by the UN Framework and elaborated by the UNGPs aims at identifying, preventing, mitigating and accounting for how companies manage their adverse impacts. This part of the UNGPs formulates the core of the risk-based due diligence that has since been adopted by the OECD's Guidelines, ISO 26000 and some other CSR initiatives.

The conceptual understanding of business responsibilities for human rights constructed by the SRSG is not simply a human rights-focused subset of CSR. Pillar Two's responsibility to respect human rights is based on a dual set of informing normative requirements and expectations: to comply with law, and to act in accordance with social expectations. The distinction and complementarity of this duality are explained in more detail in the UN Framework[85] than in the UNGPs. In addition to compliance with law, this is based on the social expectation that companies conduct themselves in such a way as not to cause human rights abuse by benefiting from weak governance, and differs from CSR because it does not leave companies discretion with regard to their responsibility. In other words, companies should respect human rights in their breadth as well as depth. The basic rationale, based on studies made under the SRSG mandate, is that all human rights may be subject to abuse by companies, directly or through complicity, and all human rights are therefore subject to the social expectation that they be respected by company conduct.

Thus, the corporate responsibility to respect human rights comprises both the obligation to comply with applicable law and a responsibility to respect social expectations. The compliance

84 Sidoti, C. (2011) 'It's our business: Ensuring inclusiveness in the process of regulating and enforcing corporate social responsibility', in K. Buhmann, L. Roseberry and M. Morsing (eds), *Corporate Social and Human Rights Responsibilities: Global Legal and Management Perspectives*, London: Palgrave Macmillan, pp. 144–164; Ruggie (2013) *Just Business*.
85 United Nations Human Rights Council (2008), para. 54.

element tends to be overlooked in discussions on the UNGPs, perhaps because it was more explicit in the UN Framework.[86] Compliance and social expectations connect, because compliance relates directly to statutory obligations that may be introduced by states, and because the boundary between what is a compliance obligation and what is a social expectation is dynamic. Governments may decide to develop statutory law that changes a social expectation into law. Issues subject to social expectation in some jurisdictions may be subject to statutory regulation and therefore compliance obligations in others. Whereas binding law often limits requirements to minimal standards, social expectations may work to drive up performance. They may therefore serve to raise the bar for firms' active steps to respect human rights, not just in terms of business ethics but also through soft law, which may gradually evolve into hard law.

From a legal perspective, the responsibility to observe social expectations may appear weaker than the obligation to comply with applicable law. Yet, from the economic perspective, the assessment may be different. Social expectations may be coupled with social or market-based sanctions. Hurting businesses' reputation, investment relations and general 'social licence to operate', such sanctions may be considerable in financial terms[87] and be significant to a company, despite often being treated as or even hidden in general operational costs, as documented by the SRSG and his team in studies that fed into the UN Framework.[88]

The priority for the type of explanatory policy document that we now refer to as the UN Framework did not rule out the possibility that a conventional international law instrument on business duties for human rights (such as a declaration or a treaty) might emerge or that such an instrument would build on the UN Framework. Indeed, the UNGPs, which like other 'principles' or 'guidelines' developed by international organisations may be understood as a type of international soft law, take their direct point of departure in the UN Framework and explain what businesses and states should do to implement the three pillars. Moreover, the unprecedented agreement in the Human Rights Council in 2008 and 2011 on a UN instrument on business and human rights, which came about based on the processes leading to the UN Framework and UNGPs and broad support among stakeholders at the time for both instruments, may be seen as an important element in paving the way for the treaty process launched in 2014. In the event that agreement on a treaty on business and human rights does materialise, business will have had some access to make its views and suggestions heard through participation in the SRSG process, even if it may not be involved to the same extent in the treaty process. Contrary to lobbying and similar conventional avenues that may be deployed to seek to influence states, the participation of businesses through the SRSG processes has been transparent through communication issued by the SRSG, typically through the UN Human Rights Council or the OHCHR as well as news shared through the internet.[89] Statements that businesses made or sent to the SRSG have also been made available online through the Business and Human Rights Resource Centre. However, as noted in Chapter 1, the inclusion of business raises important issues related to legitimacy. This relates in particular to two aspects that in the current context are deeply interconnected: legitimacy of

---

86 Ibid.
87 Kapstein, E. B. (2001) 'The corporate ethics crusade', *Foreign Affairs*, Vol. 80, No. 5, pp. 105–119.
88 United Nations (2007) *Human Rights Policies and Management Practices: Results from Questionnaire Surveys of Governments and Fortune Global 500 firms*, UN Doc. A/HRC/4/35/Add.3; Ruggie (2013) *Just Business*, at pp. 136–138; see also Davis, R. and Franks, D. (2014) *Costs of Company–Community Conflict in the Extractive Sector*, Corporate Social Responsibility Initiative Report No. 66, Cambridge, MA: Harvard Kennedy School.
89 This was done, i.e. through a dedicated SRSG portal set up by the Business and Human Rights Resource Centre, and as news published in the regular newsletters of the Resource Centre.

the process, including participation, and legitimacy of the output, including support for the output based on the process. We will revert to this topic in Chapter 5 onwards.

3.2.4 After the UN Guiding Principles

Following the successful adoption of the UN Framework and UNGPs, a discussion emerged on the legitimacy of the instruments and the processes that led to them. Part of this places the legitimacy that was indicated by the support for the texts up to and during their adoption into a more critical perspective that is instructive for legitimacy issues in relation to regulatory innovation to include non-state actors more directly in super-national law-making than is commonly the case in international law. Accordingly, this subsection notes some of the points of critique that have been raised against the UN Framework and UNGPs in terms both of substance (especially for not going beyond business responsibilities to respect human rights and stopping short of including the active fulfilment by businesses of such rights, and for not paying sufficient attention to victims of corporate-related human rights abuse) and of the process (for involving business too much and victims or representative NGOs too little).[90] It also observes that, more recently, the academic debate has become more welcoming of the UNGPs and their general contributions to guidance and expectations for business impacts on society. Next, the subsection moves on to the process for a treaty on business and human rights and the way in which that process engages with stakeholders and their participation.

3.2.4.1 Academic views of the UN Framework and UNGPs and their legitimacy

As noted, the UN Framework and UNGPs were welcomed and unanimously adopted, respectively, by the UN Human Rights Council, and avoided the intense and damaging lobbying that contributed to the dismissal of the Draft Norms. However, the UN Framework and UNGPs have been criticised on different counts by scholars from several academic disciplines, including business ethics, international human rights law and corporate law.[91] Compared to the influence of the UN Framework and UNGPs on business policies and their uptake on transnational business governance instruments including the Global Compact, ISO 26000, the OECD's Guidelines for Multinational Enterprises and the International Finance Corporation's Performance Standards, critiques made by some authors have pointed to weaknesses in terms of coverage, philosophical foundations and the non-hard legal form of the instruments.

Some business ethics scholars find the limitation of the responsibility of corporations to avoid doing harm problematic. They argue that, in considering corporations 'specialized economic organs, not democratic public interest institutions', the UN Framework overlooks

90 Kolstad, I. (2012) 'Human rights and positive corporate duties: The importance of corporate–state interaction', *Business Ethics: A European Review*, Vol. 21, No. 3, pp. 276–285; e.g. Bilchitz (2013) 'A chasm between "is" and "ought"?'; Bilchitz, D. and Deva, S. (2013) 'The human rights obligations of business: A critical framework for the future', in S. Deva and D. Bilchitz (eds), *Human Rights Obligations of Business: Beyond the Corporate Responsibility to Respect?*, Cambridge: Cambridge University Press, pp. 1–26; Nolan, J. (2013) 'The corporate responsibility to respect human rights: Soft law or not law?', in S. Deva and D. Bilchitz (eds), *Human Rights Obligations of Business: Beyond the Corporate Responsibility to Respect?*, Cambridge: Cambridge University Press, pp. 138–161; Wettstein (2013) 'Making noise about silent complicity'.
91 This subsection draws on Jonsson, J., Fisker, M. and Buhmann, K. (2016) 'Beyond "doing no harm": An "extended UN Framework" to connect political CSR with business and human rights', Paper for SAFIC 2016: The Private Sector in Development: New Perspectives on Developing Country and Emerging Market Firms, Copenhagen Business School, 6–7 April.

the political and social power of corporations, and that such firms should be assigned direct obligations, which might or should include human rights fulfilment.[92] Moreover, the texts have been criticised for adopting an instrumentalist view of firms that 'strip[s] corporate responsibility to its bare minimum'[93] by assigning only negative duties that from a philosophical perspective may be argued to apply to all agents in society. These authors reject the rationale that assigning positive duties to corporations entails a risk of external stakeholders becoming dependent on corporations to provide human rights fulfilment where the government fails to do so, or of governments leaving it to firms to lift such tasks that are often of a socio-economic character.

A moral perfectionist approach to human rights also marks some of the critique of the social risk-based due diligence promoted by the UN Framework and the UNGPs. In this case, authors argue that this approach to firms' adverse impact contrasts with human rights as perfect moral obligations that under no circumstances should be violated.[94] The critique is based on the recognition inherent in the UN Framework's and UNGPs' reasoning that business-related human rights abuse may occur despite firms' (best) efforts to perform due diligence, along with the recommendations for mitigation, because this assumes the existence of human rights abuse which (for temporal reasons or due to the character of business relations linkages) be fully prevented by the firm.

International and corporate lawyers have critiqued the UNGPs for confusing two meanings of due diligence: a standard of conduct (to discharge an obligation), and a process (to manage risks to businesses), argued to reveal a flawed inner logic.[95] Some international human rights law scholars have criticised the very conceptual foundations of the UN Framework and UNGPs, the fact that businesses are not awarded direct international legal obligations, and the fact that the instruments are not hard law.[96] The inclusiveness of the process has also been criticised for being biased towards businesses at the expense of victims.[97]

Not all scholars share the critique of the UN Framework and UNGPs, however. Both the process and the output have been commended. Olivier De Schutter, who both is an academic and has held the mandate of UN Special Rapporteur on the Right to Food, has noted that the style and what some see as limitations of the UN Framework in fact helped pave the way for the more detailed guidance provided by the UNGPs. Because the UN Framework was crafted in such a way as to generate acceptance by the Human Rights Council, the Council would be hard placed not to accept the follow-up instrument that built on the second SRSG mandate

92 Cragg, W. (2012) 'Ethics, Enlightened self-interest, and the corporate responsibility to respect human rights', *Business Ethics Quarterly*, Vol. 22, No. 1, pp. 9–36; Kolstad (2012) 'Human rights and positive corporate duties'; Wettstein (2013) 'Making noise about silent complicity'.
93 Wettstein (2015) 'Normativity, ethics, and the UN Guiding Principles on Business and Human Rights', at p. 165.
94 Fasterling, B. and Demuijnck, G. (2013) 'Human rights in the void? Due diligence in the UN Guiding Principles on Business and Human Rights', *Journal of Business Ethics*, Vol. 116, No. 4, pp. 1–16.
95 Bonnitcha, J. and McCorquodale, R. (forthcoming) 'Is the concept of "due diligence" in the Guiding Principles coherent?', *European Journal of International Law*, available at SSRN, http://papers.ssrn.com/sol3/papers.cfm?abstract_id=2208588.
96 Cernic (2010) 'Two steps forward, one step back'; Deva, S. (2010) '"Protect, respect and remedy": A critique of the SRSG's Framework for Business and Human Rights', in K. Buhmann, L. Roseberry and M. Morsing (eds), *Corporate Social and Human Rights Responsibilities: Global Legal and Management Perspectives*, Houndmills: Palgrave Macmillan, pp. 108–128; Bilchitz (2013) 'A chasm between "is" and "ought"?'; Deva (2013) 'Treating human rights lightly'.
97 Melish, T. J. and Meidinger, E. (2012) 'Protect, respect, remedy and participate: "New governance" lessons for the Ruggie Framework', in M. Radu (ed.), *The UN Guiding Principles on Business and Human Rights: Foundations and Implementation*, Leiden: Martinus Nijhoff, pp. 303–336; Deva (2013) 'Treating human rights lightly'.

prepared by the Council.[98] Others have recognised the uniqueness of the multi-stakeholder process in the UN context and its ability to break the stalemate that had stalled previous efforts to develop guidance on the social responsibilities of business.[99] The process induced even some of the businesses and organisations that were most opposed to the Draft Norms into developing their stances and recognising international human rights law as a relevant normative source for business in relation to human rights.[100] Some of these business organisations issued guidance for their members to observe international human rights law in conflict zones when or where national law and protection of human rights are deficient.[101] It has been noted that the instruments' delimitation to respecting human rights was a pragmatic choice that helped ensure broad agreement on the UN Framework,[102] and hence does not prevent or discourage firms' engagement in human rights fulfilment. Some business ethics scholars who joined in some of the early critique of the instruments have more recently recognised their potential for promoting the international regulatory as well as academic debate on a very complex sustainability issue,[103] and even the potential for the solidifying discourse on BHR to revitalise the CSR debate.[104]

Some scholars have noted the potential of the social risk-based due diligence approach within the human rights field[105] as well as beyond.[106] From a more general perspective related to whether corporations should have obligations to fulfil human rights, scholars of international development have warned that developments where non-state actors take over functions normally considered governmental responsibilities may undermine state capacity and legitimacy, leading to an unsustainable dependence on corporations to fulfil human rights.[107]

98 De Schutter (2013) 'Foreword'.

99 Knox (2012) 'The Ruggie Rules'; see also Buhmann (2012) 'The development of the "UN Framework"'.

100 For an example of this, see in particular International Organisation of Employers, International Chamber of Commerce and BIAC (2006) *Business and Human Rights: The Role of Business in Weak Governance Zones: Business Proposals for Effective Ways of Addressing Dilemma Situations in Weak Governance Zones*, December, Geneva: International Organisation of Employers, International Chamber of Commerce and BIAC, which makes reference to international human rights law as a 'fall-back' position in conflict zones where national law and its implementation are deficient.

101 Ryngaert and Buhmann (2012) 'Human rights challenges for multinational corporations working and investing in conflict zones'.

102 Buhmann (2012) 'The development of the "UN Framework"'; Knox (2012) 'The Ruggie Rules'; Sanders (2015) 'The impact of the "Ruggie Framework" and the "United Nations Guiding Principles on Business and Human Rights" on transnational human rights litigation'; see also Wettstein (2015), 'Normativity, ethics, and the UN Guiding Principles on Business and Human Rights'.

103 Wettstein (2015), 'Normativity, ethics, and the UN Guiding Principles on Business and Human Rights'; see also Backer, L. C. (2014) *The Guiding Principles of Business and Human Rights at a Crossroads: The State, the Enterprise, and the Spectre of a Treaty to Bind Them All*, Working Paper No. 7/1, July, Coalition for Peace and Ethics.

104 Wettstein, F. (2015) 'Business and human rights: Implementation challenges', in D. Baumann-Pauly and J. Nolan (eds), *Business and Human Rights: From Principles to Practice*, Abingdon: Routledge, pp. 77–89.

105 Martin-Ortega, O. (2014) 'Human rights due diligence for corporations: From voluntary standards to hard law at last?', *Netherlands Quarterly on Human Rights*, Vol. 32, No. 1, pp. 44–74; Footer, M. (2015) 'Human rights due diligence and the responsible supply of minerals from conflict-affected areas: Towards a normative framework?', in J. L. Cernic and T. Van Ho (eds), *Direct Human Rights Obligations of Corporations*, The Hague: Wolf Legal Publishers, pp. 179–228.

106 Buhmann (2015) 'Business and human rights'.

107 Idemudia, U. and Ite, U. (2006) 'Corporate–community relations in Nigeria's oil industry: Challenges and imperatives', *Corporate Social Responsibility and Environmental Management*, Vol. 13, pp. 194–206; Kolk, A. and Lenfant, F. (2013) 'Multinationals, CSR and partnerships in Central African conflict countries', *Corporate Social Responsibility and Environmental Management*, Vol. 20, pp. 43–54.

Much of the scholarly critique as well as welcoming of the UN Framework and UNGPs converges on two topical lines, which are in fact related across critique and welcoming: critics note the limited ambitions of the UN Framework and UNGPs with regard to assigning firms direct international obligations for human rights or explicitly suggesting that such obligations should be a next step in an onward process; and they note a failure to relate academically to the philosophical underpinnings of human rights. Those who welcome the documents note that they have achieved much compared to the baseline situation, which counted not only the Draft Norms but also the entire idea of a combination of economic non-state actors and responsibilities for human rights as alien. They also note that the texts manage to combine a range of diverse and often conflicting interests and speak across academic disciplines.

In retrospect, explicitly addressing the issue of business contributions or even obligations for human rights fulfilment as part of the process towards the UN Framework and UNGPs might easily have entailed opening a Pandora's box. While it was possible in the aftermath of the failed Draft UN Norms to craft agreement on reminding states of their duty to protect and explicating the corporate responsibility to respect without ruling out the possibility that firms on their own account might decide to contribute to fulfilling human rights, the issue of business obligations for human rights fulfilment is more politically sensitive. Defining such obligations is not just about moral or legal aspects of human rights. It also relates to political aspects of state sovereignty. Even if it had been possible to reach agreement on a division of economic issues between states and business, the politics of human rights and sovereignty might have stalled the process and effectively limited further progress on business and human rights for a long time, including on steps to prevent and account for business-related human rights abuse.

From this perspective, the limitations of the UN Framework and UNGPs might in fact be considered a strength, because they kept the agenda moving towards new agreements and insights, and helped spur further developments, including the current debate on the role of business with regard to human rights fulfilment, which also relates to the more general debate on so-called 'political CSR', that is, when companies contribute to the tasks of governments in delivering public goods and related services.[108]

It is part of the normative academic professions like law and philosophy to hold a case to the highest standards of achievement, yet there is reason to be wary of considering the outcome of the process of regulation to be imperfect to the extent that 'perfect' sometimes becomes the enemy of 'good'. Like much other sustainability work, human rights politics and law-making have always been an iterative process in which seemingly small steps may become game-changers. The UN Charter's brief and undetailed references to human rights (in paras 1, 13 and 55) led to the UDHR, which in turn framed much of the 20th century's comprehensive international, regional and national human rights law-making. Although we will never know for sure, it is plausible that, without the agreement generated around the UN Framework and UNGPs, the launch of a process towards a UN treaty on BHR might not have come about less than ten years after the UN dismissed the Draft Norms.

In sum, the processes that resulted in the UN Framework and UNGPs broke ground by being innovative and inclusive in a way that offers learning for the future in terms of both process and output. They also left some legitimacy issues. This also offers insights for the iterative evolution of collaborative rule-making to address sustainability concerns. In critically

---

108 Jonsson, J., Fisker, M. and Buhmann, K. (2016) *From 'Do No Harm' to Doing More Good: Extending the UN Framework to Connect Political CSR with Business Responsibilities for Human Rights*, Working Paper No. 26/2016, Copenhagen: Copenhagen Business School, Centre for Business and Development Studies; Scherer et al. (2016) 'Managing for political corporate social responsibility'.

reviewing the UN Framework and UNGPs, it must be kept in mind that, unlike the work of John Ruggie in his academic capacity, these were not scholarly products or scholarly undertakings. Rather, they were political-legal texts targeting a broad audience in which academics were only one group, and not the main target group. While in practice the texts spanned many different audiences – civil society, academics, business, media, politicians, to mention some – they first and foremost had to fulfil the format and expectations of the Human Rights Council of a report addressing members of that group and the governmental officials of states that are members of the UN. Where the documents sought to address non-state actors, the primary audience, again, were or are not scholars or university academics, but employees of firms who would need to apply the recommendations and principles, and victims of business-related human rights abuse and civil society organisations working with such victims, who would expect to see action-oriented guidance. Finally, the texts must be understood against the backdrop of the discourses on CSR and BHR as they unfolded at the time up to the establishment of each of the SRSG mandates and during the mandate terms. The main focus of the BHR discourse at the time was the capacity of firms to do harm and to cause harm because of insufficient protection of and respect for human rights. In accordance with the two mandates and their instructions for inclusive multi-stakeholder participation it was also important to preempt the lobbying that had 'killed' the Draft Norms.

3.2.4.2 From soft law to treaty on business and human rights? Policy and stakeholder inclusion

In 2014 the Human Rights Council adopted two resolutions pertaining to business and human rights. Sponsored by Ecuador and joined by South Africa, Venezuela and Cuba, one proposed the elaboration of a treaty on business and human rights.[109] The other, sponsored by Norway and joined by 21 other states, proposed an elaboration of the implementation of the UNGPs, focusing on the existing instrument.[110]

In accordance with the resolution on the treaty, the Human Rights Council decided to establish an open-ended intergovernmental working group (also referred to as the 'OEIWG') on transnational corporations and other business enterprises with respect to human rights. The mandate of the intergovernmental working group was defined as elaborating 'an international legally binding instrument to regulate, in international human rights law, the activities of transnational corporations and other business enterprises'.[111]

The mandate resolution decided that the first two sessions[112] of the intergovernmental working group were to be 'dedicated to conducting constructive deliberations on the content, scope, nature and form of the future international instrument'.[113]

---

109 United Nations Human Rights Council (2014) *Elaboration of an International Legally Binding Instrument on Transnational Corporations and Other Business Enterprises with Regard to Human Rights*, UN Doc. A/HRC/26/L.22/Rev.1, 25 June.

110 United Nations Human Rights Council (2014*) Human Rights and Transnational Enterprises and Other Business Enterprises*, UN Doc. A/HRC/26/L.1, 23 June.

111 United Nations Human Rights Council (2014) *Elaboration of an International Legally Binding Instrument on Transnational Corporations and Other Business Enterprises with Respect to Human Rights*, UN Doc. A/HRC/RES/26/9, 14 July.

112 The OEIWG held its first session on 6–10 July 2015, and the second session on 24–28 October 2016. At the time of writing, a third session has been planned for 23–27 October 2017.

113 United Nations Human Rights Council (2014*) Elaboration of an International Legally Binding Instrument on Transnational Corporations and Other Business Enterprises with Respect to Human Rights*, para. 2.

Unlike the mandates that led to the UN Framework and the UNGPs, the mandate for the intergovernmental working group does not contain instructions for multi-stakeholder consultations. In its operative part the mandate resolution '[r]ecommends that the first meeting of the open-ended intergovernmental working group serve to collect inputs, including written inputs, from States and relevant stakeholders on possible principles, scope and elements of such an international legally binding instrument'.[114] Thus, states are the only stakeholders explicitly recognised for the purposes of collecting inputs. What constitutes 'relevant stakeholders' is not defined. In the context of the wording noted above, this suggests a process set to evolve from the state-centrist international law perspective. This, too, appears to inform the preamble, which '[stresses] that the obligations and primary responsibility to promote and protect human rights and fundamental freedoms lie with the State, and that States must protect against human rights abuse within their territory and/or jurisdiction by third parties, including transnational corporations'. The preamble also '[emphasises] that transnational corporations and other business enterprises have a responsibility to respect human rights' and 'that civil society actors have an important and legitimate role in promoting corporate social responsibility, and in preventing, mitigating and seeking remedy for the adverse human rights impacts of transnational corporations and other business enterprises'. The mandate resolution preamble finally acknowledges 'that transnational corporations and other business enterprises have the capacity' of 'causing adverse impacts on human rights' as well as and in line with other international agreements, such as the SDGs, 'to foster economic well-being, development, technological improvement and wealth'.[115] Thus, apart from the mentioning of 'transnational enterprises and other business enterprises' as subjects of the prospective treaty, the resolution's mention of business is limited to the preamble, in which businesses are recognised to have a responsibility to respect human rights, and noted to have the capacity both to contribute to society and to cause adverse impacts on human rights.

NGOs in consultative status with ECOSOC may apply for accreditation for their representatives to attend the working group sessions. According to an engagement note issued by the intergovernmental working group for its second meeting, such groups in consultative status have the opportunity to engage with the working group during a round of discussion during each panel segment, following the presentations by panellists. This is to allow for interaction between participants and panellists, and is followed by general comments and discussion on the panel theme or sub-theme, for which participants might prepare their oral statements in advance.[116] Among the 18 written contributions to the intergovernmental working group's first session, one was from a business association (the IOE).[117] Among the eight contributions from groups designated as 'other relevant stakeholders' on the list, none were from business. As of late November 2016, the list of 20 written statements to the intergovernmental working group's second session contains no contributions from business associations in consultative status with ECOSOC. Among 17 contributions from 'other relevant stakeholders',

114 Ibid., para. 5.
115 Ibid., preamble and paras 8–11.
116 OHCHR, Open-Ended Intergovernmental Working Group (OEIWG) on TNCs and Human Rights (2016) *Information Note for NGOs with ECOSOC Consultative Status on Their Engagement with the Open-Ended Intergovernmental Working Group on Transnational Corporations and Other Business Enterprises with Respect to Human Rights*, http://www.ohchr.org/EN/HRBodies/HRC/WGTransCorp/Pages/IGWGOnTNC. aspx (accessed 25 November 2016).
117 OHCHR, OEIWG, *First Session Written Contributions*, http://www.ohchr.org/EN/HRBodies/HRC/WGTrans Corp/Session1/Pages/WrittenContributions.aspx (accessed 25 November 2016).

the only business contribution is from a law firm.[118] A group of academics has been formed to provide input to the process.[119]

Overall, therefore, the activities of the working group so far and the background to its work as set out in the mandate resolution appear not to be very focused on, if at all, or effective in engaging business as a stakeholder in the process towards a treaty on business and human rights.

In view of the fact that the resolution limits the understanding of business enterprises to 'enterprises that have a transnational character in their operational activities' and explicitly excludes local businesses registered in terms of relevant domestic law from the focus of the intergovernmental working group and the prospective treaty,[120] the reason for not explicitly including business as a stakeholder to be consulted need not be the immense number of businesses of all types and sizes around the world. TNCs and similar are normally assessed to number around 70,000–80,000 companies, many of which are represented in one or more business associations, which effectively reduces the number of representative organisations. Hence, this need not be an obstacle to the inclusion of business in the process, in particular through business associations, as has widely been the case for previous efforts to develop norms of conduct for business on human rights or CSR.

3.3 Multi-stakeholder hybrid initiatives for norms for business conduct: the UN Global Compact, EU processes and ISO 26000

Besides recent years' processes to develop norms of conduct for businesses with regard to human rights, several multi-stakeholder initiatives to set norms for business conduct have emerged in response to the governance gaps and limited capacity of public regulators to govern transnational business conduct. While some are primarily organised and implemented as private initiatives, others embody a strong public institutional participation. For the current purposes, we will focus on those with broad sectoral coverage.[121]

The Global Compact launched by the UN in 2000 and the ISO 26000 SR guidance standard launched in 2010 are global in their ambitions in terms of both institutional background and sectoral applicability. They also differ, because the UN is an inherently public organisation charged with the implementation of public policy objectives, while the ISO is a private organisation. Developed mainly for application by for-profit organisations, the ISO's standard-setting activities complement the norm-setting activities of public organisations. This applies to the ISO's operational standards for transforming public policy norms

---

118 OHCHR, OEIWG, *Second Session Written Contributions*, http://www.ohchr.org/EN/HRBodies/HRC/WGTransCorp/Session2/Pages/WrittenContributions.aspx (accessed 25 November 2016).

119 See, for example, note on the 'Academic Reflections' side event to the second session of the OEIWG: OHCHR, OEIWG, *Exploring the Content of Proposed Business and Human Rights Treaty: Academic Reflections*, http://www.ohchr.org/EN/HRBodies/HRC/WGTransCorp/Session2/Pages/SideEvents.aspx (accessed 25 November 2016).

120 OHCHR, Open-Ended Intergovernmental Working Group (OEIWG) on TNCs and Human Rights (2016) *Information Note for NGOs with ECOSOC Consultative Status on Their Engagement with the Open-Ended Intergovernmental Working Group on Transnational Corporations and Other Business Enterprises with Respect to Human Rights.*

121 Single-sector initiatives that incorporate collaboration with public authorities include: for the oil and gas extraction sector the Voluntary Principles on Security and Human Rights; for diamonds the Kimberley Process; for payment transparency for extractive companies in general the Extractive Industries Transparency Initiative (EITI); and for forestry the Programme for the Endorsement of Forest Certification (PEFC). Compare Chapter 2, section 2.3.

or rules on sustainability concerns – environment (ISO 14000 series), occupational health and safety (ISO 18000 OHSAS series), social responsibility (ISO 26000) – into business practice. Another set of multi-stakeholder initiatives, launched by the European Commission in 2002 and 2006 under the names of the European Multi-Stakeholder Forum (MSF) and the CSR Alliance, were also global in intended applicability, but regionally limited in terms of institutional background. Yet the European initiatives were unique as regional initiatives set up by a public institution with the aim of establishing norms on responsible business, and as early examples of such initiatives.

The initiatives share the deployment of a multi-stakeholder approach to respond to social or political pressure for regulation in a global legal environment which is becoming more specialised, transnational, politicised, and prone to apply new forms of soft law.[122] The following provides an overview of the backgrounds, processes and outputs of those initiatives, which place the above processes towards norms of conduct for business and human rights and their outputs into perspective and offer further insights for collaborative regulation.

The hybrid initiatives set out below are all related to constructing CSR as a normative concept and promoting that normative concept as a standard for business conduct. Through the process-orientated approach of each of the initiatives, various stakeholder groups were involved in constructing normative guidance for business conduct with regard to its societal impacts. Considerable varieties in outputs assessed against the ambitions and objectives underlying each of the initiatives suggest that the procedural design framing each of these law-making processes played a major part in the extent to which input was transformed into output through a process perceived as legitimate. The subsequent overview and discussion explain this. A summary is provided in Table 3.1 at the end of this chapter.

3.3.1 The United Nations Global Compact

An initiative launched under the otherwise state-centric UN, but developed from within the Secretary-General's Office with the participation of for-profit and non-profit non-state actors, the Global Compact from its origin was highly unusual in its approach to public–private norm creation. By contrast to conventional international law instruments that are formally adopted by the UN General Assembly, the Global Compact was simply mentioned and implicitly approved in biennial resolutions that set out UN processes under the joint title *Towards Global Partnerships*.[123] By setting up the Global Compact, the UN enabled itself to have direct contact with business with an objective of promoting specific types of action and discouraging others. The Compact has enabled the UN to reach out to companies and other private actors in a clearly normative way related to societal objectives and public policy concerns.

The background to the Global Compact, as mentioned, was a speech delivered at the World Economic Forum in Davos in January 1999, in which the UN's then Secretary-General Kofi Annan called on business to play an active role in upholding and implementing global public

---

122   Joerges, C., Sand, I.-J. and Teubner, G. (2004) *Transnational Governance and Constitutionalism*, Oxford: Hart.

123   The first General Assembly resolution that mentioned the Global Compact was United Nations General Assembly (2000) *Towards Global Partnerships*, Resolution adopted by the General Assembly, UN Doc. A/RES/55/215, 21 December. This was followed by United Nations General Assembly (2001) *Towards Global Partnerships*, Resolution adopted by the General Assembly, UN Doc. A/RES/56/76, 11 December, which has been followed up by resolutions every second year since.

policy goals.[124] The speech made reference to human rights, labour standards and environmental objectives already established in the UDHR, the ILO's 1998 Declaration and the Rio Declaration. Annan explained that businesses were benefiting from an international economic law regime that was not balanced by obligations for business to reduce their adverse social and environmental impact and contribute to positive impacts. He observed that, unless businesses demonstrate a willingness to adapt their conduct to accord with such objectives, policy-makers might resort to hard law to bring about the necessary change of conduct. The speech also made it clear that public regulators do have those powers and, if businesses were seen to be the problem rather than part of the solution, it would not be unrealistic for policy-makers to resort to proposing hard law. The speech offered the suggestion that, by adapting their conduct in response to global sustainability needs, businesses would be able to retain significant discretion as to how they might address their societal impacts, as compared to the likely situation of requirements imposed by public regulators. Essentially, the message was that significant self-regulation was a minimum alternative to hard law, in view of the significant public policy concerns at stake.

What came to be launched in 2000 as the Global Compact was developed through a multi-stakeholder process that included the UN Secretary-General's Office, intergovernmental organisations and business, in cooperation with civil society. The Compact was launched with nine principles on human rights, labour rights and environmental protection, which all refer to instruments of international law as their normative basis. The two human rights principles (Global Compact Principles 1 and 2) refer to the UDHR.[125] The labour standards (Principles 3 to 6) refer to the ILO 1998 Declaration on Fundamental Principles and Rights at Work.[126] Among the environmental principles (Principles 7 to 9), Principle 7 on the precautionary approach is based on the Rio Declaration.[127] Added in 2004, Principle 10 refers to the UN Convention against Corruption.[128] These international law declarations and conventions establish duties for states, not for companies or other non-state actors. Yet the rationale behind the Compact assumes that the legitimacy of those international norms of conduct lends legitimacy and strength to the Compact, as well as relevance to firms' self-regulation to honour their commitments to the Global Compact principles.

The Compact was developed over an 18-month period through a multi-stakeholder process that included companies and CEOs recognised to be 'CSR leaders'.[129] A limited number of NGOs were involved as well, selected on the basis of expertise in the Compact's issue areas (human rights, labour and environment) and invited at certain times into the general process.[130]

The institutional set-up of the Global Compact does not provide for intergovernmental or governmental organisations to compel non-state actors to participate, or to legally enforce commitment to the ten principles. Participation is by voluntary commitment from each individual participant. A Communication of Progress reporting scheme was introduced in response to critiques on its 'toothlessness' and concerns of abuse (e.g. 'blue-washing', referring to the blue

---

124 Annan (1999) 'Secretary-General proposes Global Compact on human rights, labour, environment, in address to World Economic Forum in Davos', also reprinted in McIntosh et al. (2004) *Learning to Talk*, pp. 28–31.
125 United Nations General Assembly (1948) *Universal Declaration of Human Rights.*
126 ILO (1998) *Declaration on Fundamental Principles and Rights at Work.*
127 United Nations General Assembly (1992) *Rio Declaration on Environment and Development.*
128 United Nations General Assembly (2003) *United Nations Convention against Corruption.*
129 Kell, G. and Levin, D. (2002) 'The Global Compact Network: An historic experiment in learning and action', Paper presented at the Academy of Management Annual Conference 'Building Effective Networks', Denver, CO, 11–14 August, http://www.unglobalcompact.org/docs/news_events/9.5/denver.pdf (last accessed 22 December 2016).
130 Ibid.

of the UN flag). Communication of Progress reports are not monitored (officially, at least) by the UN Global Compact Office, which runs the Compact from New York City. The reports are made accessible online at the Global Compact website through links to the company's home page, with the task of monitoring in practice left to civil society and other concerned stakeholders. Non-reporting may be sanctioned, ultimately, by a participant effectively being excluded by being taken off the list of active Global Compact participants. While the de-listing sanction was originally communicated widely through Global Compact newsletters and the website, as of mid-2016 the Compact's website does not remove non-communicating companies (despite being officially de-listed) from its participant count on the Compact's front webpage, or from the participant search site unless explicitly crossed out in a search.

Partly reflecting the novelty of the Compact as a form of public–private collaboration as well as a concern to reach agreement relatively fast against concern within and outside the UN that the organisation was putting its integrity at risk, participants in the proces to develop the Compact were selected from among companies and CEOs that already had a commitment to responsible business practices or were already seen to be CSR leaders.[131] When civil society was invited to join the process to develop the Compact, the invitation went out to only a few organisations.[132] Limited participation by civil society organisations, especially initially, caused significant apprehension among NGOs, threatening to seriously delegitimise the Compact idea among those organisations whose support was needed for the initiative to be acceptable among voices critical of company conduct. Eventually, however, the evolution of the Compact built legitimacy through a multi-stakeholder process that involved businesses as well as civil society organisations, despite the latter's representation through a few hand-picked organisations.

The initiative to develop the Global Compact was successful in transforming the original objectives that were defined following the positive reception of the Secretary-General's speech at the World Economic Forum into a set of principles that despite their brevity are based in detailed international law instruments. This normative connection is reflected in the Compact's multi-layered website, which takes the user into increasingly detailed guidance for each 'click'. Despite the 'soft' set-up, the Global Compact is clearly normative. The objective is to make companies and other participants act in accordance with the ten principles and therefore the informing instruments of international law and related concerns and objectives of the UN. The Global Compact is a hybrid regulatory instrument, which was initiated by a public international organisation and included businesses as well as civil society directly in the development and precise wording of the ten principles, and additionally in the elaboration and explanations on implications for business activity.

3.3.2 The EU Multi-Stakeholder Forum (MSF) on CSR

In 1999 the European Parliament adopted a resolution proposing a code of conduct for European TNCs.[133] As the Parliament (based on its EU treaty-based competences) did not

---

131 Ibid.
132 Three NGOs were selected in the area of human rights: Human Rights Watch, Lawyers Committee for Human Rights and Amnesty International. Four environmental NGOs joined the Compact: the World Wildlife Fund for Nature, the International Union for Conservation of Nature, the World Resources Institute and the International Institute for Environment and Development. Save the Children, the Ring Network and Transparency International were selected for their particular competencies in key areas. The ILO generally represented labour concerns. See Kell and Levin (2002) 'The Global Compact Network', at p. 10.
133 European Parliament (1999) *Resolution on EU Standards for European Enterprises Operating in Developing Countries: Towards a European Code of Conduct*, OJ C 104/180, EP Resolution A4-0508/98, adopted 15 January.

have the power to legislate on such a code of conduct on its own, the initiative was a political statement rather than a legislative act. In response, the EU Commission in 2001 issued a Green Paper on a European Framework for CSR,[134] and followed up in 2002 by issuing a Commission Communication on CSR.[135] Both documents are policy papers, but being EU Commission statements they nevertheless aimed at transforming the European Parliament's policy into specific activities.

The 2002 Communication announced the establishment of a European Multi-Stakeholder Forum on CSR. Chaired by the EU Commission, the MSF comprised organisations representing trade unions, industrial, employers' and commerce organisations, and NGOs engaged in human rights, consumers' interests and sustainable development issues. It was charged with discussing convergence on CSR practices, and to consider establishing a normative framework consisting of common guiding principles for CSR practices and instruments for European companies. The Communication recommended that such a normative framework should be aligned with international normative instruments, in particular ILO labour standards and the OECD's Guidelines for Multinational Enterprises.

In terms of organisation, the MSF shared features with the Global Compact. It was introduced by the Commission as a forum for dialogue, learning and exchanging expectations between different types of participants, which included European industry and business associations, labour organisations, and a broad range of civil society groups. The MSF held a number of meetings with all members as well as meetings in targeted working groups. As elaborated below, some types of participants or stakeholder groups turned out effectively to exercise stronger influence on the output than others.[136] In particular, business associations that enjoyed experience in EU law-making in the labour area played a role in the industry and employers' organisations being more successful than NGOs in making their preference for the normative basis, character and form of institutionalisation of European CSR prevail.

The objective of the Commission's decision to launch the MSF was regulatory, with the Commission presuming that the multi-stakeholder process could lead to a European version of the Global Compact.[137] Contrary to the Commission's announcements of the MSF's objectives at the outset, the MSF's output that was announced after two years' work did not include an actual normative framework. This had much to do with imbalanced power disparities in the process, as will be elaborated in Chapter 5.

3.3.3 The European CSR Alliance

Following the limited success of the 2002–2004 MSF, a new Commission Communication on CSR[138] issued in 2006 increased focus on intra-EU aspects of CSR, in particular with a

---

134 Commission of the European Communities (2001) *Promoting a European Framework for Corporate Social Responsibility*.

135 Commission of the European Communities (2002) *Communication from the Commission Concerning Corporate Social Responsibility*.

136 Buhmann (2011) 'Integrating human rights in emerging regulation of corporate social responsibility'; Fairbrass (2011) 'Exploring corporate social responsibility policy in the European Union'; Kinderman (2013) 'Corporate social responsibility in the EU, 1993–2013'.

137 Buhmann (2013) 'The Danish CSR reporting requirement as reflexive law'.

138 Commission of the European Communities (2006) *Communication from the Commission to the European Parliament, the Council and the European Economic and Social Committee: Implementing the Partnership for Growth and Jobs: Making Europe a Pole of Excellence on CSR*, COM(2006)136.final.

view on inclusive employment. However, it also retained human and labour rights aspects related to EU-based companies' conduct in states outside the EU. The 2006 Communication announced a new multi-stakeholder initiative to promote CSR within European companies, a 'CSR Alliance' (also known as the European Alliance for CSR). The CSR Alliance was set up to comprise European companies and the Commission but unlike the MSF not civil society organisations. Its objective was to promote business activities addressing societal needs and mainstreaming CSR into EU policies.

For setting up the CSR Alliance, the Commission changed its argumentative approach compared to when the MSF was set up, and during the MSF. Although the Alliance was announced in an EU policy document, the Annex part of that document, which describes the Alliance, talked about CSR being business-driven, explicitly recognised businesses' economic role in society, and referred to CSR as meaningful for business achieving a better image in society and therefore better conditions for entrepreneurship, innovation and economic success.[139] The Alliance came to be hosted by European business organisations with varied stances in the MSF, and to be joined by European businesses including some organised in associations that had argued against an ambitious normative output of the MSF.

The CSR Alliance was established as a learning forum for businesses, aimed at exchanging best practices, displaying models and encouraging laggards to follow. The first major collective output, a CSR 'toolbox', published in late 2008,[140] was a mapping of (best) practices rather than a novel normative product.

3.3.4 ISO 26000 Social Responsibility Guidance Standard

After several years of internal debate within the ISO organisation and its members on the relevance and pertinence of a standard related to CSR issues, the ISO in 2005 decided to launch a process towards developing a standard. A focus on social responsibility (SR) rather than *corporate* social responsibility (CSR) was adopted to signal that the standard might be applied not just by corporations or other firms but also by governmental or not-for-profit non-governmental organisations. The ISO 26000 SR guidance standard[141] was developed over a five-year period based on a multi-stakeholder process consisting of industry, government, labour, consumers, non-governmental organisations, academics and others, organised into six groups that all held similar formal powers and rights towards the objective of a consensus-based result.[142] Leadership for the process was shared between groups and committees from industrialised countries and emerging economies, under the joint leadership of a standardisation organisation from the Global South and one from the Global North.[143] This was done to ensure a balance of viewpoints from different economic and cultural contexts. As an organisation developing standards

139 Ibid., Annex.
140 CSR Alliance (2008) *Toolbox: Equipping Companies and Stakeholders for a Competitive and Responsible Europe*, Brussels: CSR Europe.
141 ISO (2010) *ISO 26000 – Social Responsibility*.
142 ISO 26000 was developed through the participation of six stakeholder groups: industry, government, consumers, labour, NGOs and others (e.g. research). See ECPAT Sweden (n.d.) *Briefing Paper: ISO 26000 Social Responsibility Guidance Standard*, http://resources.ecpat.net/EI/Pdf/ISO_26000_Guidance_Standard_Social_Responsibility_en.pdf (accessed 2 November 2016).
143 The Brazilian Association of Technical Standards and the Swedish Standards Institute were chosen by the ISO to provide the joint leadership for development of the guidance standard.

Table 3.1 Outputs assessed against objectives and procedural design

Initiative (case)	Years of process	Objective	Procedural design: inclusiveness of for-profit non-state actors (business)	Procedural design: inclusiveness of not-for-profit non-state actors (NGOs, etc.)	Procedural design: process management, including top-down/bottom-up or dialogue with stakeholders	Output assessed against stated objectives of process	Post-process acceptance of output
Draft Norms	1998–2003	Standards of conduct for companies with respect to human rights (law-in-process with the potential to evolve into a binding instrument (treaty))	Initially low, later medium	High	Top-down, some dialogue	High with drafting body, but no political adoption by Commission on Human Rights	Low with business, medium–high with NGOs
SRSG process and output: UN Framework and UNGPs	2005–2011	2005–2008: identifying and clarifying standards of corporate responsibility and accountability for transnational corporations and other business enterprises with regard to human rights; elaborating on the role of states; clarifying implications for businesses; developing methods and materials; compiling best practices for states and business 2008–2011: operationalizing the UN Framework	High	High	High degree of process management Top-down managed dialogue Invitation to stakeholders (whether included in meetings or not) to submit views in letters, in reports and online	2005–2008: high (policy framework with explicit normative substance) 2008–2011: high (normative framework of soft law-like guiding character)	High with business and governments Mixed with NGOs: high with some, medium with others Mixed with academic stakeholders: high with some, medium–low with others
UN Global Compact	1999–2000	A 'compact' for businesses to uphold human rights and labour and environmental	High	Initially low, later medium	High degree of process management	High: 2000: nine principles in three issue areas (human rights, labour, environment)	Medium–high

(continued)

Table 3.1 (continued)

Initiative (case)	Years of process	Objective	Procedural design: inclusiveness of for-profit non-state actors (business)	Procedural design: inclusiveness of not-for-profit non-state actors (NGOs, etc.)	Procedural design: process management, including top-down/bottom-up or dialogue with stakeholders	Output assessed against stated objectives of process	Post-process acceptance of output
		standards directly, in accordance with values that have been defined by international agreements including the Universal Declaration, the ILO's Declaration on Fundamental Principles and Rights at Work, and the Rio Declaration of the United Nations Conference on Environment and Development in 1992 (Corruption added in 2004)			Top-down managed dialogue	based on the Universal Declaration, the ILO's Declaration on Fundamental Principles and Rights at Work, and the Rio Declaration (2004: Principle 10 based on UN Convention against Corruption)	
EU Multi-Stakeholder Forum for CSR and output: final report	2002–2004	A European framework on CSR, comprising guiding principles on: the relationship between CSR and competitiveness (business case); the contribution of CSR to sustainable development; SME-specific aspects, codes of conduct; commonly agreed guidelines for labelling schemes supporting ILO core conventions and environmental standards;	High	High	Limited actual process management Dialogue but no procedure to balance power in terms of sector or actor privilege of access, experience or prior knowledge of a similar political process	Mixed: first part of report (formalities) reference UN Global Compact, ILO's Tripartite Declaration and OECD's Guidelines as important texts; stronger texts (UDHR, ICESCR, ICCPR, 1998 ILO Declaration) noted with comment that they 'contain values that can inspire companies when developing their CSR,	Medium–high with business Low with civil society

		CSR benchmarks that should build on the ILO fundamental conventions and the OECD Guidelines for Multinational Enterprises as a common minimum standard of reference			Top-down invitation to stakeholders (whether present in meetings or not) to submit views	which in turn can play a role in reinforcing and making tangible the values these texts represent'; substantive parts of report: little reference to normativity	Medium with business but seems to be little referenced Low with civil society
EU CSR Alliance set-up and output: best-practice collections	2006–2008 onwards	A platform for learning and exchange of best practice with companies as members, to help reconcile European economic, social and environmental ambitions through CSR and contribute to public policy objectives, such as greater respect for human rights, environmental protection and core labour standards, more integrated labour markets and higher levels of social inclusion, investment in skills development, life-long learning and employability, improvements in public health, and improved business image	High	Low (no civil society participation)	Mainly managed by a few business organisations	Low	
ISO 26000 social responsibility guidance	2005–2010	Provide guidance for social responsibility	High	High	High degree of process management Dialogue within members of process, with input from stakeholders not directly involved	High	High

for application by organisations, the ISO makes decisions based on consensus through deliberations and negotiations.

As the ISO is a private organisation, ISO standards, including ISO 26000, are not public regulatory instruments. The inclusion of governments as stakeholders in the development of ISO 26000 makes it a hybrid instrument. Influence by the UNGPs and the UN Framework and interaction with the SRSG's team to ensure coherence between the concepts applied by the ISO and those of the UN Framework led to the risk-based due diligence process becoming adopted as regards social issues.[144] Unlike other ISO standards, ISO 26000 is not certifiable (hence the 'guidance standard' title). Emerging economies successfully argued that a certifiable standard might function as a trade barrier that would favour companies from industrialised countries whose economics and institutions enable higher-level implementation of the requirements of the guidance standard. Some national certification standards are aligned with ISO 26000 and for practical purposes serve as a certification standard for the ISO guidance.

Through its process, ISO 26000 was successful in delivering an output that for many purposes corresponds to the original objectives. The broadness of its application can be limited by the fact that ISO 26000 is for sale and not publicly available.

Following an introduction in the next chapter to theoretical perspectives that frame the analysis here, the subsequent chapters will revert to the case studies, looking at legitimacy of process and output and insights for collaborative regulation.

144 ISO (2010) *ISO 26000 – Social Responsibility*, clause 5; Wood, S. (2011) 'The meaning of "sphere of influence" in ISO 26000', in A. Henriques (ed.), *Understanding ISO 26000: A Practical Approach to Social Responsibility*, London: British Standards Institution, pp. 115–130; Ruggie (2013) *Just Business*.

Part 2

Legitimacy and public–private regulation of transnational sustainability concerns

4 Theoretical perspectives on participatory law-making, 'compliance pull', communication and legitimacy

Overview: The chapter first introduces regulatory theory with a particular emphasis on socio-legal approaches to law and instrumental regulation. The basic features of reflexive law theory, developed by Gunther Teubner, are explained with examples of its previous application to sustainability related issues. The chapter proceeds to Thomas Franck's theory on legitimacy and compliance pull in international law and a discussion of the benefits of law-making with a compliance pull in regulatory contexts in which enforcement institutions and modalities are limited or weak. It moves on to introducing the deliberative turn in rule-making with a point of departure in Jürgen Habermas' theory on deliberation and legitimate law-making and expansion of this into process aspects of input, output and particularly throughput and to law-making at the super-national level. Finally, the chapter introduces theories that suggest to update international law-making towards broader public inclusion and participation in view of the contributions of Habermas and others, in particular Grainne de Burca's democratic-striving approach.*

4.1 Instrumental approaches to law

While *law as practice* is often applied reactively to sanction undesired conduct, *law as science* is fundamentally about institutionalising norms of conduct. From its inception in early civilisations, law has been about transforming moral norms into practice. Legal philosophers and socio-legal scholars are pre-occupied with the regulatory modalities that work for those purposes. Prescriptive norms and regulatory theories are as much part of jurisprudential science as studies of case law and the application of sanctions. From the socio-legal perspective, law has a strong instrumental aspect: to shape desired conduct for the future. Statutory requirements setting legal norms of conduct form part of this. The deterrent function of criminal law and of potential sanctions has a strong instrumental aspect to it, yet instrumental law is not only related to negative sanctions such as fines or imprisonment. Instrumental law aimed at promoting desired conduct is found in traffic law (whose primary objective is to prevent casualties and only secondarily to punish those who cause them), procedural administrative rules for civil servants processing applications or claims from citizens (whose primary objective is to ensure that the correct decision is made rather than to penalise those who make wrong decisions), or environmental law pertaining to production (whose primary object is simply to avoid pollution).

Regulatory theories typically have their focus on legal rules as outputs – the norms of conduct that result from a rule-making process – rather than the potential regulatory aspect of the process of making rules. However, socio-legal studies offer major exceptions to the general emphasis on enforcement and other reactive measures. Socio-legal studies consider law in an integrated relationship with society, often inspired by sociology and paying attention to how law may proactively shape conduct through instrumental or related regulatory strategies. These may include interaction with others through participatory law-making that promotes insights into an organisation's relations in society. By inducing learning among participants, such processes may stimulate self-regulation.

The socio-legal theory of '*responsive* law'[1] aims at handling societal change and complexity by being open, oriented towards purpose and result, and responsive to reality. Responsive law is based on the pragmatic idea that law must preferably concern itself with actual societal problems rather than the application of existing forms of law and regulatory modalities. To promote relevant change of conduct, regulation should apply not only institutional elements but also procedural ones, and should include modalities for deliberation and communication in developing rules.

Another socio-legal theory, '*reflexive* law', takes part of its inspiration from the responsive law elements just noted, and draws on philosophy of law as well as political and sociological theories to develop a theory for multi-stakeholder evolution of norms of conduct that work by internalising external societal needs and concerns into organisational behaviour, typically but not only of business.[2] As theory on regulated self-regulation, reflexive law offers a regulatory approach for authorities to make organisations, such as companies, reorient their behaviour towards a wider societal goal. Its focus is on stimulating the internalisation of external concerns in complex environments that include multiple groups with competing and contradictory interests.[3] While it may appear rather abstract in its theoretical basis, reflexive law is in fact a rather practical or 'hands-on' regulatory theory that has lent inspiration to the introduction by governments and other authorities of regulatory processes that involve interest groups (or stakeholders) in debating, deliberating and defining specific norms of conduct. Reflexive law emphasises the communicative aspect of a regulatory process to develop understanding of specific concerns whose solution requires changed norms of conduct. As will be further explored in Chapter 5, reflexive law theory recognises at a level of principle that power disparities must be balanced for the regulatory process and its outcome to be legitimate.[4] However, the theory does not offer directives for how to achieve this. Chapter 5 also reverts to this.

While multi-stakeholder processes are not often or indeed rarely characterised by governments or other agents as 'reflexive law', studies have indicated that participatory and inclusive processes in the fields of environmental protection, occupational health and safety, and CSR reporting – all of which are not easily categorised in terms of conventional top-down law – may be explained and understood as reflexive law. Among these, studies have applied reflexive law as an explanatory theory on environmental management and labelling as self-regulation,[5]

1 Nonet and Selznick (1978) *Law and Society in Transition*.
2 Teubner, G. (1983) 'Substantive and reflective elements in modern law'; Teubner, G. (1986) 'After legal instrumentalism?', in G. Teubner (ed.), *Dilemmas of Law in the Welfare State*, Berlin: Walter de Gruyter, pp. 299–325.
3 See also Collins, H. (1998) Reviewed work: *Reflexive Labour Law: Studies in Industrial Relations and Employment Regulation* by Ralf Rogowski, Ton Wilthagen, *Modern Law Review*, Vol. 61, No. 6, pp. 916–920, at p. 917 with specific reference to labour law regulation.
4 See especially Teubner (1983) 'Substantive and reflective elements in modern law'; Teubner, G. (1984) 'Autopoiesis in law and society: A rejoinder to Blankenburg', *Law and Society Review*, Vol. 18, No. 2, pp. 291–301; Teubner, G. (ed.) (1986) *Dilemmas of Law in the Welfare State*, Berlin: Walter de Gruyter.
5 Orts, E. W. (1995) 'A reflexive model of environmental regulation', *Business Ethics Quarterly*, Vol. 5, No. 4, pp. 779–794, at pp. 788–789; Orts, E. W. (1995) 'Reflexive environmental law', *Northwestern Law Review*, Vol. 89, No. 4, pp. 1229–1340, at pp. 1311–1313.

non-financial reporting,[6] globalisation of law and transnational private regulation,[7] and labour law,[8] including collective negotiations[9] and occupational health and safety regulation. With a more procedural perspective, other examples include environmental law in a broad sense[10] and mediation.[11] Reflexive law has also been introduced into the debate on the emerging concept of 'new governance' as a type of soft public–private regulation.[12]

In the environmental context where reflexive law-type regulation has been applied extensively (for example, in some Scandinavian local-level environmental and area planning law), public agencies set certain overall aims that are guided by policy considerations on societal needs or desired developments. In reflexive labour law, public agencies set implicit or sometimes explicit standards (such as minimum standards defined on the basis of international or national labour law) that serve as normative guidance for social partners' negotiations. This indicates that the establishment of normative guidance by public agencies is not per se an obstacle to a regulatory process being considered as reflexive law. Hence, authorities' role is not limited to setting up the procedural forum; they may also deliver substantive input, while still leaving it to the actors concerned to develop and decide on specific normative outputs.

6 Hess, D. (1999) 'Social reporting: A reflexive law approach to corporate social responsiveness', *Journal of Corporation Law*, Vol. 25, No. 1, pp. 41–84; Hess, D. (2008) 'The three pillars of corporate social reporting as new governance regulation: Disclosure, dialogue and development', *Business Ethics Quarterly*, Vol. 18, No. 4, pp. 447–482.

7 Scheuerman, W. E. (2001) 'Reflexive law and the challenges of globalization', *Journal of Political Philosophy*, Vol. 9, No. 1, pp. 81–102.

8 Rogowski, R. (1994) 'Industrial relations, labour conflict resolution and reflexive labour law', in R. Rogowski and T. Wilthagen (eds), *Reflexive Labour Law: Studies in Industrial Relations and Employment Regulation*, Deventer: Kluwer Law and Taxation Publishers, pp. 53–93; Rogowski, R. and Wilthagen, T. (1994) 'Reflexive labour law: An introduction', in R. Rogowski and T. Wilthagen (eds), *Reflexive Labour Law: Studies in Industrial Relations and Employment Regulation*, Deventer: Kluwer Law and Taxation Publishers, pp. 1–19; Rogowski, R. (2001) 'The concept of reflexive labour law: Its theoretical background and possible applications', in J. Priban and D. Nelken (eds), *Law's New Boundaries: The Consequences of Legal Autopoiesis*, Aldershot: Ashgate, pp. 179–196; Deakin, S. (2005) 'Social rights in a globalised economy', in P. Alston (ed.), *Labour Rights as Human Rights*, New York: Oxford University Press, pp. 25–60; Deakin, S. and Hobbs, R. (2007) 'False dawn for CSR? Shifts in regulatory policy and the response of the corporate and financial sectors in Britain', *Corporate Governance*, Vol. 15, No. 1, pp. 68–76; Arthurs, H. (2008) 'Corporate self-regulation: Political economy, state regulation and reflexive labour law', in B. Bercusson and C. Estlund (eds), *Regulating Labour in the Wake of Globalisation*, Oxford: Hart, pp. 19–35.

9 Rogowski, R. (1998) 'Autopoietic industrial relations and reflexive labour law', in T. Wilthagen (ed.), *Advancing Theory in Labour Law and Industrial Relations in a Global Context*, Amsterdam: North-Holland, pp. 67–81.

10 For example, Dalberg-Larsen, J. (2006) 'Perspektiver på retlig regulering, særlig i relation til selvforvaltning', in K. Buhmann (ed.), *Corporate social responsibility (CSR) som genstandsfelt for juridisk analyse: Teoretiske og metodiske overvejelser*, Roskilde: Roskilde University, Center for Værdier i Virksomheder, pp. 37–46, at pp. 42–43; see also Rehbinder, E. (1992) 'Reflexive law and practice: The corporate officer for environmental protection as an example', in G. Teubner and A. Febbrajo (eds), *European Yearbook in the Sociology of Law: State, Law and Economy as Autopoietic Systems: Regulation and Autonomy in a New Perspective*, Milano: Giuffrè, pp. 579–608; Farmer, L. and Teubner, G. (1994) 'Ecological self-organization', in G. Teubner, L. Farmer and D. Murphy (eds), *Environmental Law and Ecological Responsibility: The Concept and Practice of Ecological Self-Organisation*, Chichester: John Wiley & Sons, pp. 3–13.

11 Dalberg-Larsen (2006) 'Perspektiver på retlig regulering, særlig i relation til selvforvaltning'; Madsen, S. S. (2006) 'Mediation blandt mediatoruddannede advokater' [Mediation among Danish mediator trained advocates], *Rettid*, Vol. 2006, No. 3.

12 For example, Lobel (2005) 'The Renew Deal'; Hess (2008) 'The three pillars of corporate social reporting as new governance regulation'.

As seen, studies of environmental or CSR reporting indicate that reflexive law-based regulatory methods are not infrequently used in practice. However, studies also indicated that this, also not infrequently, occurs without reference to or perhaps even knowledge of the theory.[13] These schemes contain reflexive elements by defining procedures or recommending actions (such as a qualified stakeholder dialogue) which allow companies to learn about the expectations and demands of stakeholders and to reflect these into and through their self-regulation.[14] From this perspective, governmentally authorised and controlled eco- or sustainability labelling schemes (such as the Nordic countries' 'Svanen' ('the Swan') eco-label) contain reflexive law features in that the adoption of the scheme induces the producer to consider how to respond to societal expectations related to the product or production process. Such schemes may also stimulate company- or industry-internal reflection leading to the decision to adopt the label and self-regulate so as to honour the conditions for use of the label.

Reflexive law is one among a series of theories that seek to integrate the dynamic relationship between law and social norms. Reflexive law was among such theories that, like *responsive law* and *deliberative law-making*, to which we turn below in this chapter, were proposed in order to deal with what was perceived as a regulatory crisis in the 1970s–1980s. Much of this crisis was seen to derive from a disconnect between the market-based economy and its adverse impacts on the environment, as well as its inadequacy to handle unemployment, discrimination, poverty and other adverse social impacts. While at the time the focus was on national regulatory theory, problems have since shifted to a larger scale and to the super-national level, where they are the focus of some of the current decade's efforts at regulating sustainability. These efforts include protecting and promoting responsible business conduct and general sustainability through codes of conduct pertaining to human rights and labour conditions in global supply chains, environment and climate change mitigation.

Proposed around the same time as reflexive law was first presented by socio-legal scholar Gunther Teubner, among related theories, Sally Falk Moore's 'semi-autonomous social field'[15] emphasises the creation of rules which actors are forced or induced to comply with. Somewhat along related lines, John Griffiths's work included informal non-state normative orders in his understanding of law.[16] Sigler and Murphy's theory on interactive corporate compliance[17] argues much along the lines of reflexive law's integrative ideas. The more recently introduced theoretical approach of '*pro-active* law' recognises stakeholder engagement and communication across systemic functions as important, and notes that, for sustainability-related purposes, regulation and related interests are transnational rather than national. Yet the focus is mainly on pre-emption of legal risk from the corporate perspective, and pro-active law theory does not delve into the regulatory process as a way to promote specific norms of conduct.[18]

Beyond the field of socio-legal studies, some political and economic theories also take an instrumental approach to regulation. Not to be confused with responsive *law*, the

---

13 Orts (1995) 'A reflexive model of environmental regulation'; Orts (1995) 'Reflexive environmental law'; Buhmann (2013) 'The Danish CSR reporting requirement as reflexive law'.

14 Buhmann (2013) 'The Danish CSR reporting requirement as reflexive law'.

15 Moore, S. F. (1978) *Law as Process: An Anthropological Approach*, New York: Routledge & Kegan Paul.

16 Griffiths, J. (1986) 'What is legal pluralism?', *Journal of Legal Pluralism and Unofficial Law*, Vol. 24, pp. 1–55.

17 Sigler, J. A. and Murphy, J. E. (1988) *Interactive Corporate Compliance: An Alternative to Regulatory Compulsion*, New York: Quorum Books.

18 Berger-Walliser and Shrivastava (2015) 'Beyond compliance'.

political-economic theory of '*responsive regulation*'[19] is concerned with how a plurality of motivations for compliance interact, and proposes combined use of compliance and enforcement strategies. Also among more recent regulatory theories related to transnational or super-national sustainability challenges, orchestration theory[20] explains how intergovernmental organisations may shape business conduct in line with social policy objectives, but remains at the abstract level.

All of these examples highlight a move towards instrumental regulation in order to shape business awareness of societal impacts of their products or production processes, and induce them to internalise external concerns in their policies and practices. In view of the fact that much of this regulation and intended business uptake occurs in a regulatory sphere marked by soft law, international norms originally developed for states and now assumed to be observed by businesses, and weak enforcement, it is important for the regulatory processes to be such that they invite businesses to observe the norms without the threat of legal enforcement as a given. In other words, what is needed is norms that carry what international law scholars have referred to as a compliance pull. We will revert to regulatory theories to change organisational conduct, in particular reflexive law, in Chapter 5 and later chapters, which will elaborate on the connection to legitimacy and power in super-national rule-making.

4.2 Legitimacy and 'compliance pull' in international law

Writing in 1990, international law professor Thomas M. Franck noted that the strength of international law depends on a rule or rule-making institution 'exerting a pull towards compliance on those addressed normatively because those addressed believe that the rule or institution has come into being and operates in accordance with generally accepted principles of right process'.[21] Franck observed that one of the most extraordinary things about the international legal system is that its subjects obey its rules and accept its obligations *despite* the underdeveloped institutional structures, processes and enforcement mechanisms.[22] Focusing on state-centrist international law, Franck's hypothesis was that nations obey rules 'because they perceive the rule and its institutional penumbra to have a high degree of legitimacy'.[23] More recently, partly through adopting an 'interactional approach' to international law that takes inspiration from international relations theory, Jutta Brunnée and Stephen J. Toope have noted that what matters in law in general is the creation and effects of legal obligation rather than form or enforcement.[24] Taking up Franck's line of thought, they argue that international law and its rule-making capacity should not be judged by the standards of domestic law and its defining features of enactment by application by courts and centralised enforcement, but on its effectiveness to generate norms that affect conduct even in the absence of sanctions.[25]

19 Ayres and Braithwaite (1992) *Responsive Regulation*.
20 Abbott, K. W., Genschel, P., Snidal, D. and Zangl, B. (2015) 'Orchestration: Global governance through intermediaries', in K. W. Abbott, P. Genschel, D. Snidal and B. Zangl (eds), *International Organizations as Orchestrators*, Cambridge: Cambridge University Press, pp. 3–36.
21 Franck, T. M. (1990) *The Power of Legitimacy among Nations*, Oxford: Oxford University Press, at p. 24.
22 Ibid., at pp. 33–34.
23 Ibid., at p. 25.
24 Brunnée, J. and Toope, S. J. (2010) *Legitimacy and Legality in International Law: An Interactional Account*, New York: Cambridge University Press, at p. 7.
25 Ibid., at pp. 6–8, 24–26, 34–35.

Franck related the compliance pull to the rule and rule-making process, thereby implying that, for a rule and rule-making process to be legitimate, compliance should ideally follow without the need for effectuating sanctions *ex post*. Of course, if and when sanctions do work preventatively, the mere existence of an *ex post* sanction may help drive compliance *ex ante*. However, because of the limited existence of strong enforcement institutions in international law, the effectiveness of international law to generate the intended normative conduct relies heavily on a 'compliance pull'. Making a point of particular relevance to sustainability-related regulation even beyond the conventional state-centrist international law context, Franck explained that '[l]egitimacy exerts a pull to compliance which is powered by the quality of the rule or of the rule-making institution and not by coercive authority. It exerts a claim to compliance in the voluntarist mode.'[26]

Elaborating on the connection between legitimacy and the compliance pull, Franck noted that:

> Legitimacy is the generic label we have placed on factors that affect our willingness to comply voluntarily with commands. These commands may be direct ('go on green; stop on red') or indirect, in the sense of referring back to a more general underlying rule or principle ('each member of the [United Nations] is to be treated by all others in accordance with the principle of equal entitlement'). Such commands emanate from institutions and from rules. Those institutions and rules perceived to have a high degree of legitimacy generate a correspondingly high sense of obligation on the part of the persons or states to whom a command is addressed.[27]

The quality of a rule-making process to generate a compliance pull remains significant as international law evolves to include an increasing range of forms of non-hard law that are developed with explicit recognition of an absence of enforcement institutions but with no fewer normative ambitions than the (limited) hard law rules that enjoy strong legal enforcement institutions, such as regional human rights courts. Similar considerations may be applied to norms on responsible private conduct and sustainability, too, when such norms are subject to similarly weak enforcement institutions. While some such norms may lend themselves to market-based sanctions,[28] the effectiveness of such sanctions remains uncertain and to some extent *ex post facto* based. Owing to their often irremediable effects or long-term restoration, sustainability concerns generally call for *ex ante* compliance (including prevention of harm) rather than remedying after harm has occurred. Whether such rules are purely private or owe their creation to a hybrid public–private set-up, the process to develop the rules risks having a low impact unless the norms carry a strong compliance pull.

In time, international law in the human rights field and other sustainability-oriented areas may come to incorporate strong enforcement mechanisms. In the shorter term, however, the likelihood of this happening is limited. This speaks to the pertinence of hard and soft law in these areas being made in such a way to enjoy a compliance pull.

With regard to non-binding norms, which are common in the international legal system, Dinah Shelton has observed that a law perceived as legitimate and fair is simply more likely to be observed.[29] This is increasingly significant in the emergent role of non-state actors such as

26 Franck (1990) *The Power of Legitimacy among Nations*, at p. 26.
27 Ibid., at p. 150.
28 Cashore et al. (2004) *Governing through Markets*.
29 Shelton, D. (2006) 'International law and "relative normativity"', in M. D. Evans (ed.), *International Law*, 2nd edn, Oxford: Oxford University Press, pp. 159–185, at p. 161.

NGOs, corporations and media[30] in super-national law-making, whether hard or soft. Studies of non-binding international instruments suggest that compliance is contingent on the degree to which the procedural setting for developing the norms is perceived as legitimate in terms of reflecting the concerns and interests of stakeholders.[31] Interestingly, even at the time when the Draft UN Code of Conduct for TNCs was being developed, the UN body in charge noted that

> the effectiveness of an international instrument does not necessarily depend on its legal form. The pertinent question is: does the instrument effectively influence the decision makers – governmental or corporate – in applying the prescribed standards? The answer to this question will depend not so much on the legal characteristics of the instrument as on the extent to which its provisions are acceptable to Member States, transnational states, trade unions and other relevant groups.[32]

While the dismissal of the UN's code of conduct owed much to Cold War legacies and political North–South differences, the points on broad stakeholder acceptance do align with the critique that contributed to the failure of the Draft UN Norms to gain support. They also resemble certain elements of the critique that hurt the legitimacy of the UN Framework and UNGPs after their formal acceptance.

The focus on an inclusive process also connects to the call made by international law scholars like Wolfgang Friedmann, Jonathan Charney and more recently Sol Picciotto for companies to be involved in international law-making pertaining to norms of conduct for business, precisely for reasons of rule-making effectiveness and legitimacy.[33] Yet the legitimacy of private non-state actors' direct as well as indirect involvement in such processes may also raise concerns about such non-state actors taking over roles that belong to states.[34] At least as importantly, the risk of certain organisations capturing the process calls for rules within the process to ensure that interests and power are properly balanced.[35] Such rules, a 'proceduralisation' of the rule-making process, are the main focus of Chapters 6–8. Indeed, as further discussed below, the Human Rights Council's dismissal of the Draft UN Norms may in part have been a result of such *ex post* process capture by certain large business organisations.[36] Similarly, the EU Commission's efforts at creating an EU normative framework on CSR through a public–private multi-stakeholder process suffered from capture by certain large and well-connected business organisations.[37]

30 Brunnée and Toope (2010) *Legitimacy and Legality in International Law*.

31 Weiss, E. B. (2000) 'Conclusions: Understanding compliance with soft law', in D. Shelton (ed.), *Commitment and Compliance: The Role of Non-Binding Norms in the International Legal System*, Oxford: Oxford University Press, pp. 535–553, esp. at pp. 542–543.

32 UNCTC (1990) *Transnational Corporations, Services and the Uruguay Round*, UN Doc. ST/CTC/103, New York: United Nations, p. 185.

33 See, for example, Friedmann (1964) *The Changing Structure of International Law*; Charney (1983) 'Transnational corporations and developing public international law'.

34 See, for example, Haufler, V. (2001) *A Public Role for the Private Sector: Industry Self-Regulation in a Global Economy*, Washington, DC: Carnegie Endowment for International Peace; Reich, R. B. (2007) *Supercapitalism: The Transformation of Business, Democracy and Everyday Life*, New York: Alfred A. Knopf.

35 Compare also Lambooy (2009) 'Private regulation', at p. 116. Lambooy discusses stakeholder involvement in the UN Global Compact and some other multi-stakeholder CSR initiatives, but does not reach definite conclusions on their legitimacy.

36 See Kinley et al. (2007) 'The politics of corporate social responsibility'.

37 Buhmann (2011) 'Integrating human rights in emerging regulation of corporate social responsibility'; Fairbrass (2011) 'Exploring corporate social responsibility policy in the European Union'; Kinderman (2013) 'Corporate social responsibility in the EU, 1993–2013'.

Underscoring the significance of participation in the rule-making process as a modality to create a sense of identification and drive towards compliance from within, studies also suggest that there is a close relationship between the effectiveness of transnational schemes, and their legitimacy perceived as the degree of ownership felt by those who are subjected to the normative requirements of the scheme.[38]

A law-making process aiming at a compliance pull is not intended as a stand-alone solution. There are productive tensions between sanctions – whether punitive, reputational or economic – and compliance. This productive tension is recognised in criminal law and in various theories of regulation.[39] Novel regulatory approaches also recognise a productive tension between hard and soft law and incentives. Thus, a tension with normative directives may play out both in regard to punishments and in regard to rewards or positive effects of compliance or self-regulation. Such 'smart mix' regulation has been recognised by the UN Framework, in the EU's 2011 communication on CSR, and as an emergent field in regulatory theory.[40]

Giving non-state actors a formalised say in international law establishing duties for businesses and rights for those affected by business activities offers an alternative to a situation where non-state actors resort to other measures, such as lobbying, in order to have their views voiced in a negotiation context to which they have no direct access. This follows the analogy from the state-centrist system of international law-making and Franck's idea of international law carrying an inherent compliance pull, because its duties and rights are formulated by those to whom it pertains and made through a process considered legitimate. For a further analogy, in line with the ICJ ruling in the *Reparations for Injuries* case noted in Chapter 2, non-state actors such as businesses and their representative organisations might be granted substantive duties that correspond to their power to affect society adversely through their already existing economic rights; and civil society organisations could be granted formalised rights to represent individuals. Obviously, this can be extended beyond international law-making to transnational law-making driven by private rather than public organisations. The process towards ISO 26000 offers an example of a rule-making process in a transnational context, beyond international organisations, in which non-state and state actors were granted similar rights of participation.

Drawing on established set-ups for organisations with consultative status at international organisations such as the UN, non-state actors' participation in rule-making may be expanded in a way that provides wider and more balanced representation. The design of the institutional set-up would need to consider methods for providing representation of competing views and interests and balancing power disparities. Procedures would therefore be needed, yet the design should not only build on procedures but be aimed at supporting and promoting rule-making as an activity to deliver outputs. Thus, the process would need to be proceduralised. An elaboration of why that is so and how proceduralised equalisation of participation may be done is the main focus of the remaining chapters.

---

38 Gulbrandsen, L. (2004) 'Overlapping public and private governance: Can forest certification fill the gaps in the global forest regime?', *Global Environmental Politics*, Vol. 4, No. 2, pp. 75–99.

39 Compare Reynaers, A.-M. and Parrado, S. (2016) 'Responsive regulation in public–private partnerships: Between deterrence and persuasion', *Regulation and Governance*, DOI 10.1111/rego.1212.

40 Kinderman, D. (2016) 'Time for a reality check: Is business willing to support a smart mix of complementary regulation in private governance?', *Policy and Society*, Vol. 35, No. 1, pp. 29–41.

4.3 Input, throughput and output legitimacy: the deliberative turn in rule-making

With acute implications for sustainability-related action at the level of organisational prac-tice, legitimacy deficits may make norms as well as action that results from those norms vulnerable to lack of trust, internal and external critique and other forms of dissatisfaction among various stakeholders. Companies may perceive the pertinent norms as not reflecting the reality of business conditions or as difficult to apply in business-to-business relationships. Civil society organisations may prefer to exercise critique rather than commend compa-nies for their actions if guiding norms are perceived to have been created in a closed forum excluding significant social actors. Media, politicians, investors and other stakeholders may react in related ways. In turn, this may compromise the willingness of businesses or oth-ers to adopt the norms as part of their management policies and strategies. Legitimacy of a process is therefore a precondition for the effective creation of sustainability-related norms. Underscoring the significance of a law-making process for the perception of legitimacy, the distinction between 'input' and 'output' legitimacy is increasingly complemented by recog-nition of the process dimension, commonly referred to as 'throughput' legitimacy.

Input legitimacy is a characteristic of a procedure that is open to and takes account of views expressed by individuals and groups. Input legitimacy requires inclusiveness (as opposed to, for example, a process that excludes affected groups).[41] Social scientists are used to and often trained to think of input legitimacy in the context of a representative democracy. Indeed, the UDHR (art. 21) and the ICCPR (art. 25(1)) both recognise the right of citizens to take part in the conduct of public affairs, directly or through elected representatives. However, this is relevant not just at the top levels of the political process. The Vienna Declaration and Programme of Action, adopted by UN member states after the World Conference on Human Rights in 1993, recognised in several contexts that public participation also extends to decision-making at the community level, and that it is essentially about taking part in all aspects of society.[42] This suggests that, as societies develop and political processes evolve, we should extend our appreciation of public participation from the central level of state govern-ance both 'downwards', towards localised policy and rule-making processes, and 'upwards', such as to processes that concern policy and norms at the level above nation states.

Representative democracy ensures input through the right to vote and representation of interests through those who are elected. The current organisation of international society assumes that citizens' concerns are represented through states as the law-makers participat-ing in the UN or other international organisations. In practice, however, the representation of specific concerns and needs may be limited. For concerns that transcend state boundaries and state interests, even touching on competing interests within a state, ensuring legitimacy is not easy. From the perspective of sustainability concerns and business social responsibilities, conventional state-centred international law-making suffers from a lack of input congruency[43] in the sense that the actors represented in the decision-making process are not those affected by the rules made: companies are not directly represented, nor are actual or potential human

41 Compare Slaughter, A.-M. (2000) 'Agencies on the loose? Holding government networks accountable', in G. Bermann, M. Herdegen and P. Lindseth (eds), *Transatlantic Regulatory Cooperation, Legal Problems and Political Prospects*, Oxford: Oxford University Press, pp. 521–546, at p. 525, referring to government networks as 'illegitimate' when they exclude affected groups.

42 United Nations General Assembly (1993) *Vienna Declaration and Programme of Action*.

43 Zürn, M. (1998) *Regieren jenseits des Nationalstaates*, Frankfurt am Main: Suhrkamp, esp. at p. 237.

rights victims. From the perspective of CSR, it has been noted that these particular stakeholders along with others 'who do not normally have a voice in society', such as farmers, children and workers in poor or developing communities, are also often missing from lists of stakeholders or physically absent from stakeholders' meetings or forums.[44]

Output legitimacy refers to the quality of the rules produced through a process. Output legitimacy is two-pronged in referring to the output being both acceptable and effective in addressing the public policy need it was designed for.[45] The two are closely linked, because lack of acceptance will compromise effectiveness, especially when compliance has to work independently of sanctions. As we saw above, the Draft UN Norms were perceived by certain business associations as being illegitimate, because these associations felt inadequately included in the process of developing norms of conduct pertaining to business conduct. The UN Global Compact was predicted to be illegitimate in the eyes of civil society because of imbalanced and late representation of NGOs. The recommendations contained in the final report of the MSF were perceived by European NGOs as being an illegitimate product of the MSF process because business associations were perceived to have an advantage in terms of representation and access to the powerful EU ministry-like Directorate-General (DG) Enterprise.

Throughput legitimacy connects the process aspect of input transformation and the substantive quality and acceptance of the output. Throughput legitimacy refers to the quality of the process through which rules are made, that is, the transformation of input to output and the conditions for such transformation. It includes the design of a process of deliberation or negotiation to provide for equalised participation and decisions based on reason rather than the asymmetric power of one or more participants or networks.[46] Equalised participation in a discourse that delivers or processes input for the production of norms of conduct implies that actors recognise each other as equals and have equal access to the discourse. In addition, the discourse must be open to other participants and be open in nature.[47]

Along with inclusiveness, transparency and equality of access, deliberation is a key factor in throughput legitimacy, with particular emphasis on conditions for broad debate and scrutiny of individual interests (including those of individual groups or types of actors). Procedural norms for interaction may contribute to increased throughput legitimacy of rule-making forums, which typically suffer from limited transparency, such as governance networks.[48] It has been observed that, at the international level, throughput legitimacy

---

44 Prieto-Carron et al. (2006) 'Critical perspectives on CSR and development', at p. 984.
45 Compare, with emphasis on problem-solving potential, Hachez and Wouters (2011) *A Glimpse at the Democratic Legitimacy of Private Standards*, at pp. 7–8; Wouters, J., Marx, A. and Hachez, N. (2011) *Private Standards, Global Governance and International Trade: The Case of Global Food Safety Governance*, Working Paper, March, Leuven: Katholieke Universiteit Leuven, Leuven Centre for Global Governance Studies, at p. 24; Pauwelyn, J. (2012) 'Informal international law-making: Framing the concept and research questions', in J. Pauwelyn, R. Wessel and J. Wouters (eds), *Informal International Law-Making*, Oxford: Oxford University Press, pp. 13–34; and, with emphasis on acceptance, Schaefer, S. (2010) 'Legitimacy and the international regulation of geoengineering with solar radiation management: Prospects for normative institutional design theory', Unpublished paper on file with author. Scott et al. (2011) 'The conceptual and constitutional challenge of transnational private regulation', at p. 13 refer to *pragmatic legitimacy* as related to the acceptance of the effectiveness of a regime, and *normative legitimacy* as a measure of the 'appropriateness of processes in terms of such matters as inclusion and transparency'.
46 Deitelhoff, N. and Müller, H. (2005) 'Theoretical paradise – empirically lost? Arguing with Habermas', *Review of International Studies*, Vol. 31, pp. 167–179.
47 Risse (2000) '"Let's argue"', at p. 11.
48 Torfing, J. (2013) 'Legitimitet i netværkssamfundet: Et politologisk perspektiv på virksomheders deltagelse i styringsnetværk', in S. Holmstrøm and S. Kjærbeck (eds), *Legitimitet under forandring: Virksomheden is samfundet*, Copenhagen: Samfundslitteratur, pp. 61–88.

means that decisions are made not only through diplomatic negotiations but via a process of deliberative argumentation in which individual interests are scrutinised and debated.[49] Shifted to the level of super-national development of norms related to sustainability and organisational conduct, the combined dearth of formal rules on non-state actor participation (input legitimacy) and of formal accountability (of those involved in the process and the output that they decide) and effective enforcement methods (of compliance with the output) strengthens the need for throughput legitimacy.

Indeed, the years since around 2000 have witnessed a surge in interest among social scientists in aspects of deliberation as a qualified form of debate and its application to decision-making at the super-national level. Many scholars have noted that legitimate decision-making in a pluralist (transnationalising) international society requires decision-making institutions and processes to become more responsive to the needs and interests of non-state actors. A main point of emerging theory emanating from this is that, for super-national decision-making – including law-making – to be legitimate, the process must provide for the opportunity to offer justification and reach consensus on norms that are consistent with the idea of the common good. Indeed, the 'deliberative turn'[50] in the social sciences has focused on the creation of legitimate rules through a process allowing for deliberation as a way to turn input into a broadly representative output.

Recognising that power is inherently present in international relations and that at the super-national level participation is often not completely 'uncoerced',[51] from the empirical perspective the key question has been phrased as under what conditions actors are able to develop outputs through deliberation, and what forms of institutional design enable deliberative discourse in which alternatives are represented on an equal footing.[52] Research indicates that transparency of the process, role identities of the actors involved, and the extent to which the institutional setting enables leadership and competent authority to influence the process are among the important conditions.[53]

To appreciate this debate on deliberation and legitimacy, we will first look at deliberative law-making as developed by Jürgen Habermas, whose writing informs much other scholarship on deliberation, legitimacy and throughput, at both the national and the super-national level.

4.3.1 Legitimate rule-making through deliberation, bargaining and negotiation

In relation to the role of non-state actors in rule-making activities taking place through public–private collaboration at the super-national level, theories developed by Habermas on discourse ethics and deliberation complement international law theory on law-making. At the same time, they challenge conventional international law theory and practice on actors in law-making processes by questioning the adequacy of the UN-based international regime in a broader perspective of globalisation, sustainability, and requirements on law and policy to respond to public policy concerns of relevance to a global citizenry.

Without going into much detail in terms of how it might be operationalised, Habermas suggests that a formalised access for civil society to interact with formal law-makers at

---

49 Schaefer (2010) 'Legitimacy and the international regulation of geoengineering with solar radiation management', at p. 3.
50 Risse and Kleine (2010) 'Deliberation in negotiations', with references at p. 709.
51 Risse (2000) '"Let's argue"', at p. 16.
52 Risse and Kleine (2010) 'Deliberation in negotiations', esp. at pp. 708–710; compare Risse (2000) '"Let's argue"', at pp. 18, 32.
53 Risse and Kleine (2010) 'Deliberation in negotiations', with conclusion at p. 721.

intergovernmental level or for transnational law-making that evolves without formal frameworks may offer a way forward. This is particularly relevant against the backdrop of the concern with power disparities suggested above in reflexive law theory. The issue is introduced here from the Habermasian perspective and will be elaborated below in relation to reflexive law and past examples of public and public–private initiatives to develop new norms on sustainability-related issues.

Centred on the idea of the 'uncoerced force of the better argument', like some of his other work Jürgen Habermas's theory on legitimate law-making through deliberation[54] draws on discourse as an element in deliberative law-making. A philosopher, Habermas approaches discourse from the perspective of ethics, focusing on the ideal conditions occurring for a discourse on a political issue to evolve into norms. While Habermas is concerned with the process towards norm development as well as the given norm that is the output of the process, the process takes centre stage: without a process that is legitimate, the output – the normative product – will not be legitimate. Proceduralisation of the process is necessary to obtain the ideal conditions for the rule-making process to bring about deliberation for the formation of a common will or at least negotiations or 'bargaining' that leads to an agreed compromise. Habermas's *philosophical and ethical-regulatory* approach to discourse therefore differs from *political* discourse theories like those developed by Ernesto Laclau, Chantal Mouffe and Norman Fairclough. Habermas seeks to balance power into a broadly representative normative product, whereas the political theories analyse power as hegemony that occurs when power is not balanced.

In his major work on legitimate law-making through deliberation, which appeared in German in 1992 as *Faktizität und Geltung* and in English translation in 1996 as *Between Facts and Norms*,[55] Habermas takes his point of departure at the national level, where norms of conduct codified into law applied or enforced by the state derive legitimacy through a broad discourse among citizens and their representatives, including civil society.[56] Public discourse mobilises reason and arguments drawing on citizens' interests and values. In the ideal political process for law-making, public reason and public concerns feed into a process of formation of will and opinion in the public sphere through a deliberative process. Through the political process, citizens influence will and opinion, which are formed into law to be applied or enforced by public institutions. It presumably has a compliance pull because it is based in common will. If it is not complied with, enforcement is in place, again because the norm is based in common will and equal access to participation in deliberation on interests.

Habermas perceives legitimacy and effectiveness of law as closely related, with both being connected to a qualified participation in the law-making process by those who are subjected to the rules. This also accords with the emphasis that Shelton has attached to the relevance of non-state actors' participation in the drafting process for their willingness to comply.[57] Thus, when non-state actors' compliance is intended by a transnational norm or intergovernmentally initiated normative process or product, then participation, legitimacy and compliance pull may be intertwined.[58]

From the Habermasian perspective, deliberation is a qualified form of collective decision-making. Decisions made by deliberation are acceptable to others affected by the decisions, because they are supported by reasoned arguments based on well-informed debate

54 Habermas (1996) *Between Facts and Norms*.
55 Ibid.
56 Ibid.
57 Shelton, D. (2000) 'Introduction', in D. Shelton (ed.), *Commitment and Compliance: The Role of Non-Binding Norms in the International Legal System*, Oxford: Oxford University Press, pp. 1–18, at p. 16.
58 Habermas (1996) *Between Facts and Norms*.

and participants' openness to persuasion. Deliberation subjects different positions to reasoned debate and justification through critique, and presumes that debate is undertaken with respect for other participants' views. To provide for the conditions for such debate and prevent capture or distortion as a result of power disparities, deliberative decision-making requires procedural institutional conditions that facilitate free discussion among equal participants by providing a framework for free expression, association and debate. In a nation state, deliberative decision-making connects deliberation to the authorisation to exercise public power and in turn ties the exercise of public power to the deliberative interaction through a framework that ensures the responsiveness and accountability of political power.[59] Deliberation provides legitimacy because it encourages the expression of differences in ideas, perception and outlook towards a commonly agreed solution. Deliberation assumes that mutual reasoning will reduce disagreement and reinforce commitment to problem-solving to a higher degree than processes dominated by singular participants' strategic gaming for advantage.[60] Thus, the throughput process connecting input to output is significant for the quality of the output, and its legitimacy. This relates to the points on a compliance pull based on perceived legitimacy noted by Franck.

Bargaining represents an alternative form of legitimate decision-making where the formation of common opinion and will is not possible.[61] This typically occurs when differences between stakeholders and their concerns are too large to be met through deliberation. Habermas's recognition of bargaining entails a pragmatic recognition of the practicalities of much of collective decision-making. Decision-making by consensus may be the ideal, but disagreement is a fact of life. Bargaining is negotiation between parties who are willing to cooperate to realign views where a common will may not be formed. Aiming at identifying compromises that participants find acceptable, bargaining is founded on a perception that the compromise arrangement is more advantageous to all than no arrangement whatever.[62] Hence, bargaining processes are particularly relevant when social power relations cannot be neutralised in the way presupposed by ideal rational deliberative discourse where participants strive towards forming a common will by each attempting to convince other participants through reasoned arguments. Bargaining, therefore, recognises that conflicting interests are too strong to be completely aligned. Here, too, Habermas recognises the impact that power disparities may have on the legitimacy of the output. If framed (and contained) by a procedure that balances power disparities, bargaining may lead to results that are legitimate.[63]

In bargaining, the ideal of an uncoerced consensus can be brought to bear only indirectly through procedures which regulate bargaining by 'disciplining' non-neutralisable power so that it is equally distributed among the parties.[64] Procedures for negotiation of compromise should provide all concerned parties with an equal opportunity for influencing one another during the bargaining process. Such procedures define the equal consideration of the concerns and needs of each participant as a problem of procedurally correct agreements among power-holders.[65] This provides for what is referred to in this book as equalised participation

---

59 Cohen, J. and Sabel, C. (2001) 'Directly-deliberative polyarchy', *European Law Journal*, Vol. 3, No. 4, pp. 313–342, at p. 320.

60 Ibid.; Risse and Kleine (2010) 'Deliberation in negotiations'.

61 Habermas (1996) *Between Facts and Norms*, at pp. 165–166.

62 Ibid., at pp. 165–166; see also Habermas, J. (1998) 'Zur Legitimation durch Menschenrechte', in *Die postnationale Konstellation: Politische Essays*, Frankfurt am Main: Suhrkamp, pp. 170–194.

63 Habermas (1996) *Between Facts and Norms*, at pp. 103–104, 167–177.

64 Ibid., at pp. 166–167.

65 Ibid.

in a decision-making process, such as rule-making. Where the institutionalised procedure in the deliberative formation of common opinion and will is a matter of providing for mutual understanding among discourse participants, in bargaining it is also about providing for agreement based on equalised power among participants in the discursive process.

In practice, deliberation and bargaining may converge.[66] With the 'deliberative turn', authors have proposed the concept of arguing as a complementary explanation for negotiated arguments. Participants in negotiations seek to persuade others to change preferences by offering arguments towards a reasoned consensus.[67] Arguing is sometimes motivated by self-interest rather than consensus in the interest of all.[68] Deliberation provides an option for swaying views and reaching common decisions through a 'better argument' that seeks to achieve consensus based on shared concerns and the common interest of all. Reflexive law in principle builds on a related idea of inducing self-regulation by offering actors an opportunity to appreciate and internalise the concerns of others as a way of meeting common interests. However, as will be elaborated below through examples from the empirical cases, in practice in settings that function as reflexive law arguments based on actor-specific interests may combine with power of privilege to strategically promote the interests of some participants beyond what can be agreed to as a common interest that all participants perceive to be the result of equalised participation. As a result, the more persuasive argument – functioning through a deliberative 'better argument' as well as power of privilege – may be deficient in throughput legitimacy.

The Habermasian approach to legitimate law-making addresses the significance of legitimacy in a wide legal community comprising authorities as well as civil society, not only as bearers of rights and duties, but also as law-makers. Such a pluralistic community is closer to that which has spurred public–private development of CSR normativity and rule-making at the intergovernmental level than is the state-centrist structure of international law which Franck targeted. The state-centrist structure in traditional international law is particular in the sense that the rule-makers (states) formally enjoy the same status in the legal system and hierarchy as those subjected to the rules (which under traditional international law are also typically states). It is also particular in the sense that those subjected to the rules (states) have the power to determine whether the rules are to be enforceable, and to set up and fund (or decide not to set up or fund) enforcement institutions. The national legal order differs from this, as does the emerging transnational legal order that has spurred various regulatory initiatives towards promoting sustainable conduct (such as on business and human rights) and protecting global sustainability-related goods (such as timber and other resources). While civil society and individual citizens may partake in law-making through methods of deliberation in the national context, national authorities are still the law-makers. Authorities have the power to make rules enforceable and to set up, fund and run enforcement institutions. They are powerful, but have been granted the power legitimately to make, implement and enforce rules on behalf of citizens.

---

66 For example, Barnard, C. (2002) 'The social partners and the governance agenda', *European Law Journal*, Vol. 8, No. 1, pp. 80–101; Peruzzi, M. (2011) 'Autonomy in European social dialogue', *Law and Industrial Relations*, Vol. 27, No. 1, pp. 3–21, at p. 18.

67 Risse (2000) '"Let's argue"'.

68 Odell, J. S. (2010) 'Three islands of knowledge about negotiation in international organizations', *Journal of European Public Policy*, Vol. 17, No. 5, pp. 619–632, at p. 627 with reference to Müller, H. (2004) 'Arguing, bargaining and all that – communicative action, rationalist theory, and the logic of appropriateness in international relations', *European Journal of International Relations*, Vol. 10, No. 2, pp. 395–435.

4.3.2 Super-national law-making: civil society and equalised participation

The theory on deliberative law-making was originally developed with a national law context in mind. In some of his more recent work, Habermas has addressed some similar issues in a super-national law-making context, particularly with regard to the UN and the need for addressing global sustainability concerns.

Habermas acknowledges that the basic ideas of deliberative discourse-based democracy as a foundation for law's legitimacy cannot be directly transferred to the international level, simply because of the different composition and roles of actors and institutions and persisting state-centrist structure.[69] Yet he notes the potential value of establishing a super-national order in which individuals enjoy a status as members of a politically constituted world society.[70] As in the national system, balancing of interests must take place within the institutional governance structures of a (reformed) transnational system.[71] Obviously, this causes challenges in relation to representation as well as the practical transmission and co-creation of opinion and will.

Habermasian theory offers a set of arguments and lines of thoughts which despite their diversity are connected through decades of scholarly production and interest in proposing solutions to what he sees as legitimation crises related to the dynamic development of society, governance and law over the past half-century.[72] Habermas argues that there is a need for the UN system and other international governance systems (such as the international trade system) to better integrate the views of the world's civil society. Currently, these governance systems neither respond fully to the needs of a global public, nor are able to deliver regulation based on global will-formation created through deliberative practices that sufficiently include civil society representing the global public.[73]

Like many others, including Kofi Annan (in Global Compact speeches), John Ruggie (both as an academic and in his capacity as SRSG) and Gunther Teubner (in post-1990 writings), Habermas notes that globalisation and the growth of economic cooperation and trade place environmental and human sustainability and equitable distribution under pressure. This causes problems that require global cooperation, and consequently policy-making and regulation for which he observes that the institutional framework is currently lacking and for which recognised actors are too limited.[74] Dealing with the challenges of globalisation and the needs for globally legitimate governance requires suitable forms of a participatory and legitimate regulatory process beyond the nation state.[75]

To Habermas, law is the primary medium of social integration in modern society. Law is power that extracts obedience from its subjects. However, power by itself cannot grant legitimacy in modern society, so law must derive its validity from the consent of the governed.

---

69 Habermas, J. (2004) 'Folkeretten i overgangen til den postnationale konstellation', *Distinktion*, Vol. 8, pp. 9–17.

70 Habermas, J. (2007) 'A political constitution for the pluralist world society?', *Journal of Chinese Philosophy*, Vol. 34, No. 3, pp. 331–343.

71 Habermas (2008) 'The constitutionalization of international law and the legitimation process of a constitution for world society'.

72 Compare the point of departure noted for the broad analysis of Habermas as a legal theorist in Baxter, H. (2011) *Habermas: The Discourse Theory of Law and Democracy*, Stanford, CA: Stanford University Press.

73 Habermas, J. (1998) 'Jenseits der Nationalstaats: Bemerkungen zu Folgeprobleme der wirtschaftlichen Globalisierung', in U. Beck (ed.), *Politik der Globalisierung*, Frankfurt am Main: Suhrkamp, pp. 67–84.

74 Habermas (2007) 'A political constitution for the pluralist world society?'

75 Habermas (2008) 'The constitutionalization of international law and the legitimation process of a constitution for world society', at pp. 444–445.

For this reason, law as output must be generated through a procedure of formation of public opinion and will. To sustain their legitimacy, formal processes of law-making in modern societies must take the concerns of ordinary citizens into account. This is a matter not just of procedures for the administration's and law-makers' integration of such information into the law or other rules, but also of proceduralisation to enable citizens to develop and share views in a balanced manner among themselves and with other groups, and be able to feed this into the political and law-making process. To Habermas, civil society and its organisations are core to these processes. Civil society represents citizens who seek acceptable solutions and interpretations of their societal interests and concerns and seek influence on institutionalised formation of opinion and will.[76] Civil society organisations represent citizens' interests and concerns, and enable them to participate directly or indirectly in deliberation.[77] Civil society organisations come in a number of forms and sizes and may organise individuals as well as a diverse range of other organisations, including businesses. At the national level, the conditions for civil society's interaction with the public sphere are constituted through fundamental (or human) rights such as the freedoms of association, assembly and speech. As civil society organisations have a key role as channels for the collective views, needs and opinions of groups of citizens, their rights to participate are subject to proceduralisation to ensure that they exist and function in the deliberative process. This requires not just formal guarantees of rights to express their views, but also ensuring opportunities equally to exercise those rights.

In the emerging transnational legal order, non-state actors already enjoy certain formalised law-making powers (such as NGOs in consultative status with the UN, or non-state actors invited into the process of developing the UN Global Compact or UN Framework), which however remain limited compared to those of states. In other contexts, non-state actors have considerable informal powers (as in the case of the EU MSF, where, as elaborated below, certain business organisations because of past experience with EU rule-making and access to EU policy bodies were able to exert decisive influence during the process and therefore also over the output).

Networks that organise actors or the representation of concerns across specific types of actors often play a part in deliberative law-making or bargaining. Networks typically either serve coordination functions in social sectors, taking care of interests through bargaining, or comprise groups that give voice to interests and needs of a more general type. The latter form typically works through complex networks that have arisen among public agencies and non-state or civil society actors.[78] Networks are already frequently informal actors in international law-making processes relating to transnational policy concerns such as environmental protection, and have proven to have significant influence.[79]

---

76 Habermas (1996) *Between Facts and Norms*, at p. 367. Overall, Habermas considers human rights as a means for institutionalising conditions for communication towards a reasonable and legitimate political will formation with resulting normativity, rules and governance. Their moral character derives not from their origin, structure or contents, but because these are rights that have normative validity beyond the legal orders of nation states. See, for example, Habermas, J. (2005) 'Kant's idé om den evige fred – på en historisk afstand af 200 år', in H. Andersen (ed.), *Jürgen Habermas: Demokrati og retsstat – en tekstsamling*, Copenhagen: Hans Reitzels Forlag, pp. 149–186, esp. at pp. 173–177, translated from Habermas, J. (1996) 'Kants Idee der ewigen Friedens', in *Die Einbeziehung des Anderen: Studien zur politischen Theorie*, Frankfurt am Main: Suhrkamp, pp. 154–185; Habermas, J. (2005) 'Legitimering på grundlag af menneskerettigheder', in H. Andersen (ed.), *Jürgen Habermas: Demokrati og retsstat – en tekstsamling*, Copenhagen: Hans Reitzels Forlag, pp. 187–203, translated from Habermas, J. (1998) 'Zur Legitimation durch Menschenrechte', in *Die postnationale Konstellation: Politische Essays*, Frankfurt am Main: Suhrkamp, pp. 170–194.
77 Habermas (1996) *Between Facts and Norms*, at pp. 127, 366–368.
78 Ibid., at pp. 353–354.
79 Hajer (1995) *The Politics of Environmental Discourse*; Arts (2001) 'The impact of environmental NGOs in international conventions'.

To be legitimate, policy processes in governance networks should reflect or at least take into account the concerns, preferences and opinions of the members of involved groups.[80] Transparency, access to public dialogue with the network representing a plurality of interests, and responsiveness on the part of the network are key factors in developing the trust necessary for negotiation to be fruitful and for compliance with the negotiated output. Because concerns and priorities of the participating groups are represented through processes of communication, what takes place within the process of the negotiation is key to the representation of interests, and therefore to the output and legitimacy. Legitimacy may be supported through procedural rules ensuring inclusive and equalised representation and participation.[81] Here, too, the effectiveness of the regulatory process that takes place through negotiation may be hampered unless the process is legitimate, as will be the legitimacy of the resulting output. When governance through networks of sectoral interests or other coalitions becomes transnational not only by accident but as an intentional way for the political system to seek to govern issues that reach beyond national territorial and jurisdictional boundaries, the significance as well as challenge of ensuring legitimacy travels along.

As with the problems that led to the creation of the Global Compact, Habermas takes a point of departure in problems caused by globalisation and the growth of economic cooperation and trade, which place severe strains on environmental and social or human sustainability. To deal with this, there is a need for the governance system at the super-national level to provide channels for the voice of the world's citizens in a way that is less purely state-centrist than in current practice. Such reforms of the super-national system will be more 'legitimate' in the sense of deliberative formation of will, opinions and consequently policy and law than is the case under the current state-centrist regime. To achieve this, the role of national governments in global will-formation must be supplemented by an institutionalised participation of civil society that entails actual participation.[82] Thus, it must go beyond what is currently found. The role of organised civil society in the national constitutional state must be transplanted with due adaptations from the national to the international stage.

Habermas argues that globalisation and its effects require a form of constitutionalisation of international law that 'can secure a democratic legitimation for new forms of governance in transnational spaces'.[83] This need not be a constitution in the sense known from national documents. Rather, constitutionalisation of law and governance at the above-national level can be perceived as a process that takes account of the democratic and legitimacy deficits in international law and challenges posed by an evolving global order, which is transnational and often pluralist[84] rather than simply international. Moreover, as an evolution of constitutional principles, instruments and doctrines, transnational constitutionalism challenges but

---

80 Sørensen, E. and Torfing, J. (2005) 'The democratic anchorage of governance networks', *Scandinavian Political Studies*, Vol. 28, No. 3, pp. 195–218.

81 Ibid.

82 Habermas, J. (1998) *Die postnationale Konstellation: Politische Essays*, Frankfurt am Main: Suhrkamp, pp. 91–169; Habermas (1998) 'Jenseits der Nationalstaats'; Habermas (1998) 'Zur Legitimation durch Menschenrechte'; Habermas (2007) 'A political constitution for the pluralist world society?'; Habermas (2008) 'The constitutionalization of international law and the legitimation process of a constitution for world society'.

83 Habermas (2008) 'The constitutionalization of international law and the legitimation process of a constitution for world society', at p. 445; see also Habermas, J. (2005) 'Den postnationale konstellation og demokratiets fremtid', in H. Andersen (ed.), *Jürgen Habermas: Demokrati og retsstat – en tekstsamling*, Copenhagen: Hans Reitzels Forlag, pp. 220–273, translated from Habermas, J. (1998) *Die postnationale Konstellation: Politische Essays*, Frankfurt am Main: Suhrkamp, pp. 91–169.

84 Compare Krisch, N. (2010) *Beyond Constitutionalism: The Pluralist Structure of Postnational Law*, Oxford: Oxford University Press.

does not negate the distinction between the national and the international legal order. As opposed to the idea of 'constitution', the process-oriented concept of constitutionalism has the potential to function as a bridge between the established (and evolving) nation state constitutional law discourses and the legitimacy in global governance.[85]

A constitutionalisation of the transnational requires a shift away from the state-centrist system of super-national law-making that is associated with the conventional perception of international law-making.[86] Basically, public institutions that enjoy policy-making and regulatory competences at the super-national level need to provide channels for the voice of the world's citizens in a way that is less purely state-centrist and more 'legitimate' in the sense of deliberative formation of will, opinions and consequently policy and law than is presently the case.

Working through deliberative procedures, communities may fulfil the conditions of legitimacy at a super-national level. With necessary adaptations due to the difference in institutional structures and the sheer size of a global citizenry, these procedures should correspond to those that provide for throughput at the national level. For example, non-state actors can be involved directly in negotiations, as well as through other arrangements and procedures that promote compromises and negotiated results among independent decision-making actors.[87]

In sum, increasing the conditions for practising a deliberative discourse will enhance the ability of norm creation at the super-national level to represent the concerns, will and opinion of the global public. That means allowing not only states but also other representative entities to take part in a process of collective will-formation leading to common agreement on norms for co-existence. This may be achieved by involving NGOs and other civil society actors in international negotiations, and through other arrangements and procedures which promote compromises and negotiated results through processes that engage not only states but also non-state actors. The creation of such a procedural regulatory process contributes to establishing a legal and political order, and institutions that are appropriate at a time when social and welfare state problems have migrated from nation state level to super-national level. Yet, while his theoretical contributions not infrequently go beyond the limits of specific subfields within social sciences, Habermas often draws attention to problems without necessarily proposing specific solutions.[88] Habermas provides the overall ideal for a global or transnational legitimate process of rule-making and arguments for why inclusiveness can and must not be limited to the national level. However, apart from the point that a global

85 Zumbansen, P. (2012) 'Comparative, global and transnational constitutionalism: The emergence of a transnational legal-pluralist order', *Global Constitutionalism*, Vol. 1, No. 1, pp. 16–52.

86 Habermas (2008) 'The constitutionalization of international law and the legitimation process of a constitution for world society', at p. 445; see also Habermas (2005) 'Den postnationale konstellation og demokratiets fremtid'.

87 Habermas (1998) *Die postnationale Konstellation*; Habermas (1998) 'Jenseits der Nationalstaats'; Habermas (1998) 'Zur Legitimation durch Menschenrechte'; Habermas (2007) 'A political constitution for the pluralist world society?'; Habermas (2008) 'The constitutionalization of international law and the legitimation process of a constitution for world society'.

88 Compare McCarthy, T. (1975) 'Translator's introduction', in J. Habermas, *Legitimation Crisis*, Boston, MA: Beacon Press, pp. vii–xxiv, at p. viii, stating that Habermas 'makes unusual demands on the reader, assuming some familiarity with a wide range of disciplines (from economics to ethics), authors (from Kant to Parsons), and approaches (from systems theory to phenomenology)', and that 'it is extremely important that the reader take Habermas at his word on the status of the argument – it is meant as a *preparatory clarification* of the enormous complex issues involved, preparatory, that is, to the *empirical research* required for further resolution'. Killion, U. (2010) 'The function of law in Habermas' modern society', *Global Jurist*, Vol. 10, No. 2, article 1, pp. 1–24, at p. 1, notes based on McCarthy (above, this footnote) that it is important to recognise that Habermas does not propose finality and does not attempt to offer definitive explanations to the problems of modern society that he identifies.

citizenry can be represented by civil society organisations, he does not provide the operational or practicable 'how-to' for transnational rule-making that enjoys legitimacy through a proceduralised process of deliberation or negotiation/'bargaining'. Reading Habermas, especially his later works on deliberative law-making and the challenges facing contemporary global society, therefore offers a point of departure for a discussion on collaborative regulation to be complemented by other authors and theories.

4.4 Modernising international law: towards participation in super-national law-making

Application and further development of Habermasian ideas by social scientists confirm that social actors use strategies of negotiation and arguments to promote and protect specific interest in processes of international policy- and rule-making. This strengthens the case for understanding how actors engage in and seek to influence the construction of sustainability-related norms of conduct, whether as hard law or for practical purposes more commonly as soft law in the form of guidance or political agreements. Because political scientists often focus more on the regulatory process and decision-making than dogmatic lawyers tend to (being more preoccupied with the norms that are the results of such processes, and with the implementation and enforcement of existing norms), political science views complement the views of socio-legal and other process-oriented lawyers well.

With the emergence of the deliberative turn in international politics studies, political scientists have been paying attention to rule-making and other forms of decision-making in international and transnational contexts. Provided there is the right institutionalised procedural framework, deliberation may work towards developing reasoned consensus between states, international organisations and civil society and their networks.[89] Such an institutionalised procedure may provide equality of access by disproportionately empowering the weaker actors who have less material resources at their disposal. This may apply, for example, to smaller and less developed states, or to civil society organisations.[90] With transnational rule-making often being developed through networks that span several groups and interests, composition is an important factor in ensuring that all concerned groups are present or represented. Participation may be limited or enhanced by rules of access. Membership selection may be prone to risks of exclusion owing to social asymmetries, marginalisation, lack of financial, material or educational resources, or bias on the part of those who make the rules or decision on access. Specific mechanisms of empowerment of disadvantaged groups may be necessary to enable a network-based rule-making process to reach out and be inclusive rather than exclusive.[91] Power asymmetries and risk of capture of the debate within the network by particular interests may compromise the quality of deliberation, and therefore the legitimacy of the output.[92] This all speaks of the importance of the design of the procedural fora that frame participatory law-making, and therefore of procedures and proceduralisation.

---

89 For example, Risse (2000) "'Let's argue'"; Odell (2010) 'Three islands of knowledge about negotiation in international organizations'; Risse and Kleine (2010) 'Deliberation in negotiations'; Steffek, J. and Gomes Pereira, M. (2011) 'Transnational governance networks and democracy: What are the standards?', in O. Dilling, M. Herberg and G. Winter (eds), *Transnational Administrative Rule-Making: Performance, Legal Effects and Legitimacy*, Oxford: Hart, pp. 281–304.

90 Risse (2000) "'Let's argue'", at p. 19.

91 Steffek and Gomes Pereira (2011) 'Transnational governance networks and democracy', at pp. 290–291.

92 Ibid., at pp. 291–292.

A rule-making process has little value if it does not respond to the problems that affected or concerned citizens experience or perceive. How to devise a communication process that ensures the necessary transmission of information is an additional challenge.[93] Information and communication enable stakeholders to form informed views not only on matters discussed but also on matters for external accountability,[94] such as through the provision of information on composition, mode of operation, actual processes and decisions made.

We saw above that international law scholars Franck and Shelton have emphasised the significance of participation, and what for practical purposes amounts to throughput legitimacy for acceptance of the output and its compliance pull in relation to international law. Political scientists, too, argue that the acceptance of the output of a decision-making process is influenced by the extent to which actors affected by the output have a say in decision-making. Directly involving non-state actors therefore provides for more of an effective respect for and implementation of outputs from collective decision-making, such as the development of normative regimes. Being more effective and involving those affected, such decision-making is also held to be legitimate, even though non-state actors involved in the decision-making process do not enjoy the democratic mandate which states have.[95] The counterargument is sometimes made that involving non-state actors in, for instance, implementation of governance decisions amounts to privatisation of state functions and 'to the overtaking of governance tasks by illegitimate actors such as companies'.[96] However, such points arguably mix up the process of decision-making, and the delivery of services and other public obligations. There is a crucial difference between, on the one hand, involving businesses in rule-making pertaining to their impact on society and, on the other, shifting responsibility for delivery of state obligations to firms. Involving business organisations in processes to develop norms on responsible conduct need not imply that they take over tasks that are conventionally held by states. For example, it is widely agreed that states retain their obligations to protect, respect and fulfil human rights, even if they outsource some of the practical exercise for delivery to the private sector.

Some theories suggest that non-state actors engage in governance, including co-regulation and self-regulation, under an implicit threat of hard state regulation or enforcement. This corresponds to studies that suggest that companies self-regulate on CSR to pre-empt coercive state law.[97] Studies also show that a threat of state coercion is no precondition for multi-stakeholder-created norms to be effective.[98]

In his academic capacity as a political scientist, John Ruggie has argued that there is a need to reconstitute the 'global public domain' to accommodate the actual roles and influence of non-state actors in globalised society.[99] The concept of the public domain accords with the

---

93   Ibid., at p. 293.

94   Ibid., at pp. 297–299.

95   Rosenau, J. N. and Czempiel, E.-O. (1992) *Governance without Government: Order and Change in World Politics*, Cambridge: Cambridge University Press; Reinicke, W. H. (1998) *Global Public Policy: Governing without Government?*, Washington, DC: Brookings Institution Press; Reinicke, W. H., Deng, F. and Witte Martin, J. (2000) *Critical Choices: The United Nations, Networks, and the Future of Global Governance*, Ottawa: International Development Research Centre; Gulbrandsen (2004) 'Overlapping public and private governance'.

96   Börzel, T. A. and Risse, T. (2010) 'Governance without a state: Can it work?', *Regulation and Governance*, Vol. 4, No. 2, pp. 113–134, at p. 127; compare for example Haufler (2001) *A Public Role for the Private Sector*; and Reich (2007) *Supercapitalism*.

97   Schwartz and Carroll (2003) 'Corporate social responsibility'.

98   Börzel and Risse (2010) 'Governance without a state'.

99   Ruggie (2004) 'Reconstituting the global public domain – issues, actors and practices'.

idea of a 'public sphere' discussed by Jürgen Habermas as early as 1974 as 'a realm of our social life in which something approaching public opinion can be formed'[100] and elaborated in 1996 as 'a network for communicating information and points of view'.[101] Ruggie has explained that the non-recognition of NGOs, companies and other non-state actors (except for intergovernmental organisations) as actors or participants under the current regime of international law does not accord with the reality of the interests and concerns they represent or the power they exercise. Law-making structures at super-national level, which would include non-state actors in active roles, could provide for more legitimate norm-creation, allowing a broad range of stakeholders to have influence on the resulting norms.[102]

Studies of non-state actors in international relations have demonstrated that, despite their lack of formal role as participants in international law-making, NGOs and private non-state actors play significant roles in international law-making processes and intergovernmental rule-making in several ways. In their capacity as non-state actors that often possess information and expertise that are welcomed by intergovernmental organisations they influence political agenda-setting, law-making and other decision-making and sometimes play a part in implementation procedures, and they are part of political, policy and institutional arrangements, including some legal arrangements in the international system.[103] Research has demonstrated that NGOs and business organisations employ a variety of strategies to influence international policy- and law-making. These include peaceful means such as advocacy of special interests of public importance, active use of possibilities for speaking and dialogue in a consultative capacity, and lobbying or national-level pressuring of states to participate in treaty-making efforts. They also include formation of coalitions, mobilisation of and participation in public opinion-making, data-gathering to help frame or define a problem in ways that influence the work of intergovernmental conferences, and persuasion in general, as well as less peaceful means such as violent protests.[104] Studies also indicate that NGOs and business organisations are typically either constrained or enabled by other players as well as by contextual factors. The former include states, private non-state organisations including companies, and intergovernmental organisations. The latter include the distribution of resources and 'the rules of the game'. The ability of private non-state actors to exert influence tends to depend on two factors: the quality of their interventions (in particular expert knowledge and skills); and the similarity between their demands and existing related regulatory regimes.[105] The use of a non-appropriate approach (e.g. a violent approach or a

---

100 Habermas, J. (1974) 'The public sphere', *New German Critique*, Vol. 3, pp. 49–55, at p. 51, quoted in Steffek and Gomes Pereira (2011) 'Transnational governance networks and democracy', at p. 294.
101 Habermas (1996) *Between Facts and Norms*, at p. 360.
102 Ruggie (2004) 'Reconstituting the global public domain – issues, actors and practices'. For arguments by John Ruggie along related lines but made in his capacity as UN Assistant Secretary-General in the process of setting up the UN Global Compact or as SRSG, see Buhmann (2018) *Changing Sustainability Norms through Communication Processes*.
103 Reinalda, B., Arts, B. and Noortmann, M. (2001) 'Non-state actors in international relations: Do they matter?', in B. Arts, M. Noortmann and B. Reinalda (eds), *Non-State Actors in International Relations*, Aldershot: Ashgate, pp. 1–8.
104 Ibid.
105 For example, a study by Arts found that NGOs succeeded in putting pressure on climate negotiations in relation to the 1992 Framework Convention on Climate Change by establishing a case of similarity to the existing ozone regime and government inconsistency. Governments accepted what Arts refers to as 'strong norms' in relation to ozone regulation but refused to accept such norms in relation to climate. See Arts (2001) 'The impact of environmental NGOs in international conventions', at p. 208.

strongly defensive opposition), traditional bloc politics (e.g. North–South), and the presence of like-minded but dominant states have been among the main constraining factors. In the latter case, states tend to dominate the issue on their own without input from private non-state actors. There are indications that a consensus-oriented approach is more enabling for influence than a confrontational approach, as is the relative strength of actors compared to others, and the political relevance of the issue at stake. Studies also indicate that the ability to politicise issues and mobilise support among other groups can be decisive, and that this sometimes allows NGOs to compete with powerful business interests.[106]

Moreover, studies suggest that companies and business organisations tend to favour voluntary initiatives and oppose public regulation at first, but that they may change stances and embrace (self-)regulation for strategic reasons.[107] These include perceived opportunities for strategic restyling or potential new markets, following competitors' lead for fear of missing chances for profit, or avoiding financial or publicity risks.[108] A particularly revealing example of the latter was provided by the SRSG's invitation in December 2005 to the IOE, ICC and Business and Industry Advisory Committee (BIAC) to the OECD on effective ways for companies to deal with dilemma situations encountered in weak governance zones, and the result of that exercise. Engaging organisations that had been opposed to the Draft UN Norms, and had indicated that they had felt excluded from the process to develop that normative text in subsequently developing guidance for companies on human rights dilemmas resulted in a change in stances within those organisations and in their support at a general level for the work and recommendations of the SRSG.[109]

Coalitions have historically played strong roles in the evolution of new norms of conduct in the sustainability field, joined by shared concerns or interests that unite actors across otherwise diverse functions. Even prior to the recent process towards the Paris Climate Change Accord, the environmental and climate change areas were particularly strong examples of this.[110] Coalitions may also have strong impacts on the outputs of formalised hybrid or non-state groups or governance networks that play formalised roles spanning development of problem understanding to the formation of rules and sometimes delivering specific action to contribute to the implementation of public tasks.[111] Public regulators may seek to influence the inclusion and exclusion of actors and interests through the design of the process through which such networks are formed or by framing the issues on which they function. This may allow them to counteract the predominance of particular interests promoted by a particular coalition.[112]

Participants in a process to develop new sustainability-related norms typically try to persuade others to follow their own preferred view. They create new cognitions and develop new positions, which in turn have an impact on the normative outputs.[113] The output and

---

106   Arts, B. (1998*) The Political Influence of Global NGOs: Case Studies on the Climate and Biodiversity Conventions*, Utrecht: International Books; Reinalda (2001) 'Private in form, public in purpose'.

107   Kolk, Ans (2001) 'Multinational enterprises and international climate policy', at p. 214.

108   Ibid., at pp. 222–223.

109   International Organisation of Employers et al. (2006) *Business and Human Rights*.

110   Hajer (1995) *The Politics of Environmental Discourse*; Arts (2001) 'The impact of environmental NGOs in international conventions'; Kolk (2001) 'Multinational enterprises and international climate policy'.

111   Sørensen, E. and Torfing, J. (2005) *Netværksstyring – fra government til governance* [Network governance – from government to governance], Copenhagen: Roskilde Universitetsforlag, at pp. 15–17; Sørensen and Torfing (2005) 'The democratic anchorage of governance networks', at pp. 197–198 with references.

112   Sørensen and Torfing (2005) 'The democratic anchorage of governance networks', at p. 204.

113   Hajer (1995) *The Politics of Environmental Discourse*, at p. 53.

possibilities to create consensus, however, are not only a result of argumentative skills. They are also shaped by institutional arrangements that allow participants and their coalitions to gain access to the process and its sub-element so that their presence and arguments may shape the output. Particular institutional practices or frameworks may therefore allow for dominance to be achieved.[114] By implication, the design of a process and its elements may also counteract or prevent forms of dominance obtained not on the basis of the best argument (in accordance with the Habermasian ideal) but by privilege or other forms of power that impact the legitimacy of the process and its output negatively. As a correlative, design may also help promote legitimate rule-making as process as well as output. This, too, means proceduralisation for balancing power disparities and ensuring equalised participation.

Like political scientists, contemporary international law-interested public law scholars have taken inspiration from Habermasian theory in discussions of how international law-making can be adapted to better accommodate the increasing significance of non-state actors and respond to the transnationalisation of law that is placing the state-centrist system of international law under pressure. Discussing what they refer to as a need to devise a process that could constitute a 'normatively desirable way' to make collective decisions,[115] scholars have drawn attention to a democratic deficit in making and implementing international law under the current state-centrist regime.[116] While the importance of institutional design for ensuring equalised participation has been noted,[117] much of the debate stops short of proposing what such design might entail. Going a step further towards what might be applicable in practice, others argue that it may not be realistic or optimal to strive for a one-size-fits-all model, and that a measure of flexibility should be in place.[118] De Burca has proposed the iterative 'democratic-striving approach' to deal with the dilemma of legitimacy and transnational governance. That entails acknowledging the difficulty and complexity of adapting international law-making and transnational governance to better respond to and take account of a broad global citizenship while also insisting on the necessity to do so.[119] De Burca's proposed approach acknowledges that, in view of the current fluidity and evolving character of above-national governance, rather than turn-key solutions, processes to include non-state actors can be both dynamic and iterative.[120] Thus, developing modalities for inclusive participation in processes of rule-making can be developed in steps that take account of the situation and concerns at hand, and adapt to those along the way based on experience and learning.

114 Ibid., esp. chaps 2.4, 6.3.
115 Cohen and Sabel (2005) 'Global democracy?'
116 Goodin, R. E. and Ratner, S. R. (2011) 'Democratizing international law', *Global Policy*, Vol. 2, No. 3, pp. 241–247.
117 Black, J. (2008) 'Constructing and contesting legitimacy and accountability in polycentric regulatory regimes', *Regulation and Governance*, Vol. 2, pp. 137–164, at p. 144.
118 Burca (2008) 'Developing democracy beyond the state'; Hachez and Wouters (2011) *A Glimpse at the Democratic Legitimacy of Private Standards*, at p. 9.
119 Burca (2008) 'Developing democracy beyond the state', at p. 237 with further details from p. 249.
120 Ibid., at p. 253.

5 Power, privilege and representation of interests

Overview: Chapter 5 opens by revisiting the cases with regard to the relationship between their processes, outputs, and the influence of power interests. Following this, the chapter reverts to reflexive law, explaining the rationale of how reflexive law, in principle, aims at stimulating organisational self-regulation in accordance with public policy objectives and social expectations and needs. It emphasises the role played by communication in sharing views, and explains how the cases of public-private collaborative regulation may be perceived as reflexive law. It proceeds to expand on reflexive law's lacuna in terms of directives for how to handle power disparities despite the theory's recognition of the importance of a reflexive law process being designed to do so. After a series of illustrations by points drawn from the empirical cases the chapter finishes by summarizing how these insights highlight the pertinence of reflexive law as a regulatory strategy for super-national multi-stakeholder regulation of sustainability concerns that often escape the regulatory powers of governments on their own, and at the same time underscores the need for a theory that fills the gap in reflexive law theory in regard to power disparities. Such a theory is required for reflexive law to deliver on its potential for super-national regulation with a compliance pull as a result of legitimacy of process and output.

5.1 Why collaborative regulation? Revisiting the roles of participation and power for output

The regulatory initiatives that were discussed above differ in terms of process and output. The process towards the Draft UN Norms approximates to conventional UN-based law-making in the human rights field and the early stages towards such a product. It did not, however, succeed in the product becoming adopted. While the process within the working group that developed the Draft Norms did deliver a comprehensive law-in-process text, the process was not effective in delivering an output that enjoyed the legitimacy necessary for it to be adopted at the level of the Human Rights Commission and obtain the form of recognition required for it to become broadly applied. The hybrid initiatives display various forms and elements of public–private and multi-stakeholder collaboration and participation. Among those, the outputs vary, with the ISO 26000 and the SRSG processes delivering the most comprehensive and normatively solid output, and the UN Global Compact, the EU's MSF and the CSR Alliance some but less comprehensive results in terms of normative guidance for business in relation to their impacts on society.

The SRSG process stands out for taking a highly multi-stakeholder-oriented consultative approach to an issue that had the potential of coming to be regulated by conventional soft or hard international law. Whether that was going to be the case was unknown at the time when the SRSG took on the mandate. More than ten years later the situation may look different when we look back, now knowing what happened. However, looking ahead in 2005 there was not much cause for optimism. At that time, while the Global Compact was unique in its own right, it was also widely criticised for being far too soft and too little detailed in terms of company commitments and action. Despondency was further caused by the failure of the EU to promote an actual normative framework on CSR through its process towards a European CSR framework when the first term of the MSF ended in 2004. When even one of the regions with the most vocal politicians, TNCs and civil society on human rights issues in CSR was unable to deliver a solid normative framework, what was the likely outlook for a global process towards a global normative instrument?

This brief summary of the initiatives and their outputs leads to two major insights that will be further developed in the subsequent sections. First, the regulatory *outputs* of the hybrid initiatives may be explained as results of processes that operated along the theoretical lines of reflexive law. In other words, the initiatives all function as reflexive regulatory fora that brought together diverse stakeholders and enabled them to exchange views, concerns and needs; and this process of exchanges enabled an enhanced appreciation of such concerns and filtered into the regulatory output. Also, despite differences in terms of set-up and organisation, participants, ambitions and outputs, from the socio-legal perspective the hybrid initiatives all display various characteristics of a reflexive law *process*. Apart from ISO 26000, all were established by public authorities in response to limited political powers or regulatory fit, in order to adopt and issue the desired normative directives for business conduct and their impact on society. The fact that such processes were capable of delivering normative outputs that received support from stakeholders indicates that in principle the process of developing rules through reflexive law offers a modality for law-making at the super-national level where authorities' powers or relevant capacity may be limited.

Second, interests represented by particular stakeholders were both a major driver and in some cases a major obstacle to the normative comprehensiveness of the outputs. Damaging throughput and output legitimacy, power disparities played a part in some cases, leading to the related interests becoming dominant or distorting the process. The influence of such imbalances indicates the significance of the gap in reflexive law theory noted in Chapter 1, which concerns how power disparities might be handled.

In combination, the two findings indicate that, for reflexive law to deliver its regulatory potential, reflexive law as a regulatory strategy must be advanced to encompass directives for balancing power disparities. This confirms the pertinence of collaborative regulation as a process of involving private and public stakeholders in rule-making. Recall that collaborative regulation was described at the beginning of this book as a process, which includes a procedure aimed at balancing power disparities while allowing for the exchange of views, needs and expectations in such a way as to enable the appreciation of interests across functional categories of systems and stimulate evolution and agreement on norms.

Factors that led to the differing normative outputs of the processes framing the evolution of the Draft UN Norms, the Global Compact, the UN Framework and UNGPs, the recommendations of EU MSF, the establishment of the CSR Alliance, and ISO 26000 suggest a crucial difference in the procedural approach. All were processes of creating norms in accordance with underlying sustainability-related public policy objectives, but some were much more successful in delivering outputs in accordance with the objectives that led to the rule-making process being created.

In particular, the analysis suggests that the failure of the Draft Norms to become accepted was a perception by (certain but powerful) business associations that they were unduly excluded from the rule-making process and, similarly, that the failure of the EU MSF to create an actual normative framework in accordance with the original objectives was due to power disparities within the MSF. In the case of the MSF the power of businesses combined with their inclusion gave business associations a heightened influence as participants in the regulatory process. This hurt the legitimacy of the process as well as of the output. Internal power struggles in the EU Commission among proponents of business interests and social affairs may have added to the meagre output of the MSF process as compared to the original ambitions of DG Social Affairs.

The process towards the Global Compact, the SRSG process and the establishment of the CSR Alliance all took place against the backdrop of authorities reflecting on their regulatory capacities in regard to regulating business conduct, in particular of transnational enterprises.

The outputs demonstrate that reflexive law forums may lead to appreciation of social expectations and public policy needs that are actively transformed into norms of conduct created through a participatory process and which gain support among stakeholders. This also suggests that the general acceptance of the outputs as legitimate is conditional on actors' perception of being participants or at least represented within the forum. It is also conditional on power disparities based on privilege, for example of insight or access to authorities or the rule-making process, being constrained through procedural steering.

Importantly, the Global Compact and SRSG processes exemplify an informal institutionalisation of a role for business in international law-making, a process from which business as explained earlier is excluded under conventional international law-making. The experience of the SRSG process, particularly its lessons on the significance that inclusion of prospective subjects of rules may have for acceptance of rules, may turn out to be significant not only with regard to future intergovernmental processes of making rules pertaining to private non-state actors but also with regard to a formalisation of the inclusion of such actors. As the SRSG process and its ability to deliver a substantive output implying significant change in terms of norms of conduct for business organisations suggest, such inclusion may simply be necessary for reaching an output that will deliver on the public policy objectives involved and be accepted by those who it is intended should follow the rules – that is, an output that will enjoy a compliance pull.

Despite considerable diversity across their processes and results, the hybrid initiatives noted above demonstrate that it is possible for a diverse range of actors to reach agreement on new norms of conduct in a field marked by transnational activity relating to both public and private law, and frequent conflicts of economic and political interests. Or, one might say, it has been possible to agree on new norms *despite* the tensions between public and private regulatory objectives and actors as well as across economic and political interests. The sustainability-related field is characterised by a need to prevent harm from occurring, because repairing damage done is often not possible or takes a very long time, while secondary harm resulting from the primary harm may occur in the meantime. Regardless of the strength of enforcement institutions, this calls for regulation with a proactive focus, as opposed to a reactive approach, which to some extent presumes that reparation will re-do damage done. The proactive focus also calls for a regulatory process that caters for compliance from within. The need for such a compliance pull is further strengthened by the fact that international human rights enforcement institutions are typically weak, and that therefore any preventative effect resulting from the risk of legal sanctions is also weak.

In sum, while the cases confirm that organising collaborative regulation according to the idea that participation in the process both stimulates internal appreciation of external needs and facilitates the process of delivering agreement, they also confirm that power disparities between stakeholders are an effective obstacle. The subsequent sections develop these points in more detail through examples drawn from the processes, their effectiveness in delivering outputs corresponding to the intended objectives, and the reception of the outputs. Those issues all centre on throughput legitimacy. From the Draft UN Norms to the UNGPs, the significance of power disparities has affected the legitimacy of both process and output.

Together, the conclusions from the above analysis confirm the connection between participation in the rule-making process, legitimacy and power disparities. This call is for a participatory process that enables and induces the capacity within organisations for them to understand, appreciate and internalise external concerns and needs in the way that business organisations run and manage their societal impacts and their effects on sustainability. This, too, speaks for addressing the lacuna in reflexive law theory in order for reflexive law to be deployed in a manner that allows for the evolution of norms of conduct related to transnational sustainability concerns, which do not lend themselves to solutions developed by individual states and their governments.

To frame the discussion of constitutive elements of collaborative regulation, this chapter moves on to expand on the communicative aspects of reflexive law as an approach to developing or adapting norms of conduct. This takes place through a process entailing a qualified form of communication, which pays particular attention to exchanging perceived needs and concerns between stakeholders. It has special regard to, on the one hand, those who represent victims or other groups or stakes (such as the environment) and, on the other, those whose practices or actions are the subjects of the intended change of conduct. In that context, we will revert to specific insights that may be drawn from the regulatory processes towards the Draft UN Norms, the UN Global Compact, the SRSG process, the EU MSF and CSR Alliance, and ISO 26000 as well as throughput and output legitimacy. Following the discussion of process and legitimacy, we proceed to discussing how deliberation-oriented theory may enrich reflexive law processes towards a more fully fledged process of collaborative regulation that enhances legitimacy through a procedure that balances power disparities.

5.2 Communicating for change: inducing self-regulation by addressing the concerns and interests of stakeholders

Communicating concerns that call for change of conduct is a major element in the foundations of reflexive law. Law in general entails communication, but, whereas much other legal theory places emphasis on driving change through specific norms of conduct or sanctions in the case of non-compliance with those norms, reflexive law theory has communication as a major change agent. Communication also plays a major role in deliberative law-making, whether in the national or transnational context. Communication helps transfer ideals and perceptions of needs for specific conduct to those who set the norms and create insights and learning among participants. Additionally, communication facilitates the transfer of normative directives from those who decide to those who are expected or required to observe them. Reflexive law is concerned precisely with communicating perceived needs and demands into norms, and norms into internalisation that leads to change. Reflexive law theory responds to a need for explanation of how communication and sustainability-related self-regulation connect, in particular with regard to the promotion of public policy objectives.

5.2.1 Regulating self-regulation through reflection at several levels

Reflexive law draws on several complex theories, but the complexity of the theory and its reasoning should not be overstated. A major challenge for understanding its reasoning probably lies in the fact that, contrary to much other regulatory theory, it does not adopt an institutional but a systems thinking-oriented outlook. Reflexive law theory does not emphasise legal enforcement through courts or other legal institutions, but rather that regulators should establish communicative fora to allow diverse stakeholders to exchange their views on their needs and demands with those organisations with whom change is intended. The communication that takes place is regulatory instrumental because – if properly designed – it induces new norms and change, often through a form of self-regulation. In other words, to induce change with business, regulators (which from the reflexive law perspective are typically policy-makers) can organise procedural settings in which businesses are exposed to the needs or demands of stakeholders, such as civil society organisations and/or regulators. This regulatory method is particularly well suited to inducing normative change in contexts in which public regulators lack direct regulatory powers, for example for regulating transnational business activity where nation states (such as a firm's home state) lack the power to issue directives for conduct in host states.

Teubner's formulation of reflexive law theory was partly spurred by a desire to combine and reconcile elements of Niklas Luhmann's systems theory and Habermasian ideas on discourse ethics and law-making. As mentioned, much of Teubner's own basis is in systems thinking, but rather than opposing other approaches he sought to embrace and integrate them. Reflexive law thus combines a procedural orientation (the Habermasian element) with a systems approach towards organisational change of conduct based on internalisation of external needs or concerns (the Luhmannian element).

Reflexive law builds on the assumption that regulation is more effective and more easily accepted if created by those directly affected by it. It therefore seeks to ensure the representation of a plurality of views and to stimulate system-internal reflection and responsiveness to societal needs through procedural forums providing for participation.[1] Authorities retain control of what issues are subjected to regulation, while leaving substantive regulation of specific issues or sub-issues to other actors who are invited to participate in the reflexive regulatory process. In his 1983 seminal article in the *Law and Society Review* that introduced the theory, Teubner stated: 'Reflexive law is characterized by a new kind of legal self-restraint. Instead of taking over regulatory responsibility for the outcome of social processes, reflexive law restricts itself to the installation, correction, and redefinition of democratic self-regulatory mechanisms.'[2]

For this to come about, reflexive law assumes that a process of reflection takes place at up to three levels of governance, starting with governments or authorities, next interaction between stakeholders and organisations with which normative change is desired, and finally self-regulation with those organisations. The latter process is what really leads to change for sustainability. As a result, the framing, which is offered by what takes place at the two prior levels, is of crucial importance for the end result.

At the first level, governments or other formal regulators reflect on their regulatory capacity and/or how well the issues at stake lend themselves to the type of law that authorities may pass. If the regulatory capacity or type of law is found inadequate for the regulatory need at

---

1   Teubner, G. (1992) 'Social order from legislative noise', in G. Teubner and A. Febbrajo (eds), *European Yearbook in the Sociology of Law: State, Law and Economy as Autopoietic Systems: Regulation and Autonomy in a New Perspective*, Milano: Giuffrè, pp. 609–649, at p. 611; Teubner, G. (1993) *Law as an Autopoietic System*, Oxford: Blackwell, at pp. 68–69; see also Wilthagen, T. (1994) 'Reflexive rationality in the regulation of occupational safety and health', in R. Rogowski and T. Wilthagen (eds), *Reflexive Labour Law: Studies in Industrial Relations and Employment Regulation*, Deventer: Kluwer Law and Taxation Publishers, pp. 345–376, at p. 348 with references.
2   Teubner (1983) 'Substantive and reflective elements in modern law', at p. 239.

hand, the regulator may instead institute a type of process that will enable organisations (such as firms) or groups, for which change of conduct is needed, to engage with stakeholders to understand the needs and concerns that the latter harbour with regard to the organisation's societal impact. This is the second level of reflection. The process may be actual (such as a meeting) or virtual (such as a sustainability report that offers data to stakeholders and invites them to comment). If the process is well designed to promote and support exchanges between different stakeholders and the organisation, it will stimulate reflection within the organisation on its impact and how its practices may be changed to reduce undesired impact or enhance positive impact. Stakeholders may include private organisations and groups, such as civil society, local communities, business relations and media, as well as public organisations, such as central or local authorities that are charged with the substantive issue at hand. These exchanges ideally lead to development of new or adapted norms of conduct, which reflect external concerns and, in effect, internalise them into self-regulation. That is the third level of reflection. On this basis, reflexive law offers a regulatory strategy through which rules or norms of conduct may be developed through bottom-up processes or within organisations, while authorities remain in control at the overall level. We will revert to examples of this below in this chapter.

5.2.2 Communicating to induce self-regulation

The term 'reflexive law' can be confusing, as the theory assumes an internal process of *reflection* as a key element in generating change. Often a result of learning created by exposure to the views and concerns of the stakeholders, such active reflection may be contrasted to processes in which systems simply and more passively reflect their environment, mirroring its views without themselves reflecting upon their own actions and impact on society. It therefore differs from simply reflecting the expectations of the environment by signalling coherence but not internalising it. The distinction may be exemplified by the way in which companies engage in CSR reporting: as a communication exercise that functions as a modality to present a particular vision of the company to its environment ('CSR as process');[3] or as an avenue for internal learning about the company's impact on society as perceived by stakeholders, with a view to organisational change.[4]

While the process may be represented through three types of reflection noted above (one at each level of reflexive regulation), rendering reflexive law simply as a form of procedural regulation misses the sophisticated elements of the theory. These elements are informed by the communicative aspect, which relates to how self-regulation is produced in response to exchange of views and societal expectations in a reflection-generating learning process. Whereas the general participatory element and emphasis on procedure draw strongly on Habermasian theory, the learning and self-regulation draw much of their inspiration from systems thinking and in particular the theory of autopoiesis, as explained in the following.

---

3 See Holmstrøm, S. (2013) 'Legimiterende praksisformer: Et sociologisk perspektiv på praksisformers funktion, strategi og begrundelse', in S. Holmstrøm and S. Kjærbeck (eds), *Legitimitet under forandring: Virksomheden i samfundet*, Copenhagen: Samfundslitteratur, pp. 273–312, elaborating the distinction between reflection (internalising external expectations into adapted practices) and being reflective (communicating a particular image that corresponds to external expectations).

4 Compare Gond and Herrbach (2006) 'Social reporting as an organisational learning tool?'; and Baumann-Pauly, D., Wickert, C., Spence, L. J. and Scherer, A. G. (2013) 'Organizing corporate social responsibility in small and large firms: Size matters', *Journal of Business Ethics*, Vol. 115, pp. 693–705.

Systems thinking has had socio-legal appeal owing to its ability to conceptualise forms of complex social organisation and interaction from the macro-level perspective rather than through individuals' direct intentions or interaction.[5] Sociologist Niklas Luhmann's theory, which has been a source of influence for Teubner and many others, focuses not on institutions but on functions.[6] This is a fundamentally different way of seeing and analysing society from the institution-focused approach that social scientists are often trained to adopt. The focus on functions rather than institutions is important for an appreciation of how reflexive law-type multi-stakeholder initiatives stimulate self-regulation, as also explained in the following.

Like Habermasian theory, Luhmann's ideas tend to be somewhat abstract and may appear overly detached from real-life occurrences.[7] Yet a systems-oriented view on society that is concerned with functions rather than institutional structures offers an alternative way to see and analyse societal events, including processes of law-making and the interaction within such processes. This helps the observer note process elements that appear less significant from the institutional perspective. Systems thinking's observation that functional sub-systems may engage in self-regulation as a response to external needs and pressure rather than as an automated and often minimal reaction to institutional requirements offers a basis for ana-lytical consideration of regulatory strategy that is refreshingly different from the institutional command-and control approach.

Reflexive law builds on communication as a process connecting two (or more) involved par-ticipants. In systems thinking, communication is not a unilateral utterance but a bilateral process that requires both parties – the transmitter and the recipient – to be engaged. Systems theory perceives communications as processes which produce meaning. Meaning materialises when the information carried by the communication is understood. Communication, therefore, is not just a speech act but the understanding which it creates and which may cause further communication.[8]

In dealing with the regulatory and societal problems he observed in the 1980s, Teubner felt that a theory of law-making should include room for exchanges and discursive processes. He took inspiration from Habermasian discourse ethics as they were at the time (before the publication of *Between Facts and Norms* in its German original in 1992), including the idea that the 'uncoerced force' of the better argument prevails and that legitimate decisions result from a process in which participants develop a common will based on reasoned arguments. Teubner added elements inspired by other contemporary regulatory theories, in particular Nonet and Selznick's theory on responsive law, but going beyond these.[9] Reflexive law incorporates the systems thinking idea of how change in the norms and conduct of a func-tional sub-system may be induced by 'irritants' from the outside, and adds the Habermasian emphasis on participation in rule-making as a key component in what makes for legitimacy leading to observance of the rules – in other words, what provides a compliance pull.

5 Rehg, W. (1996) 'Translator's introduction', in J. Habermas, *Between Facts and Norms: Contributions to a Discourse Theory of Law and Democracy*, translated by W. Rehg, Cambridge: Polity Press/Blackwell, pp. ix–xxxvii, at p. xxi.

6 Nobles, R. and Schiff, D. (2012) 'Using system theory to study legal pluralism: What could be gained?', *Law and Society Review*, Vol. 46, No. 2, pp. 265–294, at p. 293.

7 Compare, on Luhmann, Schoeneborn, D. (2011) 'Organization as communication: A Luhmannian perspective', *Management Communication Quarterly*, Vol. 25, No. 4, pp. 663–689, esp. at pp. 665–671 with references.

8 Teubner (1993) *Law as an Autopoietic System*, at pp. 45–46; Teubner, G., Nobles, R. and Schiff, D. (2005) 'The autonomy of law: An introduction to legal autopoiesis', in J. Penner, D. Schiff and R. Nobles (eds), *Jurisprudence*, New York: Oxford University Press, pp. 897–954.

9 See in particular Teubner (1983) 'Substantive and reflective elements in modern law'; Teubner (1984) 'Autopoiesis in law and society'.

The fundamental idea of stimulating change across functional sub-systems is relatively simple: a system or a functional sub-system, such as the social sub-systems of the economy, politics, law or the media, is defined by a boundary between itself and its environment (that is, other functional sub-systems). The boundary allows the system to 'observe' its environment, and to adapt to irritants from the environment. For example, the political system (which includes not just policy-making but also implementation of policies once adopted) may react to changes in the economic system due to globalisation by experimenting with new forms of policy. In turn, this will cause adaptations within the legal system resulting in new forms of law. The workings of the legal system after its internalisation of the influence (the irritants) provided by the political system will then have an impact on the economic system, for example through the latter's application of new regulation on the conduct of economic activities. Functional sub-systems see the world in terms of binary codes or logics, which for practical purposes may be likened to the core concerns that are crucial for that particular sub-system. The economic sub-system perceives the world or what is important in terms of profit and loss (non-profit), the political system in terms of power and non-power, law in terms of what is legal or illegal or mandatory or voluntary, media in terms of news or non-news, and so on. Despite their differences, social sub-systems may be closely connected. This applies particularly to the sub-systems of politics and law.[10]

To appreciate the way in which reflexive law works, it should be noted that 'the legal system' does not refer to the institutions associated with the legal system in dogmatic or doctrinal legal science, but rather to communicative processes. Thus, reflexive law is not about legal institutions, such as statutes, legislatures, cases or courts per se, but about the processes in which law and norms of conduct with a significant self-regulatory intent or impact are developed, shaped, altered and modified in a process of communication in which the (self-)regulating system responds to the outside environment and reacts to its impulses. In Tamanaha's somewhat simplistic but illustrative rendering, the focus on communication and perception of law as a system of meaning (as opposed to a system of institutions) means that law 'is present whenever someone communicates, or even thinks, in legal terms'.[11]

Reflexive law was developed as a regulatory strategy for situations where policy-makers and law-makers do not have the insights or authority to develop appropriate and relevant detailed regulation applying to specific societal entities, such as businesses that form part of the economic functional sub-system. Reflexive law is not concerned with regulating the substantive outcome of a negotiation in detail, but with structuring the process of negotiation and ensuring that the process enables exchanges on needs, concerns or expectations. Through communication that may take a range of forms of interaction, those involved are exposed to needs, concerns or expectations harboured by stakeholders (or, in systems language, their 'environment') in relation to the entity's impact on society. This stimulates learning as a result of enhanced insights into external perceptions of the organisation and the resulting pressure on it. Through appreciation of the potential impact on their own interests they (ideally) come to internalise those concerns, needs and expectations and turn them into normative change that is relevant to societal needs as well as operational from the perspective of the firm. This logic may appear intuitive, but is not necessarily so. If the workings of reflexive law were intuitive, many more regulatory processes would apply that regulatory approach.

10 Nuotio, K. (2010) 'Systems theory with discourse ethics: Squaring the circle? Comment on Marcelo Neves's *Zwischen Themis und Leviathan*', *Journal of Extreme Legal Positivism*, Vol. 7, April, pp. 59–85, at p. 64.
11 Tamanaha, B. Z. (1997) *Realistic Socio-Legal Theory: Pragmatism and a Social Theory of Law*, Oxford: Oxford University Press, at p. 103.

Autopoiesis of law is a key element in reflexive law (*auto* meaning 'self' and *poiesis* from *poiein* meaning 'to create'). An autopoietic process may be induced through a (sub-) system's reception of irritants that are communicated in the specialised logic or 'code' of the (sub-)system.[12] In this respect, reflexive law draws on but also diverts from systems theory and autopoiesis as formulated by Niklas Luhmann.[13] Luhmann's theory was based on inspiration from biology.[14] Luhmann wanted to transfer knowledge of the neural system's self-reproduction and interaction with the body to social interaction. Perhaps partly owing to its background in the natural sciences, the theory of autopoiesis in social systems was received with considerable scepticism at its presentation.[15] Teubner has downplayed this part of reflexive law since the early 1990s. According to Teubner's theory, autopoiesis allows parts of the social system, that is, social sub-systems such as the political, the economic and the legal system, to adapt based on irritants transmitted by other social sub-systems. Irritants from the environment (such as consumers' expectations of a firm not to produce through exploiting workers in violation of international labour standards) may cause internal disturbance ('perturbation') that stimulates internal processes of change.[16] The reflexive law process allows social sub-systems to exchange information, which causes perturbation inside the recipient sub-system. This stimulates self-regulation in order to change that impact and, by implication, meet the concerns and needs of other social sub-systems which served as irritants. For example, the economic system may react to social expectations expressed by the political system on conduct in accordance with international labour standards so that those standards are adopted as a corrective to avoid economic loss. Owing to self-regulation, in practice the international law standards serve as minimum standards where host state law provides lower protection for workers.

Through its integration of Habermasian ideas in addition to autopoiesis, reflexive law theory's focus is on establishing procedures that allow for those involved or affected to have access to influence rules pertaining to conduct. Again, reflexive law does not directly regulate conduct to implement particular predetermined goals. Instead, it aims at encouraging processes of reflection leading to self-regulation and ideally organisational change, based on participants' learning and consideration of their impact on society, and the sharing of views, expectations and experience. To promote reflexive regulation, governmental bodies may establish procedures and organisational forums and frameworks to facilitate debate and

---

12 Teubner et al. (2005) 'The autonomy of law', at p. 912.
13 Luhmann, N. (1986) 'The self-reproduction of law and its limits', in G. Teubner (ed.), *Dilemmas of Law in the Welfare State*, Berlin: Walter de Gruyter, pp. 111–127, at p. 112.
14 The theory on autopoiesis was developed by Chilean biologists Humberto Maturana and Francisco Varela. An autopoietic system is defined as 'a unity as a closed network of productions of components that recursively, through their interactions, realize the network that produces them and constitute its boundaries by realizing the surfaces of cleavage that separate it as a composite unity in the space in which they exist'; Braten, S. (1992) 'Paradigms of autonomy', in G. Teubner and A. Febbrajo (eds), *European Yearbook in the Sociology of Law: State, Law and Economy as Autopoietic Systems: Regulation and Autonomy in a New Perspective*, Milano: Giuffrè, pp. 35–65, at p. 38 with reference to Maturana, H. (1981) 'Autopoiesis', in M. Zeleny (ed.), *Autopoiesis: A Theory of Living Organizations*, New York: North-Holland, at p. 30. See also Rottleuthner, H. (1988) 'Biological metaphors in legal thought', in G. Teubner (ed.), *Autopoietic Law: A New Approach to Law and Society*, Berlin: Walter de Gruyter, pp. 97–127; Neves, M. (2001) 'From the autopoiesis to the allopoiesis of law', *Journal of Law and Society*, Vol. 28, No. 2, pp. 242–264.
15 Blankenburg, E. (1984) 'The poverty of evolutionism: A critique of Teubner's case for "reflexive law"', *Law and Society Review*, Vol. 18, pp. 273–289.
16 Teubner et al. (2005) 'The autonomy of law', at p. 912.

exchanges among other organisations and their adaptation to external demands, concerns and expectations through self-regulation. Authorities may guide the process by providing normative guidance, but normative outputs are ideally made by those actors who will be subjected to the output and who represent the interests at stake. Through the procedures of reflexive regulation, authorities are able both to retain control and to offer other social actors a learning process enabling them to integrate societal needs and demands in their norms of conduct.

The legal system may adapt its rule-making structures to the autopoietic character of itself and its environment. For example, the legal sub-system of international law, in reflection on its own capacities and the formal limitations on engaging private non-state actors in the law-making process, may accept the emergence of new regulatory procedures which are reflexive, participatory and able to encompass the active role of private non-state actors. The system may also accept the outputs of these procedural processes including their normative messages. The latter may ultimately turn into hard law by softening the political opposition at the international level to passing conventional international law (treaties) to provide for human rights or other CSR-relevant obligations for private non-state actors.

Thus, for the political sub-system to 'regulate' businesses towards sustainable conduct, it can make it clear to business organisations that, unless they change their conduct to become more sustainable, their economic freedom is likely to be reduced. This was the type of 'irritant' that Kofi Annan's 1999 speech in Davos created, and which led companies to be interested in supporting UN goals through the Global Compact. By contrast, if the political system lets it be known that a series of new norms on business conduct have been created and that businesses may expect monitoring of their observance of the norms and some type of legal sanction, the likelihood that businesses will perceive this as related to their core concern with profit or loss is less pronounced. They will not see it as an irritant relating to themselves, but as political action that is performed in the code of politics and law. They will change their ways if they must, but not adapt to internalise the norms, and will most likely baulk at what makes it more difficult for them to deliver on their overriding goal – to make profits. The manner in which the Draft UN Norms were developed and communicated drew on political and legal interests or codes rather than economic system codes, in part because the language used did not appeal to the system-specific code of profit/loss or, to the extent that it did, signalled constraints on business that some managers assumed would lead to losses. Thus, the process managed to create strong opposition in some business organisations.[17]

Considering regulation from the perspective of autopoiesis provides an alternative angle for understanding and analysing the production of norms of conduct from that which follows from the perception of the legal system as conventional law-making institutions, actors and institutionalised legal acts (treaties, statutes, case law, etc.). Likewise, the systems thinking approach to the interaction between social sub-systems is instructive in relation to sustainability-related regulation in public–private forums. It assists us in understanding how a reflexive law-type regulatory process is a way not just of involving stakeholders in developing norms but also of making them consider and integrate societal demands or expectations in the resulting norms. In turn, this implies taking into consideration the position and power of stakeholders involved in such processes and any power imbalances that may affect the processing of input into output, and therefore legitimacy.

---

17 For details, see Buhmann (2014) *Normative Discourses and Public–Private Regulatory Strategies for Construction of CSR Normativity.*

5.2.3 The normative element in reflexive law: balancing power but lacking instructions

As noted, reflexive law theory incorporates a Habermasian element by recognising that procedure matters for the balancing of power disparities among participants. The omission to develop that point in detail has led scholars who have otherwise welcomed the contributions of reflexive law theory to express reservations as a result of its lack of specificity in explaining how to handle power disparities.[18] This highlights the importance of addressing that part of reflexive law, in order to enable regulatory processes that function as reflexive law to deliver their potential for sustainability regulation.

The procedural element builds on a normative premise that reflexive law processes should enable an exchange of views and the co-creation of a regulatory output. As part of this, they should be structured in such a way that they encompass a plurality of views, negotiating patterns and discourses.[19] To limit abuse of power by stronger participants in the process, reflexive law assumes a neutralisation of power disparities, which presumably will take place by institutional procedural mechanisms. Rather than setting strict procedures for the way that power should be used, reflexive law as regulatory strategy intends abuse of power to be restrained through the design of procedural and institutional mechanisms which aim at neutralising power inequality.[20] Thus, reflexive law as a matter of principle aims not only at making decision-making structures sensitive to externalities. It also aims at ensuring that reflexive regulatory forums deploy procedural designs that allow stakeholders, such as those that are negatively affected by the activities of other functional sub-systems, to express their concerns in a process that balances power disparities. In other words, reflexive law assumes that the induction of self-regulation takes place through an exchange of views and concerns that is balanced with regard to the power of the participants in the process. This emphasis on procedurally granted qualitative exchange adds a specific normative aspect to reflexive law. Importantly, while this has not generally been noted in the literature, it also establishes a connection to the common usage of ordinary procedural law to ensure the rights and opportunities of social actors, especially in relation to more powerful actors, such as in the relationship between citizens and authorities in human rights law and national administrative law. This connection offers a social basis for normative inspiration for an advanced version of reflexive law that includes directives for balancing power disparities. We will revert to this in Chapters 6 and 7. It also provides a connection to post-1980s Habermasian theory on proceduralisation, including the role of fundamental

---

18 Sand, I.-J. (1996) *Styring av kompleksitet: Rettslige former for statlig rammestyring og desentralisert stats-forvaltniing*, Bergen: Fagbokforlaget Vigmostad & Bjørke, at pp. 86–94, esp. p. 94; Neves (2001) 'From the autopoiesis to the allopoiesis of law', at pp. 253–264; Scheuerman (2001) 'Reflexive law and the challenges of globalization', at p. 86; compare also Dalberg-Larsen, J. (1991) *Ret, styring og selvforvaltning*, Aarhus: Juridisk Bogformidling, at pp. 15–16, 136.

19 Teubner (1992) 'Social order from legislative noise', at p. 611; Teubner (1993) *Law as an Autopoietic System*, at pp. 66–67.

20 Teubner (1983) 'Substantive and reflective elements in modern law', esp. at p. 249; Teubner (1986) 'After legal instrumentalism?', at pp. 316–319; Teubner (1993) *Law as an Autopoietic System*, at p. 94; see also Sand (1996) *Styring av kompleksitet*, at p. 94; Neves (2001) 'From the autopoiesis to the allopoiesis of law', at pp. 263–264; Scheuerman (2001) 'Reflexive law and the challenges of globalization', at p. 86; and the discussion by Koudiadaki, A. (2009) 'Information and consultation rights of employees in Britain', *International Journal of Law in Context*, Vol. 5, No. 4, pp. 393–416, esp. at pp. 411–412; compare also Dalberg-Larsen (1991) *Ret, styring og selvforvaltning*, at pp. 15–16, 136.

or human rights for participation in law-making. This means that such an advanced version of reflexive law like the original version builds on a combination of systems thinking and Habermasian theory.

Thus, the normative aspect of reflexive law comes out through the theory's emphasis on two interrelated issues: participation of societal actors in the development of norms based on exchange of needs, demands and expectations; and establishing a balance of power between participants in this process. Both require proceduralisation. Power balance should be achieved through the procedures set up for the reflexive regulatory process. In establishing reflexive regulatory processes, the organisers (typically authorities) therefore should pay attention to procedural design to ensure that power disparities are mitigated. The objective is to cater for equal possibilities for all actors to inform the substantive normativity.

Functioning as reflexive law, the hybrid initiatives that form the empirical basis for the current study demonstrate that the assumption of autopoiesis on which reflexive law rests works at the super-national level to stimulate the development of norms of conduct for businesses in relation to their impacts on society. The differences in output and procedural design between, on the one hand, the SRSG process, the development of the Global Compact and ISO 26000 and, on the other, the MSF support the previous argument on reflexive law as a relevant regulatory strategy at the super-national level, but also underscore the need for addressing power disparities. Assessed against the successes of the SRSG process, the Global Compact and ISO 26000 to deliver norms that not only were in accordance with the original objectives but also were received favourably by stakeholders and allowed to pass to a stage of formal adoption, the case of the Draft Norms further underscores that it is relevant to consider applying reflexive law as a regulatory strategy for super-national law-making on sustainability concerns.

Statements that invoke the rationality of particular functional sub-systems with which change is desired may be an effective way to cause irritation that may generate acceptance of novel ideas with normative and thus regulatory aims, and/or self-regulation (change). By way of illustration, Global Compact architects and the SRSG deployed arguments on the economic risks that businesses may encounter if they do not appreciate societal concerns with their adverse impacts on human rights and self-regulate to change conduct accordingly. Whereas the EU Commission had not had much traction with business in relation to the outputs of the MSF process in which the Commission mainly argued with reference to the concerns and rationality of authorities, the Commission was successful in achieving business support for setting up the CSR Alliance, because its statements reasoned that CSR is good for business image, innovation and entrepreneurship. Conversely, business associations successfully deflected the Commission's efforts through the MSF to develop detailed normative guidance on CSR by referring to the political tasks and legal obligations of the Commission and EU member states to deliver on public policies on employment and societal inclusiveness as well as international human rights and labour obligations.

However, for such an output to be legitimate, it is important that it comes about through a legitimate process, in other words through persuasion based on 'the better argument' rather than on privilege or greater power. The MSF recommendations were rejected by civil society as lacking in legitimacy because the process was not perceived to be balanced.

The subsequent discussion illustrates the significance of power disparities for process, output and legitimacy. The analysis suggests that reflexive law, on the one hand, offers a relevant regulatory approach to the development of norms of conduct in a field with diverse and often conflicting interests that for formal or substantive reasons or constraints does not lend itself to top-down regulation by public authorities. On the other hand, it also shows that power disparities can be utterly disruptive to the process, the outcome, and the legitimacy of both. For reflexive law-type regulatory processes to deliver on their potential, it is therefore highly important to address the normative lacuna in reflexive law theory in relation to handling power disparities. This is where Habermasian theory on legitimate law-making, having been developed after reflexive law theory, may complement the latter. That is particularly pertinent in regard to ensuring that reflexive law processes are effective in delivering normative outputs that correspond to the original idea (rather than as in the MSF being deflected into a watered-down version) and deliver rules with a compliance pull through a process based on equalised participation among stakeholders. The next sections elaborate on these points and offer additional examples from the empirical cases.

5.3 Process, reflection and outputs

For the following analysis, each of the empirical cases will be introduced through a short summary of the main points related to process and output, which will then be followed by an analysis.

Recall that the Draft UN Norms were developed through a relatively conventional process of UN law-making in the human rights field. Moreover, the process occurred against the relatively conventional backdrop of increased awareness in a UN human rights expert sub-committee of the need to target a particular type of human rights abuse, and a decision to address that need through an international law-in-process draft that might develop into a soft or even possibly a hard law international instrument. While their name was innovative ('Norms'), as law-in-process the Draft Norms were written first and foremost by a human rights expert in collaboration with other human rights expert members of the same expert sub-committee of the Human Rights Commission. Civil society organisations in consultative status (under article 71 of the UN Charter) were involved as is common for human rights law-making and law-in-process instruments. As is also common in the human rights field, consulted civil society organisations mainly consisted of organisations representing victims of human rights abuse. As a result of late inclusion of business in the process, perceived by some also to be unduly limited, the legitimacy of the process and the resulting output suffered from a legitimacy deficit that contributed to lobbying by business and opposition by some governments. Eventually, despite other companies and governments being in favour of the document and the clarification it might deliver in terms of business and human rights, the Draft Norms were dismissed. Substantive issues were part of the reason, but a perceived legitimacy deficiency of the process contributed to its output and the normative messages being severely challenged. Stakeholder participation in the process was in accordance with formalities and conventional process in the human rights law field. However, this failed to generate a broad sense of actual consultation and involvement among one group of key stakeholders, that is, those to whom the new norms of conduct were addressed.

Despite the law-making process being conventional rather than reflexive, a key lesson of the Draft Norms is that, when the concern is with promoting transnational sustainability through norms of conduct addressing non-state actors, the successful development and adoption of the output require the participation of the actors who are targeted by the intended new rules. The conventional international law process may be well suited for delivering normative outputs that gather sufficient stakeholder support to ensure agreement and eventual adoption as conventional instruments of international hard or soft law. At least, decisions on stakeholder inclusion should carefully consider what groups have important stakes in the process and output, and invite stakeholders on this basis rather than whether they are typically included for the overall issue in question. As associations of businesses can obtain consultative status with the UN and some already have, in the UN context this is fully feasible. The outcome of the Draft Norms process suggests that the need for a broadly inclusive approach to participants is particularly pertinent when the object and subjects of intended regulation exceed the state-centric sphere. Indeed, the recommendations made by the OHCHR in its 2005 report for future steps to adopt a broad multi-stakeholder approach and the explicit instructions for the holder of the SRSG mandate to consult broadly with stakeholders, including companies,[21] suggest that this was precisely what was realised within the UN's core human rights institutions in the aftermath of the dismissal of the Draft Norms.

The UN Global Compact evolved through a multi-stakeholder process organised and led by the Office of the UN Secretary-General. This was based on a selectively composed multi-stakeholder group. Business organisations and selected CEOs and NGOs were invited to form part of the group. The overall objective was defined as involving business in the implementation of the UN goals. The Global Compact was successful in constructing a normative framework commonly understood to be related to CSR, and normatively informed by specific but general international law instruments related to the original three issue areas (human rights, labour and environment). The original limited inclusion of civil society caused severe legitimacy problems that affected civil society support for the process as well as the expected output.[22] When selected civil society organisations were invited to take part in the process, the legitimacy crisis subsided somewhat but not fully. The Compact's hybrid character as very soft law-type[23] normative guidance based on international law instruments has also led academics to criticise the initiative,[24] again affecting its legitimacy.

The initiative to develop the Compact emerged from within an administrative body under the UN on the basis of a process of what amounts to reflection or stock-taking within this body (or by its head, the UN Secretary-General) on limitations of the current system of international law and international law-making to regulate corporate conduct with regard to human rights, labour rights and the environment, and a need to stimulate processes within companies to self-regulate and adapt their practices to societal needs and expectations. Its normative objectives are clear: to make companies act in accordance with the ten principles and the informing instruments of international law. Its network structure engages companies procedurally to share best practice, in other words to discuss how best to integrate the normative goals of the ten principles into daily business practice. Procedurally, the Global Compact Office and the Board are set up to guide companies and to ensure that meetings take place regularly at a global scale. In practice, therefore, the Global Compact works in a way that aims at promoting self-regulation in companies based on enhanced appreciation of the societal impact of their actions and practices that relate to their business relations.

The multi-stakeholder and participatory development process of the Global Compact, as well as its normative features and continuous networking and learning approach, displays a series of reflexive law regulatory features. The Global Compact was set up as a reflexive law

---

21 Commission on Human Rights (2005) *Human Rights and Transnational Corporations and Other Business Enterprises*, paras 2–3, 5.

22 Global Compact Critics Blog, http://www.globalcompactcritics.net/ (last accessed 31 January 2013, website has been closed).

23 Sahlin-Andersson, K. (2004) 'Emergent cross-sectional soft regulations: Dynamics at play in the Global Compact initiative', in U. Mörth (ed.), *Soft Law in Governance and Regulation: An Interdisciplinary Analysis*, Cheltenham: Edward Elgar, pp. 129–152.

24 Nolan, J. (2005) 'The United Nations' compact with business'.

forum, and it still functions as one for significant practical purposes. First suggested in early 1999 at the World Economic Forum meeting in Davos and developed during 1999–2000, the Compact was launched at the same time as the Draft UN Norms were developed. Compared to the process of the Draft UN Norms and in view of the business opposition, lobbying, and eventually the Human Rights Commission's dismissal of the Norms, the Global Compact's process was more successful in taking an initial objective of developing normative guidance for the social responsibilities of businesses into a set of principles providing guidance, and achieving agreement on the principles. The process resulted in an output that attained a formal character in terms of principles that businesses commit to. Despite legitimacy challenges, the Compact process and output therefore at an overall level present an example of a reflexive regulatory process that was effective in delivering an output that corresponded well to the original objective, achieved multi-stakeholder agreement on the output, and has generated a regular increase in participants not only among business but also in recent years from some civil society organisations as well as public authorities or organisational entities.

The Compact also gained acceptance among stakeholder groups, both those directly involved and gradually among those that were indirectly involved, by applying an argumentative strategy that was later to be adopted and further evolved by the SRSG. Many statements presented by high-level UN staff involved driving the multi-stakeholder process or explaining the Global Compact initiative within the UN system, while externally they addressed stakeholder concerns through arguments that precisely targeted the logic and interests of the specific audience. Again, this may seem intuitive, but in fact it is often not. The argumentative strategies of many actors, including some state and non-state actors, in seeking to drive initiatives within the UN or other organisations towards more formalised sustainability regulation show that many miss out on opportunities to generate support from key actors by not addressing their interests or concerns.[25] Starting with the speech that Kofi Annan delivered in Davos in 1999, the Global Compact architects helped create acceptance of the need for firms to act upon societal and policy concerns with their impact and build actions on the normative foundations of existing UN instruments. They did so by explaining that this was the best way for firms to avoid profit loss and retain the ability to largely determine by themselves what action the individual business would take that would relate to its own core activities, as opposed to formalised public direct regulation.[26]

For the establishment of the Global Compact this was effective in generating acceptance of the normative directives embodied in the nine and later ten principles, founded on international law on human rights, labour rights, environmental sustainability and anti-corruption. The Global Compact architects, similarly, helped the Compact idea gain acceptance with the state-based organs of the UN (in particular, the General Assembly) by explaining public–private multi-stakeholder regulation and collaboration on business involvement in addressing global sustainability concerns as a way to move forward to implementing UN objectives in a day and age when firms have the power to do harm in this area and have few direct obligations.[27]

---

25 Buhmann (2011) 'Integrating human rights in emerging regulation of corporate social responsibility; Kinderman (2013) 'Corporate social responsibility in the EU, 1993–2013'; Buhmann (2014) *Normative Discourses and Public–Private Regulatory Strategies for Construction of CSR Normativity.*

26 Buhmann (2014) *Normative Discourses and Public–Private Regulatory Strategies for Construction of CSR Normativity.*

27 For a detailed presentation and discussion, see Buhmann (2014) *Normative Discourses and Public–Private Regulatory Strategies for Construction of CSR Normativity,* chap. 4.

Although the Global Compact is not 'law' in the sense of positive, valid law that applies directly to companies, nor a regulatory instrument in the institutional sense, it is not without legal relevance, nor does it escape legal characterisation – *in casu* under reflexive law theory. The normative foundations are strongly based in international hard and soft law, and it does seek to regulate business conduct towards acting with respect for international human rights, labour, anti-corruption and elements of environmental law. The significance of this is particularly acute given the intergovernmental setting and the dearth of hard enforcement options for these fields of international law. The Communication of Progress reporting process and the publicised 'de-listing' sanction work through a reporting and 'naming-and-shaming' modality that resembles the ways in which international law often seeks to monitor and sanction state compliance and violations, for example under international human rights treaties and treaty body modalities. Through a partnership collaboration approach, the Global Compact also seeks to support business action that may even support the fulfilment of rights granted by international human rights instruments or other UN goals, such as during 2000–2015 the MDGs and from September 2015 the SDGs.

In 2015 the Global Compact's website was thoroughly revised, shifting the primary communicative focus from the Compact's ten principles towards contributions to fulfilling social, economic and other global and local needs in accordance with the SDGs. A softening of the 'de-listing' sanction of participant companies that neglect to submit the annual Communication of Progress report has also been introduced. This is observable, amongst other things, in that the Compact website front page for much of late 2015 and throughout 2016 listed the total number of participating companies (around 9,000) in a prominent position on the Global Compact's opening webpage, rather than the number of 'active' (communicating and not de-listed) companies (around 3,500). While the new policy focus entails a shift from 'doing no harm' to 'doing more good', the basic message of the Compact remains that companies should respect and observe the ten principles.

The SRSG process was unique in including private non-state actors – business representatives and business organisations – to an unprecedented degree in a UN regulatory context. There was a significant difference in the implications of involving business representatives in developing the Global Compact, compared with the SRSG process. The Global Compact was always presented as a multi-stakeholder initiative with no legal or normative implications beyond participants' voluntary commitment. Thus, businesses (and other non-state actors) were not involved in a process that might lead to an instrument of international law, whether hard or soft. At the time that the SRSG mandate was established in 2005, the legal nature of the outcome was uncertain. The SRSG chose for pragmatic reasons to refer to the UN Framework as a 'policy framework', but many observers were hoping for a product that (like the Draft UN Norms) had explicit hard or soft law ambitions, perhaps even a draft treaty. The output might have been a conventional product of international law-making, that is, a treaty establishing obligations for companies, or at least a set of soft law principles or guidelines. Thus, involving business in the process amounted to effectively involving potential new duty-bearers in the law-making process. As firms, being non-state actors, are normally rights-holders and not duty-bearers or participants in international law-making, such an inclusion of business entailed a major change from the past not just in terms of formalising business responsibilities for human rights but also in terms of non-state actor duty-holding subjects actively participating in the rule-making process.

While states are of course always involved in their capacity as both rule-makers and duty-bearers simply by virtue of the state-centrist character of the international legal system, involving non-state actors as participants in a process that might lead to them becoming duty-bearers was a novelty. Non-state actors are generally involved in international law-making on human rights, but typically in the capacity of rights-holders or as organisations that represent victims. Indeed, in parallel to the environmentally focused NGOs in the environmental field, several human rights-focused civil society organisations with consultative status are highly active participants in UN human rights regulation precisely in that role. Business organisations with consultative status are more commonly involved in activities that relate to international economic law rather than international human rights law.

In developing the UN Framework and UNGPs, the SRSG's method of work included consultation with civil society in many parts of the world, business organisations, governments and intergovernmental organisations. It also involved consultation and collaboration with academics and other experts, including UN human rights treaty bodies. An annual report was submitted to the Human Rights Commission/Human Rights Council, followed by the SRSG debating the reports in formal meetings and online with the Commission/Council and civil society organisations in consultative status. The gradual development of findings and recommendations was achieved in a way that allowed stakeholders the opportunity to make comments. Such opportunities arose when the SRSG made presentations to audiences representing specific stakeholder groups, as well as when SRSG presentations, statements and other texts were shared online on the website of the Business and Human Rights Resource Centre and through its newsfeeds. These approaches therefore also allowed the SRSG the opportunity to share such comments with other stakeholders or experts, receive their feedback, and integrate this into the next stages of the process and its written outputs, all while taking the opportunity to hold consultations and other meetings to stimulate the exchange of needs and concerns between and across stakeholders.

The SRSG process was not actually set up to be reflexive law, but it developed into functioning as such. This happened because the individual who became the mandate-holder adopted a particular – and by UN standards unusual – consultative approach, which went far beyond meeting with organisations and individuals that are normally involved in UN law-making. The backdrop, too, had reflexive law elements, but this does not by itself make the process reflexive law. As noted in Chapter 3, subsection 3.2.2, the 2005 report from the OHCHR had recommended a broad multi-stakeholder approach, and the 2005 mandate resolution required the SRSG to undertake such an approach. This indicates that the authorities or overall regulators in question had reflected on their regulatory capacity and the Draft UN Norms process, and found that an alternative approach was necessary. Through its different forms, the broad multi-stakeholder process contributed to developing and testing the normative outputs of the two mandate terms, which generated sufficient support for the outputs to become accepted by the Human Rights Council. Business associations and civil society were supportive initially, despite some critique of both process and output.[28] As explained in Chapter 3, that critique grew some time *after* the UNGPs were adopted.

Among the law-making processes assessed in this study, the SRSG process was among the most effective in terms of delivering an output that enjoyed a high degree of acceptance. Although the process is also subject to critique of both process and output,[29] the unanimous

28　See Chapter 3, subsection 3.2.4.1; Deva (2010) '"Protect, respect and remedy"'; compare Sidoti (2011) 'It's our business'; De Schutter (2013) 'Foreword'.

29　See Chapter 3, subsection 3.2.4.1; Parker, C. and Howe, J. (2012) 'Ruggie's diplomatic project and its missing regulatory infrastructure', in R. Mares (ed.), *The UN Guiding Principles on Business and Human Rights: Foundations and Implementation*, Leiden: Martinus Nijhoff, pp. 273–301.

'welcoming' that the 2008 UN Framework report received at the Human Rights Council implies its legitimacy in the sense of the term applied in the current work. This, and the Council's adoption of the UNGPs, had been achieved through an inclusive approach to participation in the process and a procedure which granted wide participation that included carefully managing the process towards an equalisation of participants' power. Bringing together stakeholders from groups that had displayed widely differing interests during the process towards the Draft UN Norms allowed for exchanges and probably for resolution of distrust among participants.[30] Although the debate was hardly fully fledged deliberation, it did enjoy deliberative features. Meetings including stakeholders and experts, and the sharing of experts' notes and stakeholders' submissions on the internet, served as forums for deliberation and the exchange of views among actors with insight into or interest in the issue at stake.

The EU MSF, which was launched in 2002 and delivered its first comprehensive recommendations in a report issued in 2004, involved a considerable range of European business associations for large as well as smaller companies, organisations for employers and employees, and civil society organisations with expertise in human rights, labour, environment, developmental and consumer concerns. As participants in EU 'social dialogue', an institutionalised process of industry, employers' and workers' organisations' participation in EU labour law-making, business/industry and labour participants in the MSF enjoyed experience in the politics and practices of EU labour law preparation. Participating NGOs had experience from UN work in the human rights, labour and environmental field, but less EU experience.[31]

The MSF was chaired by the EU Commission, which however mainly held a secretarial role rather than an actual managing role. The Commission specifically suggested that the MSF explore the appropriateness of establishing common guiding principles for CSR practices and instruments. The Commission also specifically suggested that the MSF consider founding such principles on what was referred to as internationally agreed principles, in particular the OECD Guidelines for Multinational Enterprises and ILO fundamental conventions.[32]

During the MSF meetings, the concerns of business and industry were promoted both by formally established networks such as organisations of employers or industry, and by informal networks sharing similar interests.[33] Representing environmental, human rights, development and consumer NGOs, civil society also worked in informal networks, particularly towards the end of the MSF process when they joined to present arguments with the objective of having one strong voice.[34] However, unintentionally, this led to their voice becoming limited to one generalised voice, causing it not to come through very strongly, whereas employers and industry still spoke with several distinct but similar voices. The effects were underscored by the fact that business and industry masterfully used their several voices to articulate their concerns in the system-specific language that appealed to the authorities to reduce claims on the private sector, while civil society organisations were less adept at articulating their concerns in a manner that would appeal to make business assume enhanced social responsibilities

---

30 Compare Deitelhoff, N. (2009) 'The discursive process of legalization: Charting islands of persuasion in the ICC case', *International Organization*, Vol. 63, Winter, pp. 33–65, at pp. 55–56 on regional conferences organised under the process of developing the International Criminal Court.

31 Buhmann, K. (2011) 'Reflexive regulation of CSR: A case study of public-policy interests in EU public–private regulation of CSR', *International and Comparative Corporate Law Journal*, Vol. 8, No. 2, pp. 38–76.

32 Commission of the European Communities (2002) *Communication from the Commission Concerning Corporate Social Responsibility*.

33 Fairbrass (2011) 'Exploring corporate social responsibility policy in the European Union'.

34 Buhmann (2011) 'Reflexive regulation of CSR'.

informed by international law. Without formalised procedures to balance power disparities, arguments that watered down the initial objective of formulating a framework on CSR normatively based on international instruments came to dominate. The eventual output was less a result of equalised bargaining than of power of access and privileged knowledge, and arguments that addressed that power and privilege. As a result, neither the process nor the output enjoyed much legitimacy in the perception of civil society, nor did the process deliver the substantive normative output that the MSF was established to deliver.[35]

Consequently, the MSF did not result in a specific normative framework as originally intended. The Final Report of the MSF made only general reference to international human rights law and other international law as part of a framework for CSR in Europe, and referred only to the ILO Tripartite Declaration, the OECD Guidelines and the UN Global Compact as directly relevant to companies, all of which are non-binding and, at the most, serve as guidance for corporations.[36] The reference to those instruments was made in the first part of the report, but in such a way that the connection to more detailed recommendations for companies, the EU Commission and the EU member states was not made explicit or explained. Mirroring arguments made by business participants in the MSF, the Final Report in effect passed responsibility for social or global concerns about business impact on society back to governments, telling them to act by themselves in order to have public policy goals implemented rather than telling governments to ask companies to act directly.

The EU MSF was set up and functioned as a reflexive law forum from the outset. Its basis was explicit recognition by the EU Commission that the EU lacked the authority to legislate on business conduct in accordance with the European Parliament's 1999 resolution on codes of conduct for EU-based companies operating outside the EU. While the reflexive law modus may have been uninformed by the theory, the organisation of a series of meetings for stakeholders to meet and exchange views on needs, concerns and expectations with the objective of having them develop a normative framework for business conduct was a clear example of reflexive law. The process, however, was not effective in delivering the objective intended by the EU authorities concerned with reducing the adverse societal impact of business operations. A combination of business associations enjoying EU law-making experience and the conflicting priorities of the two involved EU Directorates-General (similar to ministries), Social Affairs and Enterprise, played a major role in this.[37] In this case, therefore, although the reflexive law set-up was clear, power imbalances resulted in the MSF not being effective in delivering the intended output. Power disparities significantly reduced the legitimacy of the MSF process as well as its output. This was evident from a number of statements during and following the MSF.[38]

---

35 Buhmann (2014) *Normative Discourses and Public–Private Regulatory Strategies for Construction of CSR Normativity*, chaps 5, 7.
36 European Multi-Stakeholder Forum on CSR (2004) *Final Results and Recommendations*.
37 Buhmann (2011) 'Reflexive regulation of CSR'.
38 See McLaren, D. (2004) *Statement on Behalf of the Green 8*, EU Multi-Stakeholder Forum on CSR, Final High Level Meeting, 29 June, http://circa.europa.eu/irc/empl/csr_eu_multi_stakeholder_forum/info/data/en/CSR%20Forum%20040629%20speech%20G8.htm (last accessed 15 February 2013, webpage has been removed); Parent, A.-S. (2004) *Statement of the Social Platform*, EU Multi-Stakeholder Forum on CSR, Final High Level Meeting, 29 June, http://circa.europa.eu/irc/empl/csr_eu_multi_stakeholder_forum/info/data/en/CSR%20Forum%20040629%20speech%20Social%20Platform.htm (last accessed 15 February 2013, webpage has been removed); Fédération Internationale des Droits de l'Homme (2013) *Statement by FIDH*, EU Multi-Stakeholder Forum on CSR, http://circa.europa.eu/irc/empl/csr_eu_multi_stakeholder_forum/info/data/en/CSR%20Forum%20040629%20speech%20FIDH.htm (last accessed 15 February 2013, webpage has been removed).

The European CSR Alliance was launched in 2006 in partial response (or reaction) to the limited success of the MSF. The CSR Alliance was set up by the Commission as a voluntary business network to exchange best practice on CSR and other activities to promote corporate self-regulation on CSR. The normative role of international law, in particular for human rights and labour rights, was emphasised by the Commission at the launch of the CSR Alliance. In practice, its normative role has been limited in the work and products of the CSR Alliance.

The EU Commission's establishment of the CSR Alliance suggests that, after the disappointing outcome of the MSF, the Commission considered alternative approaches for it to stimulate self-regulation in European companies in accordance with EU public policy objectives related to social sustainability and environmental concerns. The Commission's insistence on the role of human rights and international law instruments as key normative sources informing CSR[39] underscores that the MSF did not deliver what EU authorities were hoping for, and that the Alliance was launched as an alternative effort towards a similar objective.

The CSR Alliance was a limited type of reflexive law initiative, set up by the Commission in response to a tension between its limited legislative powers and a determined effort to involve business in addressing specific public policy objectives affected by transnational business activity. However, whereas the MSF was intended to be inclusive, by contrast the CSR Alliance from the outset suffered a legitimacy deficit because its organisational composition made civil society and labour unions feel excluded from the on-going process of developing CSR normativity within the EU. Consisting only of business organisations, the stakeholder basis was too limited to generate the dynamic exchange of needs and concerns required for a reflexive law process to induce insights into external needs and expectations and stimulate significant learning and self-regulation. For the Alliance, the fact that it was established is the main output of relevance to the current analysis, as work within the Alliance mainly consists in meetings of business only. The establishment of a new initiative consisting of business with the aim of promoting guidance for CSR was a success for the Commission in view of the resistance that a similar regulatory aim had received from business associations in the MSF, and a success assessed against the stated objectives. The outputs of the Alliance are relatively limited but do contain some references to human rights and relevant normative guidance in guides setting forth 'best practice'.[40]

Established under the ISO organisation, ISO 26000 was developed through a multi-stakeholder process with broad representation of a series of broadly composed stakeholder groups[41] with equal formal powers. This formally designated division of stakeholders and of equality served to balance power disparities. It did not eliminate power issues, but ensured sufficient legitimacy of the process and output so that the process led to guidance comprehensively covering CSR issues, to adoption by consensus, and to ISO 26000 being applied by organisations around the globe. The process enabled an exchange of concerns and needs, and along with the consensus-oriented decision-making functioned in a manner that has reflexive law-type features. The set-up of the process was not a typical reflexive law background. Rather, like several other private CSR initiatives, the process towards ISO 26000 and its

---

39 Commission of the European Communities (2006) *Communication from the Commission to the European Parliament, the Council and the European Economic and Social Committee.*

40 CSR Alliance (2008) *Toolbox.*

41 Henriques, A. (ed.) (2011) *Understanding ISO 26000: A Practical Approach to Social Responsibility*, London: British Standards Institution.

output exemplifies a private organisation stepping into a regulatory gap resulting from the limited regulatory and political powers of national governments and international organisations to adopt detailed norms on responsible business conduct. The broad composition of stakeholder groups and the inclusion of governments and public authorities as one of the six groups supported the legitimacy of the initiative in terms of the output. The composition and consensus-oriented process may have supported throughput legitimacy, at least in terms of formal balancing of power and interests.

Assessed against the power-related scenarios described in Chapter 2, section 2.5, we are able to observe all three forms of institutionalisation. The degree of institutionalisation of corporate social responsibilities varied, with the SRSG process delivering the most comprehensive change and the MSF process's output close to the status quo. None of the initiatives led to a fully fledged hard institutionalisation. The Global Compact and ISO 26000 entail a *soft institutionalisation*, with CSR remaining understood to be 'voluntary' but significant normative guidance developed with a strong basis in international law. The SRSG process led to *a combination of a hard and soft institutionalisation*: it emphasised the legal obligations of states as well as the legal obligations of firms to comply with ensuing national law, and stressed that, in self-regulating to voluntarily honour social expectations, business should consider international human rights law. It also made explicit that this should be the case where applicable national law falls short of the pertinent state's international obligations. Set on a course of clarifying corporate responsibilities for human rights, it established a foundation for further institutionalisation based on the full range of human rights grounded in the International Bill of Rights. Resulting in a situation close to the status quo, the MSF output emphasised the 'voluntary' character of CSR and rejected formalised regulation as well as a strong normative foundation in international human rights law or the advancing of such normative guidance. A second effort by the EU Commission to develop an institutionalisation of CSR normativity, the CSR Alliance has moved towards *a slightly enhanced institutionalisation* by heeding the normative guidance provided by the Commission without doing so explicitly through direct reference to international human rights law.

Across the initiatives, the system-specific interests or logics made themselves felt in diverse ways. When system-specific interests of a particular group were perceived by one or more other groups to dominate the process and the output, the effectiveness of the process to deliver the output that was intended was severely affected, with process and output both perceived to be deficient in legitimacy. This was the case with the Draft Norms, the MSF and the CSR Alliance. By contrast, when the regulatory process and the way it was managed succeeded in establishing communication between diverse groups with a conversation that exchanged the concerns and needs associated with or by the interests of specific stakeholders across those groups, the effectiveness of the process to deliver its output was greater. This was the case with the SRSG process and the process towards ISO 26000. When the power of stakeholders was perceived to be balanced or to be managed in a way that balanced power disparities, a sense of throughput legitimacy supported the process to deliver an output that was perceived to be legitimate. This, too, was the case with the SRSG process and ISO 26000.

Differentiated interests of stakeholders made themselves felt most strongly in the MSF process and in its output. Business organisations, in particular those opposed to an institutionalisation of CSR, were more influential on the output of the process than NGOs, resulting in the interests of certain economic actors prevailing to the detriment of the ambitious original objective of the Commission and the interests of civil society actors. The Global Compact was both ground-breaking and quite effective in delivering an output aligned with the original objective. Economic system interests of having CSR guidance in a very soft form prevailed, but public policy interests related to the objectives of social and environmental international law came to be influential on the output. Public policy objectives and civil society interests were allowed to play a strong part in the output, explicated and institutionalised through basing the ten principles in international law instruments.

Constituting an even stronger contrast to the EU MSF and its output, the SRSG process was the most effective among these initiatives in regard to developing norms of conduct and guidance on business social responsibilities informed by international human rights law. Economic system interests and the concerns of business were represented throughout the process, along with civil society and other stakeholders. Originally strongly opposed to an institutionalisation of CSR and the definition of business responsibilities for human rights, business representatives were swayed to recognising that socially responsible action based on international human rights law may be in the general interest of companies. The approach and construction were approved even by those who had previously been opposed to the normative idea as well as the process. To this end, the SRSG deployed arguments that were couched in the system-specific rationality of the audience at given points of time to explain the implications of the social expectations of business to the specific audience.[42] The shift from opposing to embracing business responsibilities for human rights, which the IOE, the ICC and BIAC underwent from the time of the Draft UN Norms to their input to the SRSG process through their conflict zones report, is a case in point.

Assessed against the mandate, the SRSG process not only enjoyed output effectiveness but also delivered outputs that attracted a considerable degree of legitimacy in terms of input, throughput and output. Although some organisations as well as academics would have preferred the SRSG process to deliver a conventional international law instrument, in terms of output the UN Framework did create the foundation for further work to refine and detail business responsibilities for business, starting with the SRSG's second term, which led to the UNGPs in 2011, and followed by the more recent process towards a treaty on business and human rights.

With variations across these examples, reflexive law has proven to be a viable regulatory strategy towards inducing acceptance of social expectations among business, and towards inducing public–private co-regulation on a set of norms that may lead to self-regulation. As a result of the variations in organisational set-up and procedures, reflexive law has demonstrated that it can offer, in principle, an option for authorities at the intergovernmental level to regulate in an indirect but transparent fashion where they lack direct regulatory authority to implement public policy objectives whose implementation may be affected by the private sector. This is in line with Teubner's theory for reflexive law as a regulatory strategy at the national level. The outputs' varied quality with regard to detailed guidance for CSR normativity and the degree of change induced through the outputs, however, indicate that as a regulatory strategy reflexive law is not in all ways efficient in terms of delivering the normative output seen by an initiating agency as desirable for sustainable development.

The potential of reflexive law as a strategy to regulate transnational sustainability issues in a global world in which regulatory needs escape the jurisdictional or territorial boundaries of authorities calls for an understanding of what makes the strategy work effectively to deliver normative outputs. The analysis above shows that this must take place through a process that is sufficiently legitimate to ensure that the development of a normative product is not captured or unduly influenced by certain interests or simply cut short as a result of

---

42 See, further, Buhmann (2018), *Changing Sustainability Norms through Communication Processes.*

some stakeholders not perceiving their members and concerns to be adequately involved as participants. The selection and composition of participants must also be undertaken in such a way that legitimacy of the output is not questioned after the process. The subsequent section turns to this.

5.4 Participation, power and legitimacy

The outputs of reflexive law forums are contingent not just on the participation of a range of stakeholders and the procedural setting established for these to exchange expectations, needs and demands as a matter of technical information. They are also contingent on the participation being balanced and power disparities being managed towards an equalised access to take part in the regulatory process. These observations address the significance of the design of reflexive law forums in ensuring balanced participation.

Again, the MSF serves as a particularly strong example, which demonstrates the differences as well as potential complementarity between the Habermasian approach to legitimate law-making and the reflexive law approach. Two factors played a part for the MSF output, one legitimate, the other contributing to an illegitimate process and output.

In the MSF, the argumentative strategies of organisations opposed to a soft or hard institutionalisation of CSR differed markedly in regard to both substance and effects, compared to the most generally applied argumentative strategies of organisations that favoured such an institutionalisation. Industry and employers deployed political and legal system language to cause perturbation within the Commission and other authorities by invoking obligations of these, or expectations on these. Industry and employers were successful in returning responsibility for implementation of public policy objectives and international obligations to the authorities, and in constructing a status quo understanding of CSR as not only voluntary but also – contrary to the Commission's original objective – detached from hard international law as a normative source. Per se, this is not illegitimate. It is just clever arguing with the use of targeted deployment of language that addresses system-specific interests in order to create perturbation and acceptance of the argument within other parties. In other words, in accordance with the Habermasian ideal this serves to promote the 'uncoerced force' of the better argument (albeit one in line with the transmitters' interests), and doing so in line with the systems thinking rationale of what makes communication stimulate change. However, when that uncoerced force is diverted by privilege, such as disproportionate access to policy-makers, then the argumentative strategy turns from being clever to cunning and possibly illegitimate.

Teubner recognises that language may be deployed to promote the particular interests of a particular actor or group. Along Habermasian lines, this may serve to make the good argument that works through the better argument's 'uncoerced force' with the common good in mind. However, as the analysis above has indicated, use of language as a communication tool in a reflexive regulatory process may also be strategic, bordering perhaps on cunning in the sense of achieving particular objectives through the creation of perturbation in certain recipient sub-systems, in order to protect or promote the transmitters' interests rather than the interests of the common good. Arguments raised by business in the course of the 2002–2004 EU MSF indicate as much, as business associations used systems-specific language to invoke the logic of state duties and gain acceptance of the view that the EU should abstain from developing a detailed normative framework for CSR. The effects of such discursive usage of language may be further underscored if the power of participants in the law-making process is (or is perceived to be) skewed. This, too, was demonstrated by the EU MSF, first because business associations enjoyed prior experience in EU law-making in the CSR-related area of labour, and second as the power balance and involvement of the EU Commission's agencies shifted during the course of the MSF, and business concerns also came to enjoy enhanced support from the Directorate-General for Enterprise.

Industry and employers enjoyed the benefit of a shift of power on CSR within the Commission during the MSF. Originally launched by the Directorate-General for Employment and Social Affairs, the Commission's CSR work was gradually passed to the Directorate-General for Enterprise. Between the two, the former favoured business social responsibilities and a clear normative framework, whereas the latter favoured freedom of enterprise and few regulatory limits on business.[43] Moreover, industry and employers' organisations involved in the MSF had the advantage of experience in EU 'social dialogue' in the field of labour law. This would provide them with insight into the political mechanisms of EU negotiations and therefore an advantageous point of departure for engaging in the construction of CSR normativity under the MSF compared to civil society organisations that lacked such EU experience. Obtaining understanding and agreement through the exchange of needs and expectations is what the reflexive law process aims for. Obtaining this through power of privileged access is not what it aims for. That is precisely what reflexive law theory warns about, although it only establishes this as a normative point without explicating the procedural steps. This, too, confirms the significance of the design of reflexive law forums to address power disparities to provide for equalised participation and legitimacy of process and output.

In the end, the MSF was subjected to weak steering and authority by the EU Commission. Combined with the privilege of knowledge and access of some participants, this led to loss of substantive focus, limited output effectiveness, and loss of legitimacy, as some actors (NGOs) perceived the process to be overtaken by other actors (business) that were felt to be more powerful. Launched as an alternative with the Commission seeking to take back authority, the Alliance nevertheless started out with a legitimacy deficit because it excluded the very same actors (NGOs) that had perceived the MSF to be subject to business capture. Among the examples, the ISO 26000 and SRSG processes were the most legitimate, providing for inclusive input opportunities and connecting input to output. The SRSG process achieved this and its output effectiveness through a combination of authority (delivered, for example, through notes from the SRSG prepared prior to consultations, and the inclusion of expert knowledge) and a pragmatic ostensibly informal but effectively institutionalised process during consultations that catered for throughput legitimacy. This was complemented by internet-based communication between stakeholders and the SRSG and a high degree of transparency, through the internet-based SRSG portal. However, the subsequent critique of the UN Framework and UNGPs from some quarters, including civil society organisations, is a sign that even those processes were not perceived to be fully legitimate, and that certain input was not perceived to be adequately reflected in the output.

---

43 Compare the speeches by the two EU commissioners at the MSF high level meeting on 13 November 2013: Diamantopoulou, A. (2003) *Anna Diamantopoulou – European Commissioner Responsible for Employment and Social Affairs: Dialogue and Partnership: The Key to Successful CSR*, EU Multi-Stakeholder Forum on CSR, High Level Meetings, 13 November, http://circa.europa.eu/irc/empl/csr_eu_multi_stakeholder_forum/ info/data/en/CSR%20Forum%20031113%20speech%20AD.htm (last accessed 17 February 2013, webpage has been removed); Liikanen, E. (2003) *Erkki Liikanen – Member of the European Commission, Enterprise and Information Society*, EU Multi-Stakeholder Forum on CSR, High Level Meetings, 13 November, http:// circa.europa.eu/irc/empl/csr_eu_multi_stakeholder_forum/info/data/en/CSR%20Forum%20031113%20 speech%20EL.htm (last accessed 17 February 2013, webpage has been removed).

5.5 Outlook for collaborative regulation

Given the decisive impact of the MSF in terms of warding off a hard institutionalisation and the Global Compact's avoidance of seeking a hard institutionalisation of business social responsibilities, for the potential of future regulation and development of sustainability and norms of conduct it is significant that reflexive law as a regulatory modality was broadly accepted. It was accepted both as a practical measure (evidenced by stakeholders' active participation in the Global Compact, the MSF and the SRSG process) and as a way to promote CSR (evidenced by acceptance of proposals that were made for using labelling, reporting and incentives schemes). Interestingly, the fact that authorities (as in the case of the Global Compact and the Commission as indicated at the MSF launch) or those who act on their behalf (such as the SRSG) have considerable influence in terms of setting out normative guidance for the output does not seem to reduce non-state actors' support for the process and willingness to take part. Despite the clear element of public regulation in reflexive law, the options for broad participation appear to serve for practical purposes to mitigate concerns on the part of business of being (over-)regulated or perhaps more precisely subjected to regulation perceived to be illegitimate owing to business's non-participation in the process towards the output. The qualified participation catered for by reflexive law as regulatory strategy provides for willingness to engage, even when a reflexive regulatory forum is not formally presented as such. Again, the outcome of the Draft Norms process and apprehension among some organisations like the ICC and the IOE, allegedly as a result of having felt left out of the Draft Norms process, underscore the difference provided by regulatory mechanisms such as the Global Compact and SRSG process that built on active non-state actor participation rather than simply formal consultation.

Reflexive law not only functioned as the actual mode of regulation in the initiatives but also played a role as a modality proposed and/or accepted for the purpose of the outputs for future regulation of CSR. For example, CSR reporting (non-financial reporting) is applied by the Global Compact, recommended by the UNGPs, proposed by the MSF, and currently being implemented by EU member states based on a 2014 EU directive, which in itself was influenced by the UNGPs' recommendations. The combination of an endorsement in practice for reflexive law through engagement in the processes and of proposals for related modalities for future application indicates considerable acceptance in practice. This acceptance is not only among for-profit non-state actors, but also by civil society organisations as a regulatory modality to promote business internalisation of external concerns. These include public policy objectives and tasks that are states' obligations but whose practical implementation may be limited by governance gaps or national jurisdictional boundaries.

Reflexive law not only in theory but also in practice offers itself as a regulatory strategy where the powers of authorities are limited. This means that reflexive law offers a relevant option for public, private or hybrid development of norms of conduct pertaining to problems that are transnational in character and marked by conflicts of interests within and across stakeholder groups. However, for effectiveness, the design of the process must be complemented by measures to ensure legitimacy. The next question to be considered, therefore, is what procedural design caters for a process that provides the output with the legitimacy necessary for a 'compliance pull'.

6   Proceduralisation for legitimacy

Overview: This chapter reverts to the Habermasian inspired perspective on procedure as a modality to provide for equalised access to a rule-making process and participation in a deliberative process. The discussion connects this with Franck's perspective on legitimacy as a driver of an inherent compliance pull, and reflexive law's theory gap in terms of how to balance disparities. Drawing on the empirical cases throughout, it explains the value of reflexive regulation to fill governance gaps for regulation of transnational sustainability concerns and how the deliberative approach for legitimate law-making and the communicative approach of reflexive law complement each other. Further, it highlights how the procedural aspect of deliberative law-making is lacking in reflexive law and how the presence or absence of relevant procedure has affected of the case studies as to process legitimacy and the effectiveness of the process to deliver the intended output, as well as the legitimacy of the output. The chapter observes that for reflexive law regulation to fulfil its considerable potential for sustainability related concerns and to fill the super-national governance gap for such transnational regulatory needs, in particular in regard to non-state actors, the theory gap must be addressed. It concludes that reflexive law must be strengthened through an enhanced inclusion of proceduralisation, and that this can be done by incorporating elements of Habermasian theory developed after reflexive law was introduced.*

6.1 Complementarity of reflexive law and deliberative law-making for legitimacy

From the perspective of this study, throughput legitimacy, and particularly its assumption of the significance of *deliberation* to provide for legitimacy, offers an option to complement reflexive law theory and reflexive law-making processes in practice to cover the gap on how to balance power disparities. The aim is that such processes may deliver outputs which are legitimate in terms of responding to and reflecting concerned actors' interests in an input-legitimate way. This means both that the input must be representative of relevant concerns and that the power represented by input-providers must be balanced. Moreover, by delivering outputs perceived as legitimate (output legitimacy), the process will stand a chance of being effective in delivering on its own objective. Finally, process and output legitimacy contributes to the output enjoying an inherent compliance pull with those subjected to the rules who see their concerns represented. The output should inspire trust among those who are affected indirectly but often significantly, such as victims of business-related human rights abuse. These individuals or groups often lack resources for direct participation even where this may be technically possible. Trust requires confidence that the process leading to the output was balanced in terms of the concerns and interests represented and among participants.

Recall that Franck noted that conventional international law ideally carries an inherent compliance pull because it is developed through a legitimate process. Recall further that this process in conventional international law by default includes participation by those subjected to the resulting rules as duty-bearers, because states in their capacity as primary actors in international law are both the law-makers and those to whom duties apply. To extend this idea of compliance pull to the super-national stage for processes that aim to develop duties for a larger group of actors that include non-state actors it is therefore pertinent to consider how to include those as participants in the process. As observed and as documented by the case studies above, the inclusion of non-state actors that are the potential holders of new duties, whether (soft law) responsibilities or (hard law) obligations, offers a risk of capture if the process is not carefully designed and managed, but also a possibility for support and output legitimacy if it is well designed and managed. Participation in a process is important if participants are to perceive their needs and concerns addressed, but participation must be equalised in regard to access and power in order to avoid the risk of capture and illegitimacy due to an actual or perceived imbalance.

This then relates to deliberation as a qualified form of debate characterised by procedure as an external framework for ensuring that the 'uncoerced force' of the better argument can unfold in the internal, substantive part of the debate, which leads to the development of new norms of conduct. Recall in this context that bargaining offers an alternative where true deliberation is not possible. Here, too, procedure is as important as the external framework for the quality of the internal process leading to the negotiated result (the output). For practical purposes, bargaining and negotiation are therefore what normally occur. Going forward, the discussion of 'deliberation' covers such practically occurring situations of bargaining and negotiation as well. As explained in Chapter 4, subsections 4.3.1 and 4.3.2, for law to derive validity through the consent of the governed, not only must law be made through a process that formally allows the governed to provide input for the co-creation of joint will, but the process must be proceduralised in order to enable stakeholders actually to develop and share views in a balanced manner among themselves and with other groups and feed this into the political and law-making process. The deliberative turn in the social sciences that builds on Habermasian deliberative theory has tended to focus more on the debate that unfolds within a proceduralised forum for deliberation than on the procedure itself. In this chapter, the procedure is the key element, because it complements reflexive law, which already incorporates elements of a debate and exchange of views for co-creation of norms of conduct. The formality of procedure creates the stable and predictable framework that is necessary for the substantive elements of a qualified deliberation or other debate, which is balanced in terms of power, to unfold.

Activated at three different levels of governance, reflexive law relates to both the framing and the substance of the regulatory process. The first two levels frame the process, whereas the final level, in which the learning produced through exposure to the environment's concerns and needs leads to new norms, is dependent on the former for the input and irritation to develop the necessary perturbation for normative change. This is where reflexive law is deficient in not prescribing how the design of the process and its management must be proceduralised so as to ensure that power is balanced in such a way that it does not distort the quality of the debate and the legitimacy of the output. The case studies, in particular the MSF process, proved that this issue must be taken seriously.

In consequence, the subsequent sections will particularly look at deliberation as a law-making practice and its exercise at the super-national level.

As described earlier, Teubner's theory on reflexive law pre-dates some of the Habermasian theory on deliberative discourse as a modality for creating legitimate norms.[1] When he developed reflexive law theory in the 1980s, Teubner therefore did not have the opportunity to consider the work on legitimate law-making through deliberative discourse that Habermas developed in *Faktizität und Geltung* (1992)/*Between Facts and Norms* (1996). Habermas, on the other hand, had the benefit of almost ten years of additional debates surrounding law-making and legitimacy. This included a focus on the public's right to participate in the public processes of norm-creation which prevailed in Europe in the late 1980s and early 1990s in regard to political decision-making, including law-making. Habermasian deliberative law-making theory, given that it developed after the launch of reflexive law theory and with a somewhat different objective, therefore, may provide guidance to complement reflexive law in the crucial aspect of balancing power disparities.

While scholars are divided on the need for new or reformed institutional structures,[2] Habermas's model for a super-national deliberative decision-making system embodying a global civil society has generated considerable interest. The deliberative turn in social sciences, noted above, is largely inspired by Habermas, but also develops further theoretical implications, which in some cases are more practice-oriented than the typical work of Habermas himself. This adds applicability to the highly abstract Habermasian theory on global governance and law in the 'post-national constellation', that is, for super-national law-making, which often relates to transnational economic activity or sustainability impacts.

Like other Habermasian theory, the global governance-oriented strain does not deliver a blueprint. Some find it lacking in feasibility or lacking from a democracy perspective because, while providing for the global public to have access to influence as a matter of principle, it does not provide for actual rights of participation.[3] Moreover, there are the technical difficulties of establishing deliberation at a transnational level.[4] The possibility that Habermas's ideas of a global democracy may require further elaboration does not, however, detract from the point that broad deliberation in a transnationalising world may contribute legitimacy to the normative products of super-national rule-making, with potential beneficial effects on the effectiveness of such rules in a society with limited enforcement modalities. In this respect, Teubner's and Habermas's theories are in fact mutually complementary. Not only do post-1980 Habermasian ideas add to reflexive law, as already suggested, but, in setting out a process for communication to stimulate learning of other stakeholders' concerns that may feed into self-regulation, Teubner's reflexive law theory also adds to Habermasian theory on deliberation. For law-making at the super-national level, it helps bring a substantive and practical aspect to how to make deliberation at that level of law-making feasible. Despite reflexive law not formally requiring the participation of all affected, it implicitly assumes that those who will be affected by a rule will be involved in the process of developing it, in order for the rule to be relevant to the local context and to carry a compliance pull. Where Habermasian deliberative law-making establishes an option for the public to participate through civil and political rights, Teubner's theory

1 References here are to the English translation: Habermas (1996) *Between Facts and Norms.*
2 See, for example, Scheuerman, W. E. (2006) 'Critical theory beyond Habermas', in J. S. Dryzek, B. Honig and A. Phillips (eds), *The Oxford Handbook of Political Theory*, New York: Oxford University Press, pp. 85–105, esp. at pp. 90–92.
3 Ibid.
4 Ibid.

assumes that authorities ensure that affected actors are involved. The fact that an exchange of views and concerns at the second and third levels of reflexive law may occur through a virtual process of communication makes it technically feasible in the age of electronic communication. The SRSG process and its use of IT-based communication is a case in point.

Recall that, as noted above, Habermas recognises that involving non-state actors in negotiations, as well as through procedures that promote compromises and negotiated results among independent decision-making actors, in principle offers alternatives to state-centrist international law-making. Being inclusive beyond states – and therefore also beyond states as members of international organisations such as the UN – these methods may remedy the legitimacy gap which faces law-making with effects beyond states and those who feel represented by them.[5]

This is precisely the development that to varying degrees may be observed in the cases discussed above. In a pragmatic fashion, particularly the UN Global Compact and the SRSG have included non-state actors in developing norms that seek to regulate what the international society has not been able to agree on through conventional international law. Taking an informal path, the Global Compact and especially the SRSG processes have provided their outputs with legitimacy by including representatives of a global citizenry, including companies and human rights victims as well as other interest groups, in the development of norms on business social responsibilities. While the public–private collaboration path taken by the Global Compact was initially perceived as controversial by some human rights NGOs and scholars, and while it suffered a legitimacy critique, the Global Compact was nevertheless groundbreaking in its process, its output, and the reception of the output as legitimate. Even though NGOs were included later than companies, they were provided with considerable influence through participation in the development of the Global Compact website and its guidance on the principles. The holder of the SRSG mandate benefited from lessons learnt through the process to establish the Global Compact and by more extensive and perhaps deliberate usage of electronic communication to provide more stakeholders with access to participation. Although also innovative, the MSF adopted a path closer to that already travelled for EU labour lawmaking, but with less focus on the formal procedural conditions for equal participation than those applied by the Global Compact and the SRSG. Basically involving companies and providing little transparency, the CSR Alliance on the surface adopts a new approach, but in practice only shifts collaboration and law-making powers of states to companies, that is, from one powerful actor to another. The impact is observable in the reception of the Alliance by civil society as not legitimate, and arguably also its limited outputs to date.

The deliberative turn literature suggests that, in relation to super-national decision-making, a formalisation of civil society's participation will raise the legitimacy of process and output. It is important, however, that such civil society participation also links to decision-making processes at lower levels. As Habermas explains, those that enjoy the power to act with regard to making rules and decisions at the global level need to consider themselves as members of a community in which members take the specific concerns of others as

---

5 Habermas, J. (2005) 'Efter nationalstaten? Bemærkninger til den økonomiske globaliserings følgeproblemer', in H. Andersen (ed.), *Jürgen Habermas: Demokrati og retsstat – en tekstsamling*, Copenhagen: Hans Reitzels Forlag, pp. 204–219, translated into Danish from Habermas, J. (1998) 'Jenseits der Nationalstaats: Bemerkungen zu Folgeprobleme der wirtschaftlichen Globalisierung', in U. Beck (ed.), *Politik der Globalisierung*, Frankfurt am Main: Suhrkamp, pp. 67–84; Habermas (2008) 'The constitutionalization of international law and the legitimation process of a constitution for world society'.

well as general common interests into consideration.[6] While it has not been addressed in great detail, developing procedures for this presents a challenge that is also familiar from much national and other networked governance.

To both Habermas and Teubner, exchanges of views on needs and concerns are important elements in the regulatory process for the output to materialise. Such changes connect to language as a means of communication. However, their approaches differ here. Teubner approaches language from the perspective of systems' core concerns (expressed in their binary codes of the logic or rationality core of that concern and its opposite) and the capacity of language to provoke change through creating irritants and perturbation. Habermas sees language as a general communicative means for the exchange of views and ideas and for reaching understanding – in everyday matters and in political or legal rule-making. From Habermas's perspective, language is a modality for communicative reason and the formation of common opinion and will. Citizens communicate through the use of language to bring reason and will together to create normative positions that all concerned individuals are willing to agree to. Every claim, statement or other speech act involves the raising of validity claims aimed at recognition by others and coordinating views towards agreement. By raising a validity claim, the speaker takes on a commitment to substantiate the claim with the right kind of reasons, should this be necessary. Thus, use of language for mutual understanding functions in such a way that participants either agree on the validity claimed for their speech acts or identify points of disagreement to be taken into consideration in the course of further interaction.[7] This communicative process is about transforming input into output and therefore depends on the procedural elements that frame throughput conditions. An institutionalised procedure supports the process towards delivering the necessary framework for common will or a negotiated result to emerge. To Habermas, if the procedure provides for equal access and participation, the result will reflect the common sum of good will, intentions and interests in a balanced way.

The analysis of the empirical cases above suggests that development of sustainability norms of conduct and related rule-making at the super-national level may be strengthened in terms of process as well as output by an inclusive and balanced increased participation of stakeholders. This means allowing not only states but also other representatives of civil society to take part in the processes. This may be achieved by involving NGOs and other civil society actors, and ensuring a broad representation of interests, including as relevant economic, social or other interests. At the super-national stage, it is neither sufficient nor possible to look for the embodiment of sovereign will through individual persons and electoral acts. However, in a number of fields the state-centrist international structure has also proven inadequately adept at delivering legitimate rule creation. The Draft UN Norms process is a case is point, as are the difficulties that states had in obtaining significant legal or even political agreement on reducing greenhouse gas emissions and promoting global climate regulation until the Climate Change Accord was made in 2015. Impact on sustainability that is currently caused by business organisations and which often affects other non-state actors (individuals or groups) is often also beyond the boundary of home-state jurisdiction owing to the transnational character of the business operations or of the activity itself. There is a need for rule-making that effectively targets the activities and actors that cause this impact. This calls for a shift towards processes that allow for the participation of non-state actors.

---

6 Habermas (1998) 'Jenseits der Nationalstaats'; Habermas, J. (2005) 'Den postnationale konstellation og demokratiets fremtid', esp. at pp. 270–272.

7 Habermas (1996) *Between Facts and Norms*, esp. chap. 1.

The SRSG process and to a more limited extent the Global Compact and ISO 26000 suggest that super-national rule-making on sustainability-related issues may be possible with the inclusion and participation of a global citizenry through processes that allow for exchange of views, needs and expectations along the lines of reflexive law. Those cases also show that such processes may include options for individual persons, groups or organisations to exchange views, as well as for such views to be channelled through representative organisations or networks.

This is not to say that reflexive law forums, even those whose design provides for proceduralised equalisation among participants, are applicable to all global concerns that affect and draw on multiple actors and social sub-systems. Yet, drawing on Thomas Risse's point that those issue areas which are already subjected to a high degree of international regulation (such as human rights and the environment) appear to lend themselves particularly well to super-national deliberation based on proceduralised equalisation, it is feasible that carefully designed reflexive law forums will have a potential to contribute to problem-solving in sustainability-related issue areas. As also noted by Risse,[8] equality of access and participation in discourse may require a disproportionate empowerment of weaker actors, such as civil society organisations, at least for a time. Similarly, temporary affirmative action is already recognised by international human rights law.

Whereas Habermasian theory is sophisticated in recognising that procedures must be institutionalised to provide for equal access, Teubner's theory is equally sophisticated in recognising that outputs are shaped by playing on concerns raised by other participants and communicating in a manner that speaks to their system-specific interest and through their logic. The above chapters have shown that outputs are determined by more than a simple exchange of views and that they are driven by systems-specific concerns and priorities far beyond what may look like simple recognition or rejection of the concerns of other actors.

While Habermasian theory and Teubner's reflexive law theory are distinct, they share an objective of contributing to law-making that enjoys support from those subjected to the rules, and taking into consideration the participation of those who are to be subjected to rules. In a number of ways, Habermas and Teubner want to achieve the same ideals in terms of participatory law-making that has been created by those to whom the rules would apply. This is a reason why Teubner not only built his theory on systems theory, but also looked to Habermasian theory as inspiration for reflexive law. Habermas's legitimacy perspective feeds into reflexive law, as it is conducive to law-making in that it would be effectively implemented because it would be made by those to whom it mattered. But the theories also differ. Developed after Teubner's reflexive law, Habermas's idea of deliberative law-making differs from reflexive law theory by stressing the procedural significance for legitimacy of involving non-state actors and providing equalised participation rather than simply relying on the transmission of perturbation to cause the internalisation of externalities and (self-)regulation. Moreover, Habermas's and Teubner's theories for participatory rule-making are activated at different levels of society. Habermas's is activated at the overall level of general law-making. While Teubner's theory, as described in Chapter 5, subsection 5.2.1, assumes reflection and action at several levels of governance, the essential one for the regulatory output is the level of norm-making within a functional sub-system or its elements (such as a business). Yet through their differences the two theories may complement each other, because each contains elements that the other does not have.

---

8 Risse (2000) "'Let's argue'", at p. 19.

In a context of transnational or international law-making through multi-stakeholder-based approaches, reflexive law and legitimate law-making have much in common. The deliberative theory provides important guidance for the legitimacy of the deliberative character of the reflexive regulatory process and its outcome, while the reflexive law paradigm may provide the outer procedure to frame the process. Habermas deals not only with the procedural conditions for the 'uncoerced force' of the better argument to thrive and for rational discourse allowing parties whose interests are affected to exchange views and make joint normative decisions, but also with how such participatory law-making may be lifted from the national to the above-national level.

The challenges that face a transfer of the structure of deliberative law-making and its institutionalised procedures to law-making in the context of the UN and other intergovernmental organisations need not be obstacles to discussing or assessing rule-making procedures or outputs at this level with regard to legitimacy.[9] Habermas argues that participation makes for legitimacy of norms in regulatory instruments, that legitimacy makes for acceptance of resulting constraints, and that the above-national system must strive to accommodate these concerns. In the perspective of reflexive law-making as well as the particularities of hybrid rule-making on the social responsibilities of business enterprises, these points provide a reason both to acknowledge the potential legitimacy of informal procedures and outputs and to seek to integrate institutionalised rights-based procedures in processes of rule-making at the super-national level.

On the basis of the observations set out above, reflexive law and later Habermasian theory can be applied as mutually supporting for a comprehensive theory of collaborative regulation. Teubner's theory is concrete where Habermas is abstract; and the Habermasian focus on proceduralised access to and equality of participation in law-making adds to reflexive law where the latter is limited in terms of directives for procedural design.

By focusing on what goes on during the law-making process, Habermasian theory offers a potential solution to the power-related problems in reflexive law. While not a blueprint, Habermasian theory on deliberative law-making has the capacity to offer some of the directives that Teubner neglected to describe with regard to achieving balanced power between participants in a reflexive law forum.

The presumption that bargaining becomes necessary when involved needs and concerns are particular to specific actors and not generalisable accords with the types of situations in which needs for reflexive law-making typically arise. Considered from the reflexive law perspective, these are precisely the types of situations in which a variety of interests are at stake, representing the variety of needs and concerns of participating (sub-)systems. The 2002–2004 period of the European MSF on CSR was marked by significant and irreconcilable differences in interests and perceived objectives, and the output, a report containing a series of recommendations, was reached through a process that involved a measure of negotiation. However, it did not live up to the ideal of bargaining, because power disparities affected the debate and agreement, damaging throughput and output legitimacy. The SRSG process opened as something close to bargaining and developed into a consensus-seeking forum because the argumentative strategy deployed by the SRSG convinced actors of the common interest in reaching an output that institutionalised norms on business responsibilities for human rights.

9 Compare also Willke, H. and Willke, G. (2007) 'Corporate moral legitimacy and the legitimacy of morals: A critique of Palazzo/Scherer's communicative framework', *Journal of Business Ethics*, Vol. 81, No. 1, pp. 27–38.

Accordingly, the remainder of this chapter and particularly the following chapter apply Habermasian theory to fill the gap in reflexive law theory on how to balance power disparities by ensuring balanced participation and achieve legitimacy of the process so that it may become effective towards delivering an accepted output with an inherent compliance pull. The focus is on rule-making processes at the super-national level, with particular emphasis on involving non-state actors as participants. The following sections revert to the empirical case studies to provide examples of reflexive law instances or outputs in which legitimacy deficits were a problem owing to inadequate procedural design to balance power disparities. Chapter 7 builds on this to develop proceduralisation to fill the lacuna in reflexive law and develop a theory for collaborative regulation.

6.2 Procedural design and process management

The processes and outputs of efforts at developing norms on sustainability-related issues through the Draft UN Norms, the Global Compact, the SRSG process, the MSF, the CSR Alliance and ISO 26000 suggest that, for the effective delivery of an output that is substantively normative, representation of those interests that are the most opposed to the intended regulatory output is significant. The European MSF on CSR and the SRSG process also suggest that the establishing authority or a person appointed by the authority to be in charge must also take a strong role in the process. In the MSF, the EU Commission was formally in charge but in terms of procedure stepped out of direct participation. The Commission was unable to take direct part in balancing power disparities between participants in the MSF process, or to remind participants of the original objective of the regulatory process. As a result, the output became twisted if compared with the objective, offering less direct normative guidance and suffering legitimacy deficits in the eyes of civil society and certain other groups. The MSF process and output underscore the importance of balancing power disparities to neutralise privilege of knowledge or access in a reflexive regulatory forum for the process to be effective and legitimate. The Draft UN Norms, the Global Compact and the MSF were met with hesitation or even opposition by certain business organisations and civil society, respectively.

Those reactions to the initiatives or their outputs indicate that, unless participation of the interests of those opposed to the intended normative output is balanced by the participation of others that are in favour or neutral, the legitimacy of the process and its output may be compromised. To appreciate why this occurs it is useful to keep in mind that procedure has an objective beyond formalities. Formality by itself can stifle a process of debate and decision-making rather than support it. To be meaningful, procedures must support a process towards the qualitative decision that is to be made. Procedure establishes the outer framework for trust, without which the legitimacy of a process or an output will be inadequate.

The reactions from civil society to the original design of the process towards the Global Compact or to the design of the CSR Alliance and by certain business organisations to the stakeholder consultation process towards the Draft UN Norms suggest that legitimacy was hurt because the design did not inspire trust from the outside in what was going on within the regulatory process. Similarly, reactions by civil society to the manner in which the MSF process unfolded and to the way in which the situation of victims and remedy were addressed during parts of the SRSG's mandate indicate that trust in the process being balanced was lacking. By contrast, once composition of the Global Compact became more balanced and when the SRSG process took concerns on the situation of victims more visibly into account, trust in the process rose. As a result, the quality of the debate and exchange of views that took place within the outer framework created by procedural process design and management also increased, and the substantive output benefited both in terms of delivery on the original objective and in terms of acceptance of the output.

This demonstrates that, if the procedural design of a reflexive regulatory process does not handle power disparities, such an imbalance is likely to affect the effectiveness of the process as well as the normative output. Analysis of the Global Compact, on the other hand, suggests that power disparities can be managed by authorities when they respond to stakeholders' concerns about not being sufficiently represented, even if this means that participation is based on a selection made by the authorities. The Global Compact architects were successful in turning a legitimacy crisis around by including NGOs when it was realised that their exclusion threatened civil society's support for the prospective output. Similarly, the ISO process indicates that grouping participants into agreed designated groups – something that assumes a strong management role by the organisation in charge of the process – can serve to balance power and promote legitimacy of process and output.

What is in focus here is distinct from deliberation or bargaining in terms of cleverly arguing a case, that is, the Habermasian deliberative better argument. Power disparities may result for example from politically based power based on alliances or networks, experience with the politics and negotiation patterns of a particular organisation or institutional setting, and sometimes disproportionally favourable representation. Asymmetrical power may result in negotiation outputs that are also disproportionate to the concerns and policy needs intended to be promoted or protected through the reflexive law forum itself. The quality of management of the reflexive forum may be addressed through design of the reflexive procedure, criteria for inclusion of actors, and authorities' role in directing the process of negotiation. Whether the aim is fully fledged deliberation or bargaining, design and management of reflexive regulatory forums matter.

Several NGOs were initially very apprehensive of the Global Compact. Along with support from the international labour and employer movements, the participation by some of the largest and most respected NGOs within the issue areas, however, provided the initiative with a relatively broad participation and representation of potential victims of human and labour rights infringements. This opened options for a limited but not insignificant degree of throughput legitimacy. Eventually, this led to a softening of NGOs' original antagonistic approach to the Global Compact initiative. The steering process of the UN Secretary-General's Office and the UN Global Compact Office contributed to ensuring an element of equalisation among participants.

The production of norms through a collaborative regulatory process should be procedurally structured so as to even out formal, informal but explicit, or even implicit power disparities in order to stimulate the mutual appreciation of concerns and needs as well as knowledge with a view to creating proactive regulation. In addition, it should provide for actual participation in a balanced way. Similar to reflexive law, which contains a normative aspect in relation to balancing power disparities, proceduralised deliberation contains a normative element related to the quality of conditions for an exchange of arguments and a quality of debate to be conducive to consensus or at least bargaining, leading to common acceptance of the resulting norms. The example of the MSF demonstrates that it is not sufficient to provide the formal institutional framework for social actors to meet, make speeches, exchange reports and views on needs and interests, and so on. Within the institutional framework provided for the MSF, the debate was soon politicised into non-state participants guarding already established positions. The Commission sought to engage business in implementing public policy objectives, but its steering role in the MSF was weak. The framework was not appropriate for the exchange of arguments at a deeper level to provide for consensus, even through bargaining. The difficulties and frustrations were particularly noticeable in statements at the final high level meeting during the presentation of the Final MSF Report, as elaborated below.

Publicly available texts indicate that a number of legitimacy issues arose in relation to the SRSG process, the MSF, the Global Compact and the CSR Alliance. Several written statements or official summaries of spoken text from the MSF and CSR Alliance are particularly clear examples that suggest that these issues often arose as a result of inadequate balancing of power, whether in the form of participation, privilege or forward-looking measures to handle abuses or remedy for victims of corporate-related human rights abuse.

In the MSF, business organisations[10] noted that the MSF Final Report was a 'consensual report'[11] building on 'common understanding that [had] been gained' through the process.[12] One of these organisations referred to the process of negotiation 'taking sufficiently into account the views and opinions of all sides', suggesting a link to perceived legitimacy of the MSF, and noted that the MSF results had taken 'sufficiently into account the views and opinions of all sides'.[13] However, some hesitation was expressed towards the adequacy of the process to include the views of 'all stakeholders, including representatives from developing countries'.[14]

By contrast, NGO statements indicated that those organisations did not see the MSF as providing them (as representatives of European civil society) with as balanced an influence as they would have liked on the outcome compared to business and employers' organisations. They noted that the Final Report's contents reflected the structural imbalances that those organisations had noted with regard to the composition and process of the MSF.[15]

The views suggest that the MSF was deficient in throughput legitimacy because the procedure did not sufficiently cater for broad and balanced representation of views and interests. Although business organisations also expressed that the process had been marked by 'very different understandings and divergent views',[16] their reception of the output was positive compared to the hesitation that civil society organisations expressed. From the NGO perspective, the Final Report did not represent the consensus or common understanding that business noted.[17]

In setting up the CSR Alliance, the Commission indicated that it was aware of possible legitimacy issues. It noted that the legitimacy of the CSR Alliance, and other proposals made in the 2006 Communication, was based on the multi-stakeholder-oriented dialogue preceding

---

10 European Multi-Stakeholder Forum on CSR (2004) *Final High Level Meeting, Minutes*, 29 June, http://circa. europa.eu/irc/empl/csr_eu_multi_stakeholder_forum/info/data/en/CSR%20Forum%20040629%20minutes.htm (last accessed 17 February 2013, webpage has been removed).

11 Eurocommerce (2004) *Statement by Eurocommerce*, EU Multi-Stakeholder Forum on CSR, Final High Level Meeting, 29 June, http://circa.europa.eu/irc/empl/csr_eu_multi_stakeholder_forum/info/data/en/CSR%20Forum%20040629%20speech%20Eurocommerce.htm (last accessed 15 February 2013, webpage has been removed).

12 European Multi-Stakeholder Forum on CSR (2004), *Final High Level Meeting, Minutes*.

13 Ibid.

14 Ibid.

15 Ibid.

16 Buck, P. de (2004) *Statement by Philippe de Buck – Secretary General UNICE*, EU Multi-Stakeholder Forum on CSR, Final High Level Meeting, 29 June, http://circa.europa.eu/irc/empl/csr_eu_multi_stakeholder_forum/info/data/en/CSR%20Forum%20040629%20speech%20UNICE.htm (last accessed 15 February 2013, webpage has been removed).

17 McLaren (2004) *Statement on Behalf of the Green 8*; Parent (2004) *Statement of the Social Platform*; Fédération Internationale des Droits de l'Homme (2013) *Statement by FIDH*.

it, and that it drew on several years of public debate and consultation with all stakeholders, most particularly in the context of the European Multi-Stakeholder Forum on CSR.[18]

Some paragraphs in the Commission's 2006 Communication also suggest that the Commission was aware of the significance of involving stakeholders in order to 'enhance the effectiveness of CSR initiatives' and obtain 'credibility'. The Commission stated that 'involving stakeholders enhances the effectiveness of CSR initiatives, which is why the Commission will organise regular review meetings of the Multistakeholder Forum. To foster greater awareness of CSR and further enhance its credibility, the Commission will continue to promote and support CSR initiatives by stakeholders, including social partners and NGOs, and in particular at sectoral level.'[19]

Despite somewhat similar backdrops and normative objectives, the Global Compact was relatively more successful than the EU MSF in establishing norms on CSR, including principles on human rights. The Global Compact preparatory process led to agreement on nine and later ten specific principles, all based in international law. The MSF led to a much weaker result in terms of specific normativity on CSR, let alone a normatively principled foundation in international law. Several possible reasons explain the difference despite the fact that NGOs were involved earlier and seemingly with – at least formally – a stronger role in the MSF than in the Global Compact. First, the procedural set-up of the Global Compact provided the intergovernmental body in charge, that is, the UN Secretariat, with a stronger say in terms of both procedural steering and constructing normative substance than that which the EU Commission dealt itself with regard to the MSF. Second, business was engaged directly with the UN (this included UN organisations with mandates related to ensuring the objectives of the international law instruments that inform the nine original principles), allowing for perhaps fewer constraints in terms of getting business-politically sensitive issues on the table and discussing them frankly with the organisations and individuals representing the UN than was the case with the EU MSF. This may have strengthened the deliberative quality of the process and contributed to its effectiveness in terms of throughput legitimacy catering for agreement on the substantively fairly detailed Global Compact principles and them being based in international law instruments.

As noted, it has been argued that deliberative argumentation for the development of norms perceived to be legitimate may be particularly effective when relating to norms that are already institutionalised.[20] This, again, applies to human rights which are long institutionalised as international as well as regional (including European) human rights law. Yet comparison between the Global Compact and the MSF suggests that simple institutionalisation of norms is not sufficient to cater for the output effectiveness of a multi-stakeholder forum established with the aim of developing a particular substantive normativity. The key, rather, could be that international human rights law may be perceived to be global sustainability-related international law rather than European international (Council of Europe) law, let alone EU law.

The EU Commission's decision not to include social and environmental civil society organisations in the CSR Alliance was intended to reduce tensions between participants and

---

18 Commission of the European Communities (2006) *Communication from the Commission to the European Parliament, the Council and the European Economic and Social Committee*, at p. 3.

19 Ibid., at pp. 6–8.

20 Risse, T., Ropp, S. C. and Sikkink, K. (eds) (1999) *The Power of Human Rights: International Norms and Human Rights*, Cambridge: Cambridge University Press; Risse, T. (2005) 'Global governance and communicative action', in D. Held and M. Koenig-Archibugi (eds), *Global Governance and Public Accountability*, Malden, MA: Blackwell, pp. 164–189.

therefore stimulate interaction between business, but this composition resulted in reduced overall legitimacy. Moreover, the compositional design of the CSR Alliance carried over the power of business on further EU CSR work from the MSF, further damaging process legitimacy from the perspective of civil society.

Civil society's responses to the CSR Alliance and to the original exclusive composition of the group that developed the Global Compact underscore the observation that, unless all relevant stakeholders are involved in the process with a qualitative equality of access and actual participation in a discursive process of developing rules, the result will not be perceived as legitimate in the sense of representing interests in a balanced way. Reactions by NGOs to the Global Compact initially and to the composition of the CSR Alliance highlight that, for the development of sustainability-related norms to be legitimate, procedures should remain open for dissent and promote the expression of marginalised interests and values.[21]

Similar points are indicated by several statements from participants in the SRSG process. A September 2005 letter from Amnesty International encouraged the SRSG to engage in wide consultation and listen to affected communities, noting that this would help build consensus.[22]

A statement made by Asian civil society organisations at the SRSG's regional consultation in Bangkok in June 2006 also suggests that, in the view of this network organisation, the legitimacy of the output of the SRSG process depended on its reflection of the concerns of stakeholders broadly. This statement is an indication in practice that legitimacy and broad consultations are interdependent, that is, an understanding of legitimacy similar to the one discussed above in this study. It observed that the SRSG's recommendations would only be effective if they reflected the views, concerns, inputs, experiences and knowledge of the whole range of affected parties, including corporations, trade unions, governments, communities and civil society organisations.[23] Overall, civil society organisations expressed concern with the process adequately taking the needs of victims into account.[24] Much of this concern has continued in the critique of the UNGPs after their adoption, confirming the need to take concerns voiced by stakeholders or their representatives during a process seriously for the longer-term support for an output and therefore its legitimacy. In the SRSG process, the critique led to changes even during the first term (2005–2008), indicating a process of learning with the SRSG as an actor in the process. Concern voiced by civil society organisations that the SRSG process did not sufficiently take account of the need for remedy for victims of business-related human rights abuse played a role for the evolution of access to remedy as the third pillar.[25] This contributed to the legitimacy of the output, the UN Framework and the UNGPs, at the time of the adoption and in several

---

21 Compare Scherer, A. G. and Palazzo, G. (2007) 'Toward a political conception of corporate responsibility: Business and society seen from a Habermasian perspective', *Academy of Management Review*, Vol. 32, No. 4, pp. 1096–1120, at p. 1114.

22 Amnesty International (2005) *Letter to Professor John Ruggie*, 16 September, AI ref UN 260-2005.

23 *Asian Civil Society Statement to U.N. Special Representative on Transnational Business and Human Rights at the Asia Regional Consultation*, Bangkok, Thailand, 27 June 2006.

24 Clean Clothes Campaign (2007) *Letter to John Ruggie*, Amsterdam, 23 March, http://www.business-human rights.org/Documents/Clean-Clothes-Campaign-letter-Ruggie-23-Mar-2007.pdf (last accessed 30 December 2016); *Joint NGO Letter on Work of the Mandate*, 10 October 2007, available at the Business and Human Rights Resource Centre SRSG portal in version dated 25 October 2007.

25 Buhmann (2014) *Normative Discourses and Public–Private Regulatory Strategies for Construction of CSR Normativity*, chapter 6–7.

regards for their later application and further elaboration for practice in a range of settings, from policy-makers to civil society, business and scholars.[26]

In this respect, the Habermasian perspective on proceduralised equalised access to deliberation adds a qualitative aspect to Teubner's argument that reflexive regulatory processes should handle power disparities, allowing weaker groups real participation rather than simply formal presence. NGO opposition to the EU MSF output and to the Global Compact for lack of accountability underscores this point of the significance of the deliberative approach. NGO hesitation towards the SRSG process was expressed through the process, which allowed for oral and written submission, resembling a form of deliberation.

Yet the ability that the Global Compact and the SRSG process displayed to adapt to outside concerns, such as NGO critique about the Global Compact being too business-friendly, by engaging civil society more directly and by establishing integrity measures, and for the SRSG process to internalise concerns about the need for remedy for victims of business-related human rights abuse exemplifies the significance of the inclusive deliberative approach and the willingness of the formal 'rule-maker' to heed input from participants towards the output. This may be contrasted with the approach taken by the EU Commission when the MSF did not deliver the originally intended results. The Commission instituted a completely new and more exclusive initiative, the CSR Alliance, as a result of or perhaps response to the limited normative output of the MSF. The EU's approach went from being widely inclusive to being more exclusively business-oriented, while the Global Compact went from initially mainly engaging business to being more inclusive, also engaging civil society and more recently public institutions, cities and others as members or stakeholders. This observation underscores that a deliberative approach to hybrid law-making indeed does have the potential to add legitimacy to processes that otherwise function along the lines of the paradigm of reflexive law. In particular, it underscores that the normative quality of equalisation that is inherent in the ideal of deliberation may provide an additional normative quality to the procedural aspects of reflexive regulation. This strengthens the case for proceduralisation to provide for equalised access and participation.

6.3 Procedure, trust and legitimacy

The role of procedure for trust in order for a process and its output to enjoy legitimacy has been confirmed by studies of the development and implementation of remedy for business-related human rights abuse.

Work undertaken by the SRSG and his team during the second mandate term (2008–2011) supports the significance of perceived legitimacy for the acceptance of a normative output. A pilot testing that took place during that period of the principle of *remedy*, that is, the 'third pillar' that had been proposed by the UN Framework, established that trust among intended users of a grievance mechanism is of paramount importance if the mechanism is to achieve legitimacy. Experience from operational-level tests of the sub-principles for grievance mechanisms that were developed by the UN Framework[27]

---

26 Some academic critique voiced since the adoption of the two outputs has continued to express concern with the consideration of victims. See, in particular, Deva (2010) '"Protect, respect and remedy"'; Deva (2013) 'Treating human rights lightly'.

27 According to para. 92 of the UN Framework, which established six sub-principles for the non-judicial remedy mechanisms, such mechanisms should be legitimate, accessible, predictable, equitable, rights-compatible and transparent.

underlined that while upwards legitimacy for an operational-level grievance mechanism could provide formal legitimacy and important incentives to ensure that the mechanism worked effectively, the ultimate test was whether its intended end-users trusted it enough to use it. In other words, the perception of its legitimacy among those users was the more essential factor.[28]

This observation on perceived legitimacy in practice was found to be so important that the sub-principle on legitimacy requirements of grievance mechanisms was altered between the SRSG's 2008 and 2011 reports to accommodate it. The alteration meant less focus on formal governance structures and more on achieving trust with involved stakeholders in practice.[29] This highlights the point made above that perceived legitimacy is significant for the acceptance and application of a regulatory process and its output, and therefore for its effectiveness.

Although of course reflexive law and grievance mechanisms for corporate-related human rights violations differ in several ways, they have similarities. Both are characterised by an aim to develop solutions that take account of stakeholders' interests within a broader context of social sustainability and often business impacts, and both take place in contexts where issues of disparity of formal and actual power among participants are frequent. Moreover, both are characterised by potential differential experience between actors with such or related processes. They are also composed of groups representing diverging interests. The fact that the formal law-orientated sub-principles for the *remedy* part of the UN Framework were altered as a result of practical experience underscores that design of modalities to deliver effective regulation and change in the field of human rights and business and related sustainability contexts needs to pay close attention to the perceptions of those whose interests are directly affected as well as those who represent interests on behalf of others (such as non-state organisations, whether non-profit or for-profit). For multi-stakeholder processes for law-making on sustainability, it underlines the importance of paying attention to the interests of non-state actors in a way that transcends formal representation and/or formal organisation of reflexive law forums consisting of a range of interest groups, including social sub-systems, by providing for participation and balanced inclusiveness in practice.

Also testifying to the importance of a proper and relevant procedure to handle power disparities in a remedy process to ensure its legitimacy, power issues have been found in other practice contexts to be significant for the legitimacy of a remedy process and the appropriateness of the outputs. A remedy mechanism that was set up in 2012 by Canadian mining company Barrick Gold Corporation to offer reparations to women sexually assaulted by the security guards and other company employees at the Porgera Joint Venture gold mine in Papua New Guinea has been found to be marked by severe procedural problems affecting trust, effectiveness and ultimately legitimacy. This occurred despite some positive features in terms of consultation, measures in relation to cultural sensitivity and transparency on the

---

28 Rees, C. (2011) *Piloting Principles for Effective Company–Stakeholder Grievance Mechanisms: A Report of Lessons Learned*, CSR Initiatives, Cambridge, MA: Harvard Kennedy School, at pp. 13–14.

29 The original (2008) wording of the legitimacy sub-principle, 'An operational-level grievance mechanism should be legitimate: having a clear, transparent and sufficiently independent governance structure to ensure that no party to a particular grievance process can interfere with the fair conduct of that process', was revised to 'enabling trust from the stakeholder groups for whose use they are intended, and being accountable for the fair conduct of grievance processes'. Rees (2011) *Piloting Principles for Effective Company–Stakeholder Grievance Mechanisms*, at pp. 13–15.

procedures for the remedy process.[30] The remedy mechanism has been found not to adequately overcome the acute power inequalities in Porgera, which occurred not just between the company and the community, but also between genders and other sub-entities within the community.[31] This had a substantial effect on the trust inspired by the remedy mechanism and its effectiveness. Studies of the Barrick Porgera remedy mechanism observe that, to mitigate the risk that such power differences undermine individuals' rights, procedural safeguards must be put in place to address and manage the balance of bargaining power between corporations and rights-holders. Moreover, the Barrick remedy mechanism was found to treat the survivors as disempowered 'victims' and passive recipients rather than fully engaging them in all stages of the design and implementation of the mechanism that was intended to remedy serious human rights violations. This too undermined the mechanism's legitimacy and effectiveness in numerous ways.[32] Studies of the Porgera case have determined that joint design or appointment to the process is necessary to develop trust as a precondition for legitimacy, and in this context for ensuring free and informed choice and to take account of local context, perceptions and needs.[33]

These studies provide insights that are relevant for a regulatory process too. They underscore that, in processes which involve power relations and individuals or communities, trust is an important element for a process to be legitimate, that appropriate procedures are necessary for creating trust, and that this requires focus on the procedural conditions for creating the relevant substantive communication and development of the output. Finally, they underscore the importance of paying attention to local institutional and cultural specificities. Institutional mechanisms to be taken into account can include, for example, state-based or formal processes for decision-making and relations between the government and citizens or civil society. Cultural specificities can be related to a community as such, but may also be particular to certain entities within the community, such as members of a particular gender or other groups. As shown by the Porgera case, the multiple aspects of power not only between functional sub-systems but also within a community must be adequately taken into account in the design of a process that aims to address concerns related to sustainability and competing interests.

6.4 Summing up on findings before proceeding to the proposed solution

The above analysis indicates that relatively close procedural management of the reflexive regulatory process by the (intergovernmental) agency or individual in charge of the process may be required for a balanced process of negotiation and its output. In the case of the SRSG process, the consultations and options for organisations and individuals to submit views to the

30 Human Rights Clinic (Columbia Law School) and International Human Rights Clinic (Harvard Law School) (2015) *Righting Wrongs? Barrick Gold's Remedy Mechanism for Sexual Violence in Papua New Guinea: Key Concerns and Lessons Learned*, New York City and Boston, MA, November, http://hrp.law.harvard.edu/wp-content/uploads/2015/11/FINALBARRICK.pdf (accessed 16 November 2016).
31 Aftab, Y. (2016) *Pillar III on the Ground: An Independent Assessment of the Porgera Remedy Framework*, Enodo Rights, http://www.barrick.com/files/porgera/Enodo-Rights-Porgera-Remedy-Framework-Independent-Assessment.pdf (accessed 16 November 2016).
32 Ibid.; Human Rights Clinic (Columbia Law School) and International Human Rights Clinic (Harvard Law School) (2015) *Righting Wrongs?*
33 Aftab (2016) *Pillar III on the Ground*; Human Rights Clinic (Columbia Law School) and International Human Rights Clinic (Harvard Law School) (2015) *Righting Wrongs?*

SRSG in writing provided for a high degree of access and participation. The SRSG process and the Global Compact suggest that, in the absence of formal rights of participation for non-state actors, a process that is tightly managed by the intergovernmental institution in charge of the regulatory initiative may provide a substitute by ensuring a balancing of interests. Such tight management was absent in the Commission's role in the EU MSF.

Further, the Global Compact case suggests that hand-picking participants for a reflexive regulatory forum need not compromise the legitimacy of the normative output if participants represent a diverse range of interests and the output is based on normative sources that are themselves perceived to have a high degree of legitimacy. The fact that generally recognised expertise on the situation of those not directly represented – that is, victims or potential victims of human rights or labour rights infringements – was present through selected NGOs and UN organisations probably strengthened perceived (input) legitimacy, throughput and acceptance of a common solution that resulted in the output.

In conclusion, the analysis in this chapter has demonstrated that attention must be paid to procedure in order for a multi-stakeholder-based law-making process that presumes an exchange of views and needs to progress in a manner that is effective in delivering the intended output, and which is legitimate in terms of process as well as the output. The chapter has shown that procedure is a key element in deliberation and bargaining, but as happened to some extent and at some stage in all the empirical cases can be overlooked. The reason for such an oversight in the design and management of a regulatory process may well be a focus on the substantive quality or contents of the exchanges of views that take place within the regulatory process. However, as the chapter has shown, without procedure the quality of that debate does not support the substantive elements. As also supported by the studies of remedy processes to co-create decisions on appropriate reparation for business-related human rights abuse, without procedure to equalise participation and power disparities the arguments do not flow freely, and the better argument does not come to work through the 'uncoerced force' of its substantive quality. Rather, it may be overridden by others that have better access to the process or privileged insights, or it may override others with less such power. As a result, the process suffers in terms of trust, the effectiveness of the process to deliver the intended objective decreases, and both process and output are deficient in terms of legitimacy.

On this basis, Part 3 proceeds to develop the theory of collaborative regulation. This draws on reflexive law as well as more recent Habermasian theory for the purpose of proceduralisation to provide for equalised participation and balancing of power disparities in multi-stakeholder regulation. The theory has particular regard to super-national regulation of sustainability challenges. As will be explained in Chapter 7, the theory of collaborative regulation has validity also for regulatory processes that operate according to more conventional approaches than the instrumental and proactive co-regulation of reflexive law.

Part 3

Collaborative regulation

7 Foundations for collaborative regulation

Overview: Chapter 7 develops the theory of collaborative regulation. Collaborative regulation is proposed as a solution to the theory gap that must be remedied for reflexive law to deliver its considerable potential for regulating sustainability concerns. Moreover, this will support deliberative law-making in concrete settings of multi-stakeholder regulation at the super-national level. The chapter sets out the foundations that combine reflexive law and newer Habermasian theory with a particular focus on proceduralisation to provide for equalised participation and balancing of power disparities, elaborating on proceduralisation for the purpose of legitimate regulation. It explains what this means for the design of a regulatory process, and how proceduralisation may take inspiration from human rights and administrative law. It explains that in view of the role that substantive human rights law already plays for norms of conduct for business impacts on sustainability, it is reasonable to look for guidance from the procedural elements as well, and discusses the implications of this. Chapter 7 also discusses the deployment of IT-based communication which holds both opportunities for input as well as procedural challenges for equalising participation. Finally, the chapter discusses two future prospects for enhancing the balancing of power disparities in collaborative regulation: through a prospective treaty on procedural aspects of multi-stakeholder regulation in international law; and through an actual application pending the possible adoption of a treaty.

7.1 Scope of application

The previous chapters found that reflexive law offers an option for regulation of complex transnational sustainability concerns. In particular, applying reflexive law as a regulatory strategy may complement conventional international law-making where political or jurisdictional conditions act as practical constraints on conventional law-making. However, as seen in Chapter 6, the success depends on power disparities being equalised. This also means that participation should be equalised. When power disparities are not managed and participation is not equalised during the process, there is a risk that the regulatory process will not deliver the output that was intended, or that it will be skewed in terms of the interests that it favours and deficient in legitimacy. Thus, power disparities risk either corrupting the process and reducing its effectiveness in turning input into output, or hurting the reception and uptake of the output.

The theoretical insights and practical steps provided here are applicable beyond reflexive law. The process and fate of the Draft UN Norms demonstrate that even conventional international law-making needs to innovate in order to acknowledge and involve new actors with significant stakes in new norms of conduct. Business opposition to the Draft UN Norms shows that, when such innovation occurs, legitimacy of process and output may be compromised unless power not only is perceived to be balanced in a way that ensures equalised access to participating but also is perceived by those involved as well as observers, such as media or academics, not to favour or privilege particular interests.

From within a reflexive law context, the examples of the MSF and the aftermath of the SRSG process underscore that, if the inclusion of business helped generate support for the output among its own group, later legitimacy challenges may arise from stakeholders, such as civil society groups and academics, who did not perceive their own concerns or those of groups that they represent to be adequately addressed or included. These tell of the need to ensure that power is not perceived to be skewed in such a process.

Hence, managing power disparities is also significant for the legitimacy of conventional law-making processes and resulting outputs (including for law-in-process). As international policy- and law-making continues to address sustainability issues, whose solutions (as demonstrated by the SDGs' focus on partnerships) require cooperation between the public and the private sectors, the importance of addressing non-state actors' concerns will continue as well. The process towards the treaty on business and human rights that began in 2014 and is on-going at the time of writing is a case in point. With the establishment of the Open-Ended Intergovernmental Working Group, that process has taken off on a note that is closer to conventional international law-making than the process that resulted in the UNGPs. However, while stakeholder concerns may be voiced in diplomatic terms and benefit from insights that have arisen from numerous CSR and human rights-oriented multi-stakeholder events since the presentation and dismissal of the Draft UN Norms, underlying system-specific interests remain the same. Thus, while individual stakeholder concerns and needs may be voiced in terms relating to the institutional framework for international law and human rights protection, respect, fulfilment and remediation, businesses are still at a fundamental level concerned with making profits or suffering economic losses. Similarly, policy-oriented actors like governments and not-for-profit civil society organisations are still at a fundamental level concerned with gaining, retaining or losing power, including through seeing their proposals becoming adopted and thus demonstrating and upholding power within their immediate constituencies; and the legal system will continue to be focused on the distinction between whether something is legal or not. The empirical cases above have shown that to generate acceptance of change a communicative process is necessary that stimulates an appreciation of stakeholders' concerns and needs by addressing their significance to the underlying system-specific concerns. The analysis above also demonstrates that to develop sustainability-related norms of conduct it is therefore of paramount significance that actors in the process not only address concerns with due appreciation of the interests at stake for others involved[1] but also perceive and experience participation during the process as inclusive and balanced. This chapter addresses the latter issue through elaborating the foundations of the theory of collaborative regulation. Chapter 8 develops these foundations into a method entailing specific steps for a collaborative regulatory process to procedurally manage power disparities and deliver equalised participation.

In formal terms, the balancing of power disparities is already an entrenched part of the procedure in many processes of conventional regulation. However, the pressure on international law to expand its reach beyond the state-centric approach to duty-bearers and move towards a broader transnational focus also makes it relevant to consider power disparities

---

1 For an elaboration of argumentative strategies to address system-specific interests, see Buhmann (2018), *Changing Sustainability Norms through Communication Processes.*

and how to balance them in that context. While not a parallel to the involvement and role of states in international law-making, the inclusion of non-state actors as active participants in international law-making and as potential new duty-bearers arguably may represent an early step in a gradual integration of non-state actors in international law. Consequently, this may also be seen as an early step in providing such actors with international legal subjectivity not only in terms of being duty-bearers but also in terms of being participants in certain law-making processes. With the benefit of several decades of practical efforts in engaging business in social responsibility through formal law that provides guidance or establishes requirements, and various experiences in making such rules with and without direct business participation, the subsequent discussion and recommendations have their roots in the observations of Wolfgang Friedmann and Jonathan Charney in the 1960s and 1980s. While their observations were on the importance of involving businesses in rule-making pertaining to their conduct, the discussion and recommendations here also pertain to civil society and victims as well as stakeholders broadly, because the recent experience set out above proves that participation must be inclusive and balanced for all concerned, not just those subjected to new duties.

The theoretical foundations for collaborative regulation build on the analytical insight that a combination of newer Habermasian theory and reflexive law offers process-oriented directives applicable to multi-stakeholder regulation, whether or not organised from the perspective of reflexive law.

Accordingly, to close the theory lacuna on balancing power disparities in super-national law-making, the current chapter discusses what should be considered for a proceduralisation at an overall level of principle and concerns to be addressed in a law-making process at the super-national level, whether undertaken under state-centred international law or a hybrid transnational or multi-stakeholder process. Like conventional law-making in international law, reflexive law processes initiated under international organisations leave states with primacy as makers of international law. Collaborative regulation allows them to invite non-state actors into the law-making processes with particular significance for those actors, and to formally devise directives through procedural instructions applying to the process design and its management as a way of providing for equalised participation.

7.2 Proceduralisation

7.2.1 Procedure in Habermas's and Teubner's theories

Collaborative regulation rests on a combination of reflexive law and more recent Habermasian theory on legitimate law-making.

The foundational theory for legitimate law-making through collaborative regulation is both substantive and procedural, combining the two aspects with strong emphasis on their interrelatedness. The substantive aspects are concerned with concrete (substantive, material) outputs, such as norms of conduct, that are legitimate precisely because of the presence and quality of procedure for the throughput transfer of input into output.[2] This dual perspective on law as procedure and law as output means that the procedure of law-making draws legitimacy from a process in which citizens (as participants in the law-making process)

---

2 Habermas (1996) *Between Facts and Norms*, at pp. 103, 303–304, 448–450.

'*reach an understanding* about the rules for their living together'.[3] The procedural aspect is an inherent part of the legitimate throughput and therefore the process. Without legitimate procedure, the normative result will not be legitimate. Legitimacy of output and the process which leads to the output are therefore inextricably linked. Such legitimacy may be obtained through proceduralisation of the process, in order to ensure an equalised participation with a balanced representation of stakeholders and of their power.

Both theories recognise that in communicative processes some actors may be stronger than others. Recall that Teubner, who was inspired by earlier Habermasian theory, established the normative directive in reflexive law for power disparities to be balanced, but neglected to set out directives for how to do so.[4]

In *Between Facts and Norms* Habermas not only explicitly addresses the very power disparity issue that Teubner skirts in his theory, but also prescribes the conditions that the law-making procedure should honour in order to provide for legitimacy. Habermas explicitly recognises that divergence in strength may be due to differing social conditions and forms of organisation. For the production of law to be legitimate, participants should have equal rights not just in formal but in actual terms. Such equality requires a proceduralisation of regulatory processes that draw on discourse as a channel for input towards the production (and agreement) of a normative output. The formation of legitimate procedural regulation should include participant groups that may be disadvantaged, in order for them to take part in public discussions on the factors relevant to defining procedural equality.[5]

The combination of Habermasian theory and reflexive law confirms that organisers of reflexive and other collaboratory regulatory fora need to pay attention to power disparities between participants in order for the normative outputs not to be side-tracked into something that diverts from or even opposes the original objectives, or that is lacking in legitimacy as a result of unbalanced political power. Core theory on legitimate law-making through deliberation, bargaining or even negotiation provides qualitative guidance on how to devise a process that mitigates power disparities through proceduralisation. Such a procedure also provides for legitimate law-making through involving non-state actors in a process of agreeing on norms of common co-existence and providing them with an actual say, thus generating the throughput legitimacy required for effectiveness in terms of a compliance pull. It supplements the reflexive law paradigm through which hybrid rule-making intended to promote private self-regulation may be considered. Reflexive law provides a procedural framework within which intergovernmental or other organisations may engage societal stakeholders to develop and agree on norms for common co-existence while retaining control in order to ensure the primacy of public over private interests. Because it stresses the quality of participation in law-making through common will-formation and not just formal access, and because it notes procedural rights as elements in ensuring equalised participation, Habermasian deliberative theory can be drawn on for qualitative guidance for management of reflexive law fora on how to live up to the requirement of reflexive law theory that power disparities between participants should be balanced.

As explained in Chapter 5, subsection 5.2.2, Teubner's reflexive law theory is based on a perception of law as a functional (sub-)system, whereas Habermas understands law in the institutionalist sense. To Habermas, law includes both positive enforceable law and institutionalised

---

3   Ibid., at pp. 83–84, emphasis in original.
4   Teubner (1986) 'After legal instrumentalism?', at pp. 316–319; and Chapter 5, subsection 5.2.3.
5   Habermas (1996) *Between Facts and Norms*, esp. chaps 4, 7, 9.

rights and freedoms that enable citizens to participate in the production of opinions, formulated into policy and law. To Habermas, individual legal subjects (as members of society and subject to the law that is administered and enforced by the state and its institutions) achieve clarity and legal certainty about justified interests and standards of conduct through exercise of their political autonomy. Exercise of their political rights allows them to participate in policy-making that feeds into law-making, and to agree on the regulation of society and its members.[6] Through involvement in deliberative discourse exercised on the basis of such legal institutions, those who are or will be subjected to substantive or procedural law are able to influence its normative substance. Equal participation is significant for the formation of common will through such deliberation. To provide for equal participation, the debate and exchange of views (in the form of deliberation or bargaining) need to take place according to institutionalised procedures. Procedures to equalise participation make it clear to participants what they can expect and what rights and opportunities they have; and it provides organisers of the regulatory process – whether reflexive law or more conventional law-making – with a set list of steps to be taken and procedures to be observed.

Habermas emphasises fundamental rights that provide for the freedom of expression, association and related civil and political rights as important elements in the framework for the institutionalised procedures that are necessary for equal access to and actual participation in the process. Thus, in contrast to reflexive law theory, which relies on a virtual or actual framework organised by authorities with a view to the creation of perturbation aiming at inducing participants to develop acceptable norms, Habermasian theory relies on institutionalised procedure based on rights to grant equal and actual access to participation in the process. By emphasising institutionalised procedure in his work since the early 1990s Habermas so to speak digs a level deeper than Teubner. He does so by defining the conditions that allow not only for a participatory production of norms per se, but for the production of norms that are legitimate as a result of a qualified form of communication, which is designed or structured so as to provide for equalised participation and balance power disparities as part of throughput legitimacy.

This builds on a combination of bottom-up and top-down reach: it is about providing rule-making with relevance to those whose concerns and needs are at stake, and providing it with a support and acceptance by those to whom norms of conduct apply in a manner that may be likened to Franck's 'compliance pull'. The participatory deliberative or bargaining process makes a resulting rule relevant because it has taken the concerns and needs both of those whom it intends to protect and of those who are subject to following the rule into account. In line with this Habermasian aspect, reflexive law assumes that law-making through a process that includes those (for example, business enterprises) who will be subjected to the normative directives will ensure a dual relevance: that the rule will be relevant to address societal needs, and that it will be relevant to application by the entity that is expected or required to observe it. Habermas assumes that such a rule will generate support and acceptance because it leads to a common formation of will and opinion – at least in principle, and based on balanced participation and power. When the formation of a common will and opinion is not possible, the alternative of bargaining generates acceptance as a compromise that is balanced because all have had a say in the negotiated output. This say may be direct or indirect, but the process through which it occurs is transparent. For such a balance to be achieved, power must be equalised through procedure. For power to be equalised, participation in the

---

6 Ibid., at pp. 31, 32.

law-making process must also be equalised through procedure. Accordingly, proceduralisation is a key concept to collaborative regulation. It is through proceduralisation of the process that participation is equalised, and through the equalisation of participation that power disparities are managed. Proceduralisation sets the framework for the regulatory process so that the substantive parts of a process of exchanges of views and the collaborative development of norms through deliberation or bargaining/negotiation can occur in a climate of trust and confidence among participants as to their access to the process and prior knowledge, the concerns that they represent, and the interests at stake.

7.2.2 Equalised participation

Equalised participation entails not only that participants recognise each other as equals but also that they have equal access to the deliberation or negotiation (bargaining) that leads to new norms of conduct. The process must be open to other participants, and generally non-exclusive and transparent.[7] Proceduralisation of a process that involves deliberation or bargaining, such as law-making, is an avenue for equalising participation. In turn, law is legitimate if developed through a deliberative or bargaining process that allows participation and for the result to meet with the agreement of those affected.

Law (norms of conduct) having been developed through such a process that engages actors is assumed to exert a compliance pull because it is perceived to be valid and legitimate.[8] This Habermasian thought relates directly to Franck's ideal of legitimacy in international law. It was noted in Chapter 4 that Franck's views are pertinent also in relation to the need for compliance pull that norms on business social responsibilities encounter, especially when developed under and applied in an international and transnationalising super-national legal order with limited enforcement and sanction mechanisms. Similarly, Habermas's thoughts on the process to deliver legitimacy are pertinent for the norms required to function in such a context. The effectiveness of such norms of conduct is particularly dependent on a compliance pull that is independent of legal enforcement and sanctions. If such norms are not considered legitimate by those to be protected by them or by those subject to complying with them, even if they are formally agreed to by the actors involved, trust in the norms may be limited, the compliance pull will be reduced and effectiveness will suffer. Civil society's sentiments in relation to the MSF output (the Final Report) expressed at the final MSF meeting demonstrate how a process seen to suffer from legitimacy faults fails to generate trust from a forward-looking perspective, even if all the participants formally agree to the result.

Employing somewhat differing terminologies, but sharing the same aim of promoting the relevance and legitimacy of law-making to provide for the common good and connect specific concerns with the requirements of the law, both Habermas and Teubner are concerned with process as an element in law-making and with the formation of common will as a factor that provides the resulting norms with effectiveness in terms of a 'compliance pull'. Teubner places faith in the reflexive law forum per se to frame a communicative process and deliver an output that begs adherence. Habermas emphasises the deliberative quality of the

---

7 Risse (2000) "'Let's argue'", at p. 11.
8 Habermas, J. (2005) 'Den demokratiske retsstat: En paradoksal sammenknytning af modstridende principper?', in H. Andersen (ed.), *Jürgen Habermas: Demokrati og retsstat – en tekstsamling*, Copenhagen: Hans Reitzels Forlag, pp. 73–89, esp. at p. 89; Rostbøll, C. F. (2011) *Jürgen Habermas*, Copenhagen: Jurist- & Økonomforbundets Forlag, at pp. 59–60.

communicative process as a key element for the capacity to deliver an output that is valid in the sense of being perceived as legitimate and complied with. We saw above that, according to systems thinking, communication allows social sub-systems to learn about and react to developments in other social sub-systems. Reflexive law relies on the idea of autopoiesis for this purpose. As explained above, to Habermas communication is a more concrete and practical element of social processes. Communication is an element in processes of formation of meaning among individuals, from politicians to concrete law-makers and the citizenry. Civil society plays a core role for channelling the views and needs of individuals or communities into the process. This, too, calls for proceduralisation in order to enable a balanced representation of interests, and to balance the sometimes diverse powers of civil society organisations, such as between business and NGOs, or between diverse networks.

Habermas observed that participation need not be completely individualised. Participation can be generalised through modalities of representation. It was noted above that governance networks may be considered to be democratically legitimate to the extent that they reflect or at least take into account the interests, preferences and opinions of the members of the diverse groups involved. What takes place within a process of negotiation is key to the representation of interests, and therefore to the output and its legitimacy. That also applies when the process comprises networks or networks of networks or itself functions as a governance network. However, the external aspect matters as well. As in other contexts, access to information is pertinent for participants to be able to exercise their procedural rights in a meaningful sense. Moreover, flows of information to and from those whose interests are represented only indirectly – for example, through civil society organisations or individual spokespersons – are of paramount significance to ensuring the representativeness of such organisations or individuals.

Given the global dispersal of interests and stakeholders for issues that relate to the impact that business may have on society, information flows are highly relevant for inclusive public–private rule-making processes, in particular to enable such processes to take account of and deal with issues affecting less resourceful groups, including stakeholders in rural or poor urban areas in developing countries. Furthermore, such information should go not only from reflexive law forums to stakeholders, but also from stakeholders to networks. Such flows are necessary for the quality of a reflexive law forum to deal with problems, concerns and interests in a way that is balanced towards those groups whose interests are or should be represented. Two-way information, embodying bottom-up and top-down flows that connect to exchange and develop meaning, may contribute to connecting the internal and external dimensions of the rule-making process. It is also one of the major challenges for global rule-making.

For collaborative regulation at the super-national level, an important challenge is for the agency in charge to define criteria to ensure that relevant interests are represented, and to ensure that those who claim or are asked to represent the interests of others (whether civil society organisations or networks) do indeed represent the interests of the pertinent stakeholders. A national, regional or international business association does not necessarily represent the interests or concerns of all relevant businesses in a sector or region. Similarly, one or more existing not-for-profit civil society organisations, whether constituted as NGOs or other forms, are not necessarily representative of all relevant civil society interests. For example, competing interests in a community may require different channels of representation.

At the overall, general level, proceduralisation to ensure effective implementation of rights of participation, whether through direct or indirect representation, lends itself to elaboration and formalisation through international law. Initially this may be soft law, such as the Guiding

Principles' guidance for legitimate remedies or conventional international soft law. In due time it may become hard law. At the specific level of a collaborative law-making process, specific proceduralisation steps need to be considered, as suggested below.

7.3 Procedural design and power

7.3.1 Procedurally equalised participation in collaborative regulation: looking to procedural administrative and human rights law

Developing proceduralisation for equalised participation and balancing power disparities in super-national collaborative regulation do not occur in a vacuum, nor do the foundational ideas and needs arise only for that context. Similar issues are well known in national public law for individuals participating in decision-making processes, whether general policies or specific acts, and in procedural administrative law applying to situations where authorities make decisions pertaining to individuals. Institutionalised procedures for equalisation of power disparities may obtain inspiration from civil and political human rights as institutions, and from the institutionalised procedures that have been developed in national public law to ensure participation, access and transparency. GAL scholars have noted similar issues, but place the main emphasis on output and *ex post* accountability rather than the Habermasian emphasis on procedure and throughput legitimacy.

As noted, for deliberative law-making in a national context Habermas has emphasised the significance of rights which grant individuals the possibility of expressing their opinions. Such rights effectively form an institutional framework for exchanging views and engaging in deliberation. For many practical purposes, these correspond particularly to political human rights, such as rights of expression, information, and direct or indirect participation in political decision-making at different levels of governance. Those rights often translate into procedures for access to information, to express oneself and to participation. Procedural national administrative law is a case in point.

At the international level, procedural rights like those which Habermas refers to as fundamental rights largely correspond to civil and political human rights that have been formulated in the UDHR and detailed human rights instruments. Developed in the context of international human rights law, those rights are enjoyed by individuals, with related duties for states to respect, fulfil and protect, and the context of application is at the national level. Owing to the general non-discrimination principle of international human rights law, entrenched in article 2 of the ICCPR as well as the ICESCR, civil and political human rights are precisely suited to providing for equal participation in policy-oriented communication as well as rule-making, just as the non-discrimination principle provides for equal access to enjoy economic, social and cultural rights. International law also recognises, for example in certain international treaties,[9] that special measures may be required for the equalisation of otherwise marginalised or less empowered groups, but only until those groups have achieved the same status as others.

In his work, Habermas has noted the UDHR and human rights law as relevant not only for the national context but in a more general sense of common norms of co-existence in the 'post-national constellation'. Although more hesitant than Habermas towards the potential of

---

9 *Convention on the Elimination of All Forms of Discrimination against Women*, UN Doc. A/34/46, 1249 UNTS 13, art. 4(1); *Convention on the Elimination of Racial Discrimination*, UN Doc. A/6014, 660 UNTS 195, art. 2(2).

the UDHR and international human rights law as a sort of global constitution, Teubner, too, in his later work recognises the significance of international social and environmental law. In line with his general approach, which also marks the reflexive law theory, his main emphasis is on the substantive issue areas rather than procedure.[10]

For the current context, the development of international human rights law and its universality show that states are concerned with non-state actors' participation in political processes, and with procedures and procedural guarantees that provide for both informed participation and equality, even in some contexts equalisation. States have entered into such obligations under international law with regard to processes within their own territories. In view of the increased attention that has been paid in recent years to sustainability concerns that affect individuals and communities around the world and lead to calls for global regulation, it is logical to draw an analogy to political – and therefore law-making – processes at the super-national level. Political rights of individuals at the national level restrain governments' discretion to regulate and act as they please, and provide for participation and, following Habermas's line of thinking, for legitimate rule-making inviting respect and observation as a result of its deliberative background. Although a complete analogy is hardly possible owing to the institutional and political differences between international and national governance, an approximation of rights of participation and proceduralised equalisation in collaborative law-making may also be possible at the super-national level. Moreover, it may in fact work to the advantage of super-national rule-making through providing for a higher degree of legitimacy and, following Franck's ideas, catering for a compliance pull.

Although human rights are claimed to be universal, their universality is also disputed, as has been proved for example through the 'Asian values' discourse of the 1990s.[11] Yet the fact that human rights fed strongly into the Global Compact through its reference to the UDHR signals the general acceptance of human rights as a universal normative system that not only is developed by states in terms of the obligations of states, but also with the Global Compact has been adopted by non-state actors as a system entailing relevant normative directives for their activities. Similarly, the SRSG process and its output demonstrate broad acceptance of the relevance of the International Bill of Rights as relevant to states as well as non-state actors.

The Global Compact's and UNGPs' references to the UDHR and the full International Bill of Rights, which in addition to the former includes the ICESCR and the ICCPR, make it relevant to look to these instruments not only as directives for (business) conduct but also as entailing standards of equalised participation in the conduct of public affairs, including law-making. That is particularly apt for the development of rules pertaining to business conduct. Through their support of the Global Compact and the UNGPs businesses already recognise the International Bill of Rights as a basic source of (mainly substantive) norms of conduct to be applied to business operations, even though the International Bill of Rights was developed to set norms of conduct for states and rights for individuals. Taking the points on participation, legitimacy and compliance pull noted by Friedmann, Charney, Franck and Habermas as a point of departure, we may therefore consider how the procedural rights of participation that emerge from the International

10 Teubner, G. (2012) *Constitutional Fragments: Societal Constitutionalism and Globalization*, Oxford: Oxford University Press, at pp. 45–46. Teubner tends to address above-national law-making from the 'stateless' perspective rather than as integrated public–private regulation of the type discussed in the current study; see also Teubner, G. (1997) 'Foreword: Legal regimes of global non-state actors', in G. Teubner (ed.), *Global Law without a State*, Aldershot: Dartmouth Publishing, pp. xiii–xvii.

11 See, for example, Jacobsen, M. and Bruun, O. (2000) *Human Rights and Asian Values: Contesting National Identities and Cultural Representations in Asia*, Hong Kong: Curzon; compare Glendon, M.-A. (2001) *A World Made New: Eleanor Roosevelt and the Universal Declaration of Human Rights*, New York: Random House.

Bill of Rights as a source of normative standards may offer a basis for a role for businesses and other non-state actors to participate in law-making, especially when this occurs at the supernational level, as it often does with regard to transnational business conduct and its impacts.

The right to take part in public decision-making affecting one's interests, either directly or indirectly through representation, is entrenched as a human right in the UDHR (article 21) and the ICCPR (article 25). The World Conference on Human Rights in 1993 recognised that it is essential for states to foster participation by the poorest people in the decision-making process of the community in which they live (article 25).[12] Based on similar considerations to Franck's compliance pull and sometimes referred to as 'ownership', participation in a decision-making process is assumed to provide for a higher degree of productivity and delivery of intended outcomes in developmental projects in emerging and established economies.[13] The ownership idea and evidence of its significance also confirm the connection between participation and the success of a collaborative endeavour.

As sustainability concerns and related decision-making shifts from the national to the global level, the results come to affect a global public. Principles for rule-making that have been developed and agreed to between states as having universal application should lend themselves to application at the super-national level, with due adaptation as a result of the immensity of the public potentially involved. This takes us back to Habermas's arguments on global governance. The standards contained in the UDHR, article 21 and ICCPR, article 25 do not lend themselves to direct transposition to the global level, yet the standards express a global agreement on conditions and rights of participation. Just as international human rights law serves as a normative source for substantive CSR normativity as noted above, international human rights may serve as a normative source for the procedures framing participation in hybrid law-making at the super-national level.

Drawing on international human rights law in this procedural context may require some adaptations while staying true to the basic interest. In a longer-term perspective, it is possible that international society will approve rights of participation in super-national law-making that correspond to the ideals that human rights law currently creates for the national level. In the shorter term, it is sufficient to take the universal agreement on a series of procedural rules as a point of departure for elaborating methods for super-national law-making with due adaptations. Just as Habermas's deliberative rule-making when applied at the supernational level must be adapted essentially to be able to function and deliver in a manner that approximates to that at the national level, international human rights standards that cater for political participation may be adapted to global rule-making. The idea is to approximate to the type of equalised procedural participation that states have agreed to apply at the national level for super-national public decision-making processes that result in rule-making, but not to copy the rules. (Obviously, in order to avoid such super-national-level adaptation being abused 'downwards' to justify adaptations in national law that might limit

12 United Nations General Assembly (1993) *Vienna Declaration and Programme of Action.*
13 See, for example, Wight, A. (1997) 'Participation, ownership and sustainable development', in M. S. Grindle (ed.), *Getting Good Government: Capacity Building in the Public Sectors of Developing Countries*, Cambridge, MA: Harvard University Press, pp. 369–412; Kleemeier, E. (2000) 'The impact of participation on sustainability: An analysis of the Malawi rural piped scheme program', *World Development*, Vol. 28, No. 5, pp. 929–944; Ritchie, D., Parry, O., Gnich, W. and Platt, S. (2004) 'Issues of participation, ownership and empowerment in a community development programme: Tackling smoking in a low-income area in Scotland', *Health Promotion International*, Vol. 19, No. 4, pp. 51–59; Marks, S. J. and Davis, J. (2012) 'Does participation lead to a sense of ownership for rural water systems? Evidence from Kenya', *World Development*, Vol. 40, No. 8, pp. 1569–1576.

their scope, it is important for national law application to respect the spirit of the relevant provision as originally developed as well as dynamic evolution for state-level application through international human rights law.) In this context, the evolution of proceduralisation in above-national law-making benefits from some of the insights that have been raised by GAL scholars in regard to legitimacy, transparency and accountability.

GAL scholars have emphasised the significance of transparency and accountability in order to provide for the legitimacy of rules made at the above-national level, including normative regimes which are in practice developed through public–private collaboration. From national administrative law in states in common law as well as civil (including socialist)[14] jurisdictions across the world it is well known that transparency and accountability may be guaranteed through procedural rules granting rights of access to information, participation and consultation. The argument here is that similar procedural rules may also serve collaborative regulation to balance power disparities between state and non-state actors, or between non-state actors and their networks.

At the level of national law, procedural administrative law serves precisely to balance power between stakeholders – authorities and citizens, as well as between citizens. It not only provides for procedural rights for citizens (such as formal rights of access to information), but sets procedures to be followed by authorities in order to balance power disparities between authorities and citizens or between citizens. For example, authorities may be required under national administrative law to provide guidance on rights and processes, to consult with citizens to check factual data before making decisions, to provide information, and to place decision-making on hold pending citizens' becoming familiar with relevant information and able to provide relevant feedback to the decision-making authority.[15] Even when some stakeholders are by definition more powerful because they have the competence to make decisions pertaining to other stakeholders (decision-making authorities as opposed to, for example, citizens or businesses requesting permits or services), procedural rights and proceduralisation function to empower the weaker part (such as when citizens are entitled to process guidance, to consultations on facts, to information and to challenge a decision through administrative or judicial review). Although often not addressed in terms of human rights, there are significant parallels between the concerns that procedural administrative law seeks to protect and those of procedural human rights. Consider similarities in objectives of protecting the individual as the weaker part in the detailed proceduralisation of a process of administrative decision-making to enable citizens to be informed and provide clarifications, and the objectives that inform human rights of expression and information, and participation in public-decision making.[16] This feature provides a connection to the use and substantive direction of procedure to balancing power disparities in reflexive law forums. It also provides a link to addressing some of the procedural concerns which have been raised by GAL scholars. Similarly, proceduralisation offers a potential solution to the concerns noted in Chapter 4, subsection 4.3.2 relating to rule-making that is exercised by diverse groups

14 Buhmann, K. (2001) *Implementing Human Rights through Administrative Law Reforms*: The *Potential in China and Vietnam*, Copenhagen: Djoef Publishing.

15 For an overview, see Council of Europe (1996) *The Administration and You: Principles of Administrative Law Concerning the Relations between Administrative Authorities and Private Persons*, Strasbourg: Council of Europe.

16 See, for example, Council of Europe (1998) *The Administration and You: A Handbook*, Strasbourg: Council of Europe; compare Buhmann (2001) *Implementing Human Rights through Administrative Law Reforms*, at pp. 111–129.

(networks) with unclear internal relations, differentiated access to formal law-makers and sometimes overlapping interests. Indeed, national administrative law's procedural rules and proceduralisation may provide much inspiration for procedural guidance for balancing power disparities in reflexive law forums at above-national level.

Applying a human rights lens to proceduralisation of hybrid multi-stakeholder law-making, such as reflexive law forums pertaining to transnational issues and regulation, offers a platform for agreement on institutionalised participation across states, regions, cultures, and the political, economic and legal sub-systems. Unfolding the general observations made by Habermas in respect of human rights as an important element in global rule-making in terms of the substance and organisational justification of specific rights and the manner in which these may inform proceduralised interaction between stakeholders offers a way of concretising the abstract Habermasian theory. Thus, the basic human rights principle of equality – for example, in political and public decision-making processes – links up with equalised access to the human rights to expression, its corollary the freedom of information, and modalities for gathering to exchange views, such as the freedom of assembly, to provide an overall umbrella of human rights for reflexive law forums. Proceduralisation modalities developed in administrative law to protect and provide for these rights in practice (if not always by name, as stated above) offer ways to ensure inclusive participation on equalised terms, and expression and interaction in specific processes of exchanges and learning.

Habermas observed that proceduralisation can provide for institutionalised forms of participation within a framework enabling discursive formation of will and opinion. With variations, the reflexive law forums analysed above functioned in a more anarchistic fashion, with rule-making developing without institutionalised procedures ensuring equalised participation, and with intergovernmental as well as non-state actors having varied formal and actual power. It is logical to consider whether reflexive law forums need to function without proceduralisation in order for the creative and learning potential to be released. Observations on the process and output of the UN Global Compact and the SRSG process compared to those of the EU MSF and the CSR Alliance indicate that this need not be the case. On the contrary, the analysis above shows that proceduralisation – including strong procedural guidance by the agency in charge of the forum, such as was the case for the UN Global Compact, the SRSG processes and ISO 26000 – promotes output delivery and simultaneously supports throughput legitimacy by balancing participation and power in the process. Notably, the differences between the UN and the EU cases were not primarily due to the UN being an international organisation and the EU a regional one with somewhat differing objectives. The analysis indicates that the differences were mainly due to governance of the reflexive law forums and in particular their composition, management and iterative development and exchanges on issues to be addressed in the output. All of these issues can potentially be addressed through procedural rules on the organisation and functioning of multi-stakeholder regulatory forums, whether functioning as reflexive law or a more conventional regulatory process.

7.3.2 IT-based global communication: opportunities and increased demand for equalised access to public and hybrid decision-making

When considering law-making at the super-national level, the IT revolution has made the inclusion of a global citizenry much more practically feasible than it was just a few decades ago. However, the access to information and to share views that IT offers also highlights the need for proceduralisation.

The development and spread of IT for communication mean that information may be shared much faster, over a much greater distance and with much larger groups of individuals and networks today than was the case only a few decades ago. This provides opportunities for participation in global rule-making that are likely only to grow in the future.

IT offers tremendous opportunities for virtual inclusion and therefore participation of a global public in rule-making processes that used to take place in closed quarters in the headquarter buildings of the UN in New York and Geneva, or in similar physically closed settings in other intergovernmental organisations. Consider these examples of how development has already begun in terms of moving guidance for the application of sustainability-related norms of conduct and their evolution from the physical to the virtual sphere: the Global Compact is basically a web-based normative instrument, which, in addition to face-to-face network meetings, communicates with members and other stakeholders through the internet; the SRSG during his 2005–2008 term shared statements, papers and proposals with interested stakeholders through the internet, and during his 2008–2011 term further expanded IT communication to engage with stakeholders; the EU Commission already in 2001–2002 used the internet to consult with stakeholders on the 2001 Green Paper and to communicate broadly on the MSF, and the CSR Alliance made its 2008 'toolbox' available on the internet. Some information on the ISO 26000 SR Guidance Standard and related documents is available electronically free of charge; other elements are accessible only for a fee.[17]

Going beyond formal participation to actual interaction and collaboration requires more than simple access to IT. It is logical, however, to consider the availability of IT both for sharing knowledge to provide for informed usage of procedural rights, and actively to include groups or individuals possessing those rights in processes for developing normativity.

In the future, reflexive law forums and other forms of participatory evolution of norms are likely to become increasingly virtual. The growth and decreasing expenses of web-based spoken communication (Skype and similar technology) and the spread of video-linking facilities at private and public organisations around the world enable global dialogue to take place in real time without the cost of travel and time that used to characterise face-to-face communication and meetings involving individuals from several regions. Local representative offices of the UN, ILO, World Bank and regional development banks, EU Commission or embassies or consulates of governments may make communication facilities available to enable civil society or even individuals to communicate across the world, and to become virtual participants in decision-making. Companies as well as civil society organisations with similar facilities, including those placed in non-metropolitan or rural areas, may make them available to other companies or civil society organisations, which may then also be able to become virtual participants in reflexive law forums. Mobile phones have become common as banking and trade devices, including in several poor countries, where these devices are used by individuals in places far from financial hubs and political decision-making centres.[18] This makes it logical also to consider mobile phones

---

17 See ISO (2010) *ISO 26000 – Social Responsibility.*
18 See, for example, Hughes, N. and Lonie, S. (2007) 'M-PESA: Mobile money for the "unbanked" turning cell-phones into 24-hour tellers in Kenya', *Innovations: Technology, Governance, Globalization*, Vol. 2, No. 1–2, pp. 63–81; Aker, J. C. and Mbiti, I. M. (2010) *Mobile Phones and Economic Development in Africa*, Center for Global Development Working Paper No. 211, Tufts University – Fletcher School of Law and Diplomacy, Center for Global Development.

as a modality for provision of information, concerns and communication on global sustainability concerns that are subject to above-national rule-making. In particular, the reach and established broad deployment of mobile phone communication in places far from major cities make it fathomable to include rural populations and groups sometimes referred to as the 'bottom of the pyramid' (BOP) as participants in global decision-making.[19] This would increase access for actual or potential victims and others who are the most vulnerable to the adverse impact of global economic activities on their sustenance and daily lives.

Not only does IT offer extensive opportunities for two-way communication flows between those who may be physically present to represent the views of others within a regulatory forum and those whose interests are or may be represented by such individuals and addressed in the forum, but the decreasing costs of IT-based communication also reduce the resources necessary for communication, making a much larger source of input for a regulatory process feasible.

Yet past usage of IT-based communication demonstrates some of the complexities that also need to be considered in legitimate rule-making or policy development to go beyond formal participation to actual equalised inclusion and collaboration. For example, the SRSG's sharing of an advanced draft of the UNGPs[20] in late 2010 through the internet to gain broad input from stakeholders generated expectations that such input would become more visibly integrated into the final version of the UNGPs than may have been the case in practice.[21] And, while the use of mobile phones may be widespread and is coming to serve as a platform for economic interaction in places far from cities,[22] the cost of communication through this channel may be an obstacle to the general provision of stakeholder views from among the world's poorest, but also most vulnerable, individuals and communities. To take a policy-making example, consider the UN's electronic communication platform MY World. This was launched in 2013 to serve as a global 'survey' tool for citizens, aiming to 'capture people's voices, priorities and views'[23] towards what in 2015 became the SDGs. The idea was to gather information from citizens around the world to enable 'world leaders' to be informed of the views and needs of the global public as they worked to define global goals to end poverty and ensure sustainability after the 2000–2015 MDGs 'expired'. As a platform of the global public to communicate their views to the UN and global decision-makers, MY World was, however, not in practice easily accessible for those who are the most affected by the listed key issues, such as 'inequalities', 'governance', 'water', 'health' or 'environment'. To engage, individuals were asked to read UN-style reports and relate to other texts written in a rather formal style, and also requiring some previous substantive insight as well as familiarity with English or other UN languages.[24]

---

19 BOP refers to the large group of people with the most limited economic resources living in the poorest countries. See Prahalad, C. K. (2004) *The Fortune at the Bottom of the Pyramid: Eradicating Poverty through Profits*, Upper Saddle River, NJ: Prentice Hall.

20 United Nations Human Rights Council (2010*) Report of the Special Representative of the Secretary-General on the Issue of Human Rights and Transnational Corporations and Other Business Enterprises, John Ruggie: Guiding Principles for the Implementation of the United Nations 'Protect, Respect and Remedy' Framework*, UN Doc. A/HRC/, no date, draft for consultation released on 22 November.

21 See, for example, the discussion in Deva (2013) 'Treating human rights lightly'.

22 See, for example, Hughes and Lonie (2007) 'M-PESA'; Aker and Mbiti (2010) *Mobile Phones and Economic Development in Africa*.

23 MY World United Nations Global Survey, http://www.worldwewant2015.org/inequalities (accessed 11 March 2013).

24 Ibid.

Overall, language proficiency is a potential constraint to participation and equalised participation, despite broad internet access and electronic translation tools. Those who are not proficient in UN languages or other languages that predominate in a country or region may be excluded from participation in practice, and even if not fully excluded those with basic knowledge may be disadvantaged compared to those with full proficiency in those given languages. For example, documents related to the development of ISO 26000 were widely published on the internet, but being conducted in English the process arguably placed those groups and individuals with familiarity with English at an advantage over those who master other languages better. Along with proficiency of spoken language, creating broad IT-based access to participation in public decision-making also requires taking IT literacy into account, as well as the fact that only some IT platforms are accessible without a fee or subscription.

As a final example of the complexities in using the vast opportunities offered by electronic communication, the mere possibility of provision of a great number of views and comments from a global public creates organisational demands, and requires sorting practices and appropriate technical modalities to be developed. In some cases, such as during the SRSG's consultation on the draft UNGPs, comments may be made to and processed directly by the authority or agency in charge of the reflexive law forum. As was the case with the SRSG's consultation, a top-driven process may be perceived as lacking in legitimacy despite broad usage of online communication to reach and invite comments from many stakeholders globally.

Given the potentially very large number of individuals who may want to contribute to global rule-making processes, civil society and other representative organisations may play an important role as channels for sorting input and by making digests of views. This should be done in a manner that respects the essence of the concerned interest on behalf of those who transmit their views and demands through the organisation. This, too, calls for criteria for civil society and other representative organisations, including business associations, to be developed. Similar to representative political organisations at national level, such organisations may serve as channels to facilitate IT-based communication on individual views and demands.

7.4 Towards constitutionalisation? A prospective treaty on participation, procedure and rights of non-state actors in super-national law-making

The economic, political and even legal contexts have changed vastly since Wolfgang Friedmann and Jonathan Charney argued in the 1960s and 1980s, as described in Chapter 2, that including the business sector in international law-making intended to have implications for companies was significant for the process and for compliance. The economic and political circumstances for business in general and TNCs in particular had evolved considerably when the Global Compact was developed and the SRSG involved businesses as stakeholders on a par with others in the process towards the UN Framework and UNGPs. The fact that inclusion of companies or their representative organisations in rule-making on CSR through the Global Compact and the SRSG process and the process towards ISO 26000 led to acceptance of a change in norms on business social responsibilities indicates the relevance of the arguments that were made several decades ago on the inclusion of business. Whereas economics and politics mainly frame those regulatory processes from the outside, the inclusion of business as a partner in a regulatory process implies a possible change of the law from the inside, especially in terms of participation in law-making under an international organisation. To develop mindsets that enable changed and accepted norms of conduct, the process needs to allow for exchange of needs and concerns, as suggested by reflexive law theory.

Charney proposed that TNCs be granted limited procedural rights to enable them to participate through formal and informal avenues in the development and enforcement of international law-making relevant to their concerns. From the perspective of legitimacy, the inclusion of business in super-national rule-making pertaining to their conduct and responsibilities may be likened to the inclusion of states in conventional international law-making (which typically pertains to states and their conduct) and to the direct or indirect participation of individuals in law-making at the national level. As already noted in Chapter 1, this need not mean that business organisations should be granted rights similar to states in international law. What it does mean is that it is reasonable for the rule-making process to be designed so as formally to include those for whom the rules are made. Hence, for the purpose of legitimate super-national law-making, business as a societal actor could be formally invited to participate in the law-making process.[25] Such rights could eventually be granted by treaty, indicating criteria for inclusion in the process, such as sector relevance, geographic or supply chain connection, and/or representation of other business organisations. As the actors that make such a treaty, states would remain the key subjects of international law and retain that position by granting business organisations only limited rights. Matching such rights for business associations with similar rights for other non-state interest groups (e.g. organisations or not-for-profit groups) and networks would be important for ensuring a balance between for-profit and non-profit private interest groups, and particularly to ensure that the concerns and needs of actual or potential victims of adverse sustainability impacts (such as business-caused human rights abuse) should be represented. The case study of the Global Compact demonstrates that a selection of non-state actors based on expertise may strengthen rather than weaken the legitimacy of the resulting output. Moreover, transparency in the selection process will strengthen the legitimacy of the selection and representation.

Writing at two different time periods in terms of the global power and influence of transnational business, Charney and de Burca have both argued that, owing to conflicting interests and concerns of states and various non-state actors, independent participation of non-state actors in the creation and enforcement of international law would be best achieved through an evolutionary – and therefore iterative – process. Indeed, in view of the variety of issues, geographic span, states and stakeholders affected, and forms of law – ranging from formal to very informal – in the field of business impact on society and sustainability, the evolution of non-state actors' formal participation in super-national rule-making should be a step-by-step process. The process should be driven not only by a quest for inclusive and procedurally equalised participation in rule-making and a possible formalisation of non-state actor participation but also by a quest for learning about what works. Learning would be needed for organisers of reflexive law forums, for example in relation to criteria for inclusion, demands on interests to be presented (such as how to assess ability to represent the

---

25   Although its focus is on national law-making, UNECE (1998) *Convention on Access to Information, Public Participation in Decision-Making and Access to Justice in Environmental Matters* ('Aarhus Convention'), adopted 25 June, 2161 UNTS 447 is an example of how states may establish procedures for non-state actor participation in sustainability-related public decision-making. It is also an example that states may make treaty provisions establishing the rights of non-state actors to access to information to provide for informed decision-making, therefore effectively equalising the knowledge basis for participation.

interests of victims, business and other affected groups in a balanced and comprehensive manner), how to deal with and balance competing interests or claims to representativeness, and forms of regulation. A comprehensive learning process would be justified by its contributions to the evolution of an experience-based (and in due time evidence-based) system of inclusive super-national rule-making embodying representative and equalised participation. As the legitimacy of such processes could be damaged if participation was seen or experienced not to be balanced between interests and power, the long-term feasibility of and trust in a new inclusive system of super-national rule-making would require the system to be developed through ample opportunity for feedback and revision. Treaty provisions formalising non-state actor participation and criteria for inclusiveness and representation could and should be worded so as to set out general points that allow for flexibility as super-national reflexive law forum types and learning evolve.

Given the expanse of both the business sector and concern with sustainable development, some or even much future regulation of business impact on society may be transnational in the sense of being organised by private or economic non-state actors rather than by (inter)governmental agencies. Pending the perhaps utopian vision of global regulation that protects and promotes sustainable development to the satisfaction of all, the continued growth of such schemes is likely to take place both within and outside the auspices of (inter)governmental organisations. Effectively working through reflexive law modalities of exchanges and learning, this will be following in the steps of the evolution of the ISO 26000 SR Guidance Standard as well as other sustainability schemes organised by non-state actors with or without being joined by governments. An international treaty on non-state actor participation should take such opportunities into account and be phrased in a way that allows hybrid and private super-national law-making processes to apply its principles.

The strengthening of procedures to promote legitimate throughput and output through catering for equalised participation and managing power disparities offers a way to address some of the problems which have been raised by GAL scholars and others. In particular, proceduralised equalisation of access to and participation in GAL-style law-making would address concerns that have been raised in relation to transparency, accountability and legitimacy in terms of representation of interests, the inclusion of developing as well as developed states, privatisation of governmental tasks, and extra-parliamentary law-making.

Civil society is a rather elusive concept; its representatives are not easily identified,[26] nor do they necessarily constitute themselves through NGOs in the sense recognised by the UN Charter article 71. The mix of stakeholders involved in the currently on-going process towards a treaty on business and human rights (see Chapter 3, subsection 3.2.4.2) testifies to this. With business generally absent, other stakeholders are divided into those with consultative status and those that do not have consultative status.

Determining who should be included in a regulatory process is a highly pertinent concern for designing inclusive institutions for a pluralist global society. The exercise of determining this must consider what interests should be presented in a particular process, which individuals or organisations should participate, who should develop and decide criteria of participation for civil society, and how such criteria should be developed.[27] In the democratic nation state, the rights of individuals to participate in rule-making and decision-making processes are

---

26 See Hachez (2008) 'The relations between the United Nations and civil society', at p. 81.
27 Capps, P. and Machin, D. (2011) 'The problem of global law', *Modern Law Review*, Vol. 74, No. 5, pp. 794–810, at pp. 805–806.

typically rights guaranteed by the constitution or through procedural administrative law. The international society does not have a constitution, or a formal administrative law providing for such formalised participation for non-state actors. The instruments that are close to serving as a constitution for the international society – the UN Charter, customary international law on law-making, and the Vienna Convention on the Law of Treaties – provide states with access. While a 'global administrative law' may be emerging, for practical purposes it is primarily informal, and with great variations between institutions and governance modalities. However, constitutions may be informal (as evidenced by the case of the United Kingdom) and, as noted above, constitutionalisation may be an iterative process towards a degree of formalisation, as in the form of constitutionalism rather than an explicit constitution. As noted, the inclusion of private for-profit as well as non-profit non-state actors in the development of norms of conduct evidenced by the empirical examples discussed above may be understood as steps in an increasingly common practice of non-state actor participation in international law-making. It may also constitute a part of an informal, gradual constitutionalisation of their participation. The more common the practice becomes, arguably, the more acute the need for a formalisation of the process to ensure balanced participation and voice.

It was noted above that involving business in the processes towards the UN Framework and UNGPs amounted effectively to involving potential new duty-bearers in the law-making process. As firms, being non-state actors, are normally rights-holders and not duty-bearers or participants in international law-making, such inclusion of business entailed a major change from the past not just in terms of formalising business responsibilities for human rights but also in terms of non-state actor duty-holding subjects actively participating in the rule-making process. In view of the directives contained in the SRSG's mandate to consult broadly, this could be seen as an early step in a process towards a more direct and formalised inclusion of for-profit non-state actors in international law-making pertaining to them.

The objections that the UN Norms encountered with some business organisations and even from some states confirm Charney's point that, because transnational business organisations represent major independent powers of influence, failure to include them in negotiations under UN or other intergovernmental auspices to produce norms for TNC behaviour may cause resistance. Charney held that direct involvement in the norm-making process facilitates interaction within the international legal system, including on the interests, needs and conditions of stakeholders and those subjected to rules, and promotes commitment to the system. He also argued that greater TNC participation might strengthen the system of international law by recognising the increasing power of TNCs and reducing protection of business interests through lobbying of states. Both the case of the Draft Norms and the MSF case study confirm the significance of recognising the ability of certain groups or networks to liaise with formal regulators to the detriment of the interests of others, or such other groups' perception of the legitimacy of the process. This indicates the importance of including business as well as civil society through a procedure designed to provide for equalised participation.

From the perspective of super-national hybrid law-making, the idea of *ex ante* accountability underscores the significance of exchanges and debate as a modality towards this form of accountability in a setting where legal sanctions providing for *ex post* accountability may be limited.[28] For practical purposes, this corresponds to rule-making relating to the activities of business organisations with the aim of preventing adverse impacts: as a proactive process of regulation and self-regulation based on appreciation of the concerns and needs of other stakeholders, such a regulatory process would be strengthened by the inclusion of these

---

28 Hachez and Wouters (2011) *A Glimpse at the Democratic Legitimacy of Private Standards.*

stakeholders (or the organisations that they represent) in the law-making process. The substantive quality of law-making based on autopoiesis is likely to grow with the participants' perception of having equal power in the regulatory forum. The quality of discussion and exchanges could be strengthened through proceduralisation aiming at ensuring a balanced participation and discourse between stakeholders, whether business or other non-state actors, and even within those in recognition of the diversity of need, concerns and power-related interests that may be present within each.

At first thought, a treaty on procedures in super-national law-making, which would allow for formalised non-state actor participation, might look like a threat to the established system of international law and state sovereignty. However, in reality it could bring much-needed stability to that system as well as the role of states in future global governance. Such a treaty adopted by the UN would offer an update to the system of a limited form of participation for organisations in the consultative status that is recognised under article 71 of the UN Charter. A treaty would respond to the evolution that has already taken place in practice, particularly in the development of international environmental and climate law, in which NGOs have taken and obtained a strong role, partly as a result of their expertise. It would provide NGOs with a formal role that corresponds to their expertise and the fact that for many practical purposes they represent other stakeholders that do not have their own human voice, such as the environment, or whose voice is not easily heard, such as communities affected by business-related human rights abuse. A treaty formalising non-state actor participation would formalise a place and voice for business associations that would decrease their deployment of non-transparent modalities, such as lobbying, to have their views heard and interests taken care of through states. It would create a broader participation and input from the broad range of business sectors, types and associations that exist globally and whose views differ considerably between them. It would formalise processes to ensure that diverse concerns and interests are represented in a balanced manner by a diversity of not-for-profit or for-profit non-state actors, including networks, and ensure their voices are heard along with those of state actors.

A procedural treaty for sustainability regulation to include non-state participation and formalise the framework for their role would in fact not even be a novelty, as non-state actor participation in international environmental law has been recognised with the Aarhus Convention with regard to access to information.[29] A treaty that would be global in terms of sustainability issues could build on that model already developed for the environmental field, and expand the formalised non-state actor rights of participation by setting procedures for input provision, throughput and adoption of outputs. This would entail criteria for identification of participants, determining representatives and levels of representativeness, identification of needs for support in order to equalise participation and balance power, procedures for communication including through the use of IT, and procedures for recurrent checks on whether participation is sufficiently equalised and power disparities balanced. These points are all developed in more detail in Chapter 8.

7.5 Informal proceduralisation

The evolution of formal rights of participation and proceduralised equalisation for public–private regulation at the super-national level where non-state actors do not (yet) have formal access to formal law-making entails both a general and a specific proceduralisation.

---

29 See footnote 25 above.

The general proceduralisation means formalising the procedural rights of participants – including not-for-profit as well as for-profit non-state actors, provided they have a relevant interest in the regulatory issue at hand – to take part in such law-making processes. As importantly, it involves a general designation of procedural steps to be followed by the organising organisation in the establishment of a regulatory process as well as steps to be followed by participants during its implementation. The former may lean on political and participatory rights already developed in human rights law (albeit for other contexts and for other subjects); the latter may lean on procedural rules familiar from national administrative law. In a context with highly diverging power constellations, including experience and knowledge, formal procedural rights may not be very effective without proceduralisation to provide for equalised and informed participation to enable those with less power at the outset actively to make use of their rights. The specific proceduralisation may occur before the general proceduralisation. Owing to the variety in issues and forms, some or all elements of it will most likely also have to be considered in a more informal and more context-specific manner in every individual multi-stakeholder regulatory process organised even after a general proceduralisation has taken place.

As a general proceduralisation evolves, it will frame and feed into collaborative regulation in general and specific reflexive law forums and the proceduralisation of those. Pending general proceduralisation, specific proceduralisation at the level of individual regulatory processes is necessary to close the lacuna in reflexive law theory in terms of procedure for balancing power disparities. It may at the same time provide learning for the general process.

Pending formalisation through a prospective treaty, proceduralisation may and ideally should evolve on a softer and iterative basis. Such a process would develop important insights that may feed into the contents of a treaty on non-state actors' participation in international or transnational law-making. The overall process, which would entail a series of individual processes targeting a variety of issues set in a variety of contexts, would itself be a learning opportunity. Lessons would be developed that could take account of experience gained through reflexive law fora and other collaborative regulation processes with diverse compositions and functioning in diverse contexts. An outline for the steps to be taken is provided in the following chapter.

8 Steps for collaborative regulation

Overview: This chapter sets out specific steps for proceduralisation of a regulatory process to establish the framework for a broad and balanced, equalised multi-stakeholder participation in a process of collaborative regulation. Structured around two overall sub-processes of establishing and implementing the regulatory process, steps are set out for ensuring representation and representativeness, equalisation and general proceduralisation, including recurrent feed-back and revision. A fictitious case, structured around super-national regulation for sustainable forestry, serves as an example to provide context and details.

The proposed method for ensuring broad, balanced and equalised participation in deliberation or – for perhaps the majority of practical purposes – bargaining and negotiation through procedure entails a series of steps. The establishment and implementation of a multi-stakeholder regulatory process at the super-national level should proceed through these to ensure the institutional framework for the communicative processes to occur in collaborative regulation in a manner that provides for the resulting normative output to be legitimate as a result of throughput legitimacy. The establishment and implementation occur at stages of the process that correspond to the first and second levels of the reflexive law process as described in Chapter 5, section 5.2.1. The third level, which entails the intra-organisational development of norms in response to stimulation by irritants from other participants in the process, takes place as a result of this. This rule-making process is therefore a result of joint learning as participants draw insights from the communication that has taken place. Hence, the higher the quality of the establishment and implementation of the process in regard to proceduralised equalised participation, the better the opportunity that the input will be transformed into a legitimate output through a balanced and legitimate process that provides for an inherent compliance pull.

The *establishment phase*, which takes its point of departure in reflection corresponding to reflexive law at the first level, connects input to throughput. The *implementation phase* connects throughput and output, and if effective provides for reflection corresponding to reflexive law at the second level, which in turn may generate reflection at the third level, and therefore a change in the norms of conduct of relevant actors. The individual steps are defined around a series of key issues that have been identified in the preceding chapters to be significant for legitimate rule-making: representation and representativeness, equalisation and proceduralisation.

Collaborative regulation turns on equalised participation in deliberation (or bargaining/negotiation), with broad representation of affected interests set up in such a way that it ensures that concerns and insights of groups otherwise typically removed from public policy-making and law-making processes will be put on the table, discussed and addressed in the output. To be specific, collaborative law-making should take into account, to the extent relevant, the views of common people who may not even be aware of the law-making process or its potential implications for their lives, regardless of whether they live in the capitals of Africa, the Americas, Asia, Europe or Oceania, or in the suburbs or small towns of those regions, or in the countryside, and regardless of their degree of literacy, knowledge of major languages, and access to the internet. On the other hand, collaborative law-making should make use of available resources to ensure input from all such corners of the world, as this will provide a broad picture of the concerns and needs as well as interests that are necessary for the resulting regulatory output to be relevant to the level of implementation, issues at stake, and legitimacy in the eyes of those affected. Electronic communication, as mentioned in Chapter 7, may be an excellent source of communication, both for bottom-up flows and for top-down flows. The process needs to take account of power disparities in this context too, as well as the different backgrounds and IT resources that may frame the bottom-up feed from within the large group of citizens, and which may differ very much from those available to the top-down feed.

It is also a key element that power relations are continuously re-assessed. As is the case for issues subject to the risk-based due diligence process recommended by the UNGPs and adopted by the OECD's Guidelines and ISO 26000, power relations may dynamically change. It may also be the case that previous assessments and steps taken to ensure balance have been inadequate. Recurrent assessments should be undertaken by the agency or individual charged with managing the process. As part of this it should be considered how the process evolves and affects interests and interest-holders. To pre-empt capture of the process or output it should also be considered how a potential output at a given time may affect participants' power and power relations *after* the possible agreement on that output. If the output leads to change of current power relations, this is likely to affect views and willingness to change stances during the regulatory process. Such issues must be taken into account.

8.1 Issues to be considered in a formalised process of collaborative regulation

8.1.1 Inclusiveness and representation

Criteria for inclusion may be developed in collaboration with other organisations with insight into the substantive matter at hand. This may also offer a way to benefit from other networks and include these, so as to provide for coherence with other or related normative regimes, reflexive law or other multi-stakeholder regulatory processes. For sustainability-related issues, such as business responsibilities for human rights, it is important that the mapping of interests and identification of criteria of participation consider the situation of vulnerable groups. Those who are victims or potential victims of adverse business impact on society are often not in a position to represent their own interests in front of a reflexive law forum. This applies whether these be, for example, individual employees or local communities suffering from sub-standard employment conditions or the adverse impact of mining and resettlements, or rivers or estuaries suffering from environmental degradation or climate change-induced flooding. Following the Habermasian line of thought, such interests may be represented by civil society organisations. Indeed, some sustainability NGOs work across national or regional boundaries to draw attention to the problems and interests of vulnerable groups. Yet the very fact that the interests of the most vulnerable are being represented by others necessitates careful consideration of whether representative organisations are truly representative. It is important for legitimacy of the process and the output that such representative organisations fully consider and have insight into all the interests of stake-holders that expect or may make a claim to be represented, and to avoid trade-offs which will effectively cause some interests to become unrepresented. The issue of representation through civil society or other representative organisations, including business associations, is one of the most challenging and most important ones for the balancing of power in multi-stakeholder regulatory processes, whether this occurs in the form of 'classic' reflexive law or the advanced version offered by collaborative regulation. Careful proceduralisation offers a modality precisely towards balancing power disparities in this context too.

Developing relevant criteria may be time consuming and resource demanding, yet the effort will be worthwhile because of the significance for throughput legitimacy that true representation ensures. Careful pre-assessment and screening of pertinent interests and representative organisations need not lead to an extensive expansion in stakeholders to be included. They may just as well lead to a decrease in stakeholders or interests, because it may become clear that there are overlaps in interests or representative organisations. Ensuring representation through a careful mapping and selection from the outset may reduce arguments on stakeholder participation and interests during the forum, reduce disagreement and concerns related to input legitimacy, and contribute to the effectiveness of the forum.

For a process to be inclusive it should be open to participation by those who can explain a relevant concern or need in relation to the topic that is subject to the regulatory process and may be addressed or affected by the intended normative output. Inclusiveness also requires paying attention to language barriers and resources, whether human or financial. For representation to be balanced it is important to be aware of such issues in order to handle them during the process. This may require help to balance resource disparities, for example through making documents available in local languages and providing translation during a meeting, training in arguing a point, IT training if the process is conducted online or to ease participation in online exchanges taking place during a process, and financial assistance to enable a physical presence for a broad representation of concerns and stakeholders in the actual regulatory process.

8.1.2 Declaring interests and connections

To avoid legitimacy of the process being adversely affected by the mere suspicion that any members may have privileged knowledge or access to political or legal decision-makers, any such issues should be declared to the agency in charge of the process. That information should also be made accessible to other participants before the first meeting of the forum. The agency should also mention such issues or conflicts that it may be aware of, prior to the process. There may be solid reasons for such individuals or organisations to participate nevertheless. They may have expertise, which is both welcomed and necessary for the exchanges and learning to take place. However, declaring interests and sharing these in a transparent way will enable other participants to take account of the possible impact of this. As importantly, it will enable the agency in charge of the process to ensure that the process is not captured by such interests, ensuring at the same time that such interests may become voiced rather than simply subdued or excluded because they existed prior to the forum.

Experience with related processes or types of rule-making in organisational or (inter-)governmental settings similar to the pertinent one should also be declared at the time when the specific process is being organised. This too will enable the agency in charge to take account of whether some participants need to receive instruction or training in the functioning of reflexive law forums or negotiation technique in order to balance disparities of experience that might skew participants' power in the forum. While training may not fully provide for equalisation, it can mitigate strong disparities. Along with transparency about such experience it may enable participants and the agency or medium in charge to take issue with disparities or existing connections with formal decision-makers as they become evident. The agency in charge of the regulatory process may assist participants in discussing and agreeing on solutions to power disparities when these become apparent during the functioning of the forum.

8.1.3 Including stakeholders in preparing for interaction

To ensure equalised participation in a multi-stakeholder regulatory process, the agency or medium in charge of the process should also send out draft agendas for comments a reasonable period of time prior to any meeting and to allow participants to invite and obtain input from their constituencies. Final agendas should be circulated to allow time for participants and individual members of particular participant organisations to be able to make an informed decision on whether and how to participate, and to reach out to the constituencies that they represent for views and input for feedback. Procedural rules should clearly describe how participants may indicate points they want addressed on the agenda. Discussion and possible revision of the procedural functioning and rules for a particular regulatory process should be a point on the agenda of any meeting.

8.2 Steps for proceduralisation in a specific case of collaborative regulation

Essential steps are described with examples in the following. They are set out first for the establishment of the multi-stakeholder regulatory process, and next for its implementation. The steps are provided for a process set up as a reflexive regulatory process (comprising the three levels in whatever form it might be organised, including virtual exchanges of views such as gathering information for a sustainability report, sharing its contents, and receiving responses to the report). However, they are equally applicable to a more conventional international law-making form, whether in terms of formal structure or actual functioning. As discussed above, even these regulatory processes can do well to consider equalised participation in order to enhance throughput and output legitimacy. When a step involves 'reflection', this too can benefit the conventional law-making process. Reflection invites the organisers or participants to think about their roles, power, interests, and how best to ensure an effective process that is legitimate in considering and taking account of other participants' and stakeholders' needs and concerns.

The outline of steps to be taken in collaborative regulation set out here addresses procedure and procedural issues related to composition, organisation, and exchanges to stimulate reflection for the final law-making. Other matters, such as substantive issues and the general management of a collaborative regulatory process, will need to be addressed in a specific process, typically by the agency or individual in charge and in collaboration with the participants. This is referred to below as the management of the process.

To explain specific situations or issues, an example of collaborative public–private regulation of sustainable forestry serves as a fictitious example in the following. Forestry offers a number of social and environmental sustainability challenges, and could easily lend itself to public–private regulation at the super-national level. Various elements of sustainable forestry are already addressed by a number of intergovernmental, public–private and private initiatives, but none so far deal with the issue in a manner which is comprehensive and coordinated across the private sector, civil society and public organisations at the national and international level.[1] Important economic interests are involved, as are environmental, climate change and social interests. The latter include land and tenure rights, cultural practices, intellectual property knowledge of indigenous groups relating to forest products, and working conditions including occupational health and safety in forestry and timber processing, to mention but a few human rights issues at stake. Trade in forest products is often transnational and can be difficult to trace, with cut timber often travelling across boundaries for processing in other countries and crossing other boundaries through the supply chain to the final customer.[2] A renewable resource (at least in principle and provided they are given sufficient care), forests are hugely important for human survival. Renewal of forest in areas that are exploited economically must also be considered for sustainability. This applies not just to the economic or social benefits or needs of the people who live in or off the forest in a variety of ways, but to all of humanity in view of the importance of trees for CO_2 uptake. Given the public policy, economic and legal interests at stake, sustainable forestry might be a candidate for a UN effort to develop norms of conduct that would be transnational in reach.

In the current context, the case of sustainable forestry serves as a systemic case. Any application of the steps outlined for collaborative regulation needs to make adaptations to specific circumstances and local context pertaining to the resource, stakeholders and issues at stake.

For the sake of the fictitious example, imagine that the UN General Assembly, with administrative and technical support from the Office of the Secretary-General, decides to launch a special effort to ensure that management and usage of natural forest are exercised in a manner that is environmentally sustainable, respects the human rights (including labour rights) of forest-dependent people (whether they live in or off the forest), contributes to climate change reduction as well as the mitigation of climate change-induced changes in water levels and weather conditions affecting local communities, and finally does not involve corruption or bribery.

Table 8.1 sets out the steps for a general process in the middle column. The right column provides examples from forestry as a fictitious systemic case.

An effective collaborative regulatory process will lead to a normative output that promotes or supports change with some or all of the participants or stakeholders, depending on needs, demands, and actual perturbation that has been generated. Drawing on the insights of

---

1 Such initiatives include the World Bank's Forest Law Enforcement and Governance (FLEG) programmes, the United Nations' Reducing Emissions from Deforestation and Forest Degradation (REDD) and REDD+ schemes, the EU's Forest Law Enforcement, Governance and Trade (FLEGT) scheme, the Programme for the Endorsement of Forest Certification (PEFC) and FSC. See also Cashore (2002) 'Legitimacy and the privatization of environmental governance'; Gulbrandsen (2004) 'Overlapping public and private governance'; Meidinger (2006) 'The administrative law of global private–public regulation'; Meidinger, E. (2008) 'Multi-interest self-governance through global product certification programmes', in O. Dilling, M. Herberg and G. Winter (eds), *Responsible Business: Self-Governance and Law in Transnational Economic Transactions*, Oxford: Hart, pp. 259–291; Gulbrandsen, L. (2014) 'Dynamic governance interactions: Evolutionary effects of state responses to non-state certification programs', *Regulation and Governance*, Vol. 8, No. 2, pp. 74–92.

2 For examples of regulatory challenges, see Buhmann, K. and Nathan, I. (2013) 'Plentiful forests, happy people? The EU's FLEGT approach and its impact on human rights and private forestry sustainability schemes', *Nordic Environmental Law Journal*, Vol. 4, No. 2, pp. 53–82.

Table 8.1 Step-by-step guide for collaborative regulation

	General	Details (example: collaborative regulation of sustainable forestry)
Establishment of the regulatory process		
Step one: Reflection – level 1	An organisation or agency, such as an office or department within an intergovernmental organisation, which is charged with the implementation of policy and/or feeding into law-making related to sustainable development, reflects upon the capacities of the organisation to regulate the issue at hand.	In the case of a UN effort on sustainable forestry, the UN General Assembly, in collaboration with or based on analyses by the Secretary-General's Office, might conclude that the transnational character of the issue, the plurality of concerns, needs and interests at stake, the evidence of past efforts and results call for another regulatory modality than the international law-making in which the General Assembly normally engages.
	Debating the issue at hand, the organisation (supported by its secretariat) observes that the issue does not lend itself to regulation through conventional (hard) international law, or that this form of regulation is not sufficient to address the level of detail required. For example, conventional hard law requires implementation through governments. This can make it difficult to address and handle the practices, needs and concerns of individuals or organisations acting within or across the territorial borders of nation states.	It may be the case that the organisation observes that, despite the overall agreement on regulating sustainable forestry, sufficient political will for adopting conventional international law is not likely to be present, or it may take too many years to reach a compromise. To deal with such obstacles the organisation may decide to establish a process to move the issue towards another and less formal regulatory output without foreclosing the possibility of a future conventional law instrument.
	The organisation sets about developing a reflexive law forum. It defines the objective to be addressed through the output, including particular substantive norms to be considered.	The UN General Assembly might decide to charge the Secretary-General's Office with setting up and managing the process. The UNGPs could form a particularly relevant normative source relating to the action and impact of governmental and private actors.
Step two: Representation and representativeness	To ensure that concerned interests and stakeholders are involved and to prepare the ground for proceduralisation and equalised participation, a number of sub-steps must be taken by the organisation establishing the reflexive law forum:	

Developing criteria for inclusion for broad representation of concerns and interests related to the issue at hand.

Consideration of the plurality of interests involved to obtain an overview of the potential stakeholders.
At the top and medium levels, organisations representing a diversity of concerns, needs and interests should be involved.
At the local level these could be broken into numerous entities.

For forestry, consider the diversity of interests at stake, from the community level in tropical and non-tropical forests, to small-scale industry, larger processing facilities, and local and national governments in producing, processing, exporting and importing countries, forestry authorities, customs and border officials, traders along the value chain, buyers and consumers, business associations and civil society associations along the value chain. Consider coherent, competing or conflicting interests among all of those and how to identify and ensure adequate representation.

For forestry, organisations to be involved would likely include:

– Local communities living in or off the forest;
– Intergovernmental organisations (UN agencies with expertise in the field, including OHCHR, UNEP and ILO);
– Intergovernmental organisations charged with trade or international economic law, such as the WTO and the EU;
– Organisations representing the interests of business throughout the supply chain, including national industry organisations and SMEs in growing, processing and marketing states;
– Employers' organisations and trade unions (again in states throughout the supply chain);
– Civil society organisations and networks (international and local organisations representing civil society interests along the life cycle of a timber product, including but certainly not limited to environmental and human rights NGOs concerned with conditions at the place of growth of a tree, and climate change expertise and consumer organisations concerned with quality and sustainable disposal of a product on the end market);
– Networks around existing sustainability schemes with relevance for the sector (such as FSC, PEFC and ISO 26000);
– Academic experts; and
– Individuals with a concern for or interest in the issue through the life cycle of a tree.

(continued)

Table 8.1 (continued)

Establishment of the regulatory process	General	Details (example: collaborative regulation of sustainable forestry)
	Mapping interests and representative groups and/or networks according to interests (topic-wise, sector-wise, system-wise (economic, legal, political, etc.), geographic, developing or developed state, type of organisation) and overview of any conflicts of interest.	
Step three: Equalisation	After mapping the interests and potential stakeholders involved, potential power disparities must be identified and addressed in order to provide, as much as possible, equalised deliberation. This entails a number of sub-steps: – Assessing strengths and weaknesses of representative groups and interests in terms of access to representative organisations, knowledge and other resources. – Assessing special needs of representation and information and empowerment. – Formulation of specific criteria or reasons to select special groups or networks, such as previous experience in developing sustainability governance schemes or regional challenges. – Consultation on mapping and assessments at the meta-level.	– Assessing special needs of representation and information and empowerment, for example for indigenous groups or people living in the forest, or for estuaries or land affected by deforestation. – Assessing whether combinations of special expertise and high degrees of established networking are present among participants. For example, whether someone is on several boards (e.g. WWF and PEFC), was involved in leading FSC's evolution, and is also an expert in forestry and/or works in the private sector. It is important to understand these prior interests and power at the micro-level, because such a person could come to have influence in the process.
Step four: Ensuring a procedural framework for the onward process	Proceduralisation is about ensuring equalised participation and deliberation so that stakeholders are enabled to engage in the regulatory process in a way that balances out power disparities. Such disparities may be in the form of previous knowledge or experience, access to new information, access to specific decision-makers, or the absence or presence of other forms of privilege. The organisation establishing the regulatory forum takes the initiative, but consultation is important to provide feedback and ensure trust.	

- Development of draft criteria for representation and inclusiveness; of empowerment strategy; and of strategy for information and communication, including the use of IT-based modalities.
- Development of general principles for a draft code for interaction and communication to ensure deliberation that is equalised and provides for exchange of needs, demands and expectations to generate learning among participants and those whom they represent, and for contestation of decisions during the process to provide prospective accountability.
- Consultation of draft criteria, empowerment needs and strategy, and communication strategy including IT modalities, and of general principles for a draft code for interaction and communication, through modality that enables dialogue and face-to-face communication with the most affected groups with limited access to direct representation in the forum to be established.
- Revision of criteria, empowerment strategy and communication strategy, taking into account the responses provided through consultation.
- Development of a detailed code for interaction and communication within the reflexive law forum, including procedural rules on representation and voice, agenda development, interactive communication that ensures equalised deliberation, management roles and competences, guiding timeline for the process, recurrent assessment of sufficiency of criteria to ensure balanced representation, and guidelines for management of the forum to ensure exchange and learning to induce reflection and promote co- and self-regulation.
- Ensuring transparency of draft and final criteria, including access through IT-based platforms.
- Composition of the reflexive law forum, and ensuring communication about the code as well as transparency of equalisation steps.

- Develop a procedure ensuring rural individuals and forest-dependent communities are represented through local civil society organisations, and that information is provided in their local language.
- Provide training if necessary.
- Examine whether any conflicts of interest may be involved among such individuals, communities and civil society organisations. Even if not related to the specific issue at hand, the process may re-fuel older conflicts.

Table 8.1 (continued)

Implementation of the regulatory process to develop the output	General	Details (example: collaborative regulation of sustainable forestry)
Step one: Enabling reflection – level 2	Setting up the reflexive law forum in practice, including through the use of IT communication.	
	Inviting participants from stakeholders and networks identified as having relevant interest.	Ensuring balance in terms of language, presentation and communication skills, technical issues and financial and other resources.
Step two: Representation and representativeness	Participants introduce themselves and the groups or interests they represent.	The diversity of interests and organisational structure should be declared in detail, noting whether a participant represents: public or private interests; international, transnational, national or sub-national interests; economic or social/environmental interests; majority or minority interests; vulnerable or non-vulnerable interests at the national/regional/international scale; and other relevant information.
	In the interest of transparency, this should be made publicly available on the internet.	
	Forum participants declare existing connections, experience or insight.	Participants explain previous experience in reflexive law or similar-type forums (for example, FSC or labour unions with experience in collective negotiations) or in previous UN rule-making processes.
	This information can be logged electronically in a way that is dynamic, but without deleting old information.	
Step three: Equalisation	The management of the process assesses unmet needs of equalisation and introduces measures to balance disparities (e.g. detailed explanations, guidance, training).	
Step four: Ensuring that the procedural framework for active work is operational and recurrently adjusted if needed	The management of the collaborative regulatory process explains the code for interaction and the communication and conditions for active deliberation and the exchange of needs, demands and expectations to generate learning across participants' systems and interests.	

The regulatory forum develops an indicative and dynamic plan of action, including meetings (virtual and/or face-to-face) and milestones.

In the interest of transparency, this should be made publicly available on the internet.

Steps should be taken to ensure that potential victims as well as forest-dependent communities who do not have easy access to the internet are informed and that their views and concerns are fed back into the process of deliberation, bargaining or negotiation of the plan of action.

The management of the regulatory forum composes and circulates draft minutes and revises these based on feedback from the participants.

In the interest of transparency, the draft and final minutes should be made publicly available on the internet.

Steps should be taken to ensure that potential victims as well as forest-dependent communities who do not have easy access to the internet are informed and that their views and concerns are fed back into the process of discussion and agreeing on minutes.

Ensuring that translation is available into local languages and that documents are made available in local languages and their meanings explained.

Recurrent assessment of representation in terms of balance and power, including as a recurrent point on agendas for the forum's meetings.

Steps must be taken to ensure that the views and power-related concerns of potential victims as well as forest-dependent communities are represented and actively fed into and taken into account in the deliberation, bargaining or negotiation.

Ensuring that representative organisations such as civil society organisations fully represent affected concerns.

Recurrent assessment of the quality of deliberation and negotiation and needs for revision of procedure.

In the assessment and analysis of the minutes, consider whether all participants had an equal time to speak and voice their concerns. E.g., did the minutes identify a small cluster of people leading throughout several topic areas?

(continued)

Table 8.1 (continued)

	General	Details (example: collaborative regulation of sustainable forestry)
Implementation of the regulatory process to develop the output	Management of the regulatory process should pay attention to current and future power issues at stake, including the way in which future power issues related to a potential output deliberated on at a given point of time may reflect on the power and interests of participants in the process.	Steps must be taken to ensure that the views and power-related concerns of potential victims as well as forest-dependent communities are represented.
	The management of the process takes action to address power disparities or structures, including communication practices, to ensure active and equalised deliberation.	In cases where it is clear that a few, but highly persuasive, participants are leading, the agency or individual charged with managing the process should take an active role in bringing up the minority discussions while limiting those who have had a lot of 'air time'.
	Draft outputs communicated for consultation with stakeholder groups not directly represented in the process.	Steps must be taken to ensure that the views and power-related concerns of potential victims as well as forest-dependent communities are represented.
	Translations to be made available where possible.	Translations in local languages to be made available where possible.
		Documents to be read to participants with limited reading capacity.
		Implications explained and questions taken.
	Consultation responses collected and deliberated on to form opinions on changes and agree on changes.	Steps must be taken to ensure that the views and power-related concerns of potential victims as well as forest-dependent communities are represented.
	Additional round(s) of consultation and response collections until deliberations lead to agreement on a normative output.	

reflexive law for the communicative part of the deliberative process to exchange views and to create learning among stakeholders based on appreciation of others' needs and concerns is important for the output and intended change of conduct. The more the communicative process establishes meaning by making needs, concerns and implications clear in a way that relates to the rationality of the functional sub-system or sub-systems being targeted, the higher the likelihood that learning will occur and appreciation of the communicated issue occurs. The *process* towards the output is also important because of the exchange of needs and concerns that ideally induces reflection at the third level of reflexive law and therefore transforms external concerns and needs into new norms of conduct and acceptance of those. This supports agreement following deliberation or bargaining/negotiation. It informs change of conduct to meet the concerns of other participants in the process.

9   Summing up and looking ahead

Overview: This final chapter opens by recapitulating the backdrop for the new theory of collaborative regulation and the foundations for the theory. Concerned with a legitimate process to deliver norms of conduct that enjoy legitimacy, collaborative regulation is a theory for a broadly representative and participatory process to develop norms of conduct through a process of deliberation or bargaining that enables participants to induce appreciation of each others' needs and concerns so that this feeds into the normative output. Ideally and provided the right procedural design in accordance with the proposed collaborative regulation theory, this spurs an inherent compliance pull, making the regulatory process well suited for contexts where pro-active regulation is needed to prevent harm from occurring, or where enforcement institutions are absent or weak. Next, the chapter provides a condensed overview of the theoretical basis, analysis and arguments leading to the theory on collaborative regulation. Finally, the chapter looks to future deployment of collaborative regulation and prospects for refining of the theory through its application to specific regulatory contexts and situations.

9.1 Recapitulation

This book started out with a note on the need and challenges related to governing sustainability and particularly business impacts on sustainability concerns at a global level. At the same time, it noted legitimacy issues related to the inclusion of non-state actors, such as businesses, in super-national law-making. To respond to those issues the task here was defined as engaging in a discussion on whether and how to involve non-state actors in rule-making processes occurring at the super-national level, that is, above nation states. It was noted that such processes may take place under the auspices of international organisations, but they may also occur under the auspices of hybrid organisations that are set up or function with a combination of public and private actors. It was also observed that governance and exploitation of water, a common commodity, are among core emerging sustainability challenges, as is exploitation of the land or sea areas around the Arctic or Antarctic. Looking to a future that may not be far off, it may not be far-fetched to speculate that even outer space could be among future challenges for sustainability, for example with regard to minerals or land space.

Ultimately, these observations and the subsequent analysis led to the proposal of a new procedural theory for multi-stakeholder regulation at the super-national level, '*collaborative regulation*'. Concerned with a legitimate process to deliver norms of conduct that enjoy legitimacy, collaborative regulation is a theory for a broadly representative and participatory process to develop norms of conduct through a process of deliberation or bargaining that enables participants to induce appreciation of each others' needs and concerns so that this feeds into the normative output. Ideally and provided there is the right procedural design in accordance with collaborative regulation theory, this spurs an inherent compliance pull, making the regulatory process well suited for contexts where proactive regulation is needed to prevent harm from occurring, or where enforcement institutions are absent or weak. Collaborative regulation is explained through a foundational theory which rests on a combination of legitimate law-making through deliberation, developed by Jürgen Habermas in the 1990s and more recently advanced towards global applicability by Habermas and others, and the theory of reflexive regulation, developed by Gunther Teubner in the 1980s. A set of core steps is set out as the basic method of collaborative regulation. Collaborative regulation is essentially a regulatory process that includes non-state actors in super-national law-making combined with a proceduralisation to balance power disparities and equalise participation to ensure balanced representation of concerns and interests.

Through an analysis of six empirical cases, each representing a multi-stakeholder process of developing norms of conduct for sustainability in economic conduct, it was determined that the regulatory theory of reflexive law, which was proposed in the 1980s for national-level sustainability-related problems, in principle offers a unique and interesting modality for regulation at the super-national level of global or regional concerns through a process that may involve non-state actors, including businesses as well as NGOs. However, past experience shows that reflexive law in terms of theory as well as its practical application to global sustainability concerns suffers from a significant theory gap: reflexive law theory recognises that power disparities between participants must be balanced, but does not offer directives on how to do this. The cases proved that, while reflexive law may deliver results, this lacuna may significantly reduce the effectiveness of a regulatory process to deliver on its objectives, and it may affect the legitimacy of the process as well as the output. To remedy that theory gap, deliberative theory was introduced. Procedural elements offered by that theory added to reflexive law, leading to the theory of collaborative regulation.

To identify cases of sustainability regulation, a point of departure was taken in the evolution of the emergent business and human rights regime, because it has undergone a major turnaround from rejection of proposed norms of conduct, partly due to business hesitation to the Draft UN Norms, which were developed with limited business participation, to support and adoption of guidance to prevent and reduce adverse business impacts on society, created with the participation of business and other stakeholders, including NGOs. That emergent regime has entered a stage which embodies a process that is intended to lead to an international treaty on business and human rights. The entire process up to the current stage, including the turnaround, has not been without legitimacy challenges, emerging in part from dissatisfaction with the substantive focus as well as form of the normative outputs, in part from the inclusion of businesses as alleged or actual human rights abusers in processes to make rules to rein in the same actors. On the basis of this and other cases studies, including some on CSR in a broader sense, it was discussed what elements in a process strengthen or reduce perceived legitimacy, and what elements reflect the support or 'compliance pull' for a particular outcome resulting from a process, its procedures and its organisational management.

It was noted that as early as several decades ago international law scholars had observed that, owing to conflicting interests and concerns of states and various non-state actors, independent participation of non-state actors in the creation and enforcement of international law should be considered, and that this would be best achieved through an iterative process. The argument that has been made is that including businesses in the process of developing norms of conduct for them at the international level would be most effective in generating support from business for the resulting norms if the prospective duty-bearers were to be included (whether the resulting norms were soft law guidance on business responsibilities or hard law binding obligations). Indeed, scholars have more recently argued that a pluralist global order must recognise a plurality of actors in duties as well as in law-making, and that participation by non-state actors does not challenge the primacy of states in law-making. International law studies have also argued that the process of law-making is highly important if the resulting norms are to carry an inherent 'compliance pull'. A compliance pull is a major factor in the effectiveness of rules that, like much international law as well as much sustainability regulation, operate in an institutional context with weak or non-existent enforcement.

9.2 A condensed version of the theoretical basis, analysis, argument and new theory

A diversity of interests among public and private stakeholders affect their engagement in the efforts to debate and construct norms for business conduct and its societal impacts with regard to sustainability. To appreciate those interests and their significance for the legitimacy, power and regulation of global sustainability concerns, the book takes part of its point of departure in territorial limitations of national law and the ensuing constraints for extraterritorial regulation of transnational economic activity. An overview is given of issues that confront the inclusion of non-state actors, particularly businesses, in super-national lawmaking and particularly their role in the state-centrist international law regime. The role and rights of states in such international law processes are explained to make it clear why the inclusion of businesses is both a novelty and arguably sometimes a necessity when supernational law-making processes aim to make rules pertaining to business conduct. Political constraints affecting the expansion of international law-making to govern sustainable economic activity are discussed, along with the view under the international law doctrine that firms do not have responsibility for their impact on society unless such responsibility is established in international law instruments or customary law. Following a presentation of the dilemma that this poses for public regulation of transnational economic activity with particular regard to sustainability, the chapter discusses examples of regulatory innovation in theory and practice, with examples of how scholars have proposed addressing the limitations, and how international, private or hybrid organisations have sought to develop norms of conduct for business in practice.

Explaining the choice of empirical cases, it was observed that the SRSG process towards the UN Framework and UNGPs broke the previous stalemate in terms of UN regulatory initiatives not just on business and human rights but also for more general social responsibilities of business. The UN Framework prepared the ground for the UNGPs, which provide more detailed guidance than the UN Framework and operate as a form of soft law. The agreement that framed the UN Framework and UNGPs also helped lead towards the launch of negotiations towards a treaty on business and human rights. This makes the SRSG process highly relevant as a case for understanding how the UN or other organisations may design and lead a multi-stakeholder process for new norms in a sustainability-related field, which like the field of business and human rights may be characterised as having many divergent and often conflicting interests. A series of other multi-stakeholder efforts on broader sustainability objectives also serve as cases, representing one initiative originated by a public international organisation (the UN Global Compact), one initiative by a private organisation (ISO 26000) and two, interrelated, initiatives launched by a regional organisation (the EU's Multi-Stakeholder Forum on CSR, and the EU's CSR Alliance).

The analysis confirmed that reflexive law, originally developed for the national regulatory context, may also be applied at the above-national level. In the analysis of the UN Global

Compact, the EU's MSF and the CSR Alliance, the current study has discussed public–private regulation initiated by agencies with administrative authority at the intergovernmental level. However, the analysis of the SRSG process suggests that reflexive law may also offer a regulatory strategy for other intergovernmental agencies, including those with formal law-making powers or related authority. The development of ISO 26000 indicates that reflexive law also offers a regulatory modality for transnational regulation set in a non-state actor context. It is therefore relevant to consider how reflexive law can deliver its regulatory potential. In this context, the current study's observation and confirmation of the implications of the lacuna in reflexive law theory in terms of the limited directives for how to deal with power disparities become pertinent. Overall, the presence or absence of balance of power (or a perceived balance) has played a major role in the effectiveness of the processes observed in the empirical cases to deliver on their objectives, for the process to be seen as legitimate, and for the outputs to enjoy legitimacy. As part of this, the inclusion of both for-profit and not-for-profit non-state actors in the regulatory processes has also been shown to be important for legitimacy and a perceived balance of participation and power.

The discussion of legitimacy took a point of departure in Thomas Franck's discussion of international law as a process that generates norms with an inherent 'compliance pull'. It outlined the relevance of this line of thought for regulation and norms functioning in the absence of strong enforcement institutions. In the process, the similarities between a compliance pull and stakeholders' support for innovative regulation and norms to promote sustainable practices were explained. Franck's points were placed into a contextual perspective of debates on international soft law 'compliance pull' and the inclusion of business in international rule-making pertaining to business conduct in order to stimulate business support for the ensuing norms. The 'compliance pull' thesis emphasises the importance of process legitimacy for rule-making to deliver a normative output that gains support from core stakeholders: those bearing duties or responsibilities as well as rights-holders and civil society.

The analysis and discussion moved on to demonstrate the connection of arguments on the inclusion of business in super-national law-making pertaining to business conduct and compliance pull with recent debates that apply Habermasian-inspired ideas to transnational governance in a context in which non-state actors play an increasingly important role. Drawing on the empirical cases, the practical significance of power disparities on the legitimacy of collaborative regulatory processes and their effectiveness in delivering a normative output in accordance with the objective was highlighted. It was demonstrated that power disparities or privileged insight or access to rule-makers and rule-making distorts the legitimacy of a process, and therefore its ability to deliver an intended output.

The rationale of reflexive law is that public regulation may stimulate private self-regulation through procedural regulatory frameworks. In contexts where the regulatory powers or effects of public regulators are limited, they may instead resort to the alternative of setting up such frameworks for societal actors to engage in the creation of substantive norms on conduct to address societal needs and respond to social expectations through self-regulation. In particular, the procedures may include non-state actors, with a reasoning based on a similar type of rationale as that applied by Friedmann, Franck and Habermas: participation provides for the support for and relevance of norms, and therefore for effectiveness of a regulatory process to deliver relevant norms. Examples of regulatory processes to generate norms on CSR and business and human rights were discussed with regard to reflexive law elements. This led to a discussion and analysis of power issues, in which these cases were discussed, with particular emphasis on output delivery of initiatives, taking into account multi-stakeholder participation and the inclusion or non-inclusion of particular stakeholders as part of the throughput to process input into output. The significance of inclusion in the regulatory process was set against the need to balance power disparities during the regulatory process and for its outcome to be legitimate. However, while balancing power disparities is an important normative element in reflexive law in its own right, the theory does not offer directives for how to achieve this.

Based on the analysis of the case studies, it was observed that reflexive law may in principle offer a relevant regulatory strategy for addressing global concerns through public–private regulation at the intergovernmental level to complement conventional international law. Differences between the normative outputs indicated that power disparities within the composition of the reflexive law forums may have significant impact on the outputs. This confirms that reflexive law theory suffers from a significant gap through the lack of directives on how reflexive law forums should be organisationally and procedurally designed to handle power imbalances between participants. Reflexive law theory sets out only a basic assumption that reflexive law forums should neutralise power disparities. Thus, for reflexive law to be effective in delivering a compliance pull, this book argues and demonstrates that the theory gap it has been argued, this gap in theory must be remedied if reflexive law is to yield its regulatory potential, for example in relation to global sustainability concerns.

To remedy that gap, the development of the theory of collaborative regulation relied on later Habermasian theory on legitimate law-making, developed after reflexive law theory. A procedural theory, Habermasian deliberation offers useful insights to advance reflexive law in theory and practice to handle power disparities. Advancing the theory by addressing and covering the theory gap on balancing power disparities will make reflexive law better equipped to function as a pragmatic regulatory approach towards developing norms of conduct at the super-national level. Enhanced with effectiveness and legitimacy, reflexive law may fill governance gaps in relation to global, regional or local sustainability concerns. Advancing reflexive law into collaborative regulation equips the core of reflexive law as a regulatory strategy with huge practical potential to address global, regional or local sustainability challenges through a form of regulated self-regulation. Complementing the original theory with Habermasian theory on legitimate law-making offers a necessary proceduralised quality for delivering legitimate outputs that are conducive to carrying a compliance pull because they have been developed through a process that balanced power disparities.

Habermas's theory assumes a qualitative participation, or at least procedural conditions in place for such participation by all actors in the process. This requirement is not similarly developed in reflexive law. Hence, Habermasian theory on legitimate law-making through deliberation or bargaining arguably complements reflexive law theory by being formulated into concrete guidance for the procedural organisation of reflexive law forums. In other words, to promote the effectiveness of reflexive law forums to deliver rule-making that is perceived to be legitimate from the perspective of process (throughput) as well as resulting rules (output), authorities that organise reflexive law forums should carefully develop and prescribe procedural rules for the functioning of the forum. Providing the context for active and equalised usage of formal participation, these rules should define procedures framing expression of views and transparent criteria for ensuring that participants are representative of the interests, which are affected by the pertinent reflexive law forum, and able to interact through equalised participation. They should also provide for steps for the downwards, upwards and sideways sharing of information, views and concerns, whether in virtual or actual meetings. Moreover, the rules should provide for feedback mechanisms to learn about, monitor and address power disparities as these evolve. Finally, they should provide for steps to ensure that those participants who may be less experienced in collaborative norm-making processes or have less factual knowledge or political insight, have less relevant linguistic capacities or are affected by other factors that may place them at a disadvantage are assisted and empowered to the level of other participants.

The contribution of Habermasian focus on deliberation rather than simply debate and exchange of views on needs and expectations means that organisers of multi-stakeholder regulatory processes should recognise that the establishment of a procedural forum is not by itself sufficient to ensure legitimate law-making with representation of non-state actors. The procedural forum needs to be designed in such a way that procedural rules allow for management of power disparities in order for interests to be represented in a balanced way. Not only does this have the potential to provide for legitimacy of normativity on business impacts on society or other sustainability issues created through public–private collaboration. It may also provide current international law-making with guidance and experience on how to adapt to societal conditions at a time when non-state actors make claims to participation in law-making processes at the above-state level.

Building on Habermasian deliberative theory, the deliberative turn in the social sciences has tended to focus more on the debate that unfolds within a proceduralised forum for deliberation than on the procedure itself. Drawing on the case studies, it is argued here that procedure is a key element, which complements reflexive law that already incorporates elements of a debate and exchange of views for co-creation of norms of conduct. The formality of procedure creates the stable and predictable framework that is necessary for the substantive elements of a qualified deliberation or other debate that is balanced in terms of power to unfold. Without procedure, the quality of that debate does not support the substantive elements. Without procedure to equalise participation and power disparities, the arguments do not flow freely, and the better argument does not work through the 'uncoerced force' of its substantive quality. Rather, it may be overridden by others that have better access to the process or privileged insights, or it may override others with less such power.

Procedural rights of participation in decision-making processes are known from national constitutional law as well as international law, and they also connect to (national) administrative law through the emphasis on ensuring equalised opportunities for participation in decision-making processes. Procedural human rights are part of some of the key international declarations and treaties that businesses have supported for normative guidance on substantive issues, such as business impacts on society. Both Habermas and Teubner refer to human rights (or fundamental rights) in the context of super-national law-making. Taking international human rights law as a common normative source offers an opportunity to bridge these concerns and to frame public–private rule-making at the above-national level with procedural rights for participants. The parallel to national law-making is clear when the context is above-national rule-making seeking to establish norms of conduct for business enterprises: national law may create obligations for individuals subject to the relevant legislature. This applies to general law-making by a legislature as well as to decisions made by administrative authorities. Duties and the right to participation in the process of establishing those duties are inherently connected. Allowing non-state actors procedural rights of participation in above-national rule-making setting norms of conduct for them parallels this balancing of duties with rights of influence. Procedural rights of information and expression allow for equalisation and informed representative participation in decision-making. Detailed proceduralisation enables the active and equalised exercise of those rights.

When power disparities are not managed and equalised during a regulatory process in which diverse concerns are represented, there is a risk that the regulatory process will not deliver the output that was intended, or that it will be skewed in terms of the interests that it favours and deficient in legitimacy. Thus, power disparities risk either corrupting the process and reducing its effectiveness in turning input into output, or hurting the reception and uptake of the output.

Accordingly, bringing Habermasian theory on deliberative law-making into the context of public–private sustainability-related regulation at the intergovernmental level adds a deeper perspective on the requirements of reflexive law procedure to deliver the normative objective of balancing interests than that which is provided by reflexive law theory. It adds a legitimacy aspect to public–private norm creation at the super-national level as a new form of law-making that attempts to incorporate non-state actors into the process.

Collaborative regulation is proposed as the solution to the gaps in reflexive law theory, which will at the same time enable regulatory processes to apply the communicative approach of reflexive law to induce organisational appreciation of externalities so as to promote accept-ance of particular norms of conduct. Proceduralisation and equalised participation are key concepts of collaborative regulation.

After setting out the foundational theory that combines reflexive law and newer Haber-masian theory into collaborative regulation, two future prospects are outlined for enhancing the balancing of power disparities in multi-stakeholder regulation at the super-national level to address sustainability challenges: through a prospective treaty setting out procedural aspects for a right of participation for non-state actors; and through an actual application and iterative development, pending the possible adoption of a treaty.

9.3 Looking ahead

Global, regional or even local sustainability concerns tend to include transnational elements that are not easily governed by conventional national or international law. They often addi-tionally include elements of public and private power, roles or responsibilities that further blur the regulatory picture. Moreover, adverse sustainability impacts tend to be hard to rem-edy, and when they occur they often cause additional social or environmental adverse effects. When resources are at stake, environmental and climate change impacts may be what catch the media headlines, but, as the numerous human rights violations and conflicts related to 'conflict minerals' have proven, social and community concerns are as important. Hence, realising the ideal of 'do no harm' is of paramount importance. This calls for proactive regu-lation with an inherent compliance pull. In turn, this requires a regulatory process that allows for normative directives to be developed in a manner that ensures legitimacy.

Given the fast and dynamic emergence of sustainability concerns that has occurred in past decades it is reasonable to expect that the need for proactive regulation to promote sustaina-ble practices and prevent sustainability-related conflicts will only grow in the future. In view of the 20th and early 21st centuries' competition for both renewable and non-renewable natu-ral resources and the impact that climate change may come to have on land, it is not unlikely that competition for land and land-based resources will increase, and that conflicts may arise in regard to commodities like water and unpolluted air. In addition to being crucial for human life, the latter can also function as transportation media for sea- or airborne vessels, highlight-ing their economic significance. Whatever the background for such competition, the benefits of reaching agreement on common concerns and needs before competition leads to conflict in an increasingly interconnected world are obvious. Still, despite the interconnected character of the world, differences remain huge in terms of economic, political, legal and communica-tive resources, not only between countries but increasingly within them.

Legitimate law-making presupposes a process that allows for the concerns and views of all to be taken into account, regardless of access to resources. The current processes for international law-making and global governance as represented by the UN and other international organisations do not sufficiently provide for such formation of common will. Moreover, current international regulatory approaches tend to be reactively oriented, relying on monitoring and on enforcement that is institutionally weak and will not remedy harm done. While sanctions are needed when harm does occur as well as to the extent that the risk of a sanction may prevent a harm from being caused, prevention of harm is preferable. The current state-centrist system is not by all accounts well suited to establishing norms of conduct pertaining to non-state actors in a way that generates an inherent compliance pull. International law scholars decades ago had observed that involving non-state actors in decision-making pertaining to business conduct and societal impacts can enhance their support for the resulting output. Doing so does not have to challenge state sovereignty or indeed state obligations, as the recognition of a formal role for non-state actors can be limited to the issue at hand. Yet regulatory theory has not come up with a detailed solution to these dilemmas, and several past efforts to regulate sustainability concerns through multi-stakeholder processes have tended to become marred by imbalanced power disparities hurting the legitimacy of process and output, and trust in both.

Against this backdrop, collaborative regulation offers an advanced theoretical framework for multi-stakeholder regulation, which will deliver or help deliver outputs that are legitimate in terms of reflecting interests in an input-legitimate way, and by delivering outputs perceived as legitimate (output legitimacy) through a legitimate process (throughput legitimacy). To deliver a compliance pull among those subjected to the rules, the output should inspire trust among those who are affected, whether in terms of obligations or as direct victims of adverse business impact, such as corporate abuse of human rights. Such individuals or groups often lack resources for direct participation even where this may be technically possible. This makes it imperative to ensure that the representation of their interests is also balanced within the groups that have social or environmental impacts as their core concerns.

The process towards the so-called 'binding instrument' (treaty) on business and human rights that was begun in 2014 and is on-going at the time of writing is interesting in the light of the analysis above. With the establishment of an intergovernmental working group, (the Open-Ended Intergovernmental Working Group), that process has taken off on a note that is closer to conventional international law-making than the process that resulted in the UNGPs. However, underlying system-specific interests that impeded the Draft UN Norms from getting accepted remain basically unchanged. Individual stakeholder concerns and needs may be voiced in terms that are aligned with the institutional framework for international law and human rights protection, respect, fulfilment and remediation. However, businesses are still fundamentally concerned with economic implications, as they were at the time of the Draft UN Norms as well as during the EU's MSF. As the analysis above shows, in order to generate acceptance of change it is important to engage in a communicative process that stimulates an appreciation of stakeholders' concerns and needs by addressing their significance to the underlying system-specific logic or rationality. The analysis above has demonstrated that, to develop norms of conduct for the protection of human rights against business-related abuse and to promote business respect of human rights (or even business contributions to human rights fulfilment), it is important that actors in the process address concerns with due appreciation for the interests at stake for others involved – effectively communicating the need to change into acceptance by explaining the significance from the perspective of the concerns and interests of the actor with whom change is desired by other stakeholders. As importantly for the legitimacy and acceptance of the outputs of the regulatory process, participation in that process must be inclusive and balanced.

Pulling the proceduralisation that characterises deliberative law-making into reflexive law joins the best of both law-making theories. It promotes the opportunities for developing norms of conduct through a common formation of will based on reflection induced by the expectations, needs and demands of other participants. Ideally, this *ex ante* or prospective accountability limits the need for challenging decisions *ex post*. Contestation modalities may be established, and where they are may strengthen legitimacy. Constituting a form of internal jurisprudence, insights from contestation will also provide insights into how power concerns can be identified, managed and remedied as part of a collaborative regulatory process.

Indeed, the onward course for collaborative regulation is likely to proceed as an iterative process, fitting the prospects for a democratic-striving approach to global governance noted in Chapter 2. Testing the theoretical foundations for collaborative regulation offered above by applying them in practice will provide insights for fine-tuning, which can be applied by other processes and feed into the development of a treaty on non-state actor participation in super-national law-making.

Advancing reflexive law through the Habermasian procedural directives addresses reflexive law's theory gap in relation to the normative aspect of handling power disparities for throughput legitimacy. It equips the application of reflexive law as a regulatory strategy with an enhanced potential for delivering legitimate outputs that are conducive to carrying a compliance pull because they were developed through a process that balanced power disparities. Given that much multi-stakeholder regulation applies elements that may be understood as reflexive regulatory, advancing reflexive law into collaborative regulation will help that multi-stakeholder communication approach to regulation become better equipped towards developing norms of conduct, and therefore contribute to filling governance gaps in relation to global, regional or local sustainability concerns. In view of the frequent conflicting interests at stake in sustainability regulation, the application of the combined insights is also relevant to regulatory initiatives that aim to develop sustainability-related norms of conduct through more conventional approaches.

Managing large multi-stakeholder regulatory processes with many and diverse participants may be organisationally challenging. Working across national or regional boundaries, languages or cultures will not make the task easier. Yet, with careful organisation, development of criteria for representation and proceduralised steps to frame participation, the task is not impossible. National governance, too, deals with similar issues, for example in federal states or countries with several official languages. Certain processes of collaborative regulation are likely to be organised around issues that do not require a large group of stakeholders. This will make them more easily manageable, and such smaller forums will provide valuable experience for organising and managing larger forums. Indeed, smaller forums may well offer learning experiences for authorities charged with public policy or legal obligations whose effective implementation calls for active participation of the private sector in collaboration with civil society.

References

Academic articles and books

Abbott, K. W. and Snidal, D. (2012) 'Taking responsive regulation transnational: Strategies for international organizations', *Regulation and Governance*, Vol. 7, No. 1, pp. 95–113.

Abbott, K. W., Genschel, P., Snidal, D. and Zangl, B. (2015) 'Orchestration: Global governance through intermediaries', in K. W. Abbott, P. Genschel, D. Snidal and B. Zangl (eds), *International Organizations as Orchestrators*, Cambridge: Cambridge University Press, pp. 3–36.

Aftab, Y. (2016) *Pillar III on the Ground: An Independent Assessment of the Porgera Remedy Framework*, Enodo Rights, http://www.barrick.com/files/porgera/Enodo-Rights-Porgera-Remedy-Framework-Independent-Assessment.pdf (accessed 16 November 2016).

Aker, J. C. and Mbiti, I. M. (2010) *Mobile Phones and Economic Development in Africa*, Center for Global Development Working Paper No. 211, Tufts University – Fletcher School of Law and Diplomacy, Center for Global Development.

Andonova, L. B., Betsill, M. M. and Bulkeley, H. (2009) 'Transnational climate governance', *Global Environmental Politics*, Vol. 9, No. 2, pp. 52–73.

Anthony, G., Auby, J. B., Morison, J. and Zwart, T. (2011) 'Values in global administrative law: Introducing the collection', in G. Anthony, J. B. Auby, J. Morison and T. Zwart (eds), *Values in Global Administrative Law*, Oxford: Hart, pp. 1–16.

Arthurs, H. (2008) 'Corporate self-regulation: Political economy, state regulation and reflexive labour law', in B. Bercusson and C. Estlund (eds), *Regulating Labour in the Wake of Globalisation*, Oxford: Hart, pp. 19–35.

Arts, B. (1998) *The Political Influence of Global NGOs: Case Studies on the Climate and Biodiversity Conventions*, Utrecht: International Books.

Arts, B. (2001) 'The impact of environmental NGOs in international conventions', in B. Arts, M. Noortmann and B. Reinalda (eds), *Non-State Actors in International Relations*, Aldershot: Ashgate, pp. 195–210.

Ayres, I. and Braithwaite, J. (1992) *Responsive Regulation: Transcending the Deregulation Debate*, New York: Oxford University Press.

Backer, L. C. (2006) 'Multinational corporations, transnational law: The United Nations' Norms on the Responsibilities of Transnational Corporations as a harbinger of corporate social responsibility in international law', *Columbia Human Rights Law Review*, Vol. 37, Winter, pp. 287–389.

Backer, L. C. (2014) *The Guiding Principles of Business and Human Rights at a Crossroads: The State, the Enterprise, and the Spectre of a Treaty to Bind Them All*, Working Paper No. 7/1, July, Coalition for Peace and Ethics.

Barnard, C. (2002) 'The social partners and the governance agenda', *European Law Journal*, Vol. 8, No. 1, pp. 80–101.

Baumann-Pauly, D., Wickert, C., Spence, L. J. and Scherer, A. G. (2013) 'Organizing corporate social responsibility in small and large firms: Size matters', *Journal of Business Ethics*, Vol. 115, pp. 693–705.

Baxter, H. (2011) *Habermas: The Discourse Theory of Law and Democracy*, Stanford, CA: Stanford University Press.

Bendell, J. (2004) *Barricades and Boardrooms: A Contemporary History of the Corporate Accountability Movement*, Technology, Business and Society Programme Paper No. 13, Geneva: United Nations Research Institute for Social Development.

Berger-Walliser, G. and Shrivastava, P. (2015) 'Beyond compliance: Sustainable development, business, and pro-active law', *Georgia International Law Journal*, Vol. 46, No. 2, pp. 417–475.

Berle, A. A., Jr (1931) 'Corporate powers as powers in trust', *Harvard Law Review*, Vol. 44, No. 7, pp. 1049–1074.

Bilchitz, D. (2013) 'A chasm between "is" and "ought"? A critique of the normative foundations of the SRSG's Framework and the Guiding Principles', in S. Deva and D. Bilchitz (eds), *Human Rights Obligations of Business: Beyond the Corporate Responsibility to Respect?*, Cambridge: Cambridge University Press, pp. 107–137.

Bilchitz, D. and Deva, S. (2013) 'The human rights obligations of business: A critical framework for the future', in S. Deva and D. Bilchitz (eds), *Human Rights Obligations of Business: Beyond the Corporate Responsibility to Respect?*, Cambridge: Cambridge University Press, pp. 1–26.

Black, J. (2008) 'Constructing and contesting legitimacy and accountability in polycentric regulatory regimes', *Regulation and Governance*, Vol. 2, pp. 137–164.

Blankenburg, E. (1984) 'The poverty of evolutionism: A critique of Teubner's case for "reflexive law"', *Law and Society Review*, Vol. 18, pp. 273–289.

Bodansky, D. and Rajamani, L. (2016) 'Evolution and governance architecture of the climate change regime', in D. Sprinz and U. Luterbacher (eds), *International Relations and Global Climate Change: New Perspectives*, Boston, MA: MIT Press, available at SSRN, https://papers.ssrn.com/sol3/papers.cfm?abstract_id=2168859 (accessed 22 December 2016).

Bonnitcha, J. and McCorquodale, R. (forthcoming) 'Is the concept of "due diligence" in the Guiding Principles coherent?', *European Journal of International Law*, available at SSRN, http://papers.ssrn.com/sol3/papers.cfm?abstract_id=2208588.

Börzel, T. A. and Risse, T. (2010) 'Governance without a state: Can it work?', *Regulation and Governance*, Vol. 4, No. 2, pp. 113–134.

Braten, S. (1992) 'Paradigms of autonomy', in G. Teubner and A. Febbrajo (eds), *European Yearbook in the Sociology of Law: State, Law and Economy as Autopoietic Systems: Regulation and Autonomy in a New Perspective*, Milano: Giuffrè, pp. 35–65.

Brunnée, J. and Toope, S. J. (2010) *Legitimacy and Legality in International Law: An Interactional Account*, New York: Cambridge University Press.

Buhmann, K. (2001) *Implementing Human Rights through Administrative Law Reforms: The Potential in China and Vietnam*, Copenhagen: Djoef Publishing.

Buhmann, K. (2006) 'Corporate social responsibility: What role for law? Some aspects of law and CSR', *Corporate Governance: The International Journal of Business in Society*, Vol. 6, No. 2, pp. 188–202.

Buhmann, K. (2009) 'Regulating corporate social and human rights responsibilities at the UN plane: Institutionalising new forms of law and law-making approaches?', *Nordic Journal of International Law*, Vol. 78, No. 1, pp. 1–52.

Buhmann, K. (2011) 'Integrating human rights in emerging regulation of corporate social responsibility: The EU case', *International Journal of Law in Context*, Vol. 7, No. 2, pp. 139–179.

Buhmann, K. (2011) 'Reflexive regulation of CSR: A case study of public-policy interests in EU public–private regulation of CSR', *International and Comparative Corporate Law Journal*, Vol. 8, No. 2, pp. 38–76.

Buhmann, K. (2012) 'The development of the "UN Framework": A pragmatic process towards a pragmatic output', in R. Mares (ed.), *The UN Guiding Principles on Business and Human Rights: Foundations and Implementation*, Leiden: Martinus Nijhoff, pp. 85–105.

Buhmann, K. (2013) 'The Danish CSR reporting requirement as reflexive law: Employing CSR as a modality to promote public policy', *European Business Law Review*, Vol. 24, No. 2, pp. 187–216.

Buhmann, K. (2014) *Normative Discourses and Public–Private Regulatory Strategies for Construction of CSR Normativity: Towards a Method for Above-National Public–Private Regulation of Business Social Responsibilities*, Copenhagen: Multivers.

Buhmann, K. (2015) 'Business and human rights: Understanding the UN Guiding Principles from the perspective of transnational business governance interactions', *Transnational Legal Theory*, Vol. 6, No. 1, pp. 399–434.

Buhmann, K. (2015) 'Defying territorial limitations: Regulating business conduct extraterritorially through establishing obligations in EU law and national law', in J. L. Cernic and T. Van Ho (eds), *Human Rights and Business: Direct Corporate Accountability for Human Rights*, The Hague: Wolf Legal Publishers, pp. 179–228.

Buhmann, K. (2016) 'Juridifying corporate social responsibility through public law: Assessing coherence and inconsistencies against UN guidance on business and human rights', *International and Comparative Corporate Law Journal*, Vol. 11, No. 3, pp. 194–228.

Buhmann, K. (2016) 'Public regulators and CSR: The "social licence to operate" in recent United Nations instruments on business and human rights and the juridification of CSR', *Journal of Business Ethics*, Vol. 136, No. 4, pp. 699–714.

Buhmann, K. (2018) *Changing Sustainability Norms through Communication Processes: The Emergence of the Business and Human Rights Regime as Transnational Law*, Cheltenham: Edward Elgar.

Buhmann, K. and Nathan, I. (2013) 'Plentiful forests, happy people? The EU's FLEGT approach and its impact on human rights and private forestry sustainability schemes', *Nordic Environmental Law Journal*, Vol. 4, No. 2, pp. 53–82.

Burca, G. de (2008) 'Developing democracy beyond the state', *Columbia Journal of Transnational Law*, Vol. 46, No. 2, pp. 221–278.

Burke, R. J., Martin, G. and Cooper, C. L. (2011) *Corporate Reputation: Managing Opportunities and Threats*, Farnham: Ashgate.

Bush, S. R., Belton, B., Hall, D., Vandergeest, P., Murray, F. J., Ponte, S., Oosterveer, P., Islam, M. S., Mol, A. P. J., Hatanaka, M., Kruijssen, F., Ha, T. T. T., Little, D. C. and Kusumawati, R. (2013) 'Certify sustainable aquaculture?', *Science*, Vol. 341, No. 6150, pp. 1067–1068.

Cafaggi, F. and Renna, A. (2012) *Public and Private Regulation: Mapping the Labyrinth*, CEPS Working Document No. 370, October, Brussels: Centre for European Policy Studies.

Capps, P. and Machin, D. (2011) 'The problem of global law', *Modern Law Review*, Vol. 74, No. 5, pp. 794–810.

Carroll, A. B. (1979) 'A three-dimensional conceptual model of corporate performance', *Academy of Management Review*, Vol. 4, No. 4, pp. 497–505.

Cashore, B. (2002) 'Legitimacy and the privatization of environmental governance: How non-state market-driven (NSMD) governance systems gain rule-making authority', *Governance: An International Journal of Policy, Administration, and Institutions*, Vol. 15, No. 4, pp. 503–529.

Cashore, B., Auld, G. and Newsom, D. (2004) *Governing through Markets: Forest Certification and the Emergence of Non-State Authority*, New Haven, CT: Yale University Press.

Cassese, S. (2011) 'A global due process of law', in G. Anthony, J. B. Auby, J. Morison and T. Zwart (eds), *Values in Global Administrative Law*, Oxford: Hart, pp. 17–60.

Cernic, J. L. (2010) 'Two steps forward, one step back: The 2010 UN report by the UN Special Representative on Business and Human Rights', *German Law Journal*, Vol. 11, pp. 1264–1280.

Charlesworth, H. and Chinkin, C. (2000) *The Boundaries of International Law: A Feminist Perspective*, Manchester: Manchester University Press.

Charney, J. I. (1983) 'Transnational corporations and developing public international law', *Duke Law Journal*, Vol. 32, pp. 748–788.

Charnovitz, S. (1997) 'Two centuries of participation: NGOs and international governance', *Michigan Journal of International Law*, Vol. 18, No. 2, pp. 183–286.

Chinkin, C. (2000) 'Normative development in the international legal system', in D. Shelton (ed.), *Commitment and Compliance: The Role of Non-Binding Norms in the International Legal System*, Oxford: Oxford University Press, pp. 21–42.

Clapham, A. (2006) *Human Rights Obligations of Non-State Actors*, New York: Oxford University Press.

Cohen, J. and Sabel, C. (2001) 'Directly-deliberative polyarchy', *European Law Journal*, Vol. 3, No. 4, pp. 313–342.

Cohen, J. and Sabel, C. (2005) 'Global democracy?', *NYU Journal of International Law and Politics*, Vol. 37, No. 4, pp. 763–797.

Collins, H. (1998) Reviewed work: *Reflexive Labour Law: Studies in Industrial Relations and Employment Regulation* by Ralf Rogowski, Ton Wilthagen, *Modern Law Review*, Vol. 61, No. 6, pp. 916–920.

Council of Europe (1996) *The Administration and You: Principles of Administrative Law Concerning the Relations between Administrative Authorities and Private Persons*, Strasbourg: Council of Europe.

Council of Europe (1998) *The Administration and You: A Handbook*, Strasbourg: Council of Europe.

Cragg, W. (2012) 'Ethics, enlightened self-interest, and the corporate responsibility to respect human rights', *Business Ethics Quarterly*, Vol. 22, No. 1, pp. 9–36.

Dalberg-Larsen, J. (1991) *Ret, styring og selvforvaltning*, Aarhus: Juridisk Bogformidling.

Dalberg-Larsen, J. (2006) 'Perspektiver på retlig regulering, særlig i relation til selvforvaltning', in K. Buhmann (ed.), *Corporate social responsibility (CSR) som genstandsfelt for juridisk analyse: Teoretiske og metodiske overvejelser*, Roskilde: Roskilde University, Center for Værdier i Virksomheder, pp. 37–46.

Daniel, C., Wilde-Ramsing, J., Genovese, K. and Sandjojo, V. (2015) *Remedy Remains Rare: An Analysis of 15 Years of NCP Cases and Their Contributions to Improve Access to Remedy for Victims of Corporate Misconduct*, Amsterdam: OECD Watch.

Davis, R. and Franks, D. (2014) *Costs of Company–Community Conflict in the Extractive Sector*, Corporate Social Responsibility Initiative Report No. 66, Cambridge, MA: Harvard Kennedy School.

Deakin, S. (2005) 'Social rights in a globalised economy', in P. Alston (ed.), *Labour Rights as Human Rights*, New York: Oxford University Press, pp. 25–60.

Deakin, S. and Hobbs, R. (2007) 'False dawn for CSR? Shifts in regulatory policy and the response of the corporate and financial sectors in Britain', *Corporate Governance*, Vol. 15, No. 1, pp. 68–76.

Deitelhoff, N. (2009) 'The discursive process of legalization: Charting islands of persuasion in the ICC case', *International Organization*, Vol. 63, Winter, pp. 33–65.

Deitelhoff, N. and Müller, H. (2005) 'Theoretical paradise – empirically lost? Arguing with Habermas', *Review of International Studies*, Vol. 31, pp. 167–179.

De Schutter, O. (2010) *International Human Rights Law*, Cambridge: Cambridge University Press.

De Schutter, O. (2013) 'Foreword', in S. Deva and D. Bilchitz (eds), *Human Rights Obligations of Business: Beyond the Corporate Responsibility to Respect?*, Cambridge: Cambridge University Press, pp. xv–xxii.

Deva, S. (2010) '"Protect, respect and remedy": A critique of the SRSG's Framework for Business and Human Rights', in K. Buhmann, L. Roseberry and M. Morsing (eds), *Corporate Social and Human Rights Responsibilities: Global Legal and Management Perspectives*, Houndmills: Palgrave Macmillan, pp. 108–128.

Deva, S. (2013) 'Treating human rights lightly: A critique of the consensus rhetoric and the language employed by the Guiding Principles', in S. Deva and D. Bilchitz (eds), *Human Rights Obligations of Business: Beyond the Corporate Responsibility to Respect?*, Cambridge: Cambridge University Press, pp. 78–104.

Dodd, E. M., Jr (1932) 'For whom are corporate managers trustees?', *Harvard Law Review*, Vol. 45, No. 7, pp. 1145–1163.

Drexhage, J. and Murphy, D. (2010) *Sustainable Development: From Brundtland to Rio 2012: Background Paper Prepared for Consideration by High Level Panel on Sustainability at Its First Meeting, 19 September 2010*, New York: United Nations.

Drimmer, J. and Phillips, N. (2012) 'Sunlight for the heart of darkness: Conflict minerals and the first wave of SEC regulation of social issues', *Human Rights and International Legal Discourse*, Vol. 6, No. 1, pp. 131–158.

Elkington, J. (1998) *Cannibals with Forks: The Triple Bottom Line of 21st Century Business*, Gabriola Island, BC: New Society Publishers.

Epstein, E. M. (1993) 'Regulation, self-regulation and corporate ethics: Mutually reinforcing conditions for achieving socially responsible and publicly accountable business behaviour', in *Fundamental Subjects of the Contemporary Study of Business Administration (Essays in Honor of Professor Mizuho Nakamura)*, Japanese edn, Tokyo: Bunshindo, pp. 305–316.

Epstein, E. M. (1998) 'Business ethics and corporate social policy', *Business and Society Review*, Vol. 37, No. 1, pp. 7–39.

Fairbrass, J. (2011) 'Exploring corporate social responsibility policy in the European Union: A discursive institutionalist analysis', *JCMS: Journal of Common Market Studies*, Vol. 49, No. 5, pp. 949–970.

Farmer, L. and Teubner, G. (1994) 'Ecological self-organization', in G. Teubner, L. Farmer and D. Murphy (eds), *Environmental Law and Ecological Responsibility: The Concept and Practice of Ecological Self-Organisation*, Chichester: John Wiley & Sons, pp. 3–13.

Fasterling, B. and Demuijnck, G. (2013) 'Human rights in the void? Due diligence in the UN Guiding Principles on Business and Human Rights', *Journal of Business Ethics*, Vol. 116, No. 4, pp. 1–16.

Ferrell, C. F. (2006) *The Abolitionist Movement*, Westport, CT: Greenwood Publishing.

Footer, M. (2015) 'Human rights due diligence and the responsible supply of minerals from conflict-affected areas: Towards a normative framework?', in J. L. Cernic and T. Van Ho (eds), *Direct Human Rights Obligations of Corporations*, The Hague: Wolf Legal Publishers, pp. 179–228.

Franck, T. M. (1990) *The Power of Legitimacy among Nations*, Oxford: Oxford University Press.

Friedmann, W. (1964) *The Changing Structure of International Law*, London: Stevens & Sons.

Frynas, J. G. (2008) 'Corporate social responsibility and international development: Critical assessment', *Corporate Governance: An International Review*, Vol. 16, No. 4, pp. 274–281.

Glendon, M.-A. (2001) *A World Made New: Eleanor Roosevelt and the Universal Declaration of Human Rights*, New York: Random House.

Gond, J. P. and Herrbach, O. (2006) 'Social reporting as an organisational learning tool? A theoretical framework', *Journal of Business Ethics*, Vol. 65, pp. 359–371.

Goodin, R. E. and Ratner, S. R. (2011) 'Democratizing international law', *Global Policy*, Vol. 2, No. 3, pp. 241–247.

Griffiths, J. (1986) 'What is legal pluralism?', *Journal of Legal Pluralism and Unofficial Law*, Vol. 24, pp. 1–55.

Gulbrandsen, L. (2004) 'Overlapping public and private governance: Can forest certification fill the gaps in the global forest regime?', *Global Environmental Politics*, Vol. 4, No. 2, pp. 75–99.

Gulbrandsen, L. (2014) 'Dynamic governance interactions: Evolutionary effects of state responses to non-state certification programs', *Regulation and Governance*, Vol. 8, No. 2, pp. 74–92.

Habermas, J. (1974) 'The public sphere', *New German Critique*, Vol. 3, pp. 49–55.

Habermas, J. (1996) *Between Facts and Norms: Contributions to a Discourse Theory of Law and Democracy*, translated by W. Rehg, Cambridge: Polity Press/Blackwell.

Habermas, J. (1998) *Die postnationale Konstellation: Politische Essays*, Frankfurt am Main: Suhrkamp, pp. 91–169.

Habermas, J. (1998) 'Jenseits der Nationalstaats: Bemerkungen zu Folgeprobleme der wirtschaftlichen Globalisierung', in U. Beck (ed.), *Politik der Globalisierung*, Frankfurt am Main: Suhrkamp, pp. 67–84.

Habermas, J. (1998) 'Zur Legitimation durch Menschenrechte', in *Die postnationale Konstellation: Politische Essays*, Frankfurt am Main: Suhrkamp, pp. 170–194.

Habermas, J. (2004) 'Folkeretten i overgangen til den postnationale konstellation', *Distinktion*, Vol. 8, pp. 9–17.

Habermas, J. (2005) 'Den demokratiske retsstat: En paradoksal sammenknytning af modstridende principper?', in H. Andersen (ed.), *Jürgen Habermas: Demokrati og retsstat – en tekstsamling*, Copenhagen: Hans Reitzels Forlag, pp. 73–89.

Habermas, J. (2005) 'Den postnationale konstellation og demokratiets fremtid', in H. Andersen (ed.), *Jürgen Habermas: Demokrati og retsstat – en tekstsamling*, Copenhagen: Hans Reitzels Forlag, pp. 220–273, translated from Habermas, J. (1998) *Die postnationale Konstellation: Politische Essays*, Frankfurt am Main: Suhrkamp, pp. 91–169.

Habermas, J. (2005) 'Efter nationalstaten? Bemærkninger til den økonomiske globaliserings følge-problemer', in H. Andersen (ed.), *Jürgen Habermas: Demokrati og retsstat – en tekstsamling*, Copenhagen: Hans Reitzels Forlag, pp. 204–219, translated into Danish from Habermas, J. (1998) 'Jenseits der Nationalstaats: Bemerkungen zu Folgeprobleme der wirtschaftlichen Globalisierung', in U. Beck (ed.), *Politik der Globalisierung*, Frankfurt am Main: Suhrkamp, pp. 67–84.

Habermas, J. (2005) 'Kant's idé om den evige fred – på en historisk afstand af 200 år', in H. Andersen (ed.), *Jürgen Habermas: Demokrati og retsstat – en tekstsamling*, Copenhagen: Hans Reitzels Forlag, pp. 149–186, translated from Habermas, J. (1996) 'Kants Idee der ewigen Friedens', in *Die Einbeziehung des Anderen: Studien zur politischen Theorie*, Frankfurt am Main: Suhrkamp, pp. 154–185.

Habermas, J. (2005) 'Legitimering på grundlag af menneskerettigheder', in H. Andersen (ed.), *Jürgen Habermas: Demokrati og retsstat – en tekstsamling*, Copenhagen: Hans Reitzels Forlag, pp. 187–203, translated from Habermas, J. (1998) 'Zur Legitimation durch Menschenrechte', in *Die postnationale Konstellation: Politische Essays*, Frankfurt am Main: Suhrkamp, pp. 170–194.

Habermas, J. (2007) 'A political constitution for the pluralist world society?', *Journal of Chinese Philosophy*, Vol. 34, No. 3, pp. 331–343.

Habermas, J. (2008) 'The constitutionalization of international law and the legitimation process of a constitution for world society', *Constellations*, Vol. 15, No. 4, pp. 444–455.

Hachez, N. (2008) 'The relations between the United Nations and civil society: Past, present and future', *International Organizations Law Review*, Vol. 5, No. 1, pp. 49–84.

Hachez, N. and Wouters, J. (2011) *A Glimpse at the Democratic Legitimacy of Private Standards: Democratic Legitimacy as Public Accountability*, Working Paper, March, Leuven: Katholieke Universiteit Leuven – Leuven Centre for Global Governance Studies.

Hajer, M. A. (1995) *The Politics of Environmental Discourse: Ecological Modernization and the Policy Process*, New York: Clarendon Press.

Hannum, H. (1995) 'Human rights', in O. Schachter and C. C. Joyner (eds), *United Nations Legal Order*, Vol. I, Cambridge: Cambridge University Press, pp. 319–348.

Haufler, V. (2001) *A Public Role for the Private Sector: Industry Self-Regulation in a Global Economy*, Washington, DC: Carnegie Endowment for International Peace.

Hearne, B. (2004) 'Proposed UN Norms on human rights: Is business opposition justified?', *Ethical Corporation*, 22 March.

Henriques, A. (ed.) (2011) *Understanding ISO 26000: A Practical Approach to Social Responsibility*, London: British Standards Institution.

Hess, D. (1999) 'Social reporting: A reflexive law approach to corporate social responsiveness', *Journal of Corporation Law*, Vol. 25, No. 1, pp. 41–84.

Hess, D. (2008) 'The three pillars of corporate social reporting as new governance regulation: Disclosure, dialogue and development', *Business Ethics Quarterly*, Vol. 18, No. 4, pp. 447–482.

Higgins, R. (1994) *Problems and Process: International Law and How We Use It*, Oxford: Clarendon Press.

Hillemans, C. F. (2003) 'UN Norms on the Responsibilities of Transnational Corporations and Other Business Enterprises with Regard to Human Rights', *German Law Journal*, Vol. 4, No. 10, pp. 1065–1080.

Holmstrøm, S. (2013) 'Legitimerende praksisformer: Et sociologisk perspektiv på praksisformers funktion, strategi og begrundelse', in S. Holmstrøm and S. Kjærbeck (eds), *Legitimitet under forandring: Virksomheden i samfundet*, Copenhagen: Samfundslitteratur, pp. 273–312.

Hughes, N. and Lonie, S. (2007) 'M-PESA: Mobile money for the "unbanked" turning cellphones into 24-hour tellers in Kenya', *Innovations: Technology, Governance, Globalization*, Vol. 2, No. 1–2, pp. 63–81.

Idemudia, U. and Ite, U. (2006) 'Corporate–community relations in Nigeria's oil industry: Challenges and imperatives', *Corporate Social Responsibility and Environmental Management*, Vol. 13, pp. 194–206.

Jacobsen, M. and Bruun, O. (2000) *Human Rights and Asian Values: Contesting National Identities and Cultural Representations in Asia*, Hong Kong: Curzon.

Jägers, N. (2002) *Corporate Human Rights Obligations: In Search of Accountability*, Antwerp: Intersentia.

Joerges, C., Sand, I.-J. and Teubner, G. (2004) *Transnational Governance and Constitutionalism*, Oxford: Hart.

Jonsson, J., Fisker, M. and Buhmann, K. (2016) 'Beyond "doing no harm": An "extended UN Framework" to connect political CSR with business and human rights', Paper for SAFIC 2016: The Private Sector in Development: New Perspectives on Developing Country and Emerging Market Firms, Copenhagen Business School, 6–7 April.

Jonsson, J., Fisker, M. and Buhmann, K. (2016) *From 'Do No Harm' to Doing More Good: Extending the UN Framework to Connect Political CSR with Business Responsibilities for Human Rights*, Working Paper No. 26/2016, Copenhagen: Copenhagen Business School, Centre for Business and Development Studies.

Kapstein, E. B. (2001) 'The corporate ethics crusade', *Foreign Affairs*, Vol. 80, No. 5, pp. 105–119.

Kaufmann, C. D. and Pape, R. A. (1999) 'Explaining costly international moral action: Britain's sixty-year campaign against the Atlantic slave trade', *International Organization*, Vol. 53, No. 4, pp. 631–668.

Kell, G. and Levin, D. (2002) 'The Global Compact Network: An historic experiment in learning and action', Paper presented at the Academy of Management Annual Conference 'Building Effective Networks', Denver, CO, 11–14 August, http://www.unglobalcompact.org/docs/news_events/9.5/denver.pdf (last accessed 22 December 2016).

Killion, U. (2010) 'The function of law in Habermas' modern society', *Global Jurist*, Vol. 10, No. 2, article 1, pp. 1–24.

Kinderman, D. (2013) 'Corporate social responsibility in the EU, 1993–2013: Institutional ambiguity, economic crises, business legitimacy and bureaucratic politics', *JCMS: Journal of Common Market Studies*, Vol. 51, No. 4, pp. 701–720.

Kinderman, D. (2016) 'Time for a reality check: Is business willing to support a smart mix of complementary regulation in private governance?', *Policy and Society*, Vol. 35, No. 1, pp. 29–41.

Kingsbury, B. (2009) 'The concept of "law" in global administrative law', *European Journal for International Law*, Vol. 20, No. 1, pp. 23–57.

Kingsbury, B., Krisch, N. and Stewart, R. B. (2005) 'The emergence of global administrative law', *Law and Contemporary Problems*, Vol. 68, No. 3, pp. 15–61.

Kinley, D. and Chambers, R. (2006) 'The UN Human Rights Norms for corporations: The private implications of public international law', *Human Rights Law Review*, Vol. 6, No. 3, pp. 447–497.

Kinley, D. and Nolan, J. (2008) 'Trading and aiding human rights in the global economy', *Nordic Journal of Human Rights Law*, Vol. 7, No. 4, pp. 353–377.

Kinley, D., Nolan, J. and Zerial, N. (2007) 'The politics of corporate social responsibility: Reflections on the United Nations Human Rights Norms for corporations', *Company and Securities Law Journal*, Vol. 25, No. 1, pp. 30–43.

Kleemeier, E. (2000) 'The impact of participation on sustainability: An analysis of the Malawi rural piped scheme program', *World Development*, Vol. 28, No. 5, pp. 929–944.

Knox, J. H. (2012) 'The Ruggie Rules: Applying human rights law to corporations', in R. Mares (ed.), *The UN Guiding Principles on Business and Human Rights*, Antwerp: Brill, pp. 51–83.

Koh, H. K. (2002) 'Opening remarks: Transnational legal process illuminated', in M. Likosky (ed.), *Transnational Legal Processes: Globalisation and Power Disparities*, Colchester: Butterworths, pp. 327–332.

Kolk, A. (2001) 'Multinational enterprises and international climate policy', in B. Arts, M. Noortmann and B. Reinalda (eds), *Non-State Actors in International Relations*, Aldershot: Ashgate, pp. 211–225.

Kolk, A. and Lenfant, F. (2013) 'Multinationals, CSR and partnerships in Central African conflict countries', *Corporate Social Responsibility and Environmental Management*, Vol. 20, pp. 43–54.

Kolstad, I. (2012) 'Human rights and positive corporate duties: The importance of corporate–state interaction', *Business Ethics: A European Review*, Vol. 21, No. 3, pp. 276–285.

Koskenniemi, M. (1989) *From Apology to Utopia: The Structure of International Legal Argument*, Helsinki: Finnish Lawyers' Publishing Company.

Koudiadaki, A. (2009) 'Information and consultation rights of employees in Britain', *International Journal of Law in Context*, Vol. 5, No. 4, pp. 393–416.

Krisch, N. (2010) *Beyond Constitutionalism: The Pluralist Structure of Postnational Law*, Oxford: Oxford University Press.

Krisch, N. and Kingsbury, B. (2006) 'Introduction: Global governance and global administrative law in the international legal order', *European Journal of International Law*, Vol. 17, No. 1, pp. 1–13.

Lambooy, T. (2009) 'Private regulation: Indispensable for responsible corporate conduct in a globalizing world?', in *Law and Globalization*, Bocconi School of Law Student-Edited Papers, Saarbrucken: VDM Publishing, pp. 90–133.

Lansing, P. and Rosaria, A. (1991) 'An analysis of the United Nations proposed Code of Conduct for Transnational Corporations', *World Competition*, Vol. 14, No. 4, pp. 35–50.

Lobel, O. (2005) 'The Renew Deal: The fall of regulation and the rise of governance in contemporary legal thought', *Minnesota Law Review*, Vol. 89, pp. 7–27.

Lucke, K. (2005) 'States' and private actors' obligations under international human rights law and the Draft UN Norms', in T. Cottier, J. Pauwelyn and E. Bürgi (eds), *Human Rights and International Trade*, Oxford: Oxford University Press, pp. 148–163.

Lugt, C. van der (2004) 'Growing big, learning that small is beautiful', in M. McIntosh, S. Waddock and G. Kell (eds), *Learning to Talk: Corporate Citizenship and the Development of the UN Global Compact*, Sheffield: Greenleaf Publishing, pp. 129–145.

Luhmann, N. (1986) 'The self-reproduction of law and its limits', in G. Teubner (ed.), *Dilemmas of Law in the Welfare State*, Berlin: Walter de Gruyter, pp. 111–127.

Madsen, S. S. (2006) 'Mediation blandt mediatoruddannede advokater' [Mediation among Danish mediator trained advocates], *Rettid*, Vol. 2006, No. 3.

Mares, R. (2006) *Institutionalisation of Corporate Social Responsibilities: Synergies between the Practices of Leading Multinational Enterprises and Human Rights Law/Policy*, Lund: Lund University, Faculty of Law.

Marks, S. J. and Davis, J. (2012) 'Does participation lead to a sense of ownership for rural water systems? Evidence from Kenya', *World Development*, Vol. 40, No. 8, pp. 1569–1576.

Martin-Ortega, O. (2014) 'Human rights due diligence for corporations: From voluntary standards to hard law at last?', *Netherlands Quarterly on Human Rights*, Vol. 32, No. 1, pp. 44–74.

Matten, D. and Moon, J. (2008) '"Implicit" and "explicit" CSR: A conceptual framework for a comparative understanding of corporate social responsibility', *Academy of Management Review*, Vol. 33, No. 2, pp. 404–424.

Maturana, H. (1981) 'Autopoiesis', in M. Zeleny (ed.), *Autopoiesis: A Theory of Living Organizations*, New York: North-Holland.

Mayer, A. E. (2009) 'Human rights as a dimension of CSR: The blurred lines between legal and non-legal categories', *Journal of Business Ethics*, Vol. 88, pp. 561–577.

McCarthy, T. (1975) 'Translator's introduction', in J. Habermas, *Legitimation Crisis*, Boston, MA: Beacon Press, pp. vii–xxiv.

McCorquodale, R. (2006) 'The individual and the international legal system', in M. D. Evans (ed.), *International Law*, 2nd edn, Oxford: Oxford University Press, pp. 308–332.

McCorquodale, R. (2010) 'The individual and the international legal system', in M. D. Evans (ed.), *International Law*, 3rd edn, Oxford: Oxford University Press, pp. 284–310.

McDougal, M. (1964) 'The policy-oriented approach to law', *Virginia Quarterly Review*, Vol. 40, pp. 626–632.

McDougal, M. and Reisman, W. M. (1981) *International Law in Contemporary Perspective*, Mineola, NY: Foundation Press.

McIntosh, M., Waddock, S. and Kell, G. (eds) (2004) *Learning to Talk: Corporate Citizenship and the Development of the UN Global Compact*, Sheffield: Greenleaf Publishing.

McIntyre, O. (2012) 'The human right to water as a creature of global administrative law', *Water International*, Vol. 37, No. 6, pp. 654–669.

McIntyre, O. (2016) 'The making of international natural resource law', in C. Brölman and Y. Radi (eds), *Research Handbook on the Theory of International Lawmaking*, Cheltenham: Edward Elgar, pp. 442–465.

Meidinger, E. (2006) 'The administrative law of global private–public regulation: The case of forestry', *European Journal of International Law*, Vol. 17, No. 1, pp. 47–87.

Meidinger, E. (2008) 'Multi-interest self-governance through global product certification programmes', in O. Dilling, M. Herberg and G. Winter (eds), *Responsible Business: Self-Governance and Law in Transnational Economic Transactions*, Oxford: Hart, pp. 259–291.

Melish, T. J. and Meidinger, E. (2012) 'Protect, respect, remedy and participate: "New governance" lessons for the Ruggie Framework', in M. Radu (ed.), *The UN Guiding Principles on Business and Human Rights: Foundations and Implementation*, Leiden: Martinus Nijhoff, pp. 303–336.

Moore, S. F. (1978) *Law as Process: An Anthropological Approach*, New York: Routledge & Kegan Paul.

Müller, H. (2004) 'Arguing, bargaining and all that – communicative action, rationalist theory, and the logic of appropriateness in international relations', *European Journal of International Relations*, Vol. 10, No. 2, pp. 395–435.

Neves, M. (2001) 'From the autopoiesis to the allopoiesis of law', *Journal of Law and Society*, Vol. 28, No. 2, pp. 242–264.

Nobles, R. and Schiff, D. (2012) 'Using system theory to study legal pluralism: What could be gained?', *Law and Society Review*, Vol. 46, No. 2, pp. 265–294.

Nolan, J. (2005) 'The United Nations' compact with business: Hindering or helping the protection of human rights?', *University of Queensland Law Journal*, Vol. 24, No. 2, pp. 445–466.

Nolan, J. (2013) 'The corporate responsibility to respect human rights: Soft law or not law?', in S. Deva and D. Bilchitz (eds), *Human Rights Obligations of Business: Beyond the Corporate Responsibility to Respect?*, Cambridge: Cambridge University Press, pp. 138–161.

Nonet, P. and Selznick, P. (1978) *Law and Society in Transition: Toward Responsive Law*, New York: Harper/Colophon.

Noortmann, M. (2001) 'Non-state actors in international law', in B. Arts, M. Noortmann and B. Reinalda (eds), *Non-State Actors in International Relations*, Aldershot: Ashgate, pp. 59–76.

Nuotio, K. (2010) 'Systems theory with discourse ethics: Squaring the circle? Comment on Marcelo Neves's *Zwischen Themis und Leviathan*', *Journal of Extreme Legal Positivism*, Vol. 7, April, pp. 59–85.

Odell, J. S. (2010) 'Three islands of knowledge about negotiation in international organizations', *Journal of European Public Policy*, Vol. 17, No. 5, pp. 619–632.

Orts, E. W. (1995) 'A reflexive model of environmental regulation', *Business Ethics Quarterly*, Vol. 5, No. 4, pp. 779–794.

Orts, E. W. (1995) 'Reflexive environmental law', *Northwestern Law Review*, Vol. 89, No. 4, pp. 1229–1340.

Parker, C. and Howe, J. (2012) 'Ruggie's diplomatic project and its missing regulatory infrastructure', in R. Mares (ed.), *The UN Guiding Principles on Business and Human Rights: Foundations and Implementation*, Leiden: Martinus Nijhoff, pp. 273–301.

Pauwelyn, J. (2012) 'Informal international law-making: Framing the concept and research questions', in J. Pauwelyn, R. Wessel and J. Wouters (eds), *Informal International Law-Making*, Oxford: Oxford University Press, pp. 13–34.

Peruzzi, M. (2011) 'Autonomy in European social dialogue', *Law and Industrial Relations*, Vol. 27, No. 1, pp. 3–21.

Picciotto, S. (2003) 'Rights, responsibilities and regulation of international business', *Columbia Journal of Transnational Law*, Vol. 42, No. 1, pp. 131–152.

Picciotto, S. (2008) 'Regulatory networks and multi-level governance', in O. Dilling, H. Martin and G. Winter (eds), *Responsible Business: Self-Governance and Law in Transnational Economic Transactions*, Oxford: Hart, pp. 315–341.

Pillay, R. (2015) *The Changing Nature of Corporate Social Responsibility: CSR and Development – the Case of Mauritius*, Abingdon: Routledge.

Prahalad, C. K. (2004) *The Fortune at the Bottom of the Pyramid: Eradicating Poverty through Profits*, Upper Saddle River, NJ: Prentice Hall.

Prieto-Carron, M., Lund-Thomsen, P., Chan, A., Muro, A. and Bhushan, C. (2006) 'Critical perspectives on CSR and development: What we know, what we don't know, and what we need to know', *International Affairs*, Vol. 82, No. 5, pp. 977–989.

Rasche, A. (2010) 'Collaborative Governance 2.0', *Corporate Governance*, Vol. 10, No. 4, pp. 500–511.

Rees, C. (2011) *Piloting Principles for Effective Company–Stakeholder Grievance Mechanisms: A Report of Lessons Learned*, CSR Initiatives, Cambridge, MA: Harvard Kennedy School.

Rehbinder, E. (1992) 'Reflexive law and practice: The corporate officer for environmental protection as an example', in G. Teubner and A. Febbrajo (eds), *European Yearbook in the Sociology of Law: State, Law and Economy as Autopoietic Systems: Regulation and Autonomy in a New Perspective*, Milano: Giuffrè, pp. 579–608.

Rehg, W. (1996) 'Translator's introduction', in J. Habermas, *Between Facts and Norms: Contributions to a Discourse Theory of Law and Democracy*, translated by W. Rehg, Cambridge: Polity Press/ Blackwell, pp. ix–xxxvii.

Reich, R. B. (2007) *Supercapitalism: The Transformation of Business, Democracy and Everyday Life*, New York: Alfred A. Knopf.

Reinalda, B. (2001) 'Private in form, public in purpose: NGOs in international relations theory', in B. Arts, M. Noortmann and B. Reinalda (eds), *Non-State Actors in International Relations*, Aldershot: Ashgate, pp. 11–40.

Reinalda, B., Arts, B. and Noortmann, M. (2001) 'Non-state actors in international relations: Do they matter?', in B. Arts, M. Noortmann and B. Reinalda (eds), *Non-State Actors in International Relations*, Aldershot: Ashgate, pp. 1–8.

Reinicke, W. H. (1998) *Global Public Policy: Governing without Government?*, Washington, DC: Brookings Institution Press.

Reinicke, W. H., Deng, F. and Witte Martin, J. (2000) *Critical Choices: The United Nations, Networks, and the Future of Global Governance*, Ottawa: International Development Research Centre.

Reynaers, A.-M. and Parrado, S. (2016) 'Responsive regulation in public–private partnerships: Between deterrence and persuasion', *Regulation and Governance*, DOI 10.1111/rego.1212.

Risse, T. (2000) '"Let's argue": Communicative action in world politics', *International Organization*, Vol. 54, No. 1, pp. 1–39.

Risse, T. (2005) 'Global governance and communicative action', in D. Held and M. Koenig-Archibugi (eds), *Global Governance and Public Accountability*, Malden, MA: Blackwell, pp. 164–189.

Risse, T. and Kleine, M. (2010) 'Deliberation in negotiations', *Journal of European Public Policy*, Vol. 17, No. 5, pp. 708–726.

Risse, T., Ropp, S. C. and Sikkink, K. (eds) (1999) *The Power of Human Rights: International Norms and Human Rights*, Cambridge: Cambridge University Press.

Ritchie, D., Parry, O., Gnich, W. and Platt, S. (2004) 'Issues of participation, ownership and empowerment in a community development programme: Tackling smoking in a low-income area in Scotland', *Health Promotion International*, Vol. 19, No. 4, pp. 51–59.

Rockström, J. (2009) 'Planetary boundaries: Exploring the safe operating space for humanity', *Ecology and Society*, Vol. 14, No. 2, article 32.

Rogowski, R. (1994) 'Industrial relations, labour conflict resolution and reflexive labour law', in R. Rogowski and T. Wilthagen (eds), *Reflexive Labour Law: Studies in Industrial Relations and Employment Regulation*, Deventer: Kluwer Law and Taxation Publishers, pp. 53–93.

Rogowski, R. (1998) 'Autopoietic industrial relations and reflexive labour law', in T. Wilthagen (ed.), *Advancing Theory in Labour Law and Industrial Relations in a Global Context*, Amsterdam: North-Holland, pp. 67–81.

Rogowski, R. (2001) 'The concept of reflexive labour law: Its theoretical background and possible applications', in J. Priban and D. Nelken (eds), *Law's New Boundaries: The Consequences of Legal Autopoiesis*, Aldershot: Ashgate, pp. 179–196.

Rogowski, R. and Wilthagen, T. (1994) 'Reflexive labour law: An introduction', in R. Rogowski and T. Wilthagen (eds), *Reflexive Labour Law: Studies in Industrial Relations and Employment Regulation*, Deventer: Kluwer Law and Taxation Publishers, pp. 1–19.

Rosenau, J. N. and Czempiel, E.-O. (1992) *Governance without Government: Order and Change in World Politics*, Cambridge: Cambridge University Press.

Rostbøll, C. F. (2011) *Jürgen Habermas*, Copenhagen: Jurist- & Økonomforbundets Forlag.

Rottleuthner, H. (1988) 'Biological metaphors in legal thought', in G. Teubner (ed.), *Autopoietic Law: A New Approach to Law and Society*, Berlin: Walter de Gruyter, pp. 97–127.

Ruggie, J. G. (2004) 'Reconstituting the global public domain – issues, actors and practices', *European Journal of International Relations*, Vol. 10, No. 4, pp. 499–531.

Ruggie, J. G. (2013) *Just Business: Multinational Corporations and Human Rights*, New York: W. W. Norton & Company.

Ryngaert, C. and Buhmann, K. (2012) 'Human rights challenges for multinational corporations working and investing in conflict zones', Introductory article for special issue of *Human Rights and International Legal Discourse*, Vol. 6, No. 1, pp. 3–13.

Sahlin-Andersson, K. (2004) 'Emergent cross-sectional soft regulations: Dynamics at play in the Global Compact initiative', in U. Mörth (ed.), *Soft Law in Governance and Regulation: An Interdisciplinary Analysis*, Cheltenham: Edward Elgar, pp. 129–152.

Sand, I.-J. (1996) *Styring av kompleksitet: Rettslige former for statlig rammestyring og desentralisert statsforvaltniing*, Bergen: Fagbokforlaget Vigmostad & Bjørke.

Sand, I.-J. (1997) *Fragmented Law – from Unitary to Pluralistic Legal Systems: A Socio-Legal Perspective of Post-National Legal Systems*, Arena Working Paper No. 18, Oslo: University of Oslo.

Sand, I.-J. (2000) *Changing Forms of Governance and the Role of Law: Society and Its Law*, Arena Working Paper No. WP 00/14, Oslo: University of Oslo.

Sand, I.-J. (2012) 'Hybridization, change and the expansion of law', in N. Å. Andersen and I.-J. Sand (eds), *Hybrid Forms of Governance: Self-Suspension of Power*, Houndmills: Palgrave Macmillan, pp. 186–204.

Sanders, A. (2015) 'The impact of the "Ruggie Framework" and the "United Nations Guiding Principles on Business and Human Rights" on transnational human rights litigation', in J. Martin and K. E. Bravo (eds), *The Business and Human Rights Landscape: Moving Forward, Looking Back*, Cambridge: Cambridge University Press, pp. 288–315.

Saurwein, F. (2011) 'Regulatory choice for alternative modes of regulation: How context matters', *Law and Policy*, Vol. 33, No. 3, pp. 334–366.

Schaefer, S. (2010) 'Legitimacy and the international regulation of geoengineering with solar radiation management: Prospects for normative institutional design theory', Unpublished paper on file with author.

Scherer, A. G. and Palazzo, G. (2007) 'Toward a political conception of corporate responsibility: Business and society seen from a Habermasian perspective', *Academy of Management Review*, Vol. 32, No. 4, pp. 1096–1120.

Scherer, A. G. and Palazzo, G. (2011) 'The new political role of business in a globalized world – a review of a new perspective on CSR and its implications for the firm, governance, and democracy', *Journal of Management Studies*, Vol. 48, No. 4, pp. 899–931.

Scherer, A. G., Rasche, A., Palazzo, G. and Spicer, A. (2016) 'Managing for political corporate social responsibility: New challenges and directions for PCSR 2.0', *Journal of Management Studies*, Vol. 53, No. 3, pp. 273–298.

Scheuerman, W. E. (2001) 'Reflexive law and the challenges of globalization', *Journal of Political Philosophy*, Vol. 9, No. 1, pp. 81–102.

Scheuerman, W. E. (2006) 'Critical theory beyond Habermas', in J. S. Dryzek, B. Honig and A. Phillips (eds), *The Oxford Handbook of Political Theory*, New York: Oxford University Press, pp. 85–105.

Schoeneborn, D. (2011) 'Organization as communication: A Luhmannian perspective', *Management Communication Quarterly*, Vol. 25, No. 4, pp. 663–689.

Schwartz, M. S. and Carroll, A. B. (2003) 'Corporate social responsibility: A three-domain approach', *Business Ethics Quarterly*, Vol. 13, No. 4, pp. 503–530.

Scott, C. D., Cafaggi, F. and Senden, L. (2011) 'The conceptual and constitutional challenge of transnational private regulation', *Journal of Law and Society*, Vol. 38, No. 1, pp. 1–19.

Shaw, M. N. (2008) *International Law*, 6th edn, Cambridge: Cambridge University Press.

Sheehy, B. (2015) 'Defining CSR: Problems and solutions', *Journal of Business Ethics*, Vol. 131, No. 3, pp. 625–648.

Shelton, D. (2000) 'Introduction', in D. Shelton (ed.), *Commitment and Compliance: The Role of Non-Binding Norms in the International Legal System*, Oxford: Oxford University Press, pp. 1–18.

Shelton, D. (2006) 'International law and "relative normativity"', in M. D. Evans (ed.), *International Law*, 2nd edn, Oxford: Oxford University Press, pp. 159–185.

Sidoti, C. (2011) 'It's our business: Ensuring inclusiveness in the process of regulating and enforcing corporate social responsibility', in K. Buhmann, L. Roseberry and M. Morsing (eds), *Corporate Social and Human Rights Responsibilities: Global Legal and Management Perspectives*, London: Palgrave Macmillan, pp. 144–164.

Sigler, J. A. and Murphy, J. E. (1988) *Interactive Corporate Compliance: An Alternative to Regulatory Compulsion*, New York: Quorum Books.

Slaughter, A.-M. (2000) 'Agencies on the loose? Holding government networks accountable', in G. Bermann, M. Herdegen and P. Lindseth (eds), *Transatlantic Regulatory Cooperation, Legal Problems and Political Prospects*, Oxford: Oxford University Press, pp. 521–546.

Sørensen, E. and Torfing, J. (2005) *Netværksstyring – fra government til governance* [Network governance – from government to governance], Copenhagen: Roskilde Universitetsforlag.

Sørensen, E. and Torfing, J. (2005) 'The democratic anchorage of governance networks', *Scandinavian Political Studies*, Vol. 28, No. 3, pp. 195–218.

Stauffer, J. (2008) *Giants: The Parallel Lives of Frederick Douglass and Abraham Lincoln*, New York: Twelve Publishing.

Steffek, J. and Gomes Pereira, M. (2011) 'Transnational governance networks and democracy: What are the standards?', in O. Dilling, M. Herberg and G. Winter (eds), *Transnational Administrative Rule-Making: Performance, Legal Effects and Legitimacy*, Oxford: Hart, pp. 281–304.

Steiner, H. J., Alston, P. and Goodman, R. (2008) *Human Rights in Context*, 3rd edn, Oxford: Oxford University Press.

Suchman, M. (1995) 'Managing legitimacy: Strategic and institutional approaches', *Academy of Management Review*, Vol. 20, No. 3, pp. 571–610.

Szasz, P. C. (1995) 'General law-making processes', in O. Schachter and C. C. Joyner (eds), *United Nations Legal Order*, Vol. I, Cambridge: Cambridge University Press, pp. 35–108.

Tamanaha, B. Z. (1997) *Realistic Socio-Legal Theory: Pragmatism and a Social Theory of Law*, Oxford: Oxford University Press.

Teubner, G. (1983) 'Substantive and reflective elements in modern law', *Law and Society Review*, Vol. 17, No. 2, pp. 239–285.

Teubner, G. (1984) 'Autopoiesis in law and society: A rejoinder to Blankenburg', *Law and Society Review*, Vol. 18, No. 2, pp. 291–301.

Teubner, G. (1985) 'Corporate fiduciary duties and their beneficiaries: A functional approach to the legal institutionalization of corporate responsibility', in K. J. Hopt and G. Teubner (eds), *Corporate Governance and Directors' Liabilities*, Berlin: Walter de Gruyter, pp. 149–177.

Teubner, G. (1986) 'After legal instrumentalism?', in G. Teubner (ed.), *Dilemmas of Law in the Welfare State*, Berlin: Walter de Gruyter, pp. 299–325.

Teubner, G. (ed.) (1986) *Dilemmas of Law in the Welfare State*, Berlin: Walter de Gruyter.

Teubner, G. (1992) 'Social order from legislative noise', in G. Teubner and A. Febbrajo (eds), *European Yearbook in the Sociology of Law: State, Law and Economy as Autopoietic Systems: Regulation and Autonomy in a New Perspective*, Milano: Giuffrè, pp. 609–649.

Teubner, G. (1993) *Law as an Autopoietic System*, Oxford: Blackwell.

Teubner, G. (1997) 'Foreword: Legal regimes of global non-state actors', in G. Teubner (ed.), *Global Law without a State*, Aldershot: Dartmouth Publishing, pp. xiii–xvii.

Teubner, G. (2012) *Constitutional Fragments: Societal Constitutionalism and Globalization*, Oxford: Oxford University Press.

Teubner, G., Nobles, R. and Schiff, D. (2005) 'The autonomy of law: An introduction to legal autopoiesis', in J. Penner, D. Schiff and R. Nobles (eds), *Jurisprudence*, New York: Oxford University Press, pp. 897–954.

Torfing, J. (2013) 'Legitimitet i netværkssamfundet: Et politologisk perspektiv på virksomheders delt-agelse i styringsnetværk', in S. Holmstrøm and S. Kjærbeck (eds), *Legitimitet under forandring: Virksomheden is samfundet*, Copenhagen: Samfundslitteratur, pp. 61–88.

Warhurst, A. and Cooper, K. in association with Amnesty International (2004) *The 'UN Human Rights Norms for Business'*, 26 July, Bradford on Avon: Maplecroft.

Webb, T. (2004) 'Comment: Lobby groups and NGOs should rethink their approach to the UN Norms', *Ethical Corporation*, 23 April.

Weiss, E. B. (2000) 'Conclusions: Understanding compliance with soft law', in D. Shelton (ed.), *Commitment and Compliance: The Role of Non-Binding Norms in the International Legal System*, Oxford: Oxford University Press, pp. 535–553.

Weissbrodt, D. (2006) 'UN perspectives on "business and humanitarian and human rights obligations"', *Proceedings of the Annual Meeting (American Society of International Law)*, Vol. 100, 29 March – 1 April, pp. 135–139.

Weissbrodt, D. and Kruger, M. (2003) 'Norms on the Responsibilities of Transnational Corporations and Other Business Enterprises with Regard to Human Rights', *American Journal of International Law*, Vol. 97, No. 4, pp. 901–922.

Weissbrodt, D. and Kruger, M. (2005) 'Human rights responsibilities of businesses as non-state actors', in P. Alston (ed.), *Non-State Actors and Human Rights*, New York: Oxford University Press, pp. 315–350.

Wettstein, F. (2013) 'Making noise about silent complicity: The moral inconsistency of the "Protect, Respect and Remedy" Framework', in S. Deva and D. Bilchitz (eds), *Human Rights Obligations of Business: Beyond the Corporate Responsibility to Respect?*, Cambridge: Cambridge University Press, pp. 243–268.

Wettstein, F. (2015) 'Business and human rights: Implementation challenges', in D. Baumann-Pauly and J. Nolan (eds), *Business and Human Rights: From Principles to Practice*, Abingdon: Routledge, pp. 77–89.

Wettstein, F. (2015) 'Normativity, ethics, and the UN Guiding Principles on Business and Human Rights: A critical assessment', *Journal of Human Rights*, Vol. 14, No. 2, pp. 162–182.

Wight, A. (1997) 'Participation, ownership and sustainable development', in M. S. Grindle (ed.), *Getting Good Government: Capacity Building in the Public Sectors of Developing Countries*, Cambridge, MA: Harvard University Press, pp. 369–412.

Willke, H. and Willke, G. (2007) 'Corporate moral legitimacy and the legitimacy of morals: A critique of Palazzo/Scherer's communicative framework', *Journal of Business Ethics*, Vol. 81, No. 1, pp. 27–38.

Wilthagen, T. (1994) 'Reflexive rationality in the regulation of occupational safety and health', in R. Rogowski and T. Wilthagen (eds), *Reflexive Labour Law: Studies in Industrial Relations and Employment Regulation*, Deventer: Kluwer Law and Taxation Publishers, pp. 345–376.

Wood, S. (2011) 'The meaning of "sphere of influence" in ISO 26000', in A. Henriques (ed.), *Understanding ISO 26000: A Practical Approach to Social Responsibility*, London: British Standards Institution, pp. 115–130.

Wouters, J. and Chané, A. (2013) *Multinational Corporations in International Law*, Working Paper No. 129, Leuven: Leuven Centre for Global Governance Studies.

Wouters, J., Marx, A. and Hachez, N. (2011) *Private Standards, Global Governance and International Trade: The Case of Global Food Safety Governance*, Working Paper, March, Leuven: Katholieke Universiteit Leuven, Leuven Centre for Global Governance Studies.

Zelli, F. and Asselt, H. van (2013) 'Introduction: The institutional fragmentation of global environmental governance: Causes, consequences, and responses', *Global Environmental Politics*, Vol. 13, No. 3, pp. 1–13.

Zerk, J. A. (2006) *Multinationals and Corporate Social Responsibility: Limitations and Opportunities in International Law*, Cambridge: Cambridge University Press.

Zumbansen, P. (2012) 'Comparative, global and transnational constitutionalism: The emergence of a transnational legal-pluralist order', *Global Constitutionalism*, Vol. 1, No. 1, pp. 16–52.

Zürn, M. (1998) *Regieren jenseits des Nationalstaates*, Frankfurt am Main: Suhrkamp.

Documents from NGOs, public and international organisations and the EU (including law and policy texts)

Amnesty International (2005) *Letter to Professor John Ruggie*, 16 September, AI ref UN 260-2005.

Annan, K. (1999) 'Secretary-General proposes Global Compact on human rights, labour, environment, in address to World Economic Forum in Davos', Address of Secretary-General Kofi Annan to the World Economic Forum in Davos, Switzerland, 31 January, UN Press Release SG/SM/6881, 1 February, http://www.un.org/News/Press/docs/1999/19990201.sgsm6881.html (accessed 17 December 2016).

Asian Civil Society Statement to U.N. Special Representative on Transnational Business and Human Rights at the Asia Regional Consultation, Bangkok, Thailand, 27 June 2006.

Brundtland, G., Khalid, M., Agnelli, S., Al-Athel, S., Chidzero, B., Fadika, L., Hauff, V., Lang, I., Shijun, M., Botero, M. M. de and Singh, M. (1987) *Report of the World Commission on Environment and Development: 'Our Common Future'*, UN Doc. A/42/427 Annex, 4 August.

Buck, P. de (2004) *Statement by Philippe de Buck – Secretary General UNICE*, EU Multi-Stakeholder Forum on CSR, Final High Level Meeting, 29 June, http://circa.europa.eu/irc/empl/csr_eu_multi_stakeholder_forum/info/data/en/CSR%20Forum%20040629%20speech%20UNICE.htm (last accessed 15 February 2013, webpage has been removed).

Business and Human Rights Resource Centre, UN Secretary-General's Special Representative on Business and Human Rights (SRSG portal), https://business-humanrights.org/en/un-secretary-generals-special-representative-on-business-human-rights (last accessed 27 December 2016).

Business and Human Rights Resource Centre, UN Secretary-General's Special Representative on Business and Human Rights (SRSG portal), 'Consultations, meetings and workshops', https://business-humanrights.org/en/un-secretary-generals-special-representative-on-business-human-rights/consultations-meetings-workshops (accessed 17 December 2016).

BusinessEurope, *European Alliance for CSR*, https://www.businesseurope.eu/european-alliance-csr (last accessed 5 December 2016).

Caux Round Table, www.cauxroundtable.org (last accessed 27 December 2016).

Clean Clothes Campaign (2007) *Letter to John Ruggie*, Amsterdam, 23 March, http://www.business-humanrights.org/Documents/Clean-Clothes-Campaign-letter-Ruggie-23-Mar-2007.pdf (last accessed 30 December 2016).

Commission of the European Communities (2001) *Promoting a European Framework for Corporate Social Responsibility*, COM(2001)366.

Commission of the European Communities (2002) *Communication from the Commission Concerning Corporate Social Responsibility: A Business Contribution to Sustainable Development*, COM(2002)347.

Commission of the European Communities (2006) *Communication from the Commission to the European Parliament, the Council and the European Economic and Social Committee: Implementing the Partnership for Growth and Jobs: Making Europe a Pole of Excellence on CSR*, COM(2006)136.final.

Commission on Human Rights (2004) *Decision 2004/116*, UN Doc. E/CN.4/2004/L.73/Rev.1, 16 April.

Commission on Human Rights (2005) *Human Rights and Transnational Corporations and Other Business Enterprises*, UN Doc. E/CN.4/2005/L.87, 15 April.

Convention on Civil Liability for Oil Pollution Damage, 973 UNTS 3.

Convention on the Elimination of All Forms of Discrimination against Women, UN Doc. A/34/46, 1249 UNTS 13.

Convention on the Elimination of Racial Discrimination, UN Doc. A/6014, 660 UNTS 195.

CSR Alliance (2008) *Toolbox: Equipping Companies and Stakeholders for a Competitive and Responsible Europe*, Brussels: CSR Europe.

CSR Europe, website on CSR Alliance, http://www.csreurope.org/pages/en/alliance.html (last accessed 12 March 2013, website has been removed).

Development and International Economic Cooperation: Transnational Corporations, Draft Code of Conduct on Transnational Corporations (1990) UN Doc. E/1990/94, 12 June.

Diamantopoulou, A. (2003) *Anna Diamantopoulou – European Commissioner Responsible for Employment and Social Affairs: Dialogue and Partnership: The Key to Successful CSR*, EU Multi-Stakeholder Forum on CSR, High Level Meetings, 13 November, http://circa.europa.eu/irc/empl/csr_eu_multi_stakeholder_forum/info/data/en/CSR%20Forum%20031113%20speech%20AD.htm (last accessed 17 February 2013, webpage has been removed).

ECPAT Sweden (n.d.) *Briefing Paper: ISO 26000 Social Responsibility Guidance Standard*, http://resources.ecpat.net/EI/Pdf/ISO_26000_Guidance_Standard_Social_Responsibility_en.pdf (accessed 2 November 2016).

Eurocommerce (2004) *Statement by Eurocommerce*, EU Multi-Stakeholder Forum on CSR, Final High Level Meeting, 29 June, http://circa.europa.eu/irc/empl/csr_eu_multi_stakeholder_forum/info/data/en/CSR%20Forum%20040629%20speech%20Eurocommerce.htm (last accessed 15 February 2013, webpage has been removed).

European Commission (2011) *A Renewed EU Strategy 2011–2014 for Corporate Social Responsibility*, Communication from the Commission to the European Parliament, the Council, the European Economic and Social Committee and the Committee of the Regions, Brussels, 25 October, COM(2011)681.

European Commission DG Enterprise and Industry, website on CSR Alliance, http://ec.europa.eu/enterprise/policies/sustainable-business/corporate-social-responsibility/european-alliance/index_en.htm (last accessed 12 March 2013, website has been removed).

European Multi-Stakeholder Forum on CSR (2002–2004) EU MSF homepage through the EU Commission's website, http://circa.europa.eu/irc/empl/csr_eu_multi_stakeholder_forum/info/data/en/csr%20ems%20forum.htm (last accessed 15 February 2013, webpage has been removed).

European Multi-Stakeholder Forum on CSR (2004) *Final Results and Recommendations*, 'Final Report', 29 June, http://forum.europa.eu.int/irc/empl/csr_eu_multi_stakeholder_forum/info/data/en/CSR%20Forum%20final%20report.pdf (last accessed 15 February 2013, website has been removed).

European Multi-Stakeholder Forum on CSR (2004) *Final High Level Meeting, Minutes*, 29 June, http://circa.europa.eu/irc/empl/csr_eu_multi_stakeholder_forum/info/data/en/CSR%20Forum%20040629%20minutes.htm (last accessed 17 February 2013, webpage has been removed).

European Parliament (1999) *Resolution on EU Standards for European Enterprises Operating in Developing Countries: Towards a European Code of Conduct*, OJ C 104/180, EP Resolution A4-0508/98, adopted 15 January.

Extractive Industries Transparency Initiative (EITI), www.eiti.org (last accessed 27 December 2016).

Fédération Internationale des Droits de l'Homme (2013) *Statement by FIDH*, EU Multi-Stakeholder Forum on CSR, http://circa.europa.eu/irc/empl/csr_eu_multi_stakeholder_forum/info/data/en/CSR%20Forum%20040629%20speech%20FIDH.htm (last accessed 15 February 2013, webpage has been removed).

Global Compact Critics Blog, http://www.globalcompactcritics.net/ (last accessed 31 January 2013, website has been closed).

Global Reporting Initiative, https://www.globalreporting.org/ (last accessed 27 December 2016).

Global Sullivan Principles, http://hrlibrary.umn.edu/links/sullivanprinciples.html (last accessed 30 December 2016).

Human Rights Clinic (Columbia Law School) and International Human Rights Clinic (Harvard Law School) (2015) *Righting Wrongs? Barrick Gold's Remedy Mechanism for Sexual Violence in Papua New Guinea: Key Concerns and Lessons Learned*, New York City and Boston, MA, November, http://hrp.law.harvard.edu/wp-content/uploads/2015/11/FINALBARRICK.pdf (accessed 16 November 2016).

ILO (1998) *Declaration on Fundamental Principles and Rights at Work*, Adopted by the International Labour Conference, 86th session, Geneva, June, 37 I.L.M. 1233, http://www.ilo.org/public/english/standards/decl/declaration/text/ (last accessed 17 January 2013).

ILO, *Tripartite Declaration of Principles Concerning Multinational Enterprises and Social Policy* (MNE Declaration), originally adopted in 1977 by the ILO Governing Body, http://www.ilo.org/empent/Publications/WCMS_094386/lang--en/index.htm (last accessed 27 December 2016).

India Companies Act 2013, *Gazette of India*, New Delhi, 30 August.

Intergovernmental Panel on Climate Change (2012) 'Summary for policymakers', in C. B. Field, V. Barros, T. F. Stocker, Qin D., D. J. Dokken, K. L. Ebi, M. D. Mastrandrea, K. J. Mach, G.-K. Plattner, S. K. Allen, M. Tignor and P. M. Midgley (eds), *Managing the Risks of Extreme Events and Disasters to Advance Climate Change Adaptation*, Special Report, Cambridge: Cambridge University Press, pp. 3–22.

International Court of Justice (1949) *Reparations for Injuries*, Advisory Opinion, ICJ Reports, pp. 178–179.

International Covenant on Civil and Political Rights, GA Res. 2200A (XXI), UN Doc. A/6316 (1966), 999 UNTS 171.

International Covenant on Economic, Social and Cultural Rights, GA Res. 2200A (XXI), UN Doc. A/6316 (1966), 993 UNTS 3.

International Labour Office (2003) *Corporate Social Responsibility: Myth or Reality?*, Labour Education Series 2003/1, Geneva: ILO.

International Organisation of Employers, International Chamber of Commerce and BIAC (2006) *Business and Human Rights: The Role of Business in Weak Governance Zones: Business Proposals for Effective Ways of Addressing Dilemma Situations in Weak Governance Zones*, December, Geneva: International Organisation of Employers, International Chamber of Commerce and BIAC.

ISO (2010) *ISO 26000 – Social Responsibility*, http://www.iso.org/iso/iso_catalogue/management_standards/social_responsibility.htm (last accessed 5 December 2016).

Joint NGO Letter on Work of the Mandate, 10 October 2007, available at the Business and Human Rights Resource Centre SRSG portal in version dated 25 October 2007.

Kimberley Process, http://www.kimberleyprocess.com/ (last accessed 27 December 2016).

Koskenniemi, M. (2006) *Fragmentation of International Law: Difficulties Arising from the Diversification and Expansion of International Law*, International Law Commission – Report of the Study Group of the International Law Commission, UN Doc. A/CN.4/L.682.

Liikanen, E. (2003) *Erkki Liikanen – Member of the European Commission, Enterprise and Information Society*, EU Multi-Stakeholder Forum on CSR, High Level Meetings, 13 November, http://circa.europa.eu/irc/empl/csr_eu_multi_stakeholder_forum/info/data/en/CSR%20Forum%20031113%20speech%20EL.htm (last accessed 17 February 2013, webpage has been removed).

McLaren, D. (2004) *Statement on Behalf of the Green 8*, EU Multi-Stakeholder Forum on CSR, Final High Level Meeting, 29 June, http://circa.europa.eu/irc/empl/csr_eu_multi_stakeholder_forum/info/data/en/CSR%20Forum%20040629%20speech%20G8.htm (last accessed 15 February 2013, webpage has been removed).

MY World United Nations Global Survey, http://www.worldwewant2015.org/inequalities (accessed 11 March 2013).

OECD (1976) *OECD Guidelines for Multinational Enterprises*, Paris: OECD, http://search.oecd.org/officialdocuments/publicdisplaydocumentpdf/?cote=CES(2000)17&docLanguage=En (last accessed 27 December 2016).

OECD (2011) *Declaration on International Investment and Multinational Enterprises*, http://www.oecd.org/daf/inv/investment-policy/oecddeclarationoninternationalinvestmentandmultinationalenterprises.htm (last accessed 20 November 2016).

OHCHR, in cooperation with the Global Compact Office (2004) *Consultation on Business and Human Rights: Summary of Discussions*.

OHCHR (2005) *Report of the United Nations High Commissioner on Human Rights on the Responsibilities of Transnational Corporations and Related Business Enterprises with Regard to Human Rights*, UN Doc. E/CN.4/2005/91, 15 February.

OHCHR, OEIWG, *Exploring the Content of Proposed Business and Human Rights Treaty: Academic Reflections*, http://www.ohchr.org/EN/HRBodies/HRC/WGTransCorp/Session2/Pages/SideEvents.aspx (accessed 25 November 2016).

OHCHR, OEIWG, *First Session Written Contributions*, http://www.ohchr.org/EN/HRBodies/HRC/WGTransCorp/Session1/Pages/WrittenContributions.aspx (accessed 25 November 2016).

OHCHR, OEIWG, *Second Session Written Contributions*, http://www.ohchr.org/EN/HRBodies/HRC/WGTransCorp/Session2/Pages/WrittenContributions.aspx (accessed 25 November 2016).

OHCHR, Open-Ended Intergovernmental Working Group (OEIWG) on TNCs and Human Rights (2016) *Information Note for NGOs with ECOSOC Consultative Status on Their Engagement with the Open-Ended Intergovernmental Working Group on Transnational Corporations and Other Business Enterprises with Respect to Human Rights*, http://www.ohchr.org/EN/HRBodies/HRC/WGTransCorp/Pages/IGWGOnTNC.aspx (accessed 25 November 2016).

Parent, A.-S. (2004) *Statement of the Social Platform*, EU Multi-Stakeholder Forum on CSR, Final High Level Meeting, 29 June, http://circa.europa.eu/irc/empl/csr_eu_multi_stakeholder_forum/info/data/en/CSR%20Forum%20040629%20speech%20Social%20Platform.htm (last accessed 15 February 2013, webpage has been removed).

Report of the Sessional Working Group on the Working Methods and Activities of Transnational Corporations, 1st session, UN Doc. E/CN.4/Sub.2/1999/9.

Report of the Sessional Working Group on the Working Methods and Activities of Transnational Corporations, 2nd session, UN Doc. E/CN.4/Sub.2/2000/12.

Report of the Sessional Working Group on the Working Methods and Activities of Transnational Corporations, 3rd session, UN Doc. E/CN.4/Sub.2/2001/9.

Report of the Sessional Working Group on the Working Methods and Activities of Transnational Corporations, 4th session, UN Doc. E/CN.4/Sub.2/2002/13.

Report of the World Summit for Social Development, UN Doc. A/CONF/166/9.

Social Accountability International, Social Accountability (SA) 8000, version 2008, http://www.sa-intl.org/_data/n_0001/resources/live/2008StdEnglishFinal.pdf (last accessed 27 December 2016).

Sub-Commission on Prevention of Discrimination and Protection of Minorities (1995) *The Realization of Economic, Social and Cultural Rights: The Relationship between the Enjoyment of Human Rights, in Particular, International Labour and Trade Union Rights, and the Working Methods and Activities of Transnational Corporations*, UN Doc. E/CN.4/Sub.2/1995/11, 24 July.

Sub-Commission on Prevention of Discrimination and Protection of Minorities (1996) *The Impact of the Activities and Working Methods of Transnational Corporations on the Full Enjoyment of Human Rights, in Particular Economic, Social and Cultural Rights and the Rights to Development, Bearing in Mind Existing International Guidelines, Rules and Standards Relating to the Subject-Matter*, UN Doc. E/CN.4/Sub.2/196/12, 2 July.

Sub-Commission on Prevention of Discrimination and Protection of Minorities (1998) *The Realization of Economic, Social and Cultural Rights: The Question of Transnational Corporations*, UN Doc. E/CN.4/Sub.2/198/6, 10 June.

Sub-Commission on the Promotion and Protection of Human Rights (1998) *Resolution*, 1998/8, 20 August.

Sub-Commission on the Promotion and Protection of Human Rights (2001) *Resolution 2001/3*, UN Doc. E/CN.4/SUB.2/RES/2001/3, 15 August.

Sub-Commission on the Promotion and Protection of Human Rights (2003) *Norms on the Responsibilities of Transnational Corporations and Other Business Enterprises with Regard to Human Rights*, UN Doc. E/CN.4/Sub.2/2003/12/Rev.2.

Sub-Commission on the Promotion and Protection of Human Rights (2003) *Resolution 2003/16*, UN Doc. E/CN.4/Sub.2/2003/L.11, 15 August.

UNCTC (1990) *Transnational Corporations, Services and the Uruguay Round*, UN Doc. ST/CTC/103, New York: United Nations.

UNECE (1998) *Convention on Access to Information, Public Participation in Decision-Making and Access to Justice in Environmental Matters* ('Aarhus Convention'), adopted 25 June, 2161 UNTS 447.

United Nations (1986) *Declaration on the Right to Development*, UN Doc. A/RES/41/218, 4 December.

United Nations (2002) *Report of the World Summit on Sustainable Development*, UN Doc. A/CONF.199/20.

United Nations (2005) *Press Release: Commission Requests Secretary-General to Appoint Special Representative on Transnational Corporations*, Commission on Human Rights, 20 April, http://www.unhchr.ch/huricane/huricane.nsf/view01/F92E35AD92F360D3C1256FEA002BF653?opendocument (last accessed 19 January 2013, website has been removed).

United Nations (2007) *Human Rights Policies and Management Practices: Results from Questionnaire Surveys of Governments and Fortune Global 500 Firms*, UN Doc. A/HRC/4/35/Add.3.

United Nations Charter (1945), UNTS 993, art. 71.

United Nations Commission on Human Rights (2006) *Interim Report of the Special Representative of the Secretary-General on the Issue of Human Rights and Transnational Corporations and Other Business Enterprises*, UN Doc. E/CN.4/2006/97, 22 February.

United Nations/Conference of the Parties, Framework Convention on Climate Change (2015) *Adoption of the Paris Agreement*, UN Doc. FCCC/CP/2015/L.9/Rev.1.

United Nations General Assembly (1948) *Universal Declaration of Human Rights*, GA Res. 217A (III), UN Doc. A/810, 10 December.

United Nations General Assembly (1992) *Rio Declaration on Environment and Development* (United Nations Conference on Environment and Development: Annex 1: Declaration on Environment and Development), UN Doc. A/CONF.151/26 (Vol. I), 12 August.

United Nations General Assembly (1993) *Vienna Declaration and Programme of Action*, UN Doc. a/conf.157/23, 25 June.

United Nations General Assembly (2000) *Towards Global Partnerships*, Resolution adopted by the General Assembly, UN Doc. A/RES/55/215, 21 December.

United Nations General Assembly (2000) *United Nations Millennium Declaration*, UN Doc. A/Res/55/2, 18 September.

United Nations General Assembly (2001) *Towards Global Partnerships*, Resolution adopted by the General Assembly, UN Doc. A/RES/56/76, 11 December.

United Nations General Assembly (2003) *United Nations Convention against Corruption*, UN Doc. A/58/422, 31 October.

United Nations General Assembly (2015) *Transforming Our World: The 2030 Agenda for Sustainable Development*, UN Doc. A/Res/70/1, 21 October.

United Nations Global Compact, http://www.unglobalcompact.org/ (last accessed 27 December 2016).

United Nations Human Rights Committee (2004) *Nature of the General Legal Obligation on States Parties to the Covenant*, General Comment 31, UN Doc. CCPR/C/21/Rev.1/Add.13.

United Nations Human Rights Council (2007) *Background Paper: Mapping States Parties' Responsibilities to Regulate and Adjudicate Corporate Activities under Seven of the United Nations' Core Human Rights Treaties: Main Trends and Issues for Further Consideration, Prepared for Meeting between the SRSG on Human Rights and Business and Treaty Bodies*, 19 June.

United Nations Human Rights Council (2007) *Report of the Special Representative of the Secretary-General on the Issue of Human Rights and Transnational Corporations and Other Business Enterprises: Addendum: State Responsibilities to Regulate and Adjudicate Corporate Activities under the United Nations Core Human Rights Treaties: An Overview of Treaty Body Commentaries*, UN Doc. A/HRC/4/35/Add.1, 13 February.

United Nations Human Rights Council (2008) *Mandate of the Special Representative of the Secretary-General on the Issue of Human Rights and Transnational Corporations and Other Business Enterprises*, Human Rights Council Resolution 8/7, June.

United Nations Human Rights Council (2008) *Protect, Respect and Remedy: A Framework for Business and Human Rights*, Report of the Special Representative of the Secretary-General on the issue of human rights and transnational corporations and other business enterprises, John Ruggie, UN Doc. A/HRC/8/5 (2008), 7 April.

United Nations Human Rights Council (2010) *Report of the Special Representative of the Secretary-General on the Issue of Human Rights and Transnational Corporations and Other Business Enterprises, John Ruggie: Guiding Principles for the Implementation of the United Nations 'Protect, Respect and Remedy' Framework*, UN Doc. A/HRC/, no date, draft for consultation released on 22 November.

United Nations Human Rights Council (2011) *Guiding Principles on Business and Human Rights: Implementing the United Nations 'Protect, Respect, Remedy' Framework*, Report of the Special Representative of the Secretary-General on the issue of human rights and transnational corporations and other business enterprises, UN Doc. A/HRC/17/31, 21 March.

United Nations Human Rights Council (2014) *Elaboration of an International Legally Binding Instrument on Transnational Corporations and Other Business Enterprises with Regard to Human Rights*, UN Doc. A/HRC/26/L.22/Rev.1, 25 June.

United Nations Human Rights Council (2014) *Elaboration of an International Legally Binding Instrument on Transnational Corporations and Other Business Enterprises with Respect to Human Rights*, UN Doc. A/HRC/RES/26/9, 14 July.

United Nations Human Rights Council (2014) *Human Rights and Transnational Enterprises and Other Business Enterprises*, UN Doc. A/HRC/26/L.1, 23 June.

United States Congress, Dodd–Frank Wall Street Reform and Consumer Protection Act (2010 – H.R. 4173), https://www.govtrack.us/congress/bills/111/hr4173 (last accessed 22 December 2016).

Voluntary Principles on Security and Human Rights, http://www.voluntaryprinciples.org/files/voluntary_principles_english.pdf (last accessed 30 December 2016).

Index

Printed in Great Britain
by Amazon